Alice S. Weems

Handbook
for Effective Supervision
of Instruction

Handbook
for Effective Supervision
of Instruction

Second Edition

ROSS L. NEAGLEY

Professor
Department of Educational Administration
College of Education, Temple University

N. DEAN EVANS

President
Burlington County College

PRENTICE-HALL, INC.
Englewood Cliffs, New Jersey

To Isabel and Jacqueline

13–372664–9

Library of Congress Catalog Card Number 79–110095

Printed in the United States of America

Current printing (last digit):
12 11 10 9 8 7 6 5 4 3

PRENTICE-HALL INTERNATIONAL, INC., *London*
PRENTICE-HALL OF AUSTRALIA, PTY. LTD., *Sydney*
PRENTICE-HALL OF CANADA, LTD., *Toronto*
PRENTICE-HALL OF INDIA PRIVATE LIMITED, *New Delhi*
PRENTICE-HALL OF JAPAN, INC., *Tokyo*

Preface

Many books have been written in recent years on the theory of modern school supervision. The tasks of definition and identification of the supervisory role have been reasonably well accomplished. However, in the thinking of many supervisors and administrators, few guidelines have been developed to help reconcile the theory of supervision with the practical teaching-learning situations which school officials and teachers meet each day.

It is the purpose of this handbook, therefore, to apply the emerging concepts and principles of modern school supervision to the practical situations in which administrators, supervisors, coordinators, and teachers are working.

In Chapter I, a summary of the history, characteristics, and function of supervision in the modern public school system is presented. Chapter II explores theory and research in supervision. Chapter III outlines methods of organizing for effective supervision of instruction in small, intermediate, and large school districts. Chapters IV, V, and VI discuss the roles of various persons usually involved in the supervisory process. In Chapter VII, the implications of educational innovations for changes in instructional leadership are explored. Ways of working with individuals and groups to improve instruction are detailed in Chapters VIII and IX. The theory and process of curriculum development are discussed in Chapter X. The importance of the proper role of learning resources in improving the instructional program is stressed in Chapter XI. Evaluation and the supervisory program are analyzed in Chapter XII, and Chapter XIII explores the implications of educational change for supervisory programs of the future.

The authors hope that educators will find this handbook to be a helpful guide to the supervisory role in the following positions: superintendent or chief school administrator; assistant superintendent in charge of instruction; director or coordinator of instruction; elementary or secondary supervisor; director or coordinator of elementary or secondary education; elementary principal; secondary principal; assistant principal; team leader; department head; and special-area coordinator or supervisor. In addition, the handbook has been designed for use as a basic or supplementary text for graduate students in such fields as supervision, curriculum development, in-service education, and evaluation of the supervisory function.

R.L.N.
N.D.E.

Contents

chapter *3*

Organization and Function of Supervision in Districts
of Various Sizes   47

chapter *4*

The Superintendent, Assistant Superintendent, and
Curriculum Coordinator at Work in Supervision   83

chapter *5*

The Principal at Work in Supervision   100

chapter 11

Selecting and Using Effective Learning Resources and Techniques 261

chapter 12

The Evaluation of Supervisory Programs 278

chapter 13

A Look Ahead 289

Appendixes

Handbook
for Effective Supervision
of Instruction

chapter 1

The History,
Characteristics, and Function
of Supervision
in the Modern Public School System

Effective supervision of instruction can improve the quality of teaching and learning in the classroom. Modern supervision at its finest is both dynamic and democratic, reflecting the vitality of enlightened and informed leadership. All human beings in the educative process—students, teachers, administrators, and supervisors—are individuals of worth, endowed with unique talents and capacities. The primary aim of supervision must be to recognize the inherent value of each person, to the end that the full potential of all will be realized.

Researchers in educational theory agree that supervision exists for the primary purpose of improving instruction. A few basic definitions should clarify the scope, purpose, and nature of modern supervision. According to Burton and Brueckner, it is:

> . . . an expert technical service primarily aimed at studying and improving co-operatively all factors which affect child growth and development. . . . Its characteristics may be summarized in outline form for brevity and clarity.
>
> 1. Modern supervision directs attention toward the fundamentals of education and orients learning and its improvement within the general aim of education.
>
> 2. The aim of supervision is the improvement of the total teaching-learning process, the total setting for learning, rather than the narrow and limited aim of improving teachers in service.
>
> 3. The focus is on the setting for learning, not on a person or group of persons. All persons are co-workers aiming at the improvement of a situation. One group is not superior to another, operating to "improve" the inferior group.
>
> 4. The teacher is removed from his embarrassing position as the focus of

attention and the weak link in the educational process. He assumes his rightful position as a co-operating member of a group concerned with the improvement of learning.[1]

Wiles maintains that

Supervision consists of all the activities leading to the improvement of instruction, activities related to morale, improving human relations, in-service education, and curriculum development.[2]

Eye and Netzer state:

Supervision is that phase of school administration which deals primarily with the achievement of the appropriate selected instructional expectations of educational service.[3]

In summary, then, modern school supervision is positive, democratic action aimed at the improvement of classroom instruction through the continual growth of all concerned—the child, the teacher, the supervisor, the administrator, and the parent or other interested lay person.

A BRIEF HISTORY OF SUPERVISION

Supervision of the instructional process began in American schools with the visits of school committee or board members for "inspection" purposes, starting about 1800. It is questionable if much assistance in the improvement of instruction resulted from the visits of these lay persons who were mainly concerned that the three R's were being taught effectively. However, many a teacher was hired or fired on the basis of these inspectorial visits.

It is generally agreed that professional supervision was initiated with the organization of the county superintendent of schools office in the mid-nineteenth century. For the next seventy-five years, the county superintendent in many areas provided notable services to the schools, including direct supervision of the instructional process. In fact, for the teacher beginning work with two years of normal school or less, the county office provided most of the available on-the-job or in-service training. The county institute originated during this era as a means of improving

[1]William H. Burton and Leo J. Brueckner, *Supervision: A Social Process* (New York: Appleton-Century-Crofts, Inc., 1955), pp. 11–13. (Copyright © 1955, Appleton-Century-Crofts, Inc.)

[2]Kimball Wiles, *Supervision for Better Schools*, 3rd ed. (Englewood Cliffs, N.J.: Prentice-Hall, Inc., 1967), p. 5.

[3]Glenn G. Eye and Lanore A. Netzer, *Supervision of Instruction—A Phase of Administration* (New York: Harper & Row, Publishers, 1965), p. 12.

teachers' skills and keeping them abreast of the latest educational trends.

With the advent of the public high school in the late 1800s and the development of larger, comprehensive school systems, special supervisory personnel were often provided at the district level. Hence, the influence of the county superintendent as a supervisor was diminished. The modern intermediate or large school district assigns supervisory functions to many personnel, who often serve in specialized areas such as curriculum development and selection of learning resources. Consequently, the field of supervision has grown with the increasing complexity of education in a complex society.

There has been a gradual evolution of the concept of supervision through the years. Originally authoritarian and sometimes punitive, the process was dubbed "snoopervision" by teachers who rightly felt that the supervisor was present only to criticize and admonish. From this stage evolved the concept of "improving the teacher" through supervision, with a rather narrow focus on the teacher, to the exclusion of other elements in the teaching-learning process. Finally, the modern concept of dynamic, democratic, cooperative supervision discussed in this handbook emerged —to an extent that almost renders the word "supervision" obsolete.

THE NEED FOR SUPERVISION

American society in the 1970s is making fantastic, yet exciting demands upon the public schools. The continuing explosion of man's knowledge staggers the imagination and forces increasing intellectual and vocational specialization in a highly complex society. It is impossible for one even to be cognizant of the broad categories of man's knowledge in a lifetime, let alone master any significant amount of this accumulated knowledge of mankind. And yet man is a total being—an entity. He must be able to coordinate his various experiences into a meaningful whole if he is to lead a productive life and be reasonably adjusted physically, mentally, socially, and emotionally.

Since the school curriculum represents ideally the distillation of man's most important experiences, ideals, attitudes, and hopes, this heartland of the educational institution demands more careful study and decision making today than ever before. There is a pressing need in every school system to decide what to teach and how to teach it. Accompanying the increase of possible content is the tremendous growth in number and type of instructional media, such as computer-assisted instruction, instructional films, and dial access system. To cope with these excessive demands that are pressing on the existing school structure, such organizational patterns as team teaching, ungraded units, and advanced placement classes have been advocated and tried experimentally. All of this means an increasing rate of obsolescence in content, methods, and materials of instruction.

Supervision, then, seems destined to play an essential role in deciding the nature and content of the curriculum, in selecting the school organizational patterns and learning materials to facilitate teaching, and in evaluating the entire educational process. Effective coordination of the total program, kindergarten through high school, has never been achieved in most school systems, although this is one of the most pressing needs in American public education today.

We can no longer afford the waste of human resources that is involved in overlapping courses, duplication of teaching effort, and lack of continuity from one school level to the next. A careful curriculum plan embracing the entire school experience from initial entry to graduation is imperative and long overdue. An effective supervisory program is needed in every school district—small, intermediate, or large—to launch or coordinate this effort.

THE CHARACTERISTICS OF
MODERN SUPERVISION

The professional literature of the past decade is full of the theory of modern supervision. Terms such as "democratic," "team effort," and "group process" have been lavishly used in an attempt to show that present-day supervision is a far cry from the autocracy supposedly exhibited by the early twentieth-century administrator and supervisor. According to the theorists, all decisions of any importance in the modern school system should involve the entire staff, and each professional employee must feel that he is a part of the team. The age of group dynamics has left its imprint in that all staff members are expected to interact with considerable understanding of each other's problems and the needs of the total group. The image of democracy in action at the school and district level has been planted very firmly by the writers of almost every book in the field.

Brickell, in a classic study of the dynamics of instructional change in the schools of New York State, broke the bubble of naïve acceptance of theory.

The language which has been developed to describe school administration, a language used almost universally by practicing administrators as well as by college professors in the field of administration, is not descriptive of the actual process. Phrases like "democratic administration," "the team approach," "shared decision-making," and "staff involvement" are commonplace. Behavior to match them is rare. The phrases themselves are often used with the intention of hiding the great strength of administrative action.

The participation patterns in widespread use are very often little more than enabling arrangements, organized after an administrator has decided the general direction (and in some cases the actual details) of an instructional change. . . .

His subtle leadership—or undercover direction—is thought by the practicing administrator to be most successful when he can say at the end: "They think they thought of it themselves."[4]

It is apparent from a review of the literature that some of the theorists have strayed rather far from a workable concept of school supervision. Equally, if the above-quoted conclusion is accurate and representative, many administrators and supervisors are verbalizing democracy and the other popular terms while practicing either authoritarian control or manipulation of staff to achieve their own goals, often in the name of democracy.

What, then, should be the major principles and characteristics of modern school supervision if the full potentialities of individuals and society are to be realized and are then to be translated into the most effective learning experiences for students?

1. The establishment and maintenance of satisfactory human relations among all staff members is primary. The Judaeo-Christian ethic of the ultimate worth of each individual must be basic in the philosophy of a school system and its administrators. Any supervisory program will succeed only to the extent that each person involved is considered as a human being with a unique contribution to make in the educative process. Relationships among all personnel must be friendly, open, and informal to a great extent. Mutual trust and respect are essential, and the person in the supervisory role must set the tone. It is increasingly apparent that the realities of today's world demand better human relationships if mankind is to survive. It is therefore imperative that the school staff, potentially one of the most influential groups of individuals in society, have the opportunity to develop and maintain a high level of personal interaction. According to Wiles, "A group's productiveness is affected by the quality of its human relations, and the supervisor must work constantly for the improvement of group cohesiveness."[5]

The selection of administrators and supervisors with a fundamental philosophy of positive human relationships is obviously essential to the implementation of this principle. And it must be admitted that research is inadequate in the area of candidate evaluation.

[4]Henry M. Brickell, *Organizing New York State For Educational Change* (Albany, N.Y.: State Education Department, 1961), pp. 23–24.
[5]Kimball Wiles, "Supervision," *Encyclopedia of Educational Research*, 3rd ed. (New York: The Macmillan Co., 1960), p. 1443.

2. Modern supervision is democratic, in the most enlightened sense. "Democracy" does not mean "laissez-faire," with each staff member proceeding as he pleases. Rather, the term implies a dynamic, understanding, sensitive leadership role. Throughout the history of democratic institutions the importance of the leader is emphasized. On a school staff different individuals may assume the function at various times, but real, affirmative guidance is continually needed to focus attention on the improvement of instruction and to involve actively all concerned persons.

A healthy rapport should exist among staff members in a give-and-take atmosphere which is conducive to objective consideration of the educational theories and problems of the day and of the school. A cooperative and creative approach to topics of joint concern is basic. Ideally, no personality, including the administrator or supervisor, dominates the group, but the considered judgments of all are felt to be valuable. At times the leader may have to exercise his rightful veto power or cast the deciding vote. However, most decisions should be made by consensus after thorough research and adequate discussion in the area under study. Too many voting situations may result in division of the staff, particularly if some persons find themselves in the minority on several successive occasions.

Individuals should be included in basic policy planning, in studies of the instructional program, and in all fundamental changes which affect them or their position directly. This does not mean that everyone must or should be involved in every decision. For example, if the assistant superintendent in charge of instruction needs to change the agenda of a curriculum workday because of a consultant's schedule, he should feel free to act without total staff approval. However, the same administrator would not usually purchase a set of filmstrips for use in the Language Arts program unless he had the advice of those who would be using these materials. The person in the supervisory position has the responsibility for deciding when individuals should be consulted. This is one of his most difficult tasks and points up the need for real stature in personnel leadership. When people are involved, then, there must be evidence that their creative participation is eagerly sought and that their contributions to the group decision are significant. There is absolutely no place in democratic supervision for "window-dressing" or autocratic administrative action based on token staff consultation.

In summary, democracy in supervision means active, cooperative involvement of all staff members in aspects of the instructional program which concern them, under the leadership of a well-informed, capable, and discerning administrator or supervisor who believes in the primacy of positive human relationships.

3. Modern supervision is comprehensive in scope. As indicated earlier, it embraces the total public school program, kindergarten through the

twelfth or fourteenth years, depending on the organization of the school district. The curriculum is, or should be, a developing, ongoing process involving the child from kindergarten enrollment through high school or junior college graduation.

Almost all researchers are agreed that some district-wide coordination of the educational effort is essential. However, the means of effecting this desirable outcome and the degree of coordination necessary are areas of continuing debate, which are discussed later in this chapter.

Furthermore, modern supervision is comprehensive in its view of the teacher and the learner. Historically, as we have seen, the supervisory concept was narrow in scope, focusing mainly on criticism of the teacher in the classroom, followed sometimes by attempts to get him to improve his teaching skills. Today, supervision is directed at improving all factors involved in pupil learning. Gone are the days of attempting to improve the teacher without regard to the totality of the teaching-learning situation in the school. The modern supervisory role reaches far beyond the traditional "classroom visitation." In Chapters VIII, IX, X, and XI, various group and individual techniques in contemporary school supervision are discussed in considerable detail. Some examples will help to verify the broad scope of modern supervision in action.

Group Techniques

1. Cooperative curriculum study and development is essential to the maintenance of up-to-date and worthwhile classroom experiences for students. Every staff member should be involved in this work. Among the positive outcomes will be: improved courses of study based on latest research findings; better staff understanding and relationships; improved articulation among the various school units, such as elementary and junior high; and a general awakening of interest in newer trends, instructional media, and methods of school organization.

2. A carefully planned staff in-service program can contribute much to intellectual growth in the areas where research and experimentation are having an impact.

3. The proper orientation of teachers to the school and community is a vital supervisory function. The instructional program is vastly improved through happy, well-adjusted teachers who feel secure in their assignments and in their new homes. An alert supervisor will solve many problems before they arise by initiating a comprehensive teacher-orientation program.

4. Action research and experimentation at the district level are desperately needed in American public education. Too great a percentage

of our already inadequate research dollar is being spent on isolated laboratory experiments. What better place could be found for meaningful, controlled studies with programmed learning materials, for example, than the public school classroom? Of course, proper safeguards need to be developed to make certain that students are not continually exposed to untested materials or methods. Recent research at Temple University has revealed that the attitudes of parents and other lay persons toward research in the classroom are favorable.

5. The coordination of special services and subjects such as art, music, physical education, speech correction, and developmental reading with the total program is a supervisory problem of the first magnitude. Too many schools have not even defined the role of the art specialist, for instance. Is this individual most effective as a resource person "on call," as a teacher regularly scheduled in classrooms, or as a supervisor of art activities in the district? Or should there be several specialists to fill these roles?

6. The establishment and coordination of a program of student teaching in cooperation with neighboring colleges or universities can make a significant contribution to classroom instruction and to the individual college student as a prospective member of the teaching profession. Again, effective supervisory practice is needed if a student-teacher program is to be beneficial to all concerned.

Individual Techniques

1. Classroom visitation is still an important part of a supervisory program. In fact, there can be no real understanding of the curriculum in action unless those responsible for supervision visit classrooms regularly. If satisfactory human relations exist, as discussed earlier in this chapter, supervisors will feel free to visit classes at will and most teachers will welcome them. The main purposes of this technique are: sensing the status of the curriculum and the experiences which students are having; discovering ideas that can be shared; establishing common bases for curriculum planning or in-service education; and, sometimes, helping to improve the teaching-learning situation.

2. Individual teacher conferences should be prominent in any comprehensive supervisory plan. These are usually held after classroom visitations or at the request of the teacher or supervisor. They can be most valuable in providing for an exchange of ideas; in giving an opportunity for constructive suggestions about classroom techniques or materials of instruction; and in identifying possible areas for curriculum study or for professional growth of the teacher.

3. The selection and assignment of well-qualified professional personnel is the basis on which a sound program of supervision must be built.

This process can be quite time-consuming but will pay off when highly qualified and suitable teachers are found for the various openings. Many future teaching-learning problems can be avoided or mitigated by careful selection of classroom teachers. It is equally important that other personnel, such as principals and supervisors themselves, be chosen with regard to the demands of the position and the personal and professional qualities required.

4. The encouragement of professional writing by capable personnel who have something to report to the profession is a function of the supervisor. Local district research or experimentation can be reported, as well as findings of research on a nationwide base. Too many educational writers have little or nothing to say. There is continuing need, however, for scholarly articles and books on current trends in the areas of the curriculum and in other professional fields.

Specific suggestions for initiating and carrying out these supervisory techniques and many others will be found in Chapters VIII, IX, X, and XI. From this brief summary, it should be apparent that modern supervision is indeed comprehensive in scope. Harris further emphasizes the point in his outline of the tasks of supervision.

Instructional supervision as a major function can be divided into ten fairly distinct major tasks.

Task 1. Developing curriculum. Designing or redesigning that which is to be taught, by whom, when, where, and in what pattern. Developing curriculum guides, establishing standards, and developing instructional units or courses are examples of programs related to this task.

Task 2. Organizing for instruction. Making organizational arrangements to implement the curriculum design. Grouping students and planning class schedules are examples of programs related to this task.

Task 3. Staffing. Selecting and assigning the appropriate instructional staff member to appropriate activities in the organization. Programs related to this task include recruitment, screening, testing, and maintaining personnel records.

Task 4. Providing facilities. Designing and equipping appropriate facilities for effective use by instructional staff members. This includes programs for school building planning and developing educational specifications for equipment.

Task 5. Providing materials. Identifying, evaluating, selecting, and securing utilization of materials for instruction that make for efficient and effective instruction.

Task 6. Arranging for in-service education. Arranging for activities which will promote the growth of instructional staff members to make them more efficient and more effective.

Task 7. Orienting new staff members. Providing new staff members with necessary information and understandings to maximize their chances of initial success with a minimum of difficulties. This is closely related to in-service education.

Task 8. Relating special services.   Relating the special service programs to the major instructional goals of the school. This involves identifying those services which have the greatest contributions to make to the instructional program, developing policies and working relationships which facilitate and do not impede instruction, and organizing for the maximum utilization of special service staff competencies to facilitate instruction.

Task 9. Developing public relations.   Developing relationships with the public in relation to instructional matters. This task is concerned with informing, securing assistance, and avoiding undesirable influences from the public in relation to the instructional program.

Task 10. Evaluating.   Planning, organizing, and implementing activities for the evaluation of all facets of the educational process directly related to instruction.

All activities of supervision may be subsumed under one or more of these major tasks. These are not mutually exclusive categories of tasks, but they do provide a structure for analyzing supervision as a major function.[6]

SELECTING AND ORGANIZING PERSONNEL FOR EFFECTIVE SUPERVISION OF INSTRUCTION

It is obvious that such a concept of supervision requires a high level of educational leadership for its implementation. The supervisor must be equipped personally and professionally to handle the position of responsibility to which he is called. Although research studies in selection of supervisors and administrators are quite limited, certain conclusions seem evident.

The modern school supervisor must have the personal attributes, first of all, that make a good teacher. He needs high native intelligence, a broad grasp of the educational process in society, a likable personality, and great skill in human relations. He must have a love for children and an abiding interest in them and their learning problems. His skill in the use of group processes is vital, and he needs to show a working understanding of the team concept in democratic supervision. He must be willing to subjugate his own personal ideas to the combined judgment of the team at times; yet he must possess the ability and fortitude to hold fast to his convictions unless additional evidence is presented. A good supervisor always should be guided by the findings of educational research and should have little time for pure opinion in group discussion and individual conference.

While the supervisor cannot possibly be expert in all of the fields which he coordinates, his knowledge should include the availability of resource leaders in all the areas of school supervision and improvement of instruc-

[6]Ben M. Harris, *Supervisory Behavior in Education* (Englewood Cliffs, N.J.: Prentice-Hall, Inc., 1963), pp. 13–14.

tion. He may be a specialist in certain disciplines, but he has to be a generalist in his approach to the total school program.

Tompkins and Beckley have further defined the necessary qualities of a supervisor: "His intuition, humility, friendliness, thoughtfulness, sense of humor—his effect on others—as well as his patience are essential characteristics, because supervision deals with relationships between people. His effectiveness depends on his understanding of human behavior. . . ."[7] According to Wiles,

A supervisor is concerned with providing effective leadership within the staff. To do this, he should seek constantly to improve his sensitivity to the feelings of others, to increase the accuracy of his estimate of group opinion on important issues, to become more cooperative in his working relationships, to seek to establish higher goals for himself, and to interact more frequently with those in the group with which he works.[8]

In short, the modern supervisor must be capable, well trained in education and psychology, likable, and expert in the democratic group process. He recognizes his role as leader, and cooperatively involves his fellow administrators and teachers in all major decisions affecting them and the teaching-learning situation.

The personnel actually involved in supervision will vary according to the size of the district and the importance ascribed to supervisory activities.

The small school district, which is discussed fully in Chapter III, consists of one or two elementary schools and a small high school; or it may be a combination of small elementary or rural schools, with perhaps a common high school. The total pupil population is usually less than 2,000. In smaller organizations like this, administrative personnel usually will have the responsibility for supervisory activities as well. For example, the chief school administrator generally will be the supervisor of the total instructional program, elementary through high school. He might have a full- or part-time high school principal, but in many cases he will also assume that position himself. At the elementary level there may be a non-teaching principal or two, but often these schools will be administered by head teachers or teaching principals. These overworked professionals certainly have little or no time for supervisory activities. Even full-time principals must devote a significant portion of their workday to the administration of their buildings. Thus, it can be seen that usually no one

---

[7]Ellsworth Tompkins and Ralph Beckley, *Selected References to Secondary School Supervision* (Washington, D.C.: U.S. Department of Health, Education, and Welfare, Office of Education, Circular No. 389, February, 1954), p. 2.
[8]Wiles, "Supervision," *Encyclopedia of Educational Research*, p. 1442.

person is fully assigned to the supervision of instruction in the typical small school district. Those involved to some extent in supervision would be the chief administrator, the principals (if any), and, hopefully, the classroom teachers.

The intermediate-size school system, as defined by the authors in Chapter III, is made up of three or more elementary schools (or combinations of rural schools), one or more secondary schools, and a total pupil population of up to 10,000. Personnel with supervisory roles would include the chief school administrator, the principals of the elementary and secondary schools, and possibly one or more of the following: special-area supervisors or coordinators, department heads, team leaders (if any), assistant superintendent in charge of instruction, coordinator of elementary education, and coordinator of secondary education. Any of the last three positions would be largely supervisory in nature and the personnel appointed to them would devote full time to the direct improvement of instruction and the coordination of the educational program at all levels throughout the district.

While any such division is arbitrary, the large school system is identified in this handbook as enrolling over 10,000 pupils. This category therefore includes the large suburban district with perhaps ten elementary and several secondary schools; it also encompasses the medium-size and large cities, which support hundreds of schools.

With the trend toward decentralization of administration in the very large cities, the principles and concepts of supervision which are pertinent to the less populous urban-suburban systems will be applicable to the relatively autonomous "local" or "community" district of a large metropolis. Consequently, the authors believe that the optimum supervisory program in a large city district will be a greatly decentralized one, with considerable autonomy being given to the principals and their immediate co-workers and superiors.

Role of the Principals and Teachers

In any size district, the principal should be recognized as the educational leader of his school and immediate community, responsible for the supervision of instruction as well as for the execution of other administrative functions. On a district-wide level, the principal will cooperate with his colleagues in other schools and with all personnel who have supervisory functions. The philosophy of modern supervision which the authors advocate obviously dictates that classroom teachers in all districts should be an integral part of the supervisory program. They must have opportunities to participate in: evaluation of the district instructional program, curriculum development and revision, and analysis of their own teaching-learning situations. In other words, the professional integrity of the school principal and the classroom teacher are basic tenets of any effective program of supervision in the modern public school.

All persons who are likely to be involved in the supervisory process in various-size districts are discussed in Chapters III, IV, V, and VI. How best can these individuals be organized as a supervisory team? Are supervisors line officers or staff consultants? How much district-wide coordination is essential, and how much freedom of action should be left to principals and their staffs? Who coordinates the supervisory program? In this handbook these controversial questions and many others pertaining to the organization and function of personnel in supervision are discussed in detail. Opposing concepts are often presented, with reasons for each. Suggestions are intended to be practical, and honest differences in methods of organizing supervisory programs are explored fully. A brief discussion of some of the major issues follows.

Is District-Wide Coordination of the Educational Program Desirable?

Virtually all researchers and authorities reported in recent literature advocate some coordination of the program in a school district. The luxury of disjointed elementary and secondary curriculums can no longer be tolerated in a society where every hour spent in the classroom must be productive. It does not make sense for two junior high schools in a district to operate independently of each other. The important question to be decided is, "How much district-wide coordination is desirable?" If local building autonomy under a principal is important, how far should a staff go in merging its professional judgment with that of colleagues from other schools? There should be a cooperatively developed, flexible district policy so that each person with supervisory responsibilities will know the extent of his final authority and the areas in which he is to work cooperatively with others. The scope of a principal's independent action with his staff should be defined, for example, as well as those areas in which he would cooperate with other principals, supervisors, and chief administrators. A list of topics for district-wide coordination might include the following:

1. Curriculum study and development.
2. Evaluation of and selection of instructional media.
3. Planning of in-service programs.
4. Orientation of new teachers.
5. Action research and experimentation in newer organizational plans, teach-

ing techniques, and materials of instruction, such as team teaching and programmed learning.

6. Function of special personnel in such fields as art, music, and physical education.
7. Student-teaching procedures in the district.
8. Selection of professional staff members.
9. Evaluation of professional personnel.

The chief administrator and his administrative-supervisory team must take the lead in establishing district-wide policies for coordination of the educational program, where they seem to be needed.

Should Supervisory Personnel Be Line or Staff?

By definition,

... line organization is basically simple in that it involves a direct flow of authority upward and downward. A line officer has power and authority over subordinates. He is a generalist who executes administrative actions.

Staff officers do not stand in the direct line of descending or ascending authority although they may, on occasion, exercise line authority. They can be divided into three types in relation to the functions which they perform: *service, coordinative,* and *advisory.*

Although the line and staff concept of administration has been held in considerable disrepute, there is no way of abolishing line authority without making administration chaotic. The important point is that the operation of line authority should be consistent with reasonable goals of democratic administration. . . . (Also) the number of authority levels and line officers are kept at a minimum.[9]

The chief school administrator, assistant superintendent in charge of instruction (if any), and the full-time principals and assistant principals are generally line officials in the organization of a school district. A portion of their time and responsibilities would normally be devoted to supervisory activities, and in this work their line authority should be de-emphasized to the end that effective democratic action may arise from sound human relationships and dynamic, sensitive leadership.

A real issue arises when the positions of coordinator of elementary education, coordinator of secondary education, and special-area supervisors are considered. Some researchers emphatically conclude that general supervisors or coordinators should be line personnel, while others find that these positions should be strictly staff. Some studies advocate both line and staff functions. The research offers conflicting evidence.

[9]*Modern Practices and Concepts of Staffing Schools* (Albany, N.Y.: Cooperative Development of Public School Administration in New York State, 1956), pp. 8, 33, 35.

A study by the Cooperative Development of Public School Administration in New York State recommended that "the role of the building principal as an educational leader in his school unit should be enhanced. He should report directly to the chief school officer in all but the largest school situations, and should be responsible for the total education of the child in his school."[10] This and other studies suggest, for example, that the position of elementary supervisor or coordinator be a staff assignment, with the supervisor serving as a resource person on call of the building principals. Arguments in favor of this conclusion can be summarized briefly as follows:

1. A sound educational program demands strong building principals, reporting directly to the chief school administrator.
2. For most effective organization, the number of authority levels and line officers should be kept to a minimum.[11]
3. A principal's council, with rotating leadership, can coordinate the program, under the general direction of the chief school administrator or assistant superintendent.

On the other hand, Evans found that the position of elementary school supervisor (or coordinator) is necessary for the most effective coordination of the total elementary program.

Coordination is important in the elementary schools of a district, and the elementary supervisor is in a position to see the broad approach to curriculum and instruction district-wide. The elementary supervisor is in a line-and-staff organization but the line relationship is not overemphasized. The supervisor is responsible to the superintendent in the areas of curriculum and instruction. The principals are responsible to the elementary supervisor for matters of curriculum and instruction, and are directly responsible to the chief school official in administrative areas. The supervisor does not participate in building administration.[12]

The advantages of the general supervisor or coordinator as a line officer seem to be as follows:

1. The supervisor should have the time and the vision to offer leadership in coordinating the total program. He is in a position to see the broad approach to curriculum and instruction district-wide.
2. The principals necessarily have a limited view of one school and com-

---

[10]*Ibid.*, p. 35.
[11]*Ibid.*, p. 33.
[12]N. Dean Evans, "The Status and Function of the Public Elementary School Supervisor in the Third and Fourth Class Districts of the Pennsylvania Counties of Chester, Delaware, and Montgomery" (Doctoral dissertation, Temple University, 1958), pp. 235–36.

munity, and do not generally have the perspective or the time to work together in effective coordination of the total instructional program.

3. It is possible to have strong building principals and effective supervisors in line, if the district table of organization is democratically established and carried out. (However, it must be admitted that an autocratic supervisor coupled with poorly defined administrative staffing policy can result in weak building principals.)

Obviously, no one pattern of organization for supervision will serve all school districts. The personnel involved in administrative and supervisory roles determine to a significant extent the patterns that emerge. An autocratic and insecure elementary supervisor will often dominate young inexperienced principals, refusing to let them develop the educational leadership needed in the modern elementary school. Conversely, an experienced, well-balanced principal, with a thorough background in positive human relationships and democratic supervision, can become a most effective elementary or secondary coordinator. Each school district must decide its own pattern of organization, and select personnel accordingly.

It is hoped that suggested guidelines in the following chapters will assist administrators and supervisors in establishing or reorganizing a plan for efficient supervision of instruction. It is important that lines of responsibility be carefully, yet sensibly, established. Sound organization avoids many basic conflicts, duplication of effort, confusion, and lack of coordinated effort.

ADMINISTRATION AND SUPERVISION— DISTINCTION AND DEFINITION

Some theorists would claim that educational administration and instructional supervision are two distinct "disciplines" and should be treated as such. Most scholars, however, seem to agree with Burton and Brueckner:

The two can be separated arbitrarily only for the sake of analysis. A separation in function is impossible . . . mere inspection of the typical division between administrative and supervisory duties would indicate that the division can be only an arbitrary one for purposes of discussion. Intimate interrelationship and overlap are inherent and inevitable.[13]

It is the position of the authors of this handbook that educational administration is the comprehensive generic category, which includes super-

[13]Burton and Bruekner, *Supervision: A Social Process*, pp. 96–98. (Copyright © 1955, Appleton-Century-Crofts, Inc.).

vision of instruction as one of its major functions. Other key areas of administration, for example, are finance and facility development.

Although overlapping among major areas is inevitable, the major purpose of a particular administrative activity should determine its classification. If the *primary* aim of an act is the improvement of the teaching-learning situation, then it may well be considered as supervisory. For example, a principal might visit a teacher's classroom for the purpose of making observations that could lead to cooperative changes in this particular learning environment. Such an activity would be classified as a supervisory one. Other examples are detailed in Chapters VIII through XI of this handbook.

In summary, any leadership function that is primarily concerned with the improvement of instruction is considered supervisory, and, supervision itself is a major division of education administration.

COLLECTIVE NEGOTIATIONS AND SUPERVISION

Some of the supervisory activities and leadership roles suggested in the following chapters are topics for negotiation and contractual agreement in certain school districts. Administrators and supervisors need to carefully define and redefine their functions in the field of supervision of instruction, particularly as they relate to teaching personnel.

The following areas are often subject to negotiation in districts that have rather formalized agreements between the board of education and teacher groups:

1. Assignment of teachers.
2. Time when teacher conferences are held.
3. Time when staff meetings are held; number of meetings.
4. Evaluation of instruction.
5. Attendance at professional conferences.
6. Participation in curriculum development and selection of learning resources.
7. Participation in staff selection.
8. Time when in-service programs are scheduled.

As the reader will note, the authors believe that teachers should be involved in cooperative planning for all of the above supervisory activities, as well as many others. Indeed, if administrators provide their staffs with an enlightened, democratic climate, there will be less reason for teachers to organize for militant confrontation. If the reader accepts the proposition that all staff members should be involved in decisions that affect them, then there is no question that teachers should participate in the planning and execution of the entire supervisory program.

For the supervisor working in a district that already has formalized agreements that impose certain restrictions on supervisory activity, the challenge is clear. He must exert every voluntary effort to provide the kind of dynamic, democratic leadership that will always be respected by the professional teacher. Such a supervisor will find creative ways to motivate people to try new ideas, and he will work around the apparent limits imposed by contract provisions. In the process, he will earn the regard of most of his fellow administrators and teachers.

A CASE STUDY—THE OLD AND THE NEW

Miss Hickory was obviously enjoying her forty-fifth county teachers' institute. She had just retired during the past year after forty-four years of teaching in the same district. With other retired teachers she was attending the sessions of the annual institute (now called Staff Workshop) as an honored guest. At the coffee break between meetings, Miss Hickory spied Jane Blossom, a recent state college graduate, with whom she had taught fifth grade during her last year. Despite the disparity in age, the two teachers had established a warm friendship and close working relationship during their year together in adjoining classrooms. And so the greeting was cordial, and the conversation flowed easily. . . .

"Jane," cried Miss Hickory across the crowded cafeteria; and the two friends quickly found a table where they could chat.

"Wasn't the keynote speaker wonderful, Miss Hickory? He certainly emphasized the necessity for the team approach to improving instruction."

"He did hit the nail on the head," agreed Miss Hickory. "I only hope that Mr. Crotchett and a few other administrators were listening. Of course it's hard 'to teach an old dog new tricks,' as the saying goes."

"But is the team concept so new?" asked Jane. "I remember all the things you've told me about Mr. Goodly—how he involved teachers in decision-making 40 years ago."

"Yes," recalled Miss Hickory. "He was a gem—the county superintendent who used to visit me at Oak Hill School. I was all alone there with grades one through eight, and I used to look forward to his visits. He was so concerned about me as a person, and he loved the children. When Mr. Goodly entered that one-room school, he immediately became a part of the 'woodwork.' No one really knew he was there, and yet he took part in the reading lessons, drank coffee with me during recess, and helped me with the troublesome attendance report. Now there was the kind of man the speaker this morning was talking about. Even in those days Mr. Goodly would call all of us teachers in our section of the county together regularly to discuss the curriculum, the problems of our children, and the educational needs of the people. Without calling it that, he really used the team approach. And we all felt that we were an important part of the team."

"I guess it just proves," replied Jane, "that examples of enlightened supervision can be found in any era."

"Now you're making me feel my age, but you're right. Today, in the supposed golden age of democratic supervision, a district like this will put up with a principal like Mr. Crotchett who doesn't know the meaning of the concept, 'teacher involvement.' And of course I could tell you about a few other Crotchetts who served as county superintendents during my teaching days. But I prefer to remember Mr. Goodly and the others like him who made my teaching career so rewarding."

DEFINITION OF TERMS

Throughout this handbook the term *supervisor* is used in reference to all personnel who render supervisory services. This includes, for example, the chief school official, assistant superintendent in charge of instruction, the coordinators of elementary and secondary education, building principals, and special supervisors or coordinators.

The terms *superintendent, chief school administrator,* and *chief school official* are synonymous and are used interchangeably. The terms *supervision* and *instructional leadership* also are used interchangeably throughout this text.

To express more accurately the authors' concept of democratic supervision, the word *coordinator* will often be used instead of *supervisor* or *director* in discussing such positions as elementary supervisor and director of elementary or secondary education.

SUMMARY

Modern supervision is positive, dynamic, democratic action designed to improve instruction through the continual growth of all concerned individuals—the child, the teacher, the supervisor, the administrator, and the parent or other lay person.

There is a pressing need for improved supervision in modern school systems which must develop and evaluate instructional programs in an ever-changing society.

The major principles and characteristics of modern school supervision can be summarized as follows:

1. The establishment and maintenance of positive human relationships is essential.

2. Modern supervision is democratic, with active, cooperative involvement of all staff members under the leadership of capable, understanding, and discerning administrators. Each person must be willing to assume some responsibility in the supervisory program.
3. Modern supervision is comprehensive in scope, embracing all school experiences from kindergarten through high school or junior college. All factors involved in pupil learning are important. The totality of the teaching-learning situations is considered. The supervisory role reaches far beyond the traditional "classroom visitation" and encompasses a variety of individual and group techniques.

Effective supervision requires a high level of leadership. The successful supervisor is intelligent, well-trained in education and psychology, likable, experienced, and expert in the democratic group process.

The size of a school district and the importance it assigns to supervisory activities will determine the number and function of personnel actually involved in supervision.

Some cooperative, district-wide coordination of the educational program is thought essential by most researchers. Principals are the educational leaders of their schools, but they must work together with the other administrators and supervisors to assure an integrated program from kindergarten through high school.

With regard to line or staff organization of supervisory personnel, the research evidence is conflicting. Each district must decide its own patterns after considering the various conclusions. It is essential that areas of responsibility be carefully, yet sensibly and flexibly, established. Sound organization for supervision avoids many basic conflicts, unnecessary overlapping, and confusion of effort.

By definition, supervision is considered a major division of educational administration. Any leadership function that is primarily concerned with the improvement of instruction is called supervision.

SUGGESTED ACTIVITIES AND PROBLEMS

1. Using several sources, write a documented research paper outlining the history of supervision.
2. Interview a chief school administrator or assistant superintendent in charge of instruction to determine the philosophy of supervision that exists in the school district. Write up your findings.
3. Study the administrative structure of an intermediate or large school system. Identify all administrators who have some supervisory responsibilities. Describe their roles and relationships.
4. Interview a principal to ascertain the extent to which he is the educational leader of his school. Write a paper summarizing your findings.
5. Select a school district that has a formal collective negotiations agreement

with the teaching staff. Contact several staff members to determine the changes that have taken place in the supervisory program since formal contracts have been negotiated. Write a paper summarizing your findings.

SELECTED READINGS

Bishop, Leslee J. *Collective Negotiation in Curriculum and Instruction—Questions and Concerns.* Washington, D.C.: Association for Supervision and Curriculum Development, 1967.

Bradfield, Luther E. *Supervision for Modern Elementary Schools.* Chap. 1. Columbus, Ohio: Charles E. Merrill Books, Inc., 1964.

Brickell, Henry M. *Organizing New York State for Educational Change.* Albany, N.Y.: State Education Department, 1961.

Burton, William H., and Brueckner, Leo J. *Supervision: A Social Process.* Chaps. 1–7. New York: Appleton-Century-Crofts, Inc., 1955.

Harris, Ben M. *Supervisory Behavior in Education.* Chaps. 1, 2, 9. Englewood Cliffs, N.J.: Prentice-Hall, Inc., 1963.

Lucio, William H., and McNeil, John D. *Supervision—A Synthesis of Thought and Action.* 2nd ed., Chaps. 1–3. New York: McGraw-Hill Book Company, Inc., 1969.

Wiles, Kimball. *Supervision for Better Schools.* 3rd ed., Chaps. 1–3. Englewood Cliffs, N.J.: Prentice-Hall, Inc., 1967.

chapter 2

Theory and Research in Supervision

Every individual who engages in a supervisory activity makes particular decisions, performs specific actions, or refrains from overt actions altogether because of his beliefs, philosophy, hunches, and theories (about educational practices). If questioned, he could give you some of his beliefs about instructional leadership and even his philosophy of education, but he probably knows little about the reasons for his hunches and next to nothing about theories of supervision. His ignorance about theories of supervision is not strange because attempts to formulate theories in the field of educational administration have been quite recent. In fact, the application of theory to the area of supervision is just beginning. Several of the attempts to adapt theory to supervisory activities are reported in this chapter as well as an outline of suggested procedures for building instructional theory.

Theory and research should go hand in hand. Research can become one of the most valuable sources of content to be used in the building of administrative theory of which supervisory theory would be a very important area. Administrative theories can in turn become a basis for research. Also, research on instructional leadership is valuable for the purpose of evaluating educational practices regardless of whether or not they are based on sound theories.

The intent of this chapter is to define educational leadership theory, relate some of its characteristics, and present several theories illustrating their relationships to the tasks of supervision. Likewise, a brief discussion of instructional theory is included in the hope that individuals in a supervisory capacity will work with teachers to build instructional theories.

Pertinent research also will be reviewed with a brief discussion of its implications for the improvement of instruction and learning. Finally, it will be recommended that the instructional leader rely more on the findings of research and engage in it and/or encourage others to participate in research in an attempt to find solutions to the many perplexing problems in learning and instruction.

THEORY AND SUPERVISION

After many years of suspicion and misunderstanding, the subject of theory has become a respectable topic for discussion in texts on educational administration. The imaginary chasm between theory and practice is at last being bridged. Writers, professors, and practitioners in the field are beginning to agree that, perhaps, there is nothing as practical as theory after all.

Individuals responsible for the improvement of learning and instruction might profitably learn all they can about supervisory, instructional, and curricular theories. They should not only become familiar with the theories that have been advanced to date, but become acquainted with the theory building process itself and attempt to build their own theories. This should not only help administrative personnel immeasurably in improving their techniques of instructional leadership and curriculum development, but also enable them to assist teachers in obtaining an understanding of instructional theory and its use. A recent authoritative pamphlet highlights this concept in the following statement:

> Student teachers and experienced teachers need to be able to recognize the different types of theories and to be aware of their power, their limitations, and their appropriate uses.[1]

Theories and Their Sources

One of the most important problems to be solved in education today is that of agreeing upon a definition of theory and identifying and understanding its role in the solution of educational problems. Attempts are being made to formulate theories of educational leadership by drawing upon the resources of the humanities, social sciences, and the natural sciences and by following the examples set by public and business administration in the development of theories.

Although earlier discussions on theory building dealt with administra-

---

[1]Ira J. Gordon, ed., *Criteria for Theories of Instruction* (Washington, D.C.: Association for Supervision and Curriculum Development, NEA, 1968), p. 30.

tive theory,[2] the various aspects of educational administration are now receiving attention. Some of the most pertinent literature on the subject will be reviewed here. Each theory will be reviewed separately and its implications for instructional leadership suggested.

A Supervisory Theory Based on Leadership

A Theory of Educational Leadership, by Saunders, *et al.*, is one of the most definitive treatises on the theory of educational leadership. In this important work theory is defined as follows:

Theory is a set of assumptions or generalizations supported by related philosophical assumptions and scientific principles. These assumptions or generalizations serve as a basis for projecting hypotheses which suggest a course of action. The hypotheses are then subjected to scientific investigation. The findings of this scientific investigation are evaluated in order to validate new scientific principles and philosophical assumptions.[3]

The same authors suggest the following statement as a theory of leadership that is applicable to the improvement of instruction:

Leadership is essential to improved educational programs. Educational leadership is any act which facilitates the achievement of educational objectives. Leadership may be performed by the status leaders, by any member of the group, or by the group as a whole.

Instructional improvement is the achievement of a set of objectives which seems to be directly and purposely related to improved learning experiences for students. The objectives should be determined by the participants who make the effort and have the responsibility for improving instruction.

The political philosophy deemed most effective places responsibility for making decisions in the hands of the people who are affected by the decision. In keeping with this concept, effective educational leadership provides the people directly involved with an opportunity to participate in the development and direction of educational programs. This participation can best be attained at the local school and community level in interaction with all people concerned with instructional improvement.

Cooperative group effort is the most acceptable and effective approach in reaching a goal that is satisfactory to and meets the needs of the total group. People who work together in groups have a contribution to make to each other and each can help achieve the objective of the group. A cooperative

[2]For example, see Daniel E. Griffiths, *Administrative Theory* (New York: Appleton-Century-Crofts, Inc., 1959), and Roald F. Campbell and James M. Lipham, eds., *Administrative Theory as a Guide to Action* (Chicago: Midwest Administrative Center, 1960).

[3]Robert L. Saunders, Ray C. Phillips, and Harold T. Johnson, *A Theory of Educational Leadership* (Columbus, Ohio: Charles E. Merrill Books, Inc., 1966), p. 5.

group effort facilitates changes in the behavior of group members and changes in behavior are necessary to reach educational goals.

People are of utmost importance in efforts to improve education. A strong respect for people should permeate all relationships. Instructional improvement should be approached with the view that the individuals involved are desirous of improving their competency. Furthermore, instructional personnel are capable of identifying and solving problems and making decisions concerning the instructional program.

The dynamic and changing nature of society requires a continuous examination of educational objectives. The schools in this society serve the people to whom they belong and, therefore, must be sensitive to the desires of the people. Every effort should be made to provide for interaction between lay and professional people in determining objectives and developing an understanding of how objectives may be achieved.

The achievement of objectives in a dynamic society demands changes in the behavior of the people involved in the instructional program. Change in behavior, or learning, becomes an important consideration. Learning is more effective when the learner is directly involved in the learning process. Involvement provides for consideration of purposes of the learner as well as focusing his attitudes, feelings, and values on the learning situation. An atmosphere that is largely non-judgmental should be provided in the instructional improvement program. The learner should be free to make choices for himself and to assume major responsibility for his own learning. An atmosphere for learning which provides the above conditions will facilitate the changes in behavior required to improve instruction.

The scientific method offers the most adequate approach to the solution of educational problems. The scientific method is flexible and adaptable to a solution of various problems of the learner. However, the method requires the learner to make a conscious and systematic approach to solving his problems. The role of the central administration of the school system or any other agency outside the local school in instructional improvement is that of making its resources available and cooperating with the people involved in identifying and achieving common goals.[4]

Application of the theory. Examination of the above theory reveals that a number of hypotheses might be drawn from it. The following ones should be sufficient to illustrate the point:

1. *If* the cooperative group effort is used and *if* changes in the behavior of group members result, *then* the educational goals are more likely to be achieved.
2. *If* a strong respect for people permeates all relationships and *if* assumptions are made that individuals are desirous of improving their competency, *then* instructional improvement will result.

Individuals in supervisory roles who accept the above hypotheses might initiate and carry out practices of the following types:

[4]*Ibid.*, pp. 39–40.

1. Institute a program to improve the skills of the administrative and instructional staff members in the use of the group processes.
2. Initiate cooperative group planning of the goals for instruction and the ways to achieve them.
3. Provide a variety of opportunities for teachers to grow professionally on their own initiative.
4. Encourage teachers to experiment and support them regardless of whether or not the project is successful.

A Supervisory Theory Based on Syntheses

The late Kimball Wiles formulated a theory of supervision by taking a number of concepts and facts from appropriate related fields and developing a set of criteria that might be used for evaluating projected supervisory acts. No attempt will be made here to reproduce all of the carefully documented material found in Wiles' text; however, abstracted selected material is included below:

Assumptions

1. The function of supervision is to effect changes in the curriculum, instruction, and learning in schools.
2. Supervisors and teachers differ in function rather than in education and experience.
3. Teachers must be treated as professionals who have a code of ethics, specialized education, and a desire to be self-directing.
4. Supervisors are expected to provide leadership and competency in developing an organization and a working environment that makes possible continuous improvement in curriculum, instruction, and learning.
5. The behavioral sciences are the most valuable sources of concepts to be used in the development of an organization and a strategy for change.
6. Concepts from each of the behavioral sciences that appear to have relevance to the formation of a strategy of change should be utilized as the bases for the formulation of a theory of supervision.

Concepts About Mental Health, Counseling, and Therapy

It must be assumed that an individual behaves in the way he believes best in any given situation, and that he modifies his behavior only as he changes his perception of himself, his role, or the situation. The extent to which an individual understands himself and his purposes is probably the best single predictive indicator of his future self-adjustment. An individual who feels worthy, wanted, and adequate has readiness for change, finds a wider range of facts and experiences significant, is receptive to learning, and is becoming more mature. An individual becomes more open in a situation in which he is accepted, finds it unnecessary to be defensive and closed, and has access to a variety of new experiences. He is assisted in the process of change by others who convey a feeling of acceptance and a desire to be helpful to him in developing self-direction.

Concepts About Learning

An individual learns through his interaction with his environment, and he selects from his environment the factors with which he will interact. An individual learns what he perceives that interaction to be, and his perception is a product of past experiences, present needs, and his purposes. His learning is affected by his emotions.

Concepts About Group Development

Group cohesiveness is the result of the interaction of individuals. When common goals, values, and norms are developed by an aggregation of individuals they become a group. Members receive greater satisfaction from working in cohesive groups. Members of a group are controlled by the norms of the group to which they give their allegiance, and the greater the prestige individuals attach to a group, the stronger the influence of its norms on them. In highly cohesive groups greater effort is made to reach an agreement, behavior is more influenced by the situation, and interaction is more effective in producing influence. Groups must develop a structure and organization in order to make and implement decisions effectively. High incentive groups usually learn faster and work more efficiently than low incentive groups. An individual's behavior in a group is affected by his position in it. Usually peripheral members of a group are more susceptible to outside influences. Consensus is more likely to occur in situations in which the group thinks together than in ones in which the leader dominates the group.

Concepts About Leadership

Leadership is a function which makes possible the formulation and attainment of group goals. It is widespread and diffused throughout the group and may be fulfilled by different individuals as the situation changes. Leadership is a product of interaction within the group and the role is interchangeable with followership. The extent to which group members can use an individual's contribution determines the leadership he exerts. This in turn depends upon the group members perception of him, his motives, and his competency. Norms of the group play an important role, in that group members select leaders that they believe will understand, accept, and maintain the group norms. Other things being equal, the leadership influence exerted by an individual is determined by the frequency of his interaction with other members of the group. Individuals with and without official status exert leadership within a group; however, high-prestige individuals are more spontaneous, make more direct attempts to influence others, and are more open to behavioral contagion than those with low prestige.

Concepts About Human Relations

Self-acceptance helps the individual to accept others, and placing value on differences enables him to develop his own uniqueness. Concern for other individuals' feelings is an essential element of effective leadership.

Concepts About Communication

Good communication is essential to the improvement of instruction, learning, and the curriculum; however, it is never complete and accurate. Communication affects a group's efficiency, accuracy, organization, leadership emergence, and membership satisfactions. The position an individual occupies in a communication pattern influences his behavior while he occupies that position. An individual who is recognized as a leader in a task-oriented group is likely to emerge at the center of the communication pattern. The behavior of group members toward an individual is affected by the credibility of that individual as a source of information. In communication the language level may be extremely important. Language that seems quite adequate for superficial communication may not be adequate for understanding of deeper meanings.

Concepts About Community Power Structure

In each community may be found a power structure in which certain individuals make the decisions that influence the behavior and decisions of others; however, the overt decision-making is not always the real decision-making in a community. The decisions made and actions taken by legal bodies and community institutions usually reflect the decisions of the community power structure.[5]

Application of the theory. In referring to his complete theory from which the above has been abstracted, Wiles suggested that it should be used as a basis for advancing hypotheses about the ways in which individuals charged with the improvement of learning and instruction should work with teachers singly and in groups.

As an example of the use of the above theory, several related hypotheses have been selected to illustrate how they might affect instructional leadership procedures. The two hypotheses follow:

A. Supervision is a function of the organization. B. Many people contribute to the function of improvement—some have an official responsibility for contribution to improved instruction, and others contribute by their actions.[6]

[5]Adapted from Kimball Wiles, *Supervision for Better Schools*, 3rd ed. (Englewood Cliffs, N.J.: Prentice-Hall, Inc., 1967), pp. ix–xiii. By permission of the publisher.
[6]*Ibid.*, pp. xiii–xv.

It would seem that any individual serving in a supervisory capacity who accepted these two hypotheses would, among other practices, accept and try to implement the following practices:

1. Plan the instructional improvement program cooperatively.
2. Insure that all staff activities contribute in some way to the improvement of learning and instruction. (For example, the selection of textbooks and other learning resources can be a valuable in-service growth experience for teachers.)
3. Institute an evaluation program that is comprehensive enough to include the participation of pupils, teachers, and administration, and to examine the effectiveness of learning in light of instructional, supervisory, and other administrative procedures.

The reader is encouraged to think of many other practices in all phases of the supervisory program that relate to the above hypotheses. The important point, however, is that theory can affect practice if the practitioner is willing to take the trouble to accept or formulate theories of supervision, to infer hypotheses from these theories, and to establish procedures that are congruent with the theories and supportive of the hypotheses.

A Supervisory Theory Based on an Action Pattern

Eye and Netzer emphasize that an understanding of theory and its use is essential to the improvement of learning and instruction:

... consistency in the form of methodological attack on problems, then, becomes the result not of averaging experiences but of a series of successful and varied experiences. These experiences, whether or not verbalized, constitute the theoretical bases of behavior choices. Theory, then, is inherent in or an integral part of supervisory planning and performance.[7]

In discussing the development of a sound theoretical basis for supervisory practices, the same authors suggest that the supervisor must develop the ability "to scrutinize his own actions, to identify his own motivations, to verbalize his own value patterns to the end that he will be in a position to view, explore, and evaluate the factors involved in the choices of behaviors."[8] Eye and Netzer's development of a theory of supervision is based on the relationships of assumptions, principles, objectives, criteria, and procedures in an action pattern. To facilitate the procedure of comparing several different theories of supervision, a brief

---

[7]Glenn G. Eye and Lanore A. Netzer, *Supervision of Instruction—A Phase of Administration*, (New York: Harper & Row, Publishers, 1965), p. 34.
[8]*Ibid.*, p. 37.

review of Eye and Netzer's theory wll be given here; however, the reader is encouraged to seek the original source for a more complete understanding.

In the brief presentation of this theory of instruction, each of the terms listed will be defined and then applied.

The Action Pattern

An *assumption* is a declaration of a supposition which does not require supporting evidence but which is based upon a knowledge of practice.

A *principle* is a general statement describing a persisting relationship between two or more phenomena which gives direction to action.

An *objective* is the identity or definition of a goal accepted as the object of achievement.

A *criterion* is the referent point or condition which can serve the purpose of making valid judgments and evaluations.

A *procedure* is the systematic arrangement of behaviors designed to accomplish a stated objective.[9]

Application of the theory. The above definitions should be self-explanatory, however, they will become somewhat clearer if the examples given below are studied. The reader should attempt to list other examples in the respective categories. It also should be noted that each example has been derived from the previous one; i.e., the example in each category was derived from the example in the previous category. The examples in the last two categories were formulated by the authors.

Assumption. The major function of supervision is that of influencing situations, persons, and relationships for the purpose of stimulating change that may be evaluated as improvement.[10]

Principle. Changes occur as the relationships between situations and persons are manipulated.[11]

Objective. To prevent either the situation or the person from remaining constant in the change-process.[12]

Criterion. Is the teaching-learning environment improving as a result of the in-service education program?

Procedure. To achieve the above objective, the supervisor engages in a series of cooperatively-planned individual and group activities.

Eye and Netzer not only have proposed a theory of supervision, but in the steps listed above, they have outlined an action pattern that can be used by instructional leaders to build their own theory of supervision.

[9]*Ibid.*, p. 52.
[10]*Ibid.*, p. 39.
[11]*Ibid.*, p. 44.
[12]*Ibid.*, p. 46.

A Supervisory Theory Based on Administration as a Social Process

One of the most frequently-quoted theories of administration which appears to have relevance for instructional supervision is that of Getzels and Guba. In their model, administration is categorized as a social process. They conceive of administration *structurally* as the hierarchy of subordinate-superordinate relationships within a social system. *Functionally*, they consider this hierarchy of relationships as the locus for allocating and integrating roles, personnel, and facilities for the purpose of achieving goals of the social system.

The social system is considered as being comprised of two major dimensions or classes of phenomena:

1. *Nomothetic*, consisting of institutions with roles and expectations that satisfy the system's goals.
2. *Idiographic*, consisting of individuals with personalities and need-dispositions to be satisfied.

Under the nomothetic (institutional) dimension of the theory, it is recognized that each institution in society has its function or functions to perform. For example, schools are established to produce a literate populace which is essential under our democratic form of government. In order that this and other goals may be achieved, individuals are assigned specific roles (teachers, principals, supervisors, superintendents, etc.) to perform. Each person is expected to fulfill the role assigned to him as defined. The institution (school) maintains systems of rewards (promotions, salary increments, special assignments, praise, etc.) and punishments (withholding of rewards, demotions, refusal of tenure, etc.).

In respect to the *idiographic* (personal) dimension, it is recognized that each individual within the social system has his own unique personal need-dispositions. To a great extent these determine his behavior. If the personality and need-dispositions of the individual are not in agreement with the role the institution has assigned to him, the individual's need-dispositions are not likely to be met and dissatisfaction is likely to result.

Getzels and Guba point to three sources of conflict in administration that may be deduced from their model. These are role-personality conflict, role conflict, and personality conflict.[13] Instructional leaders will find the above deduction helpful in understanding dissatisfaction among personnel.

Application of the theory. As should be true for all theories, it is possi-

[13] Adapted from J. W. Getzels and E. G. Guba, "Social Behavior and the Administrative Process," *School Review*, LV, no. 4 (1957), 423.

ble to formulate a number of hypotheses from the above theory. Here, again, two-related hypotheses should help to clarify the use of the theory.

1. *If* the expectations of the subordinate and superordinate are congruent, *then* the goals of the institution are more likely to be achieved.
2. *If* the personality and need-dispositions of the individual are in conflict with the institutional role expectation, *then* quality performance will not result.

Individuals in supervisory positions frequently have found support for the second hypotheses when they have been required to assist in the solution of instructional problems resulting from poor teacher assignment. For example, a teacher who prepared to teach in the primary grades may have been assigned to the upper grades; or a teacher with a major in health and physical education may be required to teach a section of general science. In the examples given above, the individuals' need-dispositions would doubtless be in conflict with the institutional role expectation. Teachers can hardly be expected to do their best under these circumstances.

In summary, then, it may be hypothesized that the success of the administrative process depends upon the extent of congruency of the expectations of both the subordinate and superordinate.

Just how does the instructional leader use this theory? The following practices might be introduced and evaluated as a test of the adequacy of the theory.

1. Continually be on the alert to see that the personality and need-dispositions of each staff member are being met.
2. Plan procedures to handle conflict that may arise between the individual and institutional dimensions.
3. Cooperatively define role expectations for all positions with the individuals expected to fulfill these expectations.
4. Be certain that the role expectations for your position as supervisor are understood by all staff members and are congruent with the expectations of the central office.

A Supervisory Theory Based on Self-actualization

Hanlon has suggested an embryonic "theory of self-actualization, in which education is the self-actualization activity of the individual person and administration is the self-actualization of the organized human group."[14] His theory takes the form of a set of postulates and theorems as outlined below:

[14]James M. Hanlon, *Administration and Education* (Belmont, Cal.: Wadsworth Publishing Company, Inc., 1968), p. 3.

Postulates

1. All things subject to change are mixtures of being and becoming.
2. In human beings this state of simultaneous being and becoming may be described as autodynamic equilibrium.
3. Where there is a state of autodynamic equilibrium, there must be both an active and a passive potency for that state.
4. The active potency for autodynamic equilibrium is by nature a system, which may be given the name "proprium."
5. In the organized human group there is a state of autodynamic equilibrium, and hence a potency for that state, analogous to the state and potency found in the individual human being.
6. The activity of the individual proprium is the process of education; the activity of the organizational proprium is the process of administration.
7. The nature and purpose of the proprium are such that they demand as the primary constitutive element of the proprium a conceptual element or subsystem.
8. The conceptual subsystem consists of a world view and an ideal pattern.
9. The nature and purpose of the proprium are such that they demand two implementary elements or subsystems—a climatic subsystem and an environment subsystem.
10. The nature and purpose of the climatic element are such that they demand three structural elements: a control element, an energizing element, and a linkage element.
11. The environmental subsystem consists of a facilitative element and a supportive element.

Theorems

1. The world view is modified by every truth which is appropriated.
2. The nature and extent of the modification of the world view depend on the inclusiveness of the truth which is appropriated and the nature of its effect on truths previously appropriated.
3. The greater the permeability and flexibility of the arcs of tolerance, the greater the possibility that the world view will be modified.
4. The greater the deliberation in constructing the world view, the greater the probability that it will be satisfactorily valid and reliable.
5. Every modification of the world view is accompanied by a modification of the ideal pattern.
6. The nature and extent of the modification of the ideal pattern will follow the pattern of modification of the world view.
7. Every modification of the ideal pattern is accompanied by a corresponding modification of the level-of-aspiration hierarchy.
8. Every ideal affects the means that will be chosen to attain every other ideal.
9. The greater the deliberation in constructing the ideal pattern, the greater the probability that it will have sufficient objective validity.
10. Human behavior is deliberate to the extent that means are consciously chosen in relation to ends that are consciously intended.

11. The only means which can be chosen are those contained in the world view, and the only ends which can be intended are those contained in the ideal pattern; therefore, no plan can be more efficacious than the world view and ideal pattern on which it is based.

12. Problems can exist only in relation to intended ends and can be perceived only through the process of evaluation; therefore, the better the evaluation, the greater the probability that problems will be perceived.

13. Problems can affect both means and ends to the extent of sometimes modifying both the world view and ideal pattern.

14. The only means for solving problems are those contained in the world view, and the only ends of problem solving are those contained in the ideal pattern; therefore no solution (decision) can be more efficacious than the world view and ideal pattern on which it is based.

15. The greater the deliberation there is in problem solving (decision-making), the greater the efficacy of the solution (decision) will be.

16. The climate of optimum freedom is created through communication in the area of subordination.

17. The use of subordination in groups follows a definite sequence of laws based on the ordinant-coordinant-non-ordinant schema.

18. Reactions to the use of subordination within the organization follow the law of reciprocal expectations; reactions to the use of subordination within the individual follow the law of introspective expectation.

19. The leader of any group will be that person who fits very closely the ideal pattern of that group, has a high level of aspiration toward the goals (ideals) which the group is seeking at the moment, and has demonstrated either actual success or high potential for success in attaining these goals (ideals).

20. The climate of energy release and channeling is created through communication in the area of self-motivation.

21. Energy is released in proportion to perceived situational involvement.

22. Energy is channeled in proportion to polarization of ideals and the acceptance of structures-in-interaction.

23. The climate of acceptance and support is created through communication in the area of other-motivation.

24. Acceptance is proportional to the successful establishment of non-irritating systemic contiguity; support is proportional to the successful establishment of systemic linkage.

25. The facilitative dimension of environment is created through exploitation in the area of ancillary or instrumental processes.

26. The supportive dimension of environment is created through exploitation in the area of financing.[15]

Application of the theory. As before, no attempt will be made here to discuss this theory in detail. The entire work should be studied by those who are interested in the concept of self-actualization. The following

[15]From *Administration and Education* by James Hanlon, pp. 205–8. © 1968 by Wadsworth Publishing Company, Inc., Belmont, California. Reprinted by permission of the publisher.

applications of the theory might convince the reader of its potential value in supervision.

For the purpose of illustration let us see how the supervisor would use Theorems 10 and 15 in carrying on his work. The individual who accepted Theorem 10 would attempt to put into effect the following practices:

1. Insure that goals and objectives are cooperatively set up for all instructional, curricular, and supervisory activities.
2. Make every effort to see that all involved and concerned individuals know, understand, and, if possible, accept these goals and objectives.
3. Provide a variety of means for meeting these goals and objectives, and allow freedom of choice in selection.

Acceptance of the intent of Theorem 15 could lead to the following procedures:

1. Innovation and change in the curriculum and/or the instructional program would be made only after extensive cooperative investigation, study, experimentation, and evaluation.
2. In preparing to make decisions involving the professional future of probationary teachers, all possible evidence will be collected, the proper administrative and supervisory personnel involved, and unlimited time spent.

Here again the reader would spend his time profitably by attempting to make applications of the other theorems to the job of instructional leadership.

THEORY AND INSTRUCTION

Earlier in this chapter it was suggested that instructional leaders attempt to build theories of instruction and assist teachers to do the same. A recent publication offers some guidelines that might be used for this purpose by proposing the following set of criteria for assessing the formal properties of theories of instruction:

1. A statement of an instructional theory should include a set of postulates and definition of terms involved in these postulates.
2. The statement of an instructional theory or sub-theory should make explicit the boundaries of its concern and the limitations under which it is proposed.
3. A theoretical construction must have internal consistency—a logical set of interrelationships.
4. An instructional theory should be congruent with empirical data.

5. An instructional theory must be capable of generating hypotheses.

6. An instructional theory must contain generalizations which go beyond the data.

7. An instructional theory must be verifiable.

8. An instructional theory must be stated in such a way that it is possible to collect data to disprove it.

9. An instructional theory must not only explain past events but also must be capable of predicting future events.

10. At the present time, instructional theories may be expected to represent qualitative synthesis.[16]

The above criteria should prove useful not only in building theories of instruction, but also as a guide for evaluating theories of instruction that are presently in existence. The reader is urged to select a current theory of instruction, such as those mentioned below, to see how it conforms to the above criteria.

Nature of a Theory of Instruction

A number of interesting theories of instruction, varying in complexity and comprehensiveness, have been suggested. A recent publication of the Association for Supervision and Curriculum Development, NEA, reports among others the following titles for theories discussed at the Ninth Curriculum Research Institute.

David G. Ryans, *A Model of Instruction Based on Information Systems Concepts.*[17]

N. A. Fattu, *A Model of Teaching as Problem Solving.*[18]

Elizabeth S. Maccia, *Instruction as Influence Toward Rule-governed Behavior.*[19]

In the introduction to the same publication, Macdonald suggests that one impediment to the development of theories of instruction has been the lack of a clear definition of terms. By use of a very helpful diagram, he demonstrates the existence of separate domains for teaching, learning, instruction, and curriculum and shows a variety of relationships among them. He further defines teaching . . . "as the behavior of the teacher, learning as the change in learner behavior, instruction as the pupil-

[16]Gordon, *Criteria for Theories of Instruction*, pp. 16–23.

[17]James B. Macdonald and Robert R. Leeper, eds., *Theories of Instruction* (Washington, D.C.: Association for Supervision and Curriculum Development, NEA, 1965), p. 36.

[18]*Ibid.*, p. 62.

[19]*Ibid.*, p. 88.

teacher interaction situation and curriculum as those planning endeavors which take place prior to instruction."[20]

In his scholarly publication, *Toward a Theory of Instruction*, Bruner states:

A theory of instruction is *prescriptive* in the sense that it sets forth rules concerning the most effective way of achieving knowledge or skill. By the same token, it provides a yardstick for criticizing or evaluating any particular way of teaching or learning.

A theory of instruction is a *normative* theory. It sets up criteria and states the conditions for meeting them. The criteria must have a high degree of generality: for example, a theory of instruction should not specify in *ad hoc* fashion the conditions for efficient learning of third-grade arithmetic; such conditions should be derivable from a more general view of mathematics learning. . . .

A theory of instruction has four major features.

First, a theory of instruction should specify the experiences which most effectively implant in the individual a predisposition toward learning—learning in general or a particular type of learning. . . .

Second, a theory of instruction must specify the ways in which a body of knowledge should be structured so that it can be most readily grasped by the learner. . . .

Third, a theory of instruction should specify the most effective sequences in which to present the materials to be learned. . . .

Finally, a theory of instruction should specify the nature and pacing of rewards and punishments in the process of learning and teaching.[21]

A casual comparison of the ten criteria for assessing the formal properties of theories of instruction and Bruner's concepts of a theory of intruction reveals that as a psychologist, Bruner emphasizes learning throughout his discussion. Examination of Bruner's complete text leaves the reader with the impression that instruction cannot be divorced from learning after all.

It is hoped that the inclusion of this brief discussion of instructional theory in this handbook will encourage individuals who are serving in or preparing for positions of instructional leadership to engage in the processes of testing hypotheses derived from theories of instruction, to formulate new theories, and assist others to do the same.

The instructional leader also must be concerned with curriculum theory. This aspect of theory will be discussed in Chapter X.

A new attitude toward the importance of theory in education has necessitated the inclusion of an extensive discussion of theory in this hand-

[20]*Ibid.*, pp. 4–6.

[21]Jerome S. Bruner, *Toward a Theory of Instruction* (New York: W. W. Norton & Company, Inc., 1968), pp. 40–41.

book. It is now generally agreed that it is highly desirable for administrators, supervisors, curriculum workers, and teachers to be concerned with and experience the building of educational theory. As the challenges and problems facing educators today increase in magnitude and complexity, new and better procedures must be developed and more lasting solutions to problems will have to be found. The building and use of theory offers some promise in this respect because it encourages the formulation of hypotheses. These, in turn, stimulate research and investigation which are responsible for accumulating a body of knowledge related to educational administration. It is beginning to be acknowledged today that very little of significant and lasting value can be accomplished without the basis of a sound theory.

The reader is urged to consider and evaluate the practices suggested throughout this handbook in light of the theories presented in this chapter.

THE SYSTEMS APPROACH AND SUPERVISION

The armed services and industry have been utilizing the *systems approach* for a number of years. This has enabled them to examine and improve the structure and operation of their respective organizations. More recently, schools have adopted the systems approach for the solution of many problems. This new approach varies from a simple charting of relationships and sequences of procedures and activities to some highly complex man-machine systems. One facet of the systems approach that is much in the limelight today is *systems analysis*. Willis defines it as follows:

The analysis of a system is a process of discovering general principles and bringing together large numbers of interrelated elements. The area referred to specifically as "systems analysis" is primarily concerned with decision-oriented systems. It is concerned with social systems that have been studied in the past and, adding an important element, that of attempting to analyze the structure of the system in terms of the decisions which must be made in operating the system.[22] [See Figure 1 for the components of a simple decision-oriented system.]

Systems approach draws from Gestalt psychology which many years ago popularized the concept that "the whole is greater than the sum of its parts." Johnson, *et al.*, throw considerable light on the matter when they define systems as:

[22]Raymond E. Willis, "Systems Analysis: Reviewing Theory and Application," in *Systems Analysis in Educational Administration*, eds. Donald E. Davis and Vernon L. Hendrix (Minneapolis, Minn.: Department of Educational Administration College of Education, University of Minnesota, 1966), p. 8.

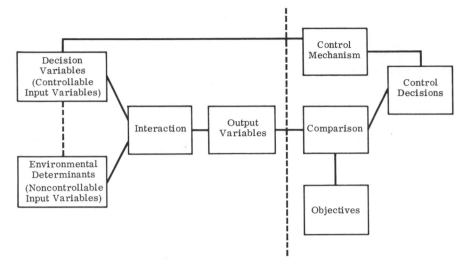

THE COMPONENTS OF A SIMPLE
DECISION-ORIENTED SYSTEM

Figure 1. Reprinted from Raymond E. Willis, "Systems Analysis: Reviewing Theory and Application," in *Systems Analysis in Educational Administration,* eds. Donald E. Davis and Vernon L. Hendricks, *op. cit.,* p. 9.

. . . *an array of components designed to accomplish a particular objective according to plan.* There are three significant points in this definition: (1) there is a design or established arrangement of materials, energy and information; (2) there is a purpose or objective which the system is designed to accomplish; and (3) inputs of materials, energy and information are allocated according to plan.[23]

In discussing the systems approach as an aid in school administration Knezevich said:

Systems, like "models," is a way of harnessing theory to the action problems of administrators. It can make the theory movement more meaningful. Rather than a bag of tricks born of raw experience, the systems approach provides a perspective for assessing challenges facing administrators. It can be classified as an approach to thinking that represents a further extension of the scientific attitude and method in administration.[24]

[23]R. E. Johnson, F. E. Kast, and J. E. Rosenzweig, *The Theory and Management of Systems,* 2nd ed. (New York: McGraw-Hill Book Co., 1967), pp. 403–4.
[24]Dr. S. J. Knezevich, *The Relevance of Systems Analysis to Educational Administration* (Philadelphia, Pa.: Address presented to the Temple University Seminar on Systems Analysis, April 18, 1968).

In attempting to clarify the confusion in terminology, the same speaker indicated that systems analysis was only one dimension of the systems approach. He added and defined other facets as follows:

"Systems design" is the creation of a new system, which may have been suggested by the analysis, for relating inputs to outputs. Alternative systems for achieving objectives in a most expeditious manner may be another outcome. "Systems operation" or "management" is a way of organizing tasks and harnessing efforts to missions. "Systems evaluation" is the culminating activity in the total systems approach. In other words, "systems analysis," "design," "operations," and "evaluation" are subsets of what I refer to as the "systems approach."[25]

What particular relevance does the systems approach have to the phase of administration known as supervision? Actually, in a simple form, individuals serving in a supervisory relationship have been recommending a systems approach when a new basal reader is selected, since a basic reading system with all of its accompanying teaching aids is a system of a sort. Meals clarifies the relevance of the systems approach to supervision when he writes:

Above all else, the systems approach is an attitude of mind—a way of seeing the world. Its concerns are with interrelated parts and with how these parts together accomplish the purpose for which the system exists.
. . . Systems analysis calls upon the educator today to see his activity as a whole—not only the whole child but also the curriculum *and* the media *and* the teacher *and* the management system for putting these and other resources together in a functional system.[26]

Feyereisen, Fiorino, and Nowak highlight the importance of the systems approach to supervision and curriculum when they state:

We can see that systems analysis makes certain demands of the supervisor or administrator which the bureaucratic table of organization ignores. A school system is a living organization whose components or parts are interacting, interdependent, and must be integrated to achieve its objectives. The interaction, interdependence, and integration of the components are analyzed in terms of the process which is the purpose of the organization. In the case of a school system, its purpose is producing educated young adults, and the process is educaton. Therefore, the supervisor using systems analysis must consider how each of the components of the system such as elementary schools, secondary schools, pupil personnel services, special education, and so on contribute to and are integrated to produce educated young adults.[27]

[25]*Ibid.*
[26]Donald W. Meals, "Heuristic Models for Systems Planning," *Phi Delta Kappan*, XLVIII, no. 5 (1967), 200.
[27]Kathryn V. Feyereisen, John Fiorino, and Arlene T. Nowak, *Supervision and Curriculum Renewal: A Systems Approach* (New York: Appleton-Century-Crofts, Educational Division Meredith Corporation, 1970), p. 40.

In summary, then, "systems approach" is a broader term than systems analysis. The systems approach in general and systems analysis in particular have implications for both supervision and curriculum. Individuals concerned with these facets of the education enterprise should acquire an understanding of the systems approach and its implications for the improvement of the curriculum and instruction. In addition, they should use this valuable tool in their work. The systems approach should prove helpful in relationship to the following areas, among others:

1. Organizing for instruction.
2. Analyzing and solving instructional problems.
3. Developing media systems for instruction.
4. Planning and scheduling in-service education activities.
5. Planning the curriculum.
6. Making comparisons of alternatives in respect to educational innovation.
7. Decision-making in certain areas related to supervision.
8. Developing instructional models.
9. Budgeting and cost studies related to instruction and the curriculum.

RESEARCH AND SUPERVISION

Theory and research are interdependent. Theory builders use research findings as their raw materials and then test and evaluate the hypotheses and educational practices by research procedures. In fact, research can play an important role in all phases of the educational enterprise. The instructional leader should be knowledgeable about research related to his sphere of competency, competent to evaluate research that has been done, familiar with good research techniques, and able and willing to utilize research findings in his work. He should also encourage and support teachers in their efforts to experiment and conduct research. There should be no fear of reprisal if the results are not satisfactory.

It will be the purpose of this section to define educational research, suggest ways that the instructional leader may use research, and relate research findings that may prove of value in the work of the supervisor.

The Nature of Research

Although the term *research* is glibly used by practitioners in the field, some individuals are over-awed by it, and others pass over it too lightly. It, therefore, seems desirable to define research before discussing it further.

Mouly defines this important process as follows:

Actually, research is simply the process of arriving at dependable solutions to problems through the planned and systematic collection, analysis, and interpretation of data. Research is a most important tool for advancing knowledge, for promoting progress, and for enabling man to relate more effectively to his environment, to accomplish his purposes, and to resolve his conflicts. Although it is not the only way, it is certainly one of the more effective ways of solving scientific problems. For our purposes, we can define educational research as the systematic and scholarly application of the scientific method, interpreted in its broadest sense, to the solution of educational problems; conversely, any systematic study designed to promote the development of education as a science can be considered educational research.[28]

If research is to be of real value to the practitioner in education, caution must be exercised that too great stress is not placed on analytically-oriented research to the detriment of clinically-oriented investigations. This danger is highlighted by Halpin when he states:

In graduate courses on research we have made such an ado about the nature of scientific evidence and the use of statistical inference that we have blinded our students to the essential issue: without fresh, viable observation all machinations of research methodology become an empty and self-deceiving ritual. There is no virtue in demonstrating that one can count or that one can compute Pearsonian correlation coefficients on the items he has counted; the trick is to know what things are worth counting in the first place.[29]

Halpin is not suggesting that research should be conducted in an unscientific manner, but he is saying that there is also a place for creativity in research. So many important things in life cannot be reduced to mathematical formulas. Take love for example. There are many different interpretations and shades of meaning for this universal human experience; mother love, the love of a young couple for each other, the mature love of a married couple, love of country, and love of God, to name but a few. Has any researcher investigated love analytically? All that is known about love has been learned through the clinical approach. The poets and philosophers have also made their contributions to an understanding of this strange phenomenon.

There is no desire on the part of the authors to belittle or de-emphasize objective research, but rather to call attention to the fact that much useful knowledge has been gained by use of the clinical method. The most creative approach to educational research may·lie in this direction.

[28]George J. Mouly, *The Science of Educational Research* (New York: American Book Company, 1963), p. 4.
[29]Andrew W. Halpin, *Theory and Research in Administration* (New York: The Macmillan Company, 1966), p. 287.

Use of Research

An adequate supervisory program must provide opportunities to investigate the various aspects of the school and its program in order to determine the strong areas and, likewise, those that require abandoning. It is impossible to plan adequately without the necessary facts, and these essential facts are discovered through study and research. In this age of teacher-awakening, it is unthinkable to plan research unless it is the cooperative type. A theme of this handbook is that supervision is a series of activities done *with* teachers and not *to* them. Research as a phase of supervision, therefore, is an activity conducted with and by teachers.

Professional growth and research. An adequate discussion of action research may be found in Chapter IX of this handbook. In this section, therefore, it will be sufficient to emphasize briefly the changing role of the supervisor in research.

Today's well-educated and enlightened teachers are assuming more and more responsibility for their own professional growth programs. The supervisor's role is changing from that of one who suggests or recommends to the role of an aid or resource person to teachers. The successful instructional leader aids teachers in discovering problems related to instruction and learning, assists them in finding procedures to use in the solution of these problems, and provides time and resources to arrive at creative solutions.

Another way in which the supervisor can be of assistance to teachers in the area of research is to keep up-to-date on the findings of research that are published in many different sources and to make these findings and sources available to staff members.

Research Findings and Supervision

Considerable research has been conducted, the findings of which can be of assistance to the instructional leader. Throughout this handbook in the appropriate places, references have been made to some of this research. The research quoted here will be confined to several studies about attitudes toward supervision.

Attitudes toward supervision. Throughout the years, a number of studies have been conducted which report attitudes of teachers toward supervisors and supervision in general. Several of the more pertinent ones will be reported here.

Negley found that there is a conclusive negative relationship between the extent of confidence held by teachers in their supervisor and the supervisor's conformity with bureaucratic practice.[30]

In a study representing teachers of all levels in the elementary schools in five different states, Claye concluded the following:

1. Effective supervision is based on sound principles of social change and group dynamics.
2. Teachers want supervision from principals as well as from those persons with titles of supervisor.
3. Principals do not supervise adequately.
4. The kinds of help that teachers want do not change significantly as the length of time in service varies.
5. All teachers need and want supervision.[31]

Campbell studied the relationships that exist between supervisory leadership and the various situational factors in the social setting where supervision takes place. Her findings revealed that teachers place a high value on those behavior actions of supervisors which seem to exemplify warmth, mutual trust, friendship, and respect.[32]

Grossman, in a study of teachers' evaluation of supervisory practices, found those considered by teachers to be useful were: helpful attitude, informal conferences, demonstration teaching, assistance with discipline, informal observations, assistance with planning, provision of books and materials, assistance to new teachers, and provision of administrative assistance.[33]

SUMMARY

The application of administrative theory to educational administration is quite recent. It has been necessary to draw upon the resources of the humanities, social sciences, and the natural sciences for concepts that can be used in theory building. At present, several theories have been advanced that may prove useful in the phase of educational administration designated as supervision. Guidelines also have been suggested that may be used in theory building.

[30]Harold H. Negley, "Effectiveness in Supervision of Social Studies in Relation to the Extent of Authoritarianism in the Practice of Supervisors" (Doctoral dissertation, Indiana University, 1962), pp. 154–55.

[31]Clifton M. Claye, "Lola Gets What Lola Wants from Supervision," *The Journal of Educational Research*, LVI, no. 7 (1963), 358.

[32]Ona L. Campbell, "The Relationship Between Eight Situational Factors and Low Scores on the Leadership Dimensions of Instructional Supervisors" (Doctoral dissertation, North Texas State College, 1961), pp. 68–69.

[33]Barney Grossman, "Teachers' Methodological Emphasis and Their Evaluation of Supervisory Practices" (Doctoral dissertation, Rutgers State University, 1967), p. 101.

Supervisors should be familiar with administrative theory, participate in the construction of new theories, and draw and test hypotheses from these theories. They, likewise, should be conversant with instructional and curriculum theories and be prepared to assist teachers in theory building and use.

Conducting, interpreting, and utilizing research are important tasks of supervision when carried on cooperatively with members of the teaching staff.

SUGGESTED ACTIVITIES AND PROBLEMS

1. Search the literature and locate a theory of administration not discussed in this handbook. Outline and discuss the theory and show its relevance for supervision.
2. Select any set of concepts found in Wiles' theory of supervision and illustrate how they apply to the content in any appropriate chapter in this handbook.
3. Select three assumptions from Wiles and then, following the action pattern of Eye and Netzer, formulate principles, objectives, crieteria, and procedures for each assumption.
4. Review the theory reported from Getzels and Guba and show its relationship to the content in any appropriate chapter in this handbook.
5. Construct an interview guide and interview ten or more teachers to determine their knowledge, opinion, and use of educational research. Write up a report including conclusions from your findings.

SELECTED READINGS

Banghart, Frank W. *Educational Systems Analysis*. New York: The Macmillan Company, 1969.

Bruner, Jerome S. *Toward a Theory of Instruction*. New York: W. W. Norton & Company, Inc., 1968.

Eye, Glen G., and Netzer, Lanore A. *Supervision of Instruction—A Phase of Administration*. Chap. 3. New York: Harper & Row, Publishers, 1965.

Fox, David J. *The Research Process in Education*. New York: Holt, Rinehart & Winston, Inc., 1969.

Getzels, Jacob W.; Lipham, James M.; and Campbell, Roald F. *Educational Administration A Social Process: Theory, Research, Practice*. Chaps. 1, 2, 3, and 4. New York: Harper & Row, Publishers, 1968.

Goldhammer, Robert. *Clinical Supervision*, Chaps. 1 and 2. New York: Holt, Rinehart & Winston, Inc., 1969.

Gordon, Ira J., ed. *Criteria for Theories of Instruction*. Washington, D.C.: Association for Supervision and Curriculum Development, NEA, 1968.

Griffiths, Daniel E. "Nature and Meaning of Theory," *In Behavioral Science and Educational Administration*. The Sixty-Third Yearbook of the National

Society for the Study of Education, Part II. Chicago: University of Chicago Press, 1964.

Halpin, Andrew W. *Administration Theory in Education.* New York: The Macmillan Company, 1967.

Halpin, Andrew W. *Theory and Research in Administration.* New York: The Macmillan Company, 1966.

Hanlon, James M. *Administration and Education.* Belmont, Calif.: Wadsworth Publishing Company, Inc., 1968.

Likert, Rensis. *The Human Organization: Its Management and Value.* New York: McGraw-Hill Book Company, Inc., 1967.

Lucio, William H., ed. *Supervision: Perspectives and Propositions.* Washington, D.C.: Association for Supervision and Curriculum Development, NEA, 1967.

Macdonald, James B., and Leeper, Robert R., eds. *Theories of Instruction.* Washington, D.C.: Association for Supervision and Curriculum Development, NEA, 1965.

Saunders, Robert L.; Phillips, Ray C.; and Johnson, Harold T. *A Theory of Educational Leadership.* Columbus, Ohio: Charles E. Merrill Books, Inc., 1966.

Wilson, L. Craig; Byar, T. Madison; Shapiro, Arthur S.; and Schell, Shirley H. *Sociology of Supervision.* Chaps. 5, 6, 7, and 8. Boston, Mass.: Allyn & Bacon, Inc., 1969.

chapter 3

Organization and Function
of Supervision
in Districts of Various Sizes

School district size is a basic factor that affects the extent and quality of supervisory programs. Research indicates that districts can be too large as well as too small to be effective. By examining some statistics that show trends in size and number of public school systems, we can draw some conclusions from the research with reference to instruction and supervision.

Despite resistance at the local level in many states, progress toward reorganization of school districts into larger units in rural and suburban areas has been dramatic. Grant's 1968 U.S.O.E. statistical analysis stated that the national total of public school systems dropped from 101,400 in 1945–1946 to 21,990 by 1967–1968.[1] In the number of districts per state, the range was from one in Hawaii to 2,171 in Nebraska (1967–68). Table 1 shows the change in number of school districts in several states from 1932 to 1968.

Table 1. Changing number of school districts in selected states.

	1932	1961	1968
California	3,589	1,650	1,105
Colorado	2,041	341	181
Illinois	12,070	1,552	1,315
Kansas	8,748	2,303	336
Michigan	6,965	1,981	718
New York	9,467	1,280	853
Pennsylvania	2,587	2,185	597
West Virginia	450	55	55

[1]Kenneth A. Simon and W. Vance Grant, *Digest of Educational Statistics, 1968 Edition* (Washington, D.C.: U.S.O.E., National Center for Educational Statistics, 1968), pp. 44–46.

An examination of 1967 census statistics reveals the following significant data:

1. Nationwide, over 58 percent of all pupils attended the 1,400 districts that enrolled more than 6,000 pupils each, and that constituted only six percent of all school systems in the country.
2. 14,000 of the 21,990 districts in 1967–1968 enrolled fewer than 600 pupils; comprised 60 percent of all districts nationwide; but enrolled less than five percent of the total number of pupils in the U.S.[2]
3. During the 1967–1968 school year, the fifteen largest cities enrolled approximately four million pupils, or over nine percent of the nation's total enrollment.[3]

Conclusions. Despite widespread and continuing school district reorganization throughout rural and suburban America, there are still thousands of very small systems. Also fifteen school districts at the other end of the scale (the very large cities) are educating approximately one-tenth of the nation's pupils. The great majority of all pupils are enrolled in school systems that fall between these two extremes (such districts are defined as "intermediate" in this handbook).

What Is the Optimum Size School District?

Research throughout the nation indicates that a school system enrolling between 8,000 and 25,000 pupils in kindergarten through high school has the best opportunity to provide a quality educational program for all of its students. Some pertinent research findings can be summarized as follows:

1. "A New York study of a uniform test for high school seniors shows a direct relationship between school size and topmost achievement in mathematics. The study reveals a significant increase when 12th grade enrollment exceeds 200 pupils." When 2,504 students from 280 New York high schools were tested, the results showed a direct and positive relationship between the size of the senior class and top achievement in this test. For example, "Schools with a senior class of less than 200 pupils produced less than their proportionate share of pupils in the top achievement brackets. Schools with senior classes of 400 or more pupils produced from three to six times their proportionate share of high achievement students."[4]

[2]*Ibid.*, p. 45.
[3]Richard H. Barr and Betty J. Foster, *Fall 1967 Statistics of Public Elementary and Secondary Day Schools* (Washington, D.C.: U.S.O.E., National Center for Educational Statistics, 1968), pp. 4–5.
[4]"Math Achievement Goes Up With Greater School Size," *Nebraska State School Boards Association Bulletin* (1964), p. 2.

2. Of the top 100 scores in the 1964 Regents' Examination given to 5,737 Nebraska high school seniors by the University of Nebraska, over half were made by seniors from the state's three largest school systems. The chairman of the State Committee for the Reorganization of School Districts concluded, "the results show not only marked differences between small and large schools but that the larger ones are pulling farther ahead all the time."[5]

3. Mayo reported the results of a six year study of high schools in San Mateo County, California, in which curriculums were examined to determine minimum enrollments necessary to provide comprehensive programs. Some conclusions were, "a school of 1000 is restricted in its offerings in several areas to an extent which adversely affects the education of the secondary pupils. . . . A reasonable guide to follow on the basis of the curriculum offerings as presented, indicates that an enrollment under 1000 is undesirable; 1500 to 2000 would be better. . . . As far as educational advantages related only to curriculum offerings are concerned, a school of 2000 seems to offer desirable maximum possibilities."[6]

Dr. C. O. Fitzwater,[7] one of the country's leading experts in school district reorganization, believes that the size of the senior high school has proven to be a significant factor in the ability of a district to provide a comprehensive, quality instructional program. Dr. Fitzwater has concluded that a multiplier of 20 is sound with respect to the ratio of high school seniors to total district enrollment. Since research definitely suggests a graduating class of 400 or more pupils, a school system should therefore enroll at least 8,000 pupils to achieve the capability of sustaining an educational program that will really meet individual needs.

At the other end of the spectrum, the Committee for Economic Development, in a nationally recognized study, concluded, "Substantial educational advantages continue to accrue until a school system has perhaps 25,000 students. There are advantages of many kinds in even larger units, although other problems begin arising in an extremely large system."[8] Districts approaching 75,000 pupils are advised to consider decentralization or autonomous subsidiary districts.

The classic studies of Havighurst in Chicago and Odell in Philadelphia during the mid-sixties marked the beginning of a trend toward decen-

[5]"Accredited Schools Have Nebraska's Top Scholars," *Nebraska State School Boards Association Bulletin* (1964), p. 8.

[6]S. S. Mayo, "What Size High School?" *American School Board Journal* (1962), pp. 32–33.

[7]Dr. C. O. Fitzwater is currently Chief, Upper Midwest Program Operations Branch, Division of State Agency Cooperation, U.S. Office of Education.

[8]*Paying for Better Public Schools* (New York: Research and Policy Committee, Committee for Economic Development, 1960), pp. 6–7.

tralization in the very large cities.[9] Although various patterns of administrative organization are emerging, one trend is clear: more authority for the development and supervision of the instructional program is being delegated to relatively autonomous regional districts within the largest city systems.[10]

It should be obvious from this brief review of research and practice that the size of a school district is a very important factor in the development of an effective supervisory program. The remainder of this chapter is devoted to an analysis of the supervisory function in small, intermediate, and large districts.

CHARACTERISTICS OF THE SMALL SCHOOL DISTRICT

The small district is usually found in rural areas, or in suburban communities whose total geographic area provides no room for additional growth. The K-12 pupil population of the entire district is generally less than 2,000. In some cases, the people live close together within the boundaries of a small town. In others, the inhabitants may be spread throughout an entire rural county of several hundred square miles. Schools might be organized into one county unit or into several tiny districts.

Although small school systems do vary widely in many respects, the typical small district can be defined in terms of usual plant and staff resources.

School-Plant Facilities

At the elementary level, there are one or more complete unit schools, with one or two sections of each grade, kindergarten (or first) through sixth. In more sparsely settled areas, there may be a number of one- to four-teacher rural schools, or a combination of one complete elementary school and several of the rural buildings.

A small junior-senior high school, serving pupils in grades seven through twelve, is usually the only secondary facility in the small district, if any is provided at all. Many school systems of this size operate elementary

[9]Robert J. Havighurst, "The Chicago School Survey," *Phi Delta Kappan*, XLVI, no. 4 (1964), 162–66; William R. Odell, *Educational Survey Report for the Philadelphia Board of Public Education* (Philadelphia, Pa.: The Board of Public Education, School District of Philadelphia, 1965).

[10]The fifteen largest city school systems: New York, Chicago, Los Angeles, Philadelphia, Detroit, Baltimore, Houston, Cleveland, Washington, St. Louis, San Francisco, Milwaukee, Boston, Dallas, and San Diego.

schools only and have no high schools of their own. Pupils must be sent on a tuition basis to other secondary schools that have space and are willing to receive them. In some instances, several of these small elementary districts join together at the secondary level to provide a common high school.

Staff Requirements

Thirty-five or fewer teachers make up the total elementary staff and sufficient secondary personnel are employed to staff the junior-senior high school, if one is maintained. In addition, there might be several special teachers, generally in art, music, and physical education, who serve both elementary and secondary pupils.

Administrative and supervisory personnel. To be functioning at optimum efficiency on the administrative level, a small district employs a full-time superintendent or supervising principal as chief administrator. In very small districts, the chief administrator may be principal of the high school and/or one of the elementary schools, in addition to his general administrative responsibilities.[11]

There is or should be a full-time principal of the junior-senior high school. (However, some small secondary schools operate with part-time principals who teach several periods per day.) If the enrollment is larger than 600 because of tuition pupils from other districts, the principal undoubtedly needs a full-time assistant administrator.

Each elementary school should have a full-time, non-teaching principal. Ideally, no elementary school ought to exist if it is not large enough to support a full-time principal. The lowest ratio that usually can be supported is one principal to twelve classroom teachers, or to approximately two sections of each grade.[12] If the elementary grades are scattered in smaller buildings and cannot be consolidated in one school, they should be arranged in administrative units of approximately 12 to 20 teachers, with a full-time principal in charge of each unit. It is almost impossible to have a comprehensive program of supervision and curriculum development in a district where the individual elementary schools have no administrative head, or at best employ a teaching principal or head teacher. In such situations, at least one area is bound to suffer: the principal's classroom teaching, building administration, or the supervision of instruc-

[11]*Modern Practices and Concepts of Staffing Schools* (Albany, N.Y.: Cooperative Development of Public School Administration in New York State, 1956), pp. 20–23.
[12]Educational Service Bureau, Temple University, *A Report of Findings, Conclusions and Recommendations of a Survey of the Solanco Area Schools* (Philadelphia: The Bureau, 1957) (Mimeographed), p. 23.

tion. Therefore, the first step toward effective supervision at the elementary level is the organization of schools geographically into units that can be directed by full-time, non-teaching principals.

In the small school district, no one person has full-time responsibility for supervision. All administrators must be responsible for improvement of instruction and the administration of their schools. They are generalists and not specialists in curriculum development, school finance, or in-service training, for example. Or, at least, they cannot function as specialists in the small district. Because of the comprehensive nature of their positions, each administrator should be fully qualified and certified for the position he holds. Of course, this is not the existing situation in many smaller systems, but it is the key to effective supervision of instruction. An administrator must be well-trained, experienced, and personable. Most important of all, he must have the ability to work cooperatively and positively with his fellow administrators, teachers, pupils, and parents. Then he will have a reasonable chance of developing an adequate program of supervision for the small school district he serves.

ORGANIZING FOR SUPERVISION

Lack of effective coordination of the elementary and secondary curriculums in many of the nation's school systems was cited in Chapter I as a major supervisory problem. According to Evans, this is particularly true in small districts. "There is apparently little concerted effort made to coordinate the total program of many districts from kindergarten through twelfth grade."[13]

How can a small school district organize for good supervision? Although he wears many hats, the chief school administrator must assume leadership as the coordinator of instruction and curriculum. It certainly is true that budgets, bus schedules, board meetings, custodial direction, endless reports to the state, and other administrative functions seem to dominate the daily calendar. Yet research has shown that the chief administrator, by his initiative, sets the tone for instructional improvement.[14] If he devotes time and effort to the organization and operation of the supervisory program, it has a good chance of success. If he does not assume this responsibility in the small district, effective supervision will be nonexistent or limited to individual schools with first-rate principals.

[13]Evans, "The Status and Function of the Public Elementary School Supervisor in the Third and Fourth Class Districts of the Pennsylvania Counties of Chester, Delaware, and Montgomery," p. 238.
[14]Brickell, *Organizing New York State For Educational Change*, p. 24.

Specifically, the chief administrator should assume leadership in the following areas:

1. Whenever there is more than one school unit in a district, it is essential that all administrators be called to meet on a top-level, executive basis. Here is the opportunity to share ideas, to plan joint curriculum evaluation and development, and to work out common district policy on problems and issues that require thinking beyond the confines of one principal's building and staff. The chief school official would normally chair this administrative council, although the chairmanship could rotate.

2. Constructive classroom visitation is one of the basic supervisory techniques. The chief administrator should schedule observations so that he can visit each teacher at least once or twice a year. If he also is a building principal, he should be in each classroom for an extended period three or four times per year. A comprehensive plan of teacher visitation, detailing the responsibilities of all district administrators, should be developed by the administrative council.

3. The recruitment, selection, orientation, and assignment of teachers is an important function, requiring definition of policy and procedures.

4. The chief administrator must be concerned with his own professional growth through continuing graduate work, participation in conventions and conferences, and occasional college teaching if he has the opportunity.

5. The professional growth of the administrative and teaching staffs through in-service programs, graduate work, and conferences is largely influenced by the interest of the chief administrator.

6. Through the administrative council, or independently, if there is only one district administrator, policies on special services to pupils, promotion and grouping, evaluation of pupil progress, and public relations must be developed and carried out with the teaching staff.

(See Chapters VIII, IX, X, and XI for further ideas on various supervisory techniques.)

Many chief school administrators of small districts are aware of their supervisory roles but are often short of time and assistance to accomplish the various tasks. In the matter of time, one must make a basic decision. Is curriculum development as important as the cafeteria account? Shouldn't classroom visitation to observe the present instructional program take precedence over a lengthy conference with a salesman who has no appointment? In other words, can't time be found for supervision if it is really considered important? Occasionally it is a good idea for a chief administrator to run an analysis of the time he spends on various activities during a week. In the small district, such a survey will usually show a deficiency in time devoted to the direct improvement of instruction through supervision.

There is considerable resource help available to the chief school official who wants to move ahead in his supervisory program. Curriculum consultants, in-service ideas, research services, and valuable publications may be obtained, often without charge, from the following organizations and offices.

1. The United States Office of Education.
2. The National Education Association and its affiliated state associations.
3. State departments of education and county superintendents' or intermediate unit offices.
4. Nearby colleges and universities with good schools of education.
5. Study councils, although these must be evaluated carefully. Some are very good; others are not worth the time and money spent for affiliation. In any event, they never take the place of a district program of curriculum development. Their studies can be helpful if applied to local needs and problems in supervision.
6. Courses of study and curriculum materials from nearby districts of comparable size and effort. Some guides from big-city school districts with full-time curriculum staffs are valuable, too. For example, the physical education courses of study developed by the Los Angeles City Schools would be quite useful to any chief administrator who plans to evaluate the physical education program of his district.
7. Special projects and studies, such as the small-high school study conducted in New York State.[15]

The chief administrator, of course, must expect and receive strong support from the building principals who make up the administrative council in the small district. If some of these principals are part-time or head teachers, every effort should be made to establish school units large enough to support full-time principals. Failing in this, the chief administrator should involve his part-time administrators in supervisory activities to the maximum extent possible. This would include, for example, the hiring of substitute teachers so that teaching principals could attend administrative council meetings and otherwise work as supervisors.

To be a leader in supervision, the chief school administrator of the small district needs vision, courage, and resourcefulness. However, the job can be done, and it must be done.

The supervisory role of the principals in the small district is of vital importance to the success or failure of the program to improve instruction. The individual principal, as the educational leader of his school, is directly responsible to the chief school administrator for the instructional program in his building. He serves on the administrative council and

[15]*Catskill Area Project in Small School Design* (Oneonta, N.Y.: Catskill Area Project in Small School Design, 1959).

cooperates with other district administrators in determining policy matters that concern all schools.

Primarily the principal leads his own faculty in the improvement of instruction. He is largely responsible for the morale of his staff members and their general attitudes toward the school program and its enrichment. To be effective, he must be vitally interested in his teachers and be able to assess their strengths, needs, and individual abilities to function as members of a professional staff. Not all will be (or will want to become) master teachers. The good principal maintains close working relationships with all his colleagues, however, and does not permit the poorest or laziest to set the tone for the instructional program.

The principal, too, needs to find a balance between supervision and other administrative functions. At least half of his time should be planned for such supervisory activities as the following:

1. Individual teacher conferences, mostly informal.
2. Regular classroom visitations.
3. Action research in the classroom.
4. Coordination of special subjects (art, music, and physical education) with the academic curriculum (see Chapter VI).
5. Demonstration and substitute teaching on occasion.
6. Participation in principals' organizations and conferences.
7. An active role in district-wide curriculum development.
8. Planning and presenting in-service programs.

(Principals should find Chapters V, VIII, IX, X, and XI to be helpful in planning their supervisory activities.)

The chief school administrator who also is building principal in the small district must divide his time between the general supervisory functions described earlier in this chapter and the more intimate role of the principal working with his staff. Such a position is most certainly demanding, but often challenging and satisfying.

Can a building principal in a small district do anything to improve instruction if his chief administrator pays little attention to the instructional program? Usually the answer is "yes." Often a superintendent will encourage a principal who desires to take some initiative in district-wide supervision. At the very least, a building principal can work extensively with his own staff to improve their own teaching-learning situations, within the framework of district policy, if any. In the absence of positive direction from the chief administrator, an alert principal can do much to stimulate good teaching and learning within his own school. The limitations of such an effort are, of course, recognized, and every attempt should be made to involve the superintendent in supervision of instruction. Indeed, it is the responsibility of a conscientious principal to try regularly and persistently to interest his chief administrator in supervisory activities. Some of the following techniques may help:

1. Send pertinent research findings, pamphlets, and summaries of curriculum studies to his desk.
2. Arrange for many informal and formal conferences to discuss various phases of the instructional program.
3. Take advantage of every contact with the chief administrator to talk supervision and its importance. Tell him what neighboring districts and leaders in other areas are doing.

The teaching principal faces a particularly difficult task in trying to provide leadership in the improvement of instruction. First of all, he has a full- or part-time job as a classroom teacher. At the elementary level, he may teach a self-contained classroom all day. As a secondary principal, he may teach several periods per day. Before and after school he must administer his building. Often it is almost impossible to find time for supervisory activities. The following suggestions may help:

1. Try to handle routine administrative matters by bulletin or note, and use staff-meeting time before or after school for discussion of curriculum and other instructional matters.
2. Request a substitute teacher for the principal's class or classes on a regular basis (a minimum of one day per week), to permit time for classroom visitation, teacher conferences, professional meetings outside the school system, and administrative council meetings in the district.
3. Teach pupils to handle certain responsibilities, such as counting lunch money, answering the phone, and communicating with the custodian. (The elementary teaching principal should always have a sixth-grade class whenever possible.)

As indicated earlier, the most effective supervision of instruction demands the elimination of the head teacher or teaching principal. Persons in this position should do everything possible to convince their superiors of the hopelessness of the job. This may be done by keeping a list of important tasks that cannot be accomplished from day to day because of the pressure of the total load.

How Two or More Small Districts May Organize for Supervision

Chief school administrators should try to work cooperatively with their counterparts in neighboring small districts in the joint improvement of instruction.

In some cases, several elementary school systems send their pupils to a common high school. The superintendent or supervising principal of the district maintaining the secondary program is often considered the chief administrator of the area, and would therefore direct the overall program of supervision, kindergarten through the twelfth or fourteenth grade. If no chief school official in a group of contiguous districts is so designated, then one of the number should be elected as chairman of an administrative council, to consist of all administrators in the group. Certainly every effort should be made to include all sending and receiving districts.

For example, since District A (Figure 2) does not operate a secondary program but sends its pupils on a tuition or joint-district arrangement to neighboring District B's high school, it is the responsibility of the two chief school officials involved to work together in establishing a K-12 curriculum. This they have done by organizing an administrative council with the chief administrator of District B as chairman and all of the principals of both districts and the chief school official of District A as members. This team can function in the coordination and improvement of instruction throughout the two districts. The following could be possible administrative council activities:

1. Determination of basic educational philosophy and resulting curricular needs.
2. A K-12 program of curriculum development, using consultants and resources that neither district alone could afford. (This activity is essential, since all nine elementary schools feed the same high school. See Chapter X for suggestions.)
3. Identification of areas in which overall joint policy should be developed and those which should be the prerogative of each district and principal.
4. Development of joint program for special areas, such as art, music, physical education, speech, and reading (see Chapter VI).

(Many of the individual and group supervisory techniques described in Chapters VIII and IX could be profitably discussed by the administrative council.)

Failure of chief administrators to provide for such coordination as is shown in Figure 2 and described above results in elementary units of teaching that are duplicated in the high school; widely varying curriculums at the same level in different elementary schools; and many other evidences of poor supervision. It should be emphasized, however, that within this broad framework of coordination of instruction, there should be considerable latitude for each administrator to work with his own staff, pupils, and parents in evolving a curriculum that is particularly appropriate for his school and community. Effective supervision involves both district-wide planning and coordination and local school autonomy.

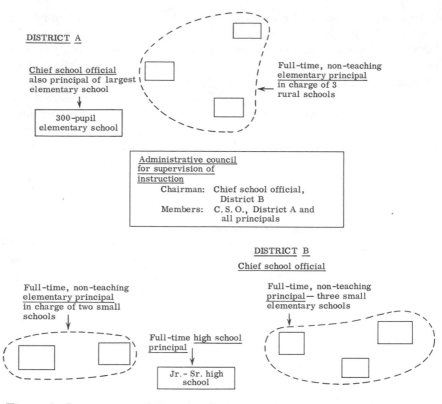

Figure 2. Organization of Two Small Districts for Supervision of Instruction. (Note: All pupils from both districts attend District B's Jr.-Sr. high school.)

CHARACTERISTICS OF THE INTERMEDIATE-SIZE SCHOOL DISTRICT

The intermediate-size district is found most commonly in the fast-growing suburban areas surrounding large cities and in rural regions where reorganization of school districts into larger units is underway. Usually there are mounting problems of mushrooming population, rapid expansion of all municipal services, and the direct concern of increased enrollments which complicate the task of effective instructional leadership. In these districts it is important that planning for supervision keep pace with the growth patterns.

An *intermediate-size system* is defined as enrolling up to 10,000 pupils from kindergarten through secondary school. Some intermediate-size districts operate only elementary schools and others are unified high school districts, serving secondary pupils only and receiving students from a number of elementary districts.

School-Plant Facilities

There are three or more complete-unit elementary schools, usually with at least two sections of each grade, kindergarten (or first) through sixth. Or there may be combinations of smaller rural schools into administrative units under full-time principals. Thus, some of the elementary buildings might be quite small while others are consolidated or neighborhood schools with 400 or more pupils. In rapidly expanding suburban communities, most of the elementary plants are new buildings housing at least two sections of each grade.

At the secondary level, the intermediate-size district will usually have at least one junior high school and one senior high school plant. Smaller intermediate systems may house all secondary pupils in one comprehensive junior-senior high school.

Staff Requirements

Personnel needs in the intermediate district may be summarized as follows.

Regular and special teachers. Depending on such variables as actual pupil population and class size, the elementary teaching staff would number approximately 40 to 250. Special teachers or coordinators in such subject areas as art, music, physical education, and possibly science and foreign languages would serve the elementary schools. Under certain plans of elementary-school organization, specialists would be required in other areas of the curriculum. In addition, guidance services might be available.

The teaching staff at the secondary level might number up to 200, with considerable variation possible owing to the size of the secondary student body, the organization of the curriculum, and the special services provided. The intermediate-size district will usually supply adequate guidance and psychological specialists to complement the instructional staff.

Administrative and supervisory personnel. There are at least two major points of view regarding the selection and organization of persons for optimum supervision of instruction in the intermediate district. Both philosophies are presented, with advantages and disadvantages of each.

Under *Plan 1* the following personnel would be directly involved in the supervisory program:

1. Chief school official.
2. Full-time elementary-school principals. (If some small buildings still exist and cannot be consolidated, they should be arranged in administrative units of approximately 12 to 20 teachers, with a full-time principal in charge of each unit.)
3. Full-time secondary-school principals.
4. Full-time assistant principals in schools with more than 600 pupils.
5. Special-area coordinators (if any).

It is recognized that flat charts are an imperfect and incomplete way of expressing organizational patterns and human relationships in supervision. At some risk of rigidity and oversimplification, then, the accompanying diagram (Figure 3, p. 61) shows the personnel in *Plan 1* and their line responsibilities. This plan provides for the coordination and supervision of instruction by the superintendent and the principals working with their staff members. A flat chart tends to appear inflexible in its delineation of line authority. Furthermore, it is impossible to indicate the flow of staff relationships that are an integral part of effective supervision. Therefore, the characteristics and principles of modern supervision outlined in Chapter I should be considered in the implementation of the organizational plans that follow.

Under *Plan 1*, the chief school official and the principals are both administrators and supervisors. The superintendent assumes the responsibility for district-wide coordination of instructional supervision and curriculum development. He can fill this role effectively if he has the training and experience and the time for the job. Some assistance is needed in the areas of business and personnel administration if the chief school official plans to coordinate the instructional program.

As indicated in the *Plan 1* chart (Figure 3), the principals are, in the total sense, educational leaders of their respective schools. They are responsible directly to the superintendent in all supervisory and other administrative matters. This does not mean that the principals will have no contact with other administrators. If the chief school official has administrative assistants, they will work closely with the building principals in such areas as attendance, selection and direction of custodians, and scheduling of buses. However, in this plan the primary line responsibility devolves from the superintendent to the principals.

Special-area coordinators in art, music, and physical education, for example, are directly responsible to the superintendent, and to the principal when working in a building. The chief school official coordinates their district-wide activities, and the principals work cooperatively with the specialists in scheduling and carrying out their programs in the various schools.

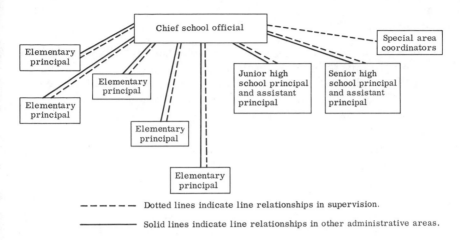

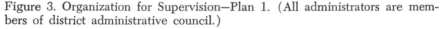

Figure 3. Organization for Supervision—Plan 1. (All administrators are members of district administrative council.)

The district administrative council provides the key to the strong role of the school principals in the supervision and improvement of instruction. The chief school official usually chairs this group, which consists of all principals. On occasion assistant principals, secondary-school department heads (if any), special subject-area teachers or coordinators, and curriculum committee chairmen take part in administrative council meetings. All major issues affecting the instructional program are discussed by the council. The various principals assume group-delegated responsibilties on a district-wide level, such as organizing staff committees for curriculum study, conducting experimental research, and planning other in-service education programs. All of these activities are coordinated by the chief school official and the administrative council.

Advantages of Plan 1

1. The principals, who are closest to their staffs, pupils, and communities, have the main responsibilities in supervision of instruction. There is no intermediate line position between the chief school official and the principals. They have direct authority and responsibility.

2. The superintendent has the opportunity to coordinate directly the instructional program, and many experts say that this is, or should be, his main function.

3. Teachers work with a minimum of supervisory personnel, and thus should not be confused by a number of classroom visitors and coordinators. Furthermore, the table of organization is simple and should be easy to understand.

Disadvantages of Plan 1

1. In a district of this size, the chief school official usually will not have the time necessary to be coordinator of instruction.

2. It is most difficult or impossible for a principal to have the perspective to understand district-wide problems, since his view is of necessity limited to one school and one portion of the total community.

3. Full-time building principals do not have time to be district curriculum coordinators, committee chairmen, and experimental research leaders. Futhermore, their background and experience often are not extensive enough to enable them to offer district-wide leadership in these areas.

4. The varied supervisory activities of an intermediate-size district need full-time coordination and leadership. Under *Plan 1*, no one has full-time responsibility for supervision of instruction.

     ✻   ✻   ✻   ✻   ✻   ✻   ✻

Plan 2, as charted in the accompanying illustrations (Figure 4, 5, and 6), provides the following personnel for supervision.

1. Chief school official.
2. Assistant superintendent in charge of instruction
AND/OR
3. Coordinator of elementary education.
4. Coordinator of secondary education. (This position is occasionally found in larger intermediate districts.)
5. Full-time elementary-school principals.
6. Full-time secondary-school principals.
7. Full-time assistant principals in schools with more than 600 pupils.
8. Special-area coordinators (if any).

The three accompanying charts (Figures 4, 5, and 6) indicate possible organization patterns for supervision of instruction in typical intermediate-size districts employing the personnel listed above. It can be seen that *Plan 2*, with its suggested variations, usually involves at least one line administrator or coordinator between the chief school official and the principals in the performance of the supervisory function.

In *Plan 2*, the chief school official delegates considerable authority and responsibilty to the assistant superintendent in charge of instruction, or to the coordinator of elementary education if there is no assistant superintendent. (In this instance, the chief school official continues to serve as the coordinator of the secondary-school program.) Curriculum coordination and development and the general improvement of classroom instruction are the areas usually assigned to these persons by the superintendent. In larger intermcdiate districts, there is a corresponding delegation of authority and responsibility from the assistant superintendent to the co-

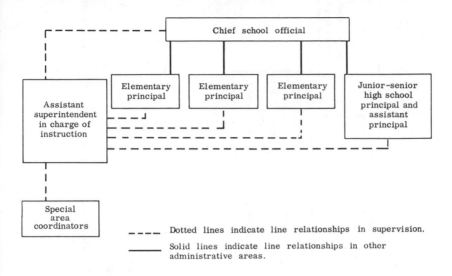

Figure 4. Organization for Supervision—Plan 2. District with assistant superintendent in charge of instruction. (All administrators and coordinators are members of district administrative council.)

ordinator of elementary education and the coordinator of secondary education for their respective fields.

Although supervisory relationships are discussed in detail in Chapters IV and V, a brief summary of the function of the assistant superintendent in charge of instruction and the coordinators of elementary and secondary education follows.

1. They are both line and staff officers, but the line relationship is not overemphasized. They are responsible to their superior in the areas of curriculum and instruction. The principals are responsible to the coordinator or assistant superintendent (if any) in matters of curriculum and instruction but are directly responsible to the chief school official or another assistant superintendent for other administrative areas.

2. The supervisory function is cooperative and democratic, and is shared under the overall coordination of the assistant superintendent in charge of instruction or the coordinator of elementary education. In districts with no assistant superintendent or coordinator of secondary education, the chief school official himself will coordinate instruction with the principals at the secondary level. (See the organization charts above.) In such cases, the junior and senior high school principals are directly responsible to the superintendent in the areas of supervision *and* other administrative responsibilities.

Regardless of the personnel available, all administrators and super-

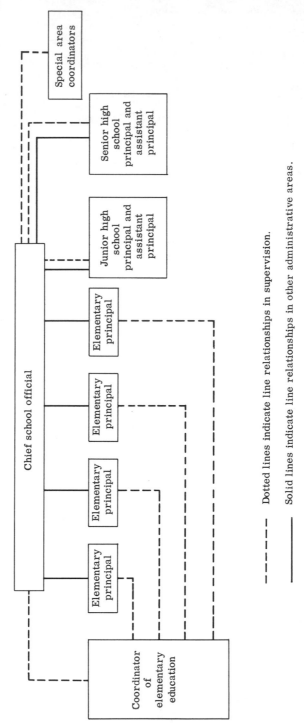

Figure 5. Organization for Supervision—Plan 2. District with coordinator of elementary education. (All administrators and coordinators are members of district administrative council.)

- - - - Dotted lines indicate line relationships in supervision.

———— Solid lines indicate line relationships in other administrative areas.

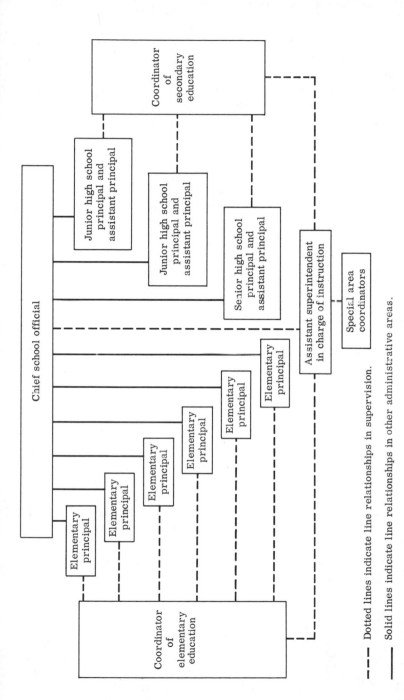

Figure 6. Organization for Supervision—Plan 2. District with assistant superintendent in charge of instruction, coordinator of elementary education, and coordinator of secondary education. (All administrators and coordinators are members of district administrative council.)

--- Dotted lines indicate line relationships in supervision.

—— Solid lines indicate line relationships in other administrative areas.

visors work together cooperatively in classroom visitation, curriculum development, other in-service program planning, workshops, and all other facets of the supervisory function.

3. The building principals are the educational leaders of their schools, exercising supervisory and administrative responsibility with their staffs. The assistant superintendent in charge of instruction and the coordinators (if any) work through and with the principals. They do not, however, participate in building administration, which is the province of the principal.

4. The assistant superintendent and the coordinators of elementary and secondary education serve also as resource persons who are on call to assist principals and classroom teachers in the improvement of instruction.

In *Plan 2*, then, at least one administrator or coordinator is assigned full-time responsibility for the instructional program. All supervisory functions are coordinated by the assistant superintendent in charge of instruction and/or the coordinators of elementary and secondary education, if these positions are filled.

The district administrative council is comprised of the chief school official, the assistant superintendent in charge of instruction, the coordinators of elementary and secondary education, and the elementary and secondary principals. At certain times the assistant principals, special-area coordinators, high school department heads (if any), curriculum committee chairmen, team leaders (if any), and other personnel play an active role in administrative council meetings. This group discusses and develops over-all district policy and guidelines for the supervision of the instructional program.

Under *Plan 2*, special-area coordinators (if any) are directly responsible to the chief school official or to the assistant superintendent in charge of instruction. Their function is primarily to provide coordination in the special areas they represent, and they are not line officers. When working in a school, they report directly to the principal and work as resource persons for teachers and administrators. (The role and function of the special supervisory personnel are detailed in Chapter VI.)

Advantages of Plan 2

1. The positions of assistant superintendent in charge of instruction and coordinators of elementary and secondary education are necessary for the most effective coordination of the total supervisory program, because these persons have district-wide perspective, kindergarten through twelfth grade. One of the most serious problems in American education today is the failure of elementary and junior and senior high

schools to provide a unified, integrated K-12 program in a school district.

2. With the tremendous explosion of knowledge in our society, curriculum development and revision demand full-time attention. Superintendents and principals do not have enough time to devote to the instructional program, which is the heart of the school system. This plan provides experienced and well-educated leaders with the time needed for regular and efficient review of the district curriculum.

3. Curriculum research and resource materials can be obtained and utilized more effectively through a district office.

Disadvantages of Plan 2

1. The building principal's authority must be shared in the areas of curriculum and improvement of instruction.

2. Problems may occur between principals and the assistant superintendent or the coordinators regarding areas of responsibility and authority. It is often difficult, for example, to separate supervisory and other administrative functions, as noted in Chapter I.

3. The classroom teacher may not understand his relationship to all those who visit his classroom and who direct the in-service and curriculum-development programs.

In selecting a plan of organization for supervision, a district must consider its objectives, its personnel, and its aspirations for improvement of instruction in the future. The qualifications and personalities of present and prospective administrators and coordinators will help determine, to a large extent, the nature of the evolving supervisory organization.

Important leadership note. The preceding discussion and diagrams outline several possible methods of organizing for supervision in the intermediate-size school district. As a system approaches eight to ten thousand pupils, or the upper limits of the intermediate category, the following considerations should be noted:

1. Be wary of having too many persons reporting to the superintendent or any other line administrator. Research and experience in industry and education indicate a range of from four to ten individuals reporting to one superior, with five to seven probably being the optimum number.[16] Districts of this size will probably employ several assistant superintendents, with delegated responsibilities for instruction, business and finance, personnel, or other areas as determined by the superintendent, administrative council, and the board of education. As a result, building principals would often report to several of the assistant superintendents for various areas of administrative concern.

[16]Galen N. Drewry, *The Administrative Team: What It Is and How It Works* (Athens, Ga.: Institute of Higher Education, University of Georgia, 1967), p. 3.

2. In the larger intermediate district not all principals can serve on the administrative council at one time. Consequently, the elementary and secondary principals should elect representatives to the council. This responsibility can be rotated to give everyone an opportunity to serve over a three- or four-year period.

ORGANIZING FOR SUPERVISION

In any intermediate-size district, the administrative council plays an important role in the coordinated K-12 program of instruction. Here is provided the opportunity for the chief school official or the assistant superintendent in charge of instruction to lead the executive team in policy decisions, in the development of district philosophy, and in the planning of various supervisory activities. The superintendent is involved at least to this extent in supervision, and he is therefore aware of any contemplated major changes or improvements in the school program.

The council includes the personnel previously listed plus the administrators of any elementary or secondary feeder districts who send pupils on a tuition or contract basis.

The administrative council functions are as follows:

1. The areas of district-wide responsibility and concern in the instructional program, and the corresponding limits of the individual building principals' authority must be determined. The district framework should be flexible enough to permit considerable latitude in principal-teacher interaction at the building level. Each professional employee needs to have a certain independence in his classroom or building, but each must also feel himself to be an integral part of the total district effort in the improvement of instruction.

For example, a fifth-grade teacher may want to initiate individualized reading in his classroom. May he do this independently; in consultation with his principal; or only after discussion with the coordinator of elementary education (if any) or the administrative council?

To take another case, are field-study trips planned by the classroom teacher; the building principal and his staff; or by these persons and others in the district?

2. General limits of authority and responsibility must be established so that all members of the supervisory staff are enabled to function effectively as team members. Job descriptions should be written, although it is recognized that these are only guides. Again, it is important to have broad-minded, competent personnel who share modern democratic concepts of supervision.

3. The administrative council approves all plans for in-service work,

including curriculum development, to insure coordination of district activities.

4. All matters pertaining to supervision of instruction clear through the council. Agenda items are suggested by teachers, the chief school official, or any member of the council. There is constant communication between the individual school faculties and their principals regarding agenda topics. All professional staff members have ample opportunity to react to proposals before these are finally accepted by the administrative council.

To illustrate the organization and function of supervision in the intermediate-size district, the Moorestown Township Public Schools in fast-growing Burlington County, New Jersey, has been selected as an example.

THE MOORESTOWN TOWNSHIP PUBLIC SCHOOLS, MOORESTOWN, NEW JERSEY, ORGANIZE FOR SUPERVISION

Moorestown Township, an upper middle-class residential community, is located eight miles east of Camden in a rapidly-growing suburban area. The Township covers approximately fifteen square miles of which only about one-third was developed in 1969. There is a small business area in the town which had its origins in colonial times. A large shopping mall and about a dozen light industrial establishments have been located in the Township. Moorestown's future undoubtedly will be influenced by the burgeoning population of the Delaware Valley area. The 1960 census listed 12,497 residents; by 1966 there were 14,060; and as many as 43,000 persons are expected to reside in the Township by 1985.

Under the leadership of Superintendent Arthur G. Martin, the Moorestown Township Public Schools have planned well for the 1970s and beyond. After a complete review of educational program needs, a master building plan was developed to phase out older structures and to provide modern school plants where required. By 1970, there were four elementary schools (K–4) with an enrollment capacity of 1750; one middle school (grades 5–8) with provisions for 1400 students; and one high school (grades 9–12) with a 1400-pupil capacity. In 1970, there were over 4,000 pupils (K–12) and over 250 professional employees in the district.

As seen in Figure 7, page 70, Superintendent Martin heads the supervisory team in the Moorestown Schools. He believes that the chief school administrator ought to be the instructional leader of the school district. The principals report directly to the superintendent, who considers them to be the educational leaders of their schools. The Assistant Superintendent in Charge of Curriculum reports to the superintendent and works in a staff relationship with the principals and teachers to provide K–12

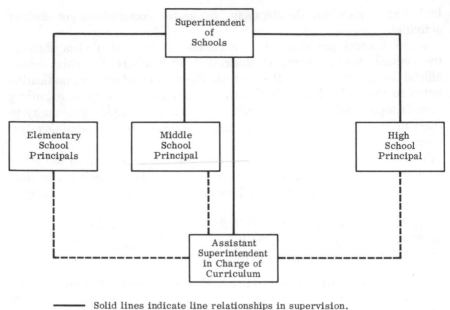

- Solid lines indicate line relationships in supervision.
- - - - Dotted lines indicate staff relationships in supervision.

Figure 7. Organization for supervision of instruction. Moorestown Township Public Schools, Moorestown, N.J.

articulation of the educational program. Completing the supervisory staff are the multi-media coordinator, subject coordinators and chairmen, and the coordinator of special services.

The Administrative Council coordinates the administration and supervision of the school system. Meeting twice a month under the chairmanship of the superintendent, this council assists in the planning of in-service programs, curriculum development, and other supervisory activities. Membership includes all principals and the central office staff.

The Faculty Advisory Council plays an important role in the administration of the supervisory program. This group consists of two teachers from each of the schools, one elementary-school principal selected on a rotating basis, middle- and high-school principals, the coordinator of special services, the president of the Moorestown Township Teachers Association, the Assistant Superintendent in Charge of Curriculum, and the Superintendent of Schools. The Council meets monthly to consider matters of general interest to the staff and school system. Its purposes have been defined as follows:

1. To serve as a coordinating group for curriculum projects and studies.
2. To act as a sounding board for staff problems and needs in areas of general concern.
3. To act as a channel of communication between elementary and secondary schools and between the teaching staff and the administration.
4. To act as an advisory committee to the superintendent in matters of general school welfare.

In summary, the Moorestown Township Public Schools are well organized for effective supervision of instruction. The Superintendent assumes a major leadership role, the principals are recognized as the instructional leaders of their schools, and the Assistant Superintendent in Charge of Curriculum provides K–12 coordination. Both the Administrative Council and the Faculty Advisory Council are key agents in the total supervisory process. Enlightened, democratic leadership is very much in evidence throughout this intermediate school system.

CHARACTERISTICS OF LARGER DISTRICTS

The large school district is an elusive designation, even when we exclude, say, the fifteen largest city school systems in the nation. For purposes of discussion in this chapter, "large" includes districts that fall, in pupil enrollment, between the intermediate-size school system previously analyzed and the very large city school systems. These larger districts are found in small- and medium-size cities and in suburban communities with a large geographic area and a rapid growth pattern where the range in pupil enrollment, kindergarten through twelfth grade, is from 10,000 to approximately 130,000.

School-Plant Facilities

In larger districts, the number of schools will range from about twelve elementary buildings and four secondary-school plants up to about 150 buildings in the largest systems in this category.

Staff Requirements

Staff needs for school districts of this size vary tremendously, depending upon the extent of curricular offerings, class size, organizational patterns for teaching, and the quantity and quality of administrative and special services.

Regular and special teachers. The total elementary teaching staff will include more than 250 regular classroom or team teachers. Special teachers or coordinators in art, music, physical education, and possibly other subject areas, often serve each of the larger schools or may be shared by several smaller buildings. In addition, resource teachers and other instructional consultants are often available.

The total teaching and guidance staff in the secondary schools will number more than 200, and other specialists or resource consultants are provided by many larger districts.

Administrative and supervisory personnel. Because of the wide range of school systems included in this category, the number and type of administrative and supervisory personnel will vary greatly. However, the positions and their function will be similar regardless of the size of the district. In actual practice, the city district which employs decentralization of administration will replicate the positions listed below in the various sub-districts. The following personnel are considered essential for effective supervision of instruction in a larger school district:

1. Superintendent of schools.
2. One or more associate superintendents or assistant superintendents in charge of instruction and/or instructional services.
3. Assistant superintendent for elementary education or coordinator of elementary education.
4. Assistant superintendent for secondary education or coordinator of secondary education.
5. Full-time non-teaching principals for each elementary school. If the staff exceeds 25 and the student enrollment reaches 600, a full-time assistant principal should be provided.
6. One full-time principal for each secondary school. When the enrollment exceeds 600, a full-time assistant principal should be provided for each additional 600 pupils or 25 teachers, or major fraction thereof. (Large city high schools need several assistant principals to assume major areas of responsibility.)
7. Subject area coordinators (K–12), team leaders, and/or department heads, depending on organization for instruction.

The associate superintendent(s), the assistant superintendent(s), and the coordinators of elementary and secondary education should work almost exclusively in curriculum development and the coordination and improvement of instruction. They would not normally be involved in other administrative matters.

In this size school district, the superintendent of schools will be kept fully informed on supervisory matters, but he has little time to participate actively in supervision. He plays a very important supportive role and delegates the responsibility for the instructional program to his associate or assistant superintendent(s).

The principals and assistant principals are responsible for administration of their schools and direct participation in the various phases of the supervisory programs. They are considered in all respects the educational leaders of their respective schools. Under no circumstances should they be by-passsed by any of the general supervisory personnel in the development and execution of the program for improvement of instruction.

ORGANIZING FOR SUPERVISION

The associate or assistant superintendent in charge of instruction plays the key role in organizing the staff for improvement of instruction. He must see that line and staff relationships are carefully defined. Although the line organization should not be overstressed, it must exist to provide the framework for overall district-wide policy in a school system this size. Such policy is essential to insure a highly-organized and well-coordinated program of instruction. The larger the organization, the more difficult it is to implement. The associate superintendent will take the lead in organizing the administrative council, which should be the basic policy-developing group in the district. The functions of this council were outlined earlier in this chapter on pages 61–68 in the discussion of intermediate-size districts. Membership in the larger district should include all associate and/or assistant superintendents in charge of instruction or instructional services, the assistant superintendents or coordinators for elementary and secondary education, and representatives of the elementary and secondary principals. Other personnel concerned with various phases of the instructional program will be invited to join the administrative council, either on an *ad hoc* or permanent basis.

The principals, as educational leaders at the building level, work with their teaching staffs to implement district-wide policies and to suggest improvements in the instructional program. Hopefully, there is considerable latitude for principals and teachers to innovate, experiment, and otherwise influence instruction at the building and classroom level. It is particularly important in the larger district to keep the lines of communication open among all levels of supervisory personnel in the schools, the district, and sub-district offices. This is especially necessary so that the teacher knows exactly where he stands in the process of instructional improvement. For example, it is imperative that the principals and their staffs receive regular reports of topics on the administrative council agenda and of action taken at each meeting of the council.

Only then can individual teachers and principals express their views to council members, and take an active part in the decision-making process.

A description of the pattern of organization for supervision in a rather large school district follows.

THE SAN DIEGO UNIFIED SCHOOL DISTRICT, SAN DIEGO, CALIFORNIA, ORGANIZES FOR SUPERVISION[17]

In 1969 San Diego, with a population of 657,775, was the fifteenth largest city in the United States, and the eighth largest city school district, with a total K–12 enrollment of 128,779. The area of the San Diego Unified School District is 196 square miles, and the system has 153 schools.

As the third largest city in both California and the Far West, San Diego is the county seat, seaport, rail and air terminal, and financial and commercial center of San Diego County. The city has four major sources of basic income: manufacturing, mainly in defense and space-related industries; the military, especially the navy; tourism; and agriculture.

Figure 8 depicts the organization of the San Diego Unified School District. There are three associate superintendents, all with instructional responsibilities. As seen in Figure 8, there are assistant superintendents for the elementary-schools division and the secondary-schools division, reporting to the associate superintendent for operation of schools. Figure 9 shows the assignment of line responsibilities in the secondary-schools division. Regions A, B, and C are composed of four senior high schools and six junior high schools each, with the director for each region reporting to the assistant superintendent of the secondary-schools division. In this manner, the administrative function is effectively decentralized, yet coordinated in a sensible line organization.

The Curriculum Services Division

The San Diego City Schools are well structured for improvement of instruction. Figure 10 lists the leadership roles of the Curriculum Services Division. As stated in the description of functions and services:

The purpose of the establishment of the Curriculum Services Division is to provide supporting services relative to the development, initiation and improvement of all instructional programs. In order to administer its assigned responsibilities, the Curriculum Services Division is organized into five sub-

[17]Adapted from *An Analysis and Summary of District Functions and Services for Secondary Schools,* San Diego Unified School District, San Diego, Calif., Feb., 1969; and *Activities of the Curriculum Services Division, 1968–1969,* February 6, 1969.

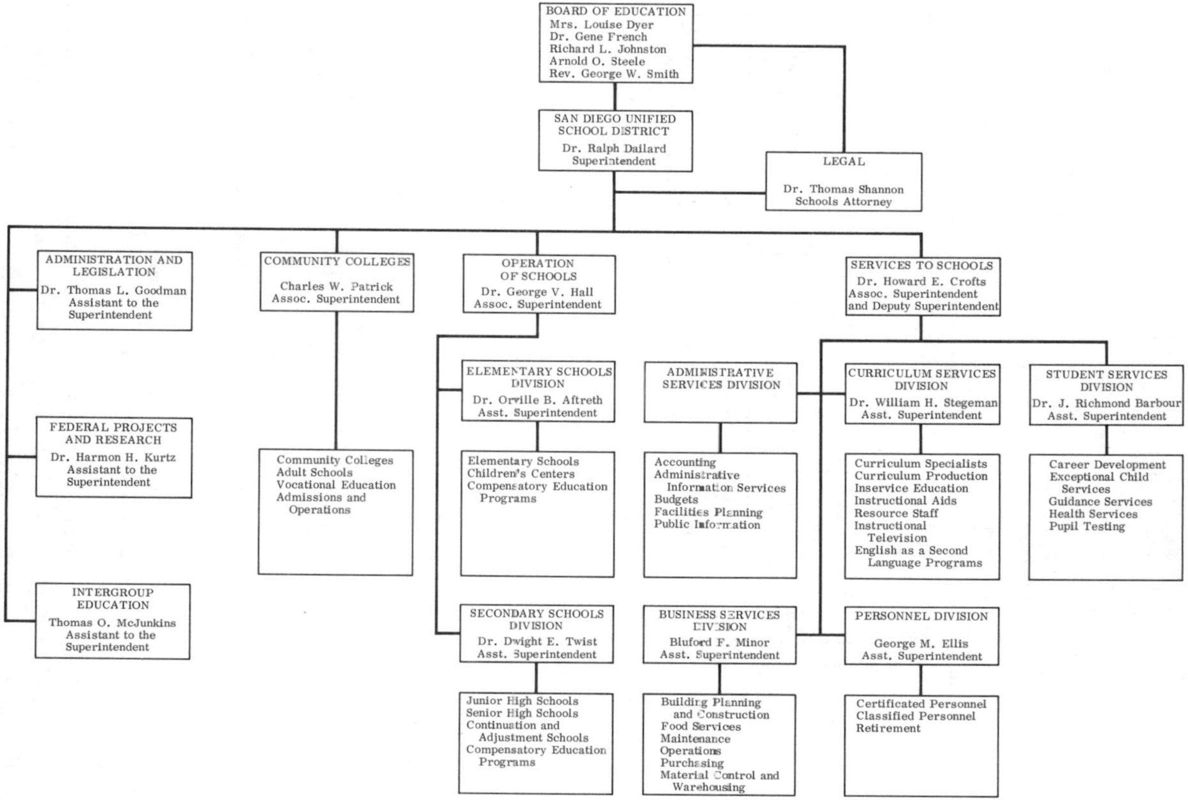

BOARD OF EDUCATION
Mrs. Louise Dyer
Dr. Gene French
Richard L. Johnston
Arnold O. Steele
Rev. George W. Smith

SAN DIEGO UNIFIED SCHOOL DISTRICT
Dr. Ralph Dailard
Superintendent

LEGAL
Dr. Thomas Shannon
Schools Attorney

ADMINISTRATION AND LEGISLATION
Dr. Thomas L. Goodman
Assistant to the Superintendent

FEDERAL PROJECTS AND RESEARCH
Dr. Harmon H. Kurtz
Assistant to the Superintendent

INTERGROUP EDUCATION
Thomas O. McJunkins
Assistant to the Superintendent

COMMUNITY COLLEGES
Charles W. Patrick
Assoc. Superintendent

- Community Colleges
- Adult Schools
- Vocational Education
- Admissions and Operations

OPERATION OF SCHOOLS
Dr. George V. Hall
Assoc. Superintendent

ELEMENTARY SCHOOLS DIVISION
Dr. Orville B. Aftreth
Asst. Superintendent

- Elementary Schools
- Children's Centers
- Compensatory Education Programs

SECONDARY SCHOOLS DIVISION
Dr. Dwight E. Twist
Asst. Superintendent

- Junior High Schools
- Senior High Schools
- Continuation and Adjustment Schools
- Compensatory Education Programs

SERVICES TO SCHOOLS
Dr. Howard E. Crofts
Assoc. Superintendent and Deputy Superintendent

ADMINISTRATIVE SERVICES DIVISION

- Accounting
- Administrative Information Services
- Budgets
- Facilities Planning
- Public Information

BUSINESS SERVICES DIVISION
Bluford F. Minor
Asst. Superintendent

- Building Planning and Construction
- Food Services
- Maintenance
- Operations
- Purchasing
- Material Control and Warehousing

CURRICULUM SERVICES DIVISION
Dr. William H. Stegeman
Asst. Superintendent

- Curriculum Specialists
- Curriculum Production
- Inservice Education
- Instructional Aids
- Resource Staff
- Instructional Television
- English as a Second Language Programs

PERSONNEL DIVISION
George M. Ellis
Asst. Superintendent

- Certificated Personnel
- Classified Personnel
- Retirement

STUDENT SERVICES DIVISION
Dr. J. Richmond Barbour
Asst. Superintendent

- Career Development
- Exceptional Child Services
- Guidance Services
- Health Services
- Pupil Testing

Figure 8. Organization Chart, San Diego Unified School District.

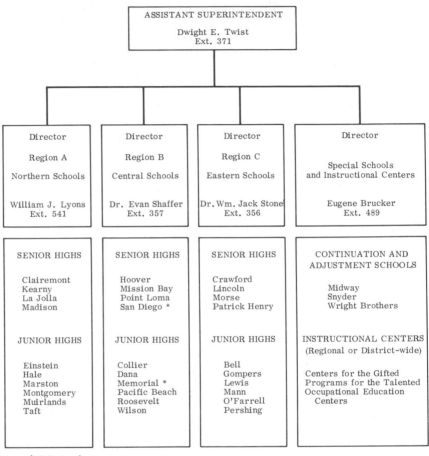

*Liaison only

Figure 9. Assignment of line responsibilities, San Diego City Schools, Secondary Schools Division.

units: (1) Curriculum Development, (2) Instructional Improvement, (3) Instructional Aids (materials and equipment), (4) In-service Education, and (5) Curriculum Production.

As seen under *Instructional Improvement,* a resource staff, consisting of instructional consultants and district resource teachers, is available to assist the school principals and faculties in the improvement of the educational program. Specifically the district resource staff performs the following functions:

1. Assists the principal in planning the instructional improvement program.

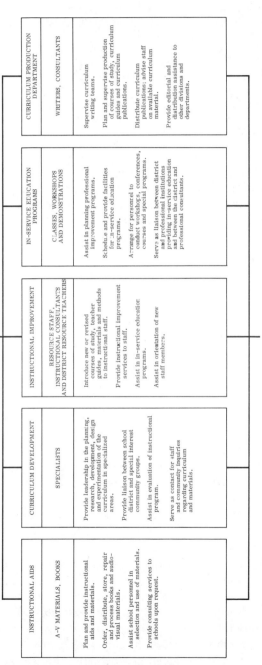

COORDINATION

Directs the curriculum services program

Coordinates activities and programs with other divisions

Coordinates curriculum materials, methods and programs

Coordinates curriculum research, development, design and experimentation

Evaluates curriculum program, Grades K–14

INSTRUCTIONAL AIDS	CURRICULUM DEVELOPMENT	INSTRUCTIONAL IMPROVEMENT	IN-SERVICE EDUCATION PROGRAMS	CURRICULUM PRODUCTION DEPARTMENT
A–V MATERIALS, BOOKS	SPECIALISTS	RESOURCE STAFF, INSTRUCTIONAL CONSULTANTS AND DISTRICT RESOURCE TEACHERS	CLASSES, WORKSHOPS AND DEMONSTRATIONS	WRITERS, CONSULTANTS
Plan and provide instructional aids and materials.	Provide leadership in the planning, research, development, design and experimentation of the curriculum in specialized areas.	Introduce new or revised courses of study, teacher guides, materials and methods to instructional staff.	Assist in planning professional improvement programs.	Supervise curriculum writing teams.
Order, distribute, store, repair and process books and audio-visual materials.	Provide liaison between school district and special interest community groups.	Provide instructional improvement services to staff.	Schedule and provide facilities for in-service education programs.	Plan and supervise production of courses of study, curriculum guides and curriculum publications.
Assist school personnel in selection and use of materials.	Assist in evaluation of instructional program.	Assist in in-service education programs.	Arrange for personnel to conduct workshops, conferences, courses and special programs.	Distribute curriculum publications; advise staff on available curriculum material.
Provide consulting services to schools upon request.	Serve as contact for staff and community inquiries regarding curriculum and materials.	Assist in orientation of new staff members.	Serve as liaison between district and professional institutions providing in-service education and between the district and professional consultants.	Provide editorial and distribution assistance to other divisions and departments.

STAFF AND RESOURCE TEACHERS IN SCHOOLS

Figure 10. Curriculum Services Division.

2. Assists experienced and probationary teachers with the instructional program.
3. Participates in faculty or area meetings.
4. Meets with small groups of teachers on instructional needs or problems.
5. Participates in workshops.
6. Teaches lessons for teacher observation.
7. Introduces new guides, texts, materials, or programs.
8. Prepares displays of materials and helps prepare room environments.
9. Assists in exploring new techniques and methods of teaching.
10. Obtains instructional materials for teachers.
11. Holds conferences with individual teachers on instructional needs or problems.
12. Works to improve the total district program.

In San Diego the principal is responsible for the instructional program in his building. The above-listed services provided by the district resource staff are available to each principal as needed. In a large city district then, the leadership role of the principal is upheld, while the necessary resources for improvement of instruction are made available to all schools.

SUMMARY

School district size is a basic factor that affects the extent and quality of the supervisory program, since research indicates that districts can be too large as well as too small to be effective. Despite continuing school district reorganization throughout rural and suburban America, there are still thousands of very small systems. At the other end of the scale, fifteen large city systems are educating approximately one-tenth of the nation's pupils. Research indicates that a school district enrolling between 8,000 and 25,000 pupils in kindergarten through high school has the best opportunity to provide a quality educational program for all of its students. There are educational advantages in even larger units, although problems arise in extremely large systems. Districts approaching 75,000 pupils are advised to consider decentralization or autonomous subsidiary districts.

The typical small district has one or more elementary schools or a number of one- to four-teacher rural buildings. The staff probably numbers 35 or less at the elementary level. A junior-senior high school is usually the only secondary facility, if any is provided at all.

No person has full-time responsibility for supervision in the small district. The chief administrator sometimes serves as elementary or secondary principal. Some small high schools operate with part-time principals who teach several periods per day. Although administrators should not be part-time teachers if they are to provide maximum instructional leadership, many elementary schools also employ teaching principals.

If the elementary grades are scattered in smaller buildings and cannot be consolidated in one school, they should be arranged in administrative units of approximately 12 to 20 teachers, with a full-time principal in charge of each unit.

If the small district is to organize effectively for supervision, the chief administrator must assume leadership in organizing an administrative council; in visiting teachers; in selecting and orienting new staff members; in providing in-service growth experiences for teachers; and in cooperatively developing policies on special pupil services, promotion and grouping, evaluation of pupil progress, and public relations. Considerable resource help is available to the chief school official who wants to improve instruction.

The supervisory role of the principals in the small district is very important. As the educational leader of his school, the individual building principal is directly responsible to the chief administrator in administration and supervision. At least half of the principal's time should be planned for teacher conferences, classroom visitations, action research, curriculum development, and other supervisory activities.

Neighboring small school districts should work cooperatively in the improvement of instruction. If they send elementary pupils to the same high school, for example, a joint administrative council should be established to coordinate the programs kindergarten through high school.

The small district can make progress in the improvement of instruction if the principles and practices of modern, democratic supervision are evident.

The intermediate-size district is usually found in fast-growing suburban areas and in rural regions where reorganization of school systems is under way. A total enrollment of up to 10,000 pupils from kindergarten through high school identifies this size district. In terms of plant facilities, there are generally three or more complete-unit elementary schools and at least one junior high and one senior high school.

The elementary teaching staff will number approximately 40 to 250. At the secondary level, there might be as many as 200 teachers, with considerable variation possible owing to the size of the student body, the organization of the curriculum, and any special services provided.

There are at least two major points of view regarding the selection and organization of administrative and supervisory personnel in the intermediate-size district. Under *Plan 1,* the superintendent assumes the responsibility for district-wide coordination of instructional supervision and curriculum development. The principals are, in the total sense, educational leaders of their respective schools, reporting directly to the chief school official in all supervisory and other administrative matters.

Plan 2 usually involves at least one line administrator or coordinator between the superintendent and the principals in the performance of the supervisory function. Under this plan, the chief school official delegates considerable authority and responsibility to an assistant superintendent in charge of instruction or to a coordinator of elementary education, for example. The principals are then responsible to the coordinator or assistant superintendent in the areas of curriculum and instruction but are directly responsible to the chief school official in other areas of administration. The supervisory function is cooperative and democratic, and is shared. The building principals are the educational leaders of their schools, exercising supervisory and administrative responsibility with their staffs. However, in *Plan 2*, it is recognized that at least one administrator or coordinator is assigned full-time responsibility for the coordination of instruction on a district-wide basis.

The administrative council plays an important role in coordinating the K–12 program. All supervisors and administrators are members, and other persons are invited to participate on occasion. Council functions include the determination of areas of district-wide concern in the instructional program and the corresponding limits of the authority of building principals. The framework should be flexible enough to permit considerable latitude in principal-teacher interaction. Each professional employee needs to have a certain independence in his classroom or building, but each must also feel himself to be an integral part of the total district effort in the improvement of instruction. Also, general limits of authority and responsibility should be established and job descriptions written as guides to action. The administrative council approves all plans for in-service work, including curriculum development, to insure coordination of district activities. In fact, all matters pertaining to the supervision of instruction clear through the council. Agenda items may be suggested by teachers, the chief school official, or any member of the council. Everyone has ample opportunity to react to proposals before final action is taken.

The intermediate-size district has the potential to organize effectively for supervision. The results will be determined primarily by the quality of the educational leadership at the building and district level.

The large school district, for purposes of discussion in this chapter, includes systems that fall, in pupil enrollment, between the intermediate-size school districts and the very large cities. These larger school systems are found in small and medium-size cities and in suburban communities with a large geographic area and a rapid growth pattern. The range in pupil enrollment is from 10,000 to approximately 130,000.

In larger districts the number of schools will range from about twelve elementary buildings and four secondary school plants up to about 150 buildings in the largest systems in this category. Staff needs will vary greatly, depending upon the curricular offerings, class size, organizational patterns for teaching, and the quantity and quality of administrative and special services. The elementary teaching staff will number more than 250 regular classroom or team teachers, and the total secondary school teaching and guidance staff will exceed 200.

The necessary administrative and supervisory personnel include: the superintendent of schools; one or more associate or assistant superintendents in charge of instruction; assistant superintendents for elementary and secondary school principals and assistant principals; and subject area coordinators (K–12), team leaders, and/or department heads.

In the larger district, the superintendent of schools will be kept fully informed on supervisory matters, but he has little time to participate actively in supervision. He plays a very important supportive role and delegates the responsibility for the instructional program to his associate or assistant superintendent(s). The principals are responsible for the administration of their schools and are considered in all respects the educational leaders of their faculty and students.

In organizing for supervision in the larger district, the associate or assistant superintendent in charge of instruction plays the key role. He must see that line and staff relationships are carefully defined. He will take the lead in organizing the administrative council and directing its activity.

There must be plenty of latitude in the large district for principals and teachers to innovate, experiment, and otherwise influence instruction at the building and classroom level. It is particularly important to keep lines of communication open among all levels of supervisory personnel in the schools, the district and sub-district offices.

SUGGESTED ACTIVITIES AND PROBLEMS

1. Interview a teaching principal in a small district and jointly evaluate his effectiveness in improving instruction. Summarize your findings. Then interview the chief school administrator to confirm or disprove your previous conclusions.
2. Locate several neighboring small school districts and develop a master plan for the coordination of supervision from kindergarten through high school.
3. Locate an intermediate-size school district in your area and carry out the following:
   A. Describe the characteristics of the district in a short summary.
   B. Interview the superintendent or assistant superintendent in charge of

instruction and explore in depth the district philosophy of supervision and the organization for improvement of instruction. Be sure to identify the roles of all personnel who have any supervisory responsibilities. Write up your findings.

4. In a short paper, prove the superiority of either *Plan 1* or *Plan 2* as a method of organizing for supervision in an intermediate-size district. Document your conclusions from:
   A. Interviews with supervisory personnel.
   B. Supplementary reading.
   C. Your own experience, if pertinent.

5. Interview three teachers in a large school system to ascertain how they perceive the respective roles of three different supervisory officials in the improvement of instruction. Write up your findings.

6. Write to a large school system and request an organizational chart. Draw up a plan for involving all staff members of this district in the improvement of some aspect of the instructional program.

SELECTED READINGS

Activities of the Curriculum Services Division and *An Analysis and Summary of District Functions and Services for Secondary Schools*. San Diego, Calif.: San Diego Unified School District, 1969.

Bair, Medill. "One Superintendent's Answer to a City's Education Problems." *Phi Delta Kappan*, L, no. 5 (1969), 274–79.

Barr, Richard H., and Foster, Betty J. *Fall 1967 Statistics of Public Elementary and Secondary Day Schools*. U.S.O.E., National Center for Educational Statistics. Washington, D.C.: U.S. Government Printing Office, 1968.

Odell, William R. *Educational Survey Report for the Philadelphia Board of Public Education*. Philadelphia, Pa.: School District of Philadelphia, 1965.

Paying for Better Public Schools. New York: Committee for Economic Development, 1960.

Simon, Kenneth A., and Grant, W. Vance. *Digest of Educational Statistics, 1968 Edition*. U.S.O.E., National Center for Educational Statistics. Washington, D.C.: U.S. Government Printing Office, 1968.

Wiles, Kimball. *Supervision for Better Schools*. 3rd ed., Chap. 8. Englewood Cliffs, N.J.: Prentice-Hall, Inc., 1967.

chapter 4

The Superintendent, Assistant Superintendent, and Curriculum Coordinator at Work in Supervision

As is true of the administrative aspects of an educational enterprise, curriculum development and the improvement of instruction can be successfully accomplished only if a staff adequate to do the job is assembled. However, adequacy of numbers is not easy to determine. Students of educational administration have been struggling over the years to determine the optimum number of administrative and supervisory personnel required to get the job done effectively. Unfortunately, up to the present time no one has come up with a magic formula that works equally well in all organizations. This may be due to the fact that situations differ greatly and individuals vary tremendously in their energy output and effectiveness.

In Chapter III the authors have discussed the organization and function of supervision in small, intermediate, and large school districts. In this chapter the positions, job analysis, qualifications, and supervisory interrelationships of personnel above the rank of principal will be discussed.

THE SUPERINTENDENT OF SCHOOLS

Throughout this handbook the terms "superintendent of schools," "chief school administrator," and "chief school official" are used interchangeably to designate the executive officer of the board of education. This official is considered to be a key figure in the improvement of instruction and the curriculum, as the authors have stated in earlier chapters.

Job Analysis

The role of the superintendent of schools in American education has been changing radically during the past few years. The school organization itself and the social and economic problems that confront it are becoming so complex that a new role has been carved out for the superintendency. Fensch and Wilson delineate this new role when they write:

> The new concept states, however, that the function of the superintendent is primarily that of a coordinating officer who marshals many functions and specialists toward the accomplishment of the system's goals. It recognizes the chief school administrator as a generalist in all aspects of school operations but a specialist only in the skill of coordinating.[1]

According to this interpretation, the role of the superintendent of schools is that of the coordinator of the superintendency team.

This new role of the superintendent, in addition to requiring skill as a coordinator, also demands expertise in planning. The needs to be met, problems to be solved, and interrelationships of education to other community functions require skill in both short-range and long-range planning.

Finally, the superintendent is a decision maker. Both coordinating and planning ultimately lead to the need for decision making and the implementation of the decisions. Although decisions are, it is hoped, arrived at cooperatively, in the final analysis the superintendent is held responsible for these decisions.

Instructional leadership and curriculum improvement. In the roles of coordinator, planner, and decision maker the superintendent can have a tremendous influence on instruction and curriculum. He also can serve as a stimulator and innovator. In fact, everything the chief school official does affects the curriculum and the instructional program.

Much is heard today about innovation and change (see Chapter VII). The superintendent plays important roles in these areas. Unless he enthusiastically supports educational change, it will not take place. In fact, he does much more than support change—he initiates it. According to the following statement from a recent study, innovations in instructional programs are introduced by administrators:

> Instructional changes which call for significant new ways of using professional talent, drawing upon instructional resources, allocating physical facilities,

[1]Edwin A. Fensch and Robert E. Wilson, *The Superintendency Team* (Columbus, Ohio: Charles E. Merrill Books, Inc., 1964), p. 13.

scheduling instructional time or altering physical space—*rearrangements* of the *structural elements of the institution*—depend almost exclusively upon administrative initiative.[2]

Not only is the superintendent an innovator, but according to a study by Gross and Herriott, empirical support was found for the hypothesis that the stronger the higher administration's approval of a principal's introducing educational change, the greater his executive professional leadership (EPL).[3]

If the superintendent is to be effective in his role as an instructional leader, there must be a similarity between the role which staff members believe the superintendent *should* assume and the one which they think he *is* carrying out. This apparently is more important than what he actually does.[4]

The roles of the chief school official in the improvement of instruction and in curriculum development may be quite different in the small district from the roles engaged in by this official in the other two categories of districts. In small school districts, the superintendent must either personally perform all the appropriate district-wide duties carried on in intermediate- and larger-size districts by the assistant superintendent in charge of instruction and the coordinators, or he must assign them to the principals. Although all of the superintendent's duties related to curriculum development and the improvement of instruction are not shown, Becker lists the following duties as performed by superintendents when there are no assistants or coordinators:

1. To conduct studies of need, determine policies and manageable projects.
2. To make the work of teachers more effective through such things as improved working conditions, better materials of instruction, improved methods of teaching, and in the preparation of courses of study.
3. To coordinate the efforts of principals, supervisors, helping teachers, and special service personnel.
4. To recognize individual group potential for continued growth and improvement.
5. To organize workshops and study groups that benefit all teachers in all grades either directly or indirectly.
6. To utilize consultants in the implementation of the in-service education program.

[2]Henry M. Brickell, *Organizing New York State For Educational Change* (Albany, N.Y.: State Education Department, 1961), p. 23.
[3]Neal Gross and Robert E. Herriott, *Staff Leadership in Public Schools: A Sociological Inquiry* (New York: John Wiley & Sons, Inc., 1965), p. 118.
[4]Andrew W. Halpin, *The Leadership Behavior of School Superintendents*, The School Community Development Study, Monograph No. 4 (Columbus: College of Education, The Ohio State University, 1956), pp. 74–78.

7. To supervise instruction through direct contact with the classroom teacher.

8. To evaluate the effectiveness of the instructional program in terms of what it does to the pupil.[5]

The same author depicts how the role of the superintendent changes when he assigns these duties to the principals or the assistant superintendent in charge of instruction. Under this arrangement, the superintendent:

1. Assigns the function to the principals or assistant superintendent.

2. Utilizes the board of education and the administrative staff in defining the duties for this function.

3. Holds each principal responsible for the educational program in his building or the assistant superintendent responsible for it from kindergarten through grade twelve.[6]

In addition to the above list of specific duties of the superintendent in the areas of curriculum improvement and instructional leadership, it seems desirable to suggest some additional responsibilities related to this phase of his job. Because of his key position, the superintendent is the one individual who can insure the development of a district-wide climate that is most favorable to the improvement of the curriculum and the instructional program. Therefore, he should use all the resources at his disposal to make certain that the following conditions and practices prevail in the school district for which he is responsible:

1. A carefully selected staff of competent teachers is secured and retained.
2. A sufficient number of supervisory personnel to get the job done adequately has been engaged.
3. Members of the superintendency team are carefully selected and retained.
4. Improved procedures for the orientation of new professional personnel have been formulated.
5. Good working conditions, including released time for curriculum work, exist.
6. Belief in and practice of democratic school administration by the superintendent is assured.
7. Regular delegation of authority with responsibility is practiced.
8. An honest desire on the part of the superintendent to see the instructional program improved is present.
9. Enthusiastic encouragement and support of curriculum projects by the superintendent is guaranteed.

[5]James W. Becker, "Processes Used by Superintendents for the Improvement of Education in Selected School Districts" (Doctoral dissertation, Temple University, 1958), p. 120.
[6]*Ibid.*, pp. 117–18.

10. An atmosphere in which teachers feel free to experiment is present.
11. Belief on the part of the superintendent that research has much to contribute to the solution of curricular and instructional problems is assured.
12. Ample instructional materials and learning resources that fit the needs of children and youth on all levels of learning ability are made available.
13. Adequate functional physical plant facilities that make good instruction and learning possible are provided, maintained, and modernized when necessary.
14. Community support for existing programs and for innovation and change are sought and encouraged.
15. Caution and good common sense are exercised in the evaluation and study of "band wagon" practices before deciding to adopt or reject them.
16. Outside consultant help is provided when necessary.
17. The superintendent practices continuous self-improvement.

One superintendent in a school system of 70,000 students who faced up to his responsibilities (as an instructional leader) scheduled one day each week for the specific task of improving instruction. On the specified day he, the superintendent, essentially became team leader of selected central office instructional staff members to visit schools, using the following operational procedures:

1. The superintendent and instructional team members visited a particular school and met with the principal and the principal's leadership members (having previously arranged for and indicated the purpose of the proposed visit).
2. The principal, in a discussion section, was asked to give the purpose of the school as well as indicate his objectives as key person in the school.
3. The principal and his school leadership staff were asked to indicate candidly the strengths and weaknesses of their school program and in turn the superintendent's team responded with objective evaluations of strengths and weaknesses of the school's instructional program.

The reactions to both the initial and follow-up work were quite favorable. Teachers and administrators agreed that here was an example where a superintendent put first things first.[7]

Qualifications

Numerous suggestions have been made concerning the qualifications necessary for success as a chief school official. The position varies so much from school district to school district that the qualifications needed for success in one situation might not be identical to those required in another school system. However, the personal characteristics and recommended professional preparation which are considered essential for dynamic leadership in the improvement of the curriculum and the instructional program will be listed.

[7]William H. Lucio, ed., *Supervision: Perspectives and Propositions* (Washington, D.C.: Association for Supervision and Curriculum Development, NEA, 1967), p. 51.

Personal characteristics. More individuals fail because of deficiencies in the personal characteristics needed for the job than because of insufficient skills. The following personal characteristics are among those considered essential for the job:

1. ". . . intelligent and decisive, penetrating, yet flexible, a sophisticated analyst and a vigorous actor."[8]
2. ". . . the ability to see the whole picture . . . each problem in its broader context."[9]
3. Excellent physical and mental health with good emotional stability and self-control.
4. A sensitivity to and understanding of people and skill in human relations that enable him to work successfully with individuals and with groups.
5. A high degree of curiosity and infectious enthusiasm for education and what it can do for individuals and society.
6. A high degree of organizational skill.
7. Creative in his approach, with broad vision, abundant courage, and great integrity.
8. Open-minded and always exercises suspended judgment, but never vacillates in making decisions.
9. Enjoys responsibility and recognizes the magnitude of his job—he is concerned but seldom worries.
10. Personal magnetism that attracts a corps of like-minded assistants who complement each other to form a superior administrative team.

Professional background. Great strides are being made in the upgrading of the programs for the preparation of chief school officials. The American Association of School Administrators, University Council on Educational Administration, and state departments of education are all assuming active roles in insuring that better qualified individuals occupy this important position.

Departments of Educational Administration in major universities throughout the nation have had their programs for preparation of chief school administrators scrutinized by visitation teams from NCATE, UCEA, and state departments. When the programs meet the criteria, some state departments are now willing to issue certificates to any individuals who have completed satisfactorily an approved program. Membership in the AASA is at present contingent on the completion of a stipulated approved educational program.

Although these programs vary somewhat from institution to institution and state to state, the basic requirements are along the following lines:

---

[8]Roald Campbell *et al., Improving Preparatory Programs for Educational Administrators in the United States: Some Action Guides* (Columbus: University Council for Educational Administration, 1962), p. 11.

[9]American Association of School Administrators, *Professional Administrators for America's Schools,* Thirty-eighth Yearbook (Washington, D.C.: National Education Association, 1960), p. 45.

1. Certification as a teacher.

2. Five or more years of successful experience in education several of which must be in a lower echelon administrative or supervisory capacity.

3. Doctor's degree or 60 to 70 semester hours of approved graduate work (including a Master's degree) with 30 to 36 semester hours in educational administration.

4. Graduate work in the related fields of Curriculum, Foundations of Education, Educational Psychology, Group Processes, and Research and Statistics.

5. A minimum of 18 semester hours of graduate work selected from three or more of the following areas: Public Finance, Economics, Sociology, Political Science, and Public Administration.[10]

Because of the increasing numbers of sociological, political, and economic problems facing school districts today, it would seem advisable for the superintendent to have considerably more background in the social sciences. Social Psychology, Cultural Anthropology, and Urban Sociology should be high on the list as required background for the big-city superintendent. The chief school administrator also should be knowledgeable in the field of planning, including community planning.

THE ASSISTANT SUPERINTENDENT IN CHARGE OF INSTRUCTION

The assistant superintendent in charge of instruction should be made responsible to the chief school official for the character and quality of the total instructional program in the school district. It should be his responsibility to provide the quality of leadership for a team of teachers, principals, supervisors, and other special resource persons that will result in a superior instructional program. To accomplish this, he must be adept at discovering, developing, and coordinating the various abilities, competencies, energies, and efforts of the members of his team. It, however, must be kept in mind that many of the responsibilities and duties listed below are related to items that are being negotiated in teacher contracts. The assistant superintendent may be held responsible in terms of his job, but teachers are increasingly making the decisions that determine the outcomes.[11]

Job Analysis

The responsibilities and duties of the assistant superintendent in charge of instruction are many and varied. No attempt will be made here to

[10] Program approved by Department of Education, Commonwealth of Pennsylvania.

[11] For example, see William F. Young, "Curriculum Negotiations: Present Status—Future Trends," *Educational Leadership*, XXVI, no. 4 (1969), 341.

enumerate all of them, but the most important areas will be pointed out. These responsibilities and duties may be grouped as follows:

1. Those relative to the instructional program.
2. Those connected with staff leadership and professional growth.
3. Those relative to the obtaining of instructional materials, resources, and special services.

Under each of these areas may be listed a number of specific items which point up the role of the assistant superintendent in charge of instruction.

Instructional program. The development, coordination, and improvement of the instructional program is one of the most important tasks of the assistant superintendent. However, it is assumed that he will work democratically with a large number of persons in fulfilling his role. Some of these responsibilities and duties are:

1. To assist the superintendent as he works with the staff to formulate an adequate philosophy of education that is acceptable to the board of education, the professional staff, and the community.
2. To assume leadership for providing a continuous program of curriculum improvement.
3. To work with the staff in the development of instructional goals for the various levels and curriculum areas—kindergarten through grade twelve.
4. To work with the staff in the development of a system-wide program of evaluation and appraisal.
5. To be responsible for the development and supervision of programs for atypical children.
6. To work with the staff in the formulation of policies relative to pupil classification, marking, reporting, and promoting, and to execute the policies which are finally adopted.
7. To assume responsibility for determining the need for instructional-staff specialists and other resource personnel, and to direct, coordinate, and supervise their work so that they function as a smooth-working team.
8. To assume responsibility for the development, direction, and supervision of adult education programs in the district.

Staff leadership. The assistant superintendent in charge of instruction must be concerned with all district-wide matters pertaining to the instructional staff. However, he does not work alone. In carrying out all of the following responsibilities, he works with the superintendent, coordinators, building principals, and teachers.

1. To jointly assume responsibility for the recruitment, selection, and assignment of instructional personnel.
2. To assume responsibility for developing a comprehensive policy and program of in-service education for all professional staff members.

3. To jointly assume responsibility for the establishment and application of policies relative to promotion, transfer, and dismissal of instructional personnel.
4. To jointly assume responsibility for the promotion and supervision of experimentation with curriculum organization, instructional techniques, and instructional materials including the designing and/or coordinating of proposals for funded projects.
5. To assume responsibility for the development and operation of a comprehensive district-wide orientation program for new instructional personnel.
6. To jointly assume responsibility for the evaluation of all instructional personnel.
7. To serve by request as a consultant to principals, their staff, and individual teachers, but always with the approval of the building principal.
8. To assume responsibility to keep up to date professionally by reading widely, attending professional meetings, visiting other school systems, and any other means that will contribute to professional growth.

Instructional materials. The third and final area in which the assistant superintendent in charge of instruction operates is concerned with instructional materials, resources, and special services. The following responsibilities are included under this category:

1. To assume responsibility for the selection, procurement, and distribution of textbooks, library books, and all categories of instructional supplies; learning resources and equipment and the preparation of the section of the budget related to them. This responsibility must be carried out in close cooperation with the business manager, if there is one.
2. To assume responsibility for advising the superintendent on all budget items related to the instructional program.
3. To assume responsibility for serving as a consultant in school plant design on all matters affecting curriculum and instruction and for the cooperative preparation of the educational specifications.
4. To assume responsibility for the establishment and operation of a district-wide curriculum materials, audio-visual, and professional library center.
5. To assume responsibility for editing and publishing curriculum bulletins, guides, courses of study, pamphlets, and so forth, for use by the instructional staff.
6. To assume responsibility for the preparation of adequate reports and materials to provide the superintendent and board of education with summary information relative to the instructional personnel and program.
7. To assume responsibility for the preparation, with the approval of the superintendent, of bulletins, brochures, and reports on the instructional program for distribution to lay groups, P.T.A. committees, and the general public.
8. To assume responsibility for the identification and use of community, county, state, and national agencies and resources for the improvement of the instructional program.[12]

[12]The job analysis was revised and adapted from: Educational Service Bureau, Temple University, *A Survey of The Cornwall-Lebanon Schools* (Philadelphia: The Bureau, 1962) (Mimeographed), pp. 111–15.

Qualifications

The assistant superintendent in charge of instruction needs to possess many of the personal characteristics listed for the superintendent. The scope of this position also demands a broad background of training and experience.

Personal characteristics. Dynamic leadership in the improvement of the instructional program and the curriculum requires, in addition to intelligence, a high degree of creativity. In a recent research report, the creative administrator was characterized as follows: He is an individual of curiosity and discontent, with unlimited enthusiasm for his work. He is a restless, intense, and strongly motivated person. He has the ability to create an atmosphere of excitement and urgency among his associates. He is open-minded and willing to listen to new ideas. He is unorthodox in his thinking, and he questions conventional ideas; he is goal-oriented rather than method-oriented.[13]

In addition, the following characteristics and competencies are highly desirable:

1. A sane, workable, consistent philosophy of education and the ability to translate it in terms of instructional purposes, programs, and procedures.
2. A person who receives a high degree of satisfaction in assisting others to develop their potential, possesses great skill in motivating others to action, and has the ability to be an astute observer of human personality.
3. Ability to establish rapport quickly with his peers, and a personality that encourages others to respect his professional competence and utilize his services.
4. Demonstrated ability in democratic leadership and effective decision making.[14]
5. Ability to supervise subordinates and to serve as an advisor to other line officers.
6. Competence in research methodology and the ability to interpret research.
7. Ability to write and speak effectively and to communicate with both lay and professional personnel.

Professional background. The assistant superintendent in charge of instruction is one of the most influential members of the superintendency

[13] Adapted from: E. Paul Torrance, "The Teacher as a Team Member: Team Leadership Through Creative Administration," in *Professional Growth for Administrators*, April 1961 (Arthur C. Croft Publications).

[14] For example, see Herbert A. Searle, "A Role Study of Decision-Making Reported by Personnel Carrying Titles as Assistant Administrative and Supervisory Functionaries in the District Superintendency of Education in Selected New Jersey School Districts" (Doctoral dissertation, Temple University, 1964).

team. In order to qualify for a position of this scope and importance, the individual must have a broad educational background and experience preferably on both the elementary and secondary schools levels. The authors believe that requirements similar to the following should be met by those seeking this important position:

1. Certification as a teacher.
2. Five or more years of successful teaching and/or administrative experience on both the elementary- and the secondary-school level.
3. Doctor's degree or 60 to 70 semester hours of approved graduate work (including a Master's degree) with 18 to 24 semester hours in educational administration incorporating courses in Supervision and Instructional Leadership.
4. Graduate work 18 to 24 semester hours in curriculum (elementary and secondary), curriculum theory, and instructional media.
5. Graduate work in the related fields of Foundations of Education, Educational Psychology, Group Processes, and Research and Statistics.
6. Graduate work selected from the humanities, social sciences, and natural sciences.[15]

The authors assume the viewpoint that the position of assistant superintendent in charge of instruction is an administrative one and, therefore, the aspirant for this post should have a good background in educational administration.

RELATIONSHIP OF ASSISTANT SUPERINTENDENT TO OTHER ADMINISTRATIVE PERSONNEL

The assistant superintendent in charge of instruction is directly responsible to the superintendent and subordinate to him. As his right-hand man in charge of instruction, he serves in a line relationship to other administrative and supervisory personnel in carrying out his responsibilities. The assistant superintendent in charge of instruction is the recognized official head of the instructional leadership team. However, in working with other officials, he respects their leadership role in improving the instructional program and the curriculum. He considers district-wide coordination of the educational program kindergarten through grade twelve an important part of his assignment. In accomplishing this, he serves in a line relationship to the coordinators of elementary and secondary education and to other assistants. The assistant superintendent is an important member of the administrative council.

[15] Department of Education, Commonwealth of Pennsylvania, now has identical requirements for all central office personnel.

THE ASSISTANT SUPERINTENDENT
FOR BUSINESS

On first thought, this official seems far removed from the tasks of improving learning and instruction and updating the curriculum. On second thought, however, it becomes clear that to a limited extent the assistant superintendent for business can in various ways control the purse strings. In the dual system which (thank goodness) is disappearing from the American scene, he is "lord of the exchequer." There is general agreement among educators that the unit control system is by far the most satisfactory.

Job Analysis

The authors take the position that the assistant superintendent for business is subordinate to the superintendent of schools. He works in a staff relationship with the assistant superintendent in charge of instruction on matters relating to the budgeting and purchasing of instructional supplies, learning resources, and instructional media. Likewise, these two assistant superintendents should work together on any other matters pertaining to the improvement of instruction and curriculum that require special financing.

The assistant superintendent for business should never exert sole decision-making power over the purchase of items related to instruction and the curriculum. His role in the budget-making process for the above area should be supportive and advisory to the work of the assistant superintendent in charge of instruction.

Qualifications

Since this official is only indirectly, although importantly, involved in the improvement of learning, instruction, and the curriculum, very brief comments will be made here concerning the necessary qualifications for this position.

Probably the most desirable personal characteristic of a successful assistant superintendent for business is that he is a good team member. He must be willing to play a supporting role and not try to carry the ball. He cannot be a star or the community's champion who tries to keep the tax rate down by slashing the budget.

At present, many individuals who perform the work of this office carry the title of business manager. Their qualifications vary greatly with some individuals not holding a baccalaureate degree, while others may have a Master's degree or even the doctorate. At present, there is a movement to make this a position equal in rank to the other assistant superintendents. The authors support this movement.

Professionally, the assistant superintendent in charge of business should be an educator first and an individual intrigued and enamored by figures and dollar signs second. He, however, should have competencies in business management developed through a broad educational background and, perhaps, some experience in the business world. The authors believe that if the status of this position is to be raised, a Doctor's degree or 60 to 70 semester hours of approved graduate work will be necessary. A Master's degree in educational administration with emphasis on business management should be the minimum education for this position.

COORDINATORS OF ELEMENTARY AND SECONDARY EDUCATION

These supervisory personnel are directly responsible to the superintendent in small districts and to the assistant superintendent in charge of instruction in intermediate- and large-size school districts.

Job Analysis

In intermediate- and large-size districts, the coordinators are the right-hand men of the assistant superintendent in charge of instruction. As coordinators in their respective fields, they function as line personnel on a district-wide basis; however, they operate only in a staff relationship to principals when they work in the individual buildings. When there is no assistant superintendent in charge of instruction, the coordinators assume his responsibilities and duties. Even in an organization which has an assistant superintendent, many of the duties of the coordinators are similar to those of their immediate superior except that the coordinators work only on their respective levels of the school system.

Duties and responsibilities. Although they may vary from district to district, the following types of duties and responsibilities may be performed successfully by the coordinators.

1. Assist in the development of a consistent philosophy of elementary or secondary education.
2. Provide leadership in developing a continuous program of curriculum improvement on their respective levels.
3. Work with the staff in the development of goals in the various curriculum areas on their respective levels.

4. Assist the principals in a staff capacity in evaluating the quality of teaching and learning.
5. Aid the principals as consultants on discipline, guidance, diagnosis of learning problems, and psychological referrals.
6. Aid the principals as consultants in the organization of instruction, teaching procedures, and experimentation.
7. Assist the principals, upon request, in supervising the work of teachers.
8. Aid the assistant superintendent and principals in the recruitment, selection, orientation, and assignment of new teachers.
9. Aid the assistant superintendent and the principals in the development of a sound program of evaluation.
10. Assist the assistant superintendent and principals in developing and executing procedures relative to pupil classification, marking, reporting, and promoting.
11. Aid the assistant superintendent and principals on curricular needs, and in formulating and administering the budget in the areas of curriculum and instruction.
12. Aid the assistant superintendent and the principals in determining the need for instructional staff specialists and in directing and supervising their work.
13. Aid the assistant superintendent and principals in developing a comprehensive policy and program of in-service education for all professional staff members.
14. Aid the assistant superintendent and principals in the establishment and execution of policies relative to promotion, transfer, and dismissal of instructional personnel.
15. Assume responsibility for keeping up to date professionally.
16. Aid the assistant superintendent and principals in the selection, procurement, and distribution of textbooks, library books, and all categories of instructional supplies and equipment.
17. Aid the assistant superintendent in the establishment of a district-wide instructional materials center including a professional library.
18. Assist in the editing and publishing of curriculum bulletins, guides, courses of study, and pamphlets.
19. Aid in the preparation of adequate reports and materials to provide the assistant superintendent, superintendent, and board of education with summary information relative to the instructional program.
20. Aid in the preparation of materials relative to the instructional program for distribution to lay groups.

Qualifications

The qualifications of the coordinator of elementary or secondary education should be similar to those of the assistant superintendent in charge of instruction, except that the coordinator should have extensive graduate work in curriculum and teaching on the level on which he expects to serve as a coordinator. His teaching experience also should have been largely in the division in which he will be serving as a coordinator.

RELATIONSHIP OF THE COORDINATORS TO OTHER ADMINISTRATIVE PERSONNEL

The coordinators are directly responsible and subordinate to the assistant superintendent in charge of instruction in districts employing this official. In districts without assistant superintendents, coordinators assume this relationship with the superintendent. As it has been stated elsewhere in this handbook, coordinators serve in a line relationship in carrying out district-wide responsibilities, but they function in a staff capacity when providing service and assistance to principals. Consequently, all requests for coordinators to work in individual schools should be made through the principal. The coordinators also are members of the administrative council.

Important leadership notes. In order to have an effective supervisory team, school districts should give serious consideration to the following suggestions:

1. Members of the supervisory team should be carefully selected in terms of their personal and professional qualifications.
2. The superintendent must always be aware of his key role in the improvement of the curriculum and instruction. His encouragement, cooperation, and support are essential if improvement in teaching and learning is to take place. The superintendent also must carry out his role as an initiator of change.
3. Written job descriptions for all positions should be available with a clear delineation of responsibilities and relationships in the areas of instructional improvement and curriculum revision.
4. Teachers should have a clear understanding of the supervisory roles of various administrative personnel and also their own roles in the improvement of instruction, learning, and the curriculum.

SUMMARY

The superintendent of schools is the key individual in the improvement of the curriculum and the instructional program. This leadership role calls for a person who is intelligent, perceptive, and decisive. He must be able to visualize the whole picture and see each problem in its broader context. He must possess excellent physical and mental health and have great skill in working with people.

He must be broadly educated, with a knowledge of society and the forces that play upon it. He must have a sane, forward-looking philosophy of education and a respect for and knowledge of research.

The assistant superintendent in charge of instruction has numerous and varied responsibilities in connection with the curriculum and the instructional program. In addition to the usual characteristics necessary for educational leadership, this individual must possess a high degree of creativity.

He also must be broadly educated and have expert knowledge of the curriculum on all levels of the elementary and secondary school. Teaching and/or administrative experience on both the elementary- and secondary-school level seem(s) to be a desirable prerequisite.

The assistant superintendent for business is subordinate to the superintendent of schools and he works in a staff relationship with the assistant superintendent in charge of instruction.

He should be an educator first and an accountant second. He must be a good team member.

His preparation should include courses in educational administration with special emphasis on business management.

Coordinators of elementary or secondary education have important roles to play in the improvement of the curriculum and the instructional program. With qualifications similar to those of the assistant superintendent, they can be of great assistance to him and to the principals in their respective fields.

SUGGESTED ACTIVITIES AND PROBLEMS

1. Secure the certification requirements from four states and examine the requirements for each of the positions discussed in this chapter. Write a paper illustrating how these requirements qualify each of the individuals for their respective positions.
2. Interview three chief school officials to ascertain what they consider to be the most significant contributions they make to the improvement of instruction and the curriculum. Evaluate their responses in light of current research and authoritative opinion.
3. Write a case study that illustrates the roles of the superintendent, assistant superintendent, and coordinators in the solution of a specific instructional problem.
4. Select a school system in which there is an assistant superintendent in charge of instruction. Interview this official, a principal, a teacher, and a parent to determine the different viewpoints held concerning the role of the assistant superintendent in the improvement of the instructional program and the curriculum.
5. Write a letter of application to the superintendent of schools that will convince him of your fitness for the position of elementary or secondary curriculum coordinator. Include some supporting evidence if you do not wish to incorporate it all in the body of the letter.
6. Write a case study that illustrates how an assistant superintendent for

business can adversely affect a program planned to improve the curriculum or instruction in a school system.

SELECTED READINGS

American Association of School Administrators. *The Superintendent as Instructional Leader.* Thirty-fifth Yearbook. Washington, D.C.: National Education Association, 1957.

Fensch, Edwin A., and Wilson, Robert E. *The Superintendency Team.* Columbus, Ohio: Charles E. Merrill Books, Inc., 1964.

Lane, Willard R.; Corwin, Ronald G.; and Monahan, William G. *Foundations of Educational Administration.* Chap. 11. New York: The Macmillan Company, 1967.

Leeper, Robert R., ed. *Role of Supervisor and Curriculum Director in a Climate of Change.* Chaps. 3 and 5. Washington, D.C.: Association for Supervision and Curriculum Development, 1965.

Mickelson, John M.; Appel, Marilyn B.; and Prusso, Kenneth W. "The Director of Curriculum and Instruction." *Educational Leadership*, XXVI, no. 4 (1969), 371.

Miller, Van. *The Public Administration of American School Systems.* Chap. 8. New York: The Macmillan Company, 1965.

Neagley, Ross L., and Evans, N. Dean. *Handbook for Effective Curriculum Development.* Chap. 5. Englewood Cliffs, N.J.: Prentice-Hall, Inc., 1967.

Neagley, Ross L.; Evans, N. Dean; and Lynn, Clarence A., Jr. *The School Administrator and Learning Resources: A Handbook for Effective Action.* Chaps. 2 and 4. Englewood Cliffs, N.J.: Prentice-Hall, Inc., 1969.

Torrance, E. Paul. *Guiding Creative Talent.* Chap. 10. Englewood Cliffs, N.J.: Prentice-Hall, Inc., 1962.

Wilson, Robert E. *Educational Administration.* Chap. 10. Columbus, Ohio: Charles E. Merrill Books, Inc., 1966.

Young, William F. "Curriculum Negotiations: Present Status—Future Trends." *Educational Leadership*, XXVI, no. 4 (1969), 341.

chapter 5

The Principal at Work
in Supervision

Elementary- and secondary-school principals are in strategic positions to assume leadership roles on their respective levels. The reorganization of smaller rural and suburban school districts into larger ones and the decentralization of large city school systems into smaller units have increased the potential of the principalship as a position of leadership.

A second opportunity to exert leadership has arisen as a result of the increasing interest of teachers in all phases of the school program. If this challenge is not met by a display of high quality professional leadership by principals, they may be relegated to a managerial role of clerical minutiae and the disciplining of uncooperative students. Unfortunately, this is a role too many principals have been satisfied to play.

FACTORS INFLUENCING THE ROLE OF THE PRINCIPAL

In addition to rural and suburban school reorganization and big city decentralization, the following factors have been responsible for affecting the role and status of the principalship:

1. Higher certification requirements.
2. Improved preparation programs for the principalship.
3. Efforts of professional organizations to upgrade the principalship.
4. Higher salaries and twelve months employment which make the principalship a desirable career position.

5. Better prepared teachers who are specialists in their fields and, consequently, demand an equal role in the decision-making process.
6. New plans of organizing for instruction.
7. New curricula and increased educational offerings.
8. New learning resources and instructional media.
9. The community school movement in which schools become the centers for other community services and activities.
10. Recognition of the importance of the principalship by the superintendent and boards of education.
11. The demands of parents and students to participate in the determination of the educational program.

The involvement of pupils, parents, and teachers in the solution of educational problems has created a need for a kind of leadership that is skillful in the use of group processes in the improvement of the curriculum and the instructional program.

Other factors that have broadened the scope of the principal's job are: (1) population explosion, (2) increased complexities of the American way of life, (3) changes in society, (4) automation, and (5) the inadequately defined line between the role of the school and other community agencies. In respect to the latter factor, the school has assumed more and more of the responsibilities formerly carried by the home and other community agencies, as, for example: health services, psychological services, guidance services, speech therapy, special education, adult education, driver education, safety education, and recreation.

THE JOB AND THE MAN

The thesis of this handbook is that, irrespective of the type of school organization, a good supervisory program is more likely to result if specifications are prepared for each position and if the qualifications desired for personnel to serve in those positions are stipulated. These qualifications and specifications, the authors believe, may vary somewhat from school district to school district, because the essential outstanding characteristic of a superior supervisory program is that the staff operates as a smoothly coordinated team. This team concept and the role of the principal in the team will be discussed later in this chapter.

Job Analysis

The principal in present-day public school organization is the chief school administrator's representative in the actual day-to-day administration and supervision of the school system's building units. As the administrative head of a building unit, the principal in effect is the local superintendent of schools. Therefore, if the principal does his job effectively, he will assume on the local building level many of the same responsibilities and duties carried by the central office staff on a district-wide basis. In assuming his leadership role, then, the principal must accept responsibility for the following major tasks: (1) instructional leadership and curriculum improvement, (2) personnel administration, (3) business management, (4) plant management, (5) school-community relations, (6) administration of routine duties, and (7) professional, personal, and cultural growth.

This handbook is concerned mainly with the first task, namely, instructional leadership and curriculum improvement.

Instructional leadership and curriculum improvement. Writers in the field of educational administration have been saying for years that the improvement of the instructional program and the curriculum is the most important task of the principal. The following statement by Jones, Salisbury, and Spencer represents this viewpoint concerning the job of the secondary school principal:

> The prime justification for the position of principal in the school is to give leadership to the teaching-learning process. If the principal spends the major portion of his time at that endeavor, he is placing the emphasis where it belongs. If, however, he spends most of his time counting lunch money, seeing that the playing field is lined, and other similar housekeeping chores, he is not fulfilling the major role his profession and society expect him to play.[1]

The same position is taken by Jenson *et al.*, when they write in respect to the elementary principalship:

> As one reviews the areas of principal activity—administrative management, instructional leadership, school-community relations, child guidance, plant supervision, staff personnel—instructional leadership emerges as the area which should have number one priority.[2]

Most elementary principals in the field agree with this conclusion. A research study by the Department of Elementary School Principals, NEA reports that 75 principals in 100 of the total sample believe that they have primary responsibility for supervision and the improvement of instruction

[1]James J. Jones, C. Jackson Salisbury, and Ralph L. Spencer, *Secondary School Administration* (New York: McGraw-Hill Book Company, 1969), p. 209.
[2]Theodore J. Jenson, James B. Burr, William H. Coffield, and Ross L. Neagley, *Elementary School Administration*, 2nd ed. (Boston: Allyn & Bacon, Inc., 1967), p. 104.

within their own schools. In the instance of those designated as supervising principals, 82 percent acknowledge this to be true.[3]

In the same research study, respondents were asked to select from the statements below the one way in which they thought they were most effective in improving instruction within their schools:

1. By organizing committees of teachers to study and report on how to get more time for teaching.
2. By working with specialists and teachers in making the best use of available sources.
3. By helping individual teachers identify, study, and take action on problems in their own classes.
4. By my own careful study of individual children and by making the findings available to teachers.
5. By giving lectures to the staff on methods of teaching and related topics.
6. By helping to create a climate in which teachers, individually or collectively, are encouraged to experiment and to share ideas.
7. By working with teachers to discover and use better instructional materials.
8. By continuous study of the factors in our school which affect learning or instruction and reporting findings to teachers.
9. By keeping abreast of research and school developments and seeking to interpret these to the staff.[4]

It is interesting to note that more than half (53.7 percent) of the total sample selected item 6 as their most effective technique for improving instruction.[5]

It is not difficult to understand why principals consider creating a climate which encourages experimentation and sharing as their most effective contribution to the improvement of instruction. Research in the area of organizational climate has tended to show that more good things happen in an open climate. The environment Halpin describes below would certainly be conducive to the improvement of instruction and learning:

The Open Climate depicts a situation in which the members enjoy extremely high Esprit. The teachers work well together without bickering and griping (low Disengagement). They are not burdened by mountains of busy-work or by routine reports; the principal's policies facilitate the teachers' accomplishment of their tasks (low Hindrance). On the whole, the group members enjoy friendly relations with each other, but they apparently feel no need for an extremely high degree of Intimacy. The teachers obtain

[3]*The Elementary School Principalship in 1968—A Research Study* (Washington, D.C.: Department of Elementary School Principals, NEA, 1968), p. 78.
[4]*Ibid.*, p. 84.
[5]*Ibid.*, p. 85.

considerable job satisfaction, and are sufficiently motivated to overcome difficulties and frustrations. They possess the incentive to work things out and to keep the organization "moving." Furthermore, the teachers are proud to be associated with their school.[6]

Teachers apparently like to teach in Open Climate schools. According to research by Boisen, teachers in all 71 schools studied hoped for optimum Open Climate. She found, however, that principals perceived climates of their schools to be more open than teachers perceived them.[7]

It would seem in view of the fact that principals believe Open Climate contributes to the improvement of instruction and teachers hope for it, that principals' and teachers' perceptions of the degree of openness will have to become more congruent. A lesson to be learned here is that principals must become more aware of teachers' perceptions; the view from a mountain top always seems more beautiful than the view from the valley. It is amazing how quickly some individuals lose the perspectives they had as teachers when they assume supervisory roles. Perhaps Olson is right when he prophetically states:

If teachers and administrators of public school systems don't understand each other, it is partly because some administrators are drifting away from the realities of the classroom. *And if they continue to drift away from these realities, administrators may become obsolete. . . .*

A main function of administration is to help improve the quality of the teaching-learning process. I believe that administrators who are aloof from the realities of the process cannot significantly contribute to its improvement.[8]

A possible solution is having a principal take over a class now and then thereby giving teachers extra free time to prepare their work or just to rest if they do not feel up to par. Principals might also substitute occasionally for a full day and acquaint themselves with teaching under present conditions of unrest. Periodically, principals might be invited in as a guest speaker, lecturer, or panel member, not to demonstrate as a superior, but to participate as a member of a teaching team.

Important leadership notes. The principal who takes the instructional leadership aspects of his job seriously will be interested in the following suggestions:

[6]Andrew W. Halpin, *Theory and Research in Administration* (New York: The Macmillan Company, 1966), pp. 174–75.

[7]Angeline G. Boisen, "Relationships Among the Perceptions and Expectations Held by Principals and Teachers for the Organizational Climate of Elementary Schools" (Doctoral dissertation, University of Maryland, 1966).

[8]Carl O. Olson, Jr., "Administrators Should Teach," *NEA Journal*, LVII, no. 3 (1968), 41.

1. The personal characteristics of a principal frequently determine his success as an instructional leader. The image he presents is very important in his relationships with others.
2. The role of the principal is changing and probably will continue to change. Principals in service must be aware of these changes and learn to assume the appropriate roles.
3. The principal must recognize the new role of the teacher in matters relating to instruction and curriculum. He should applaud this new spirit and encourage its direction in channels that will benefit the students.
4. The principal must develop and exercise skill in making the climate of the school he heads as open as possible.
5. Principals should consider seriously the suggestion that they regularly participate in actual instruction. The manager who plays on the ball team is more likely to be an effective leader than the one who manages from the bench.

In performing the following duties and responsibilities, the principal always should be aware that he is working with a team of technical specialists who are his professional equals in every respect:

1. To strive to create an Open Climate in which teachers, individually or collectively, feel free to utilize their creative talents and share them with each other to improve teaching and learning.
2. To work with the staff in the formulation and execution of an adequate philosophy of education consistent with the district-wide philosophy.
3. To work with the staff within his building unit in the development of instructional goals consistent with district goals for the various levels and curriculum areas.
4. To assume leadership for providing, within his building unit, a continuous program of curriculum improvement which will at the same time contribute to district-wide curriculum improvement.
5. To assume responsibility for seeing that a continuous program of supervision is carried on within his unit.
6. To work with the staff in the development and execution of a system-wide program of evaluation and appraisal.
7. To ascertain the need for instructional staff specialists and to see that the most efficient use is made of their time and talents.
8. To assume responsibility, within the framework of the district plan, for a continuous program of in-service education for the staff members in his unit.
9. To work with the staff in the development, application, and supervision of programs for atypical children.
10. To work with the staff in the formulation and execution of district-wide policies relative to pupil classification, marking, reporting, and promoting.
11. To provide for the interchange of information and ideas among teachers and other staff personnel.
12. To see that the necessary facilities, equipment, supplies, books, and other learning resources are available when required.

13. To keep abreast of new educational developments on the local, state, and national levels and to inform his staff concerning them.

It may be inferred from the above list that the competence of the principal will be judged on the basis of his ability to create an Open Climate and the interpersonal skills he demonstrates as he works with teams of teacher specialists.

Qualifications

The demands made upon the intellect, mental health, physical stamina, and creativity of the principal in today's modern elementary or secondary school require personal and professional qualifications of a somewhat higher order than were expected a decade or two ago. In particular, the leadership role of the elementary- and secondary-school principal in instructional improvement and curriculum development requires a broadly educated and thoroughly experienced individual with the personal characteristics that will fit him for this role.

Personal characteristics. The above duties and responsibilities listed give some hints concerning the following personal attributes that will prove valuable in the principalship:

1. Above-average intellectual ability.
2. Demonstrated ability to exercise sound, mature judgment.
3. Good conceptual ability—the capacity to view the total situation.
4. Sound mental and physical health coupled with abundant energy.
5. Great tolerance for frustration.
6. Ability to face and resolve conflict.
7. A personality that encourages others to respect his professional competence and to seek his counsel and assistance.
8. A sane, workable, consistent philosophy of education and the ability to translate it in terms of instructional purposes, programs, and procedures.
9. Dedicated commitment to the tasks of education in general and administration in particular.
10. Ability to derive great satisfaction from assisting others to develop their potential and skill in motivating others to realize their greatest potential.
11. Demonstrated ability in democratic leadership and effective decision making.
12. Ability to work well with others in a peer-group relationship.
13. Ability to communicate effectively through the use of both the written and spoken word.
14. Creative talent that discovers creativity in others and accords them recognition for it.

The manner in which the principal uses these attributes in the improvement of the instructional program and the curriculum will be described in some detail in Chapters VII, VIII, IX, and X.

Professional background. As the principalship has increased in complexity the need for additional professional background has become evident. Then too, the solution of problems associated with the large-city principalship requires knowledge and skills not formerly emphasized in preparatory programs for this important position.

As was mentioned in Chapter IV, state departments of education are certificating individuals on the basis of approved university programs in educational administration. The approved program for the elementary- or secondary-school principalship of one large university is outlined below:

1. Valid teaching certificate on the level the principalship is desired.
2. Five years of successful teaching experience.
3. Forty-five (45) semester hours of graduate study, including a Master's degree.
4. Course work distributed as follows:
   (1) A minimum of fifteen (15) semester hours in educational administration including the introductory course and courses in administration and supervision on the level the candidate plans to serve.
   (2) A course in K–12 curriculum.
   (3) Graduate study in developmental and remedial reading.
   (4) Twelve (12) semester hours preferably selected from the following academic fields: Business Administration, Economics, Political Science, and Sociology.
   (5) Documentary evidence of proficiency in English.

On completion of the above-approved program and upon recommendation of the institution a Provisional Elementary or Secondary Principal's Certificate will be issued.

Permanent certification may be secured after the applicant has completed three (3) years of successful experience as a principal and received the recommendation of his superintendent or supervisor.[9]

Although not stipulated at present, there is considerable sentiment for including field experience as an additional requirement.

Principals for inner-city schools need additional preparation for their difficult jobs. According to Levine:

School boards in urban districts should provide a minimum of one semester of full-time training to candidates preparing to take administrative positions in inner-city schools.[10]

---

[9] Program approved by Department of Education, Commonwealth of Pennsylvania.

[10] Daniel U. Levine, "Training Administrators for Inner-City Schools: A Proposal," *The National Elementary School Principal,* XLVI, no. 3 (1967), p. 17. Copyright © Department of Elementary School Principals, National Education Association. All rights reserved.

He suggests the following purposes and activities:

1. It should force potential administrators to confront their own motives and assist them to assess administrative behavior from the perspective of the teachers and students with whom they will work.
2. It must enable candidates to acquire direct knowledge of conditions in inner-city schools.
3. All candidates, with the exception of those who have taught disadvantaged students as recently as a year ago, should be required to teach for three or four weeks in the most difficult schools in the district.
4. The trainees also should be given the opportunity to observe for three or four weeks in inner-city schools in other school districts.
5. Through self-study and by working with consultants the candidates should be exposed to the best available thinking on how to educate disadvantaged youth. Material for study and discussion should be drawn from the works of sociologists, psychologists, and educators who have made significant contributions to our understanding of the meaning of educational disadvantage and of ways schools can compensate for it.
6. After acquiring background material related to sound educational practice in schools in low-income areas, the candidates should be scheduled to observe in classes taught by the district's outstanding inner-city teachers.
7. Administrative candidates should be provided with three or four weeks' experience in direct contact with low-income parents in the latter's own environment.
8. Experiences in the final three or four weeks of the training program would be tailored to the needs of each particular candidate.[11]

Levine's training program makes a lot of sense; however, it seems to the authors that the order of experiences might be changed and, perhaps, some of the activities take place simultaneously. It would seem that candidates who will be required to teach for three or four weeks in the most difficult schools in the district (item 3) would be much better prepared to face this task after having had the other experiences in the training program. Perhaps Levine is suggesting the "shock treatment," but beneficial as that may have proved to be in the past in psychiatry, it seems more like "throwing the sheep to the wolves" in this instance. It also would seem that it might be advantageous to combine some background study (item 5) with direct contact with low-income parents (item 7). Direct contact (item 7) with the parents of their pupils during the teaching stint (item 3) also might prove quite profitable to the candidates.

The Instructional Leadership Team

It should be readily apparent to the reader that the principal performs as a member of a team. The job of educational leadership is so immense

[11]*Ibid.*, pp. 18–19.

today that it no longer can be accomplished successfully by individuals working independently. The more successful chief school administrators surround themselves with a corps of well-prepared specialists and likewise see that principals are provided with sufficient assistance. The ability to work with individuals and to utilize their special skills and talents thus becomes a top priority in the qualities essential for dynamic educational leadership.

Elementary- and secondary-school principals serve as valuable members of the school district's instructional leadership team, and, in addition, they are the responsible leaders of their own teams.

Team and *teamwork* are well-known, commonly understood terms. Because they are central to the vocabulary of every sport, individuals learn quite early in life that good teamwork wins games. Although star athletes often execute spectacular plays, every coach knows that behind each star stands the teamwork of the supporting players.

The application of these terms to the industrial, scientific, and political world is a less understood but equally important concept best typified by research teams that have made possible the many new wonders of the scientific age. By tapping the creative genius of many persons working cooperatively as research teams, the life span of man has been increased, many diseases have been wiped out, thousands of new products and labor-saving devices have been invented, the marvels of television and air travel have been made possible, and the comforts and luxuries of man have been multiplied a thousand-fold.

In the field of government, the team concept has long been practiced. In fact, our democratic system of government provides for participation in decision-making by teams of individuals. This is one of the distinctive features of our form of government. Decisions are formulated by groups, not by individuals. True, individuals exert a powerful influence, but they must secure the support of the other members of the team before a decision is finally made.

Unique aspects of educational administration. The team concept has been explored briefly in relation to the sports, industrial, scientific, and political world. There are, however, certain unique aspects of educational administration which influence the way that teamwork functions in this sphere. The reader is reminded that in this handbook supervision has been defined as a phase of educational administration. In the ensuing discussion, *educational administration* is used in its broadest sense to encompass both supervisory and administrative functions. This handbook is, of course, concerned with the improvement of instruction and the curriculum, although the authors have emphasized several times that it it difficult to draw a fine line between supervisory and other administrative functions. Campbell ably describes the following peculiarities which he believes make educational administration (and, consequently, instructional leadership) a special case:

1. School administrators have almost no legal status.
2. They are responsible to lay boards of education which know little about education.
3. School administrators cannot choose their own clients.
4. Many staff members have had as much formal education as the administrators.
5. Many teachers have tenure, and they can resist direction from school administrators without being guilty of outright insubordination.
6. Nonprofessional personnel are in the minority.
7. There are wide differences in the professional worker's perception of the role of administration in education.
8. School administrators are directly responsible to a large number of diverse sub-publics.
9. An educational administrator has to serve as the administrative officer of his school, and he needs constantly to reshape his organization in order that it shall achieve its purposes more adequately.[12]

Although all of the above items may not necessarily influence the formation and functioning of administrative teamwork, some of them, such as items 4, 5, 7, and 9, are particularly crucial and make the job of the educational administrator more difficult than that of administrators in other fields. For example, the fact that most teachers probably know more about their jobs than the principal does has many serious implications for the team concept. Likewise, item 7 presents a difficult challenge to the administrator who desires to use the team approach to school administration. Unless the majority of the professional staff have similar images of the role of the principal, little success will be achieved in the development of a professional team.

Essentials of teamwork. An authoritative text in administration raises the following questions and lists five essentials of teamwork:

Why do some teams win and others lose? What elements are present in good teamwork and absent in poor? How can the creativity in each team member be tapped and utilized to the fullest extent? These, and others, are questions to which satisfactory answers must be found. What, then, are the essentials of good teamwork? First, the team must have a goal, purpose, cause, or objective identified, accepted, understood, and desired by all members of the team. Second, the team must have spirit, morale, and the desire to win even at considerable individual sacrifice. Third, the lines of authority and

[12]Adapted from: Roald F. Campbell, "What Peculiarities in Educational Administration Make It a Special Case?", in *Administrative Theory in Education*, ed. by Andrew W. Halpin (Chicago: The Midwest Administration Center, University of Chicago, 1958), pp. 173–84.

responsibility must be both clearly defined and understood. Fourth, channels of communication must be established. Fifth, leadership must discover and utilize to the fullest extent the creative abilities of each of the individuals and weld them into a smooth working team.[13]

The Principal Works in His Building Unit

The principal of even a small school has a large number of individuals with whom he has to work, and the larger the school, the more complicated the human relations problem becomes. As an essential prerequisite for providing in his school the best possible educational program for the boys and girls under his charge, the principal must build a team that will cooperatively develop and work to achieve a set of objectives and outcomes. He must assist a group of persons with widely different backgrounds to work together for a common cause. This is no mean achievement and requires leadership of a rare type.

Assistant principal. According to a research study, only 8.4 percent of 2,318 elementary principals reporting indicated that services of an assistant principal were available to them.[14] This would seem to indicate that the position of assistant principal is not very common in the elementary schools of the United States. On the secondary level, many principals have assistant principals.

If carefully selected, the assistant principal can become a valuable member of the team. Rather than assigning him routine clerical responsibilities or placing him in charge of attendance or discipline, the wise principal will pick an assistant who can complement him and thus help to build a stronger team. Usually, there are areas in school administration, including supervision, in which the principal is not so proficient as in other areas. The selection of an assistant principal with these particular skills will greatly strengthen the team.

Regardless of his special areas of responsibility, the assistant principal should be given opportunities to participate in all aspects of school administration. When the principal is out of the building, the assistant principal is the logical person to be placed in charge.

The position of assistant principal not only affords valuable assistance to the principal, but it provides a much-needed training ground for the principalship. In this capacity young men and women can receive excellent experience in school administration.

The scope of activities and responsibilities of the assistant principal

[13]James B. Burr, William H. Coffield, T. J. Jenson, and Ross L. Neagley, *Elementary School Administration* (Boston: Allyn & Bacon, Inc., 1963), p. 402.
[14]*The Elementary School Principalship in 1968—A Research Study*, p. 73.

should be clearly defined in writing and made known to all staff personnel, pupils, and parents.

Regular classroom teachers. The present generation of better-prepared teachers consider themselves to be educational specialists, and many of them deserve this title. This new breed of teacher refuses to acknowledge that by virtue of his title and responsibilities the principal should be assigned an authoritarian role. On the other hand some of the older teachers will mistakenly assume that this is the principal's role. Past experiences with autocratic principals, images of the role of the principal dating from their own elementary-school days, and concepts developed as they observed the actions of persons in authority in various walks of life are difficult to eradicate. The principal should make every effort to create a less authoritarian image in their minds.

The key as to whether or not the principal can survive as a professional leader in his school is the way he works with teachers. According to English:

Two things must occur if we are to avoid complete neutralization of the principalship. First, principals must work for new organizational relationships with teachers in the decision-making process at the school level. Teachers must become partners; they must be involved with their principals in the shaping of school policies, curriculum decisions, and mutual evaluation of colleagues. Perhaps the concept of the academic senate may be modified and used with success in this function. Second, differentiated staffing must be employed to release teachers to serve in varying capacities within the organization.[15]

The teaching team as discussed in Chapter VI is certainly a form of differentiated staffing. There are, however, many models and their essential ingredients differ somewhat. It therefore seems appropriate here to list the principles of the Temple City (California) Plan as described by Fenwick English, its director:

1. Differentiated staffing is a means of producing more relevant student learning.
2. Teaching must be the primary function of all teachers.
3. Teachers must become formal professional partners with administrators in the decision-making process.
4. Teachers must be relieved of many nonprofessional functions now required of them.
5. Teachers must perform the self-disciplining or regulating activities of their own profession.
6. Organizational flexibility must be created through the use of flexible scheduling.

[15]Fenwick English, "The Ailing Principalship," *Phi Delta Kappan*, L, no. 3 (1968), 160.

7. New kinds of teacher in-service and preservice programs need to be developed to prepare teachers to be able to function in different roles.

8. The advanced positions in the teacher hierarchy are service rather than supervisory positions.

9. Some teachers earn more than school administrators.[16]

It is interesting to note that in item 8, English stresses the service aspect of positions in the teacher hierarchy rather than the supervisory role. The authors of this handbook take the position that supervision is largely a service function and, therefore, no dichotomy exists.

Taylor and McPherson agree with English that differentiated staffing is essential and add a new dimension of principal teaming when they suggest that if the principal is to be effective as a supervisor, models of individualizing and teaming must be utilized. First, there must be a differentiation of assignments for teachers. While some assume supervisory functions for a part of the day, others will take on team-leadership functions, and still others will engage in in-service education of teachers. Second, the teaming of principals will be utilized. Each principal in the district will be a specialist in one subject and principals work in each other's schools in the cooperative diagnosis of the teaching-learning situations.[17]

Involvement of teachers in the development of the organizational plan also is important according to the following statement by Morphet, Johns, and Reller:

The organizational plan lays the basis for the procedures by which the principal works with his staff, both instructional and noninstructional. Therefore, all members of the staff should participate in the development of the plan of organization. They should understand it and accept it.[18]

As a consequence of the previous discussion in this section, it would seem that the following list, although incomplete, characterizes the team concept of working with staff members:

1. The principal recognizes that leadership is a function shared by many persons rather than the sole prerogative of the status individual.
2. Staff members are encouraged to participate in the administrative and supervisory activities of the school.
3. The talents and special abilities of staff members are utilized to the fullest extent.

[16]Fenwick English, "Questions and Answers on Differentiated Staffing," *Today's Education*, LVIII, no. 3 (1969), 53.

[17]Lloyd L. Taylor and Philip E. McPherson, "The Superintendent and the Principal," *The National Elementary Principal*, XLVII, no. 6 (1968), 83.

[18]Edgar L. Morphet, Roe L. Johns, and Theodore L. Reller, *Educational Administration: Concepts, Practices, and Issues* (Englewood Cliffs, N.J.: Prentice-Hall, Inc., 1959), p. 288.

4. Faculty meetings and staff committees are chaired by faculty members.
5. Faculty members participate in making all decisions of policy that affect them.
6. The principal assumes a peer relationship when he participates in staff discussions.
7. Decisions are made by consensus rather than by majority rule.
8. The principal clearly defines with staff members the limits of their operation. That is, they know when they have the authority to make a decision ("budget of power") and when they can only recommend.
9. The principal never vetoes "budget of power" decisions, and when recommendations cannot be implemented, he sees that staff members understand the reasons.
10. Suggestions and recommendations are freely made by staff members.
11. The principal believes in the democratic process, but he realizes that, in the final analysis, he is the responsible leader of the school.

Other professional personnel. This category would vary considerably from school to school, with the greatest differences to be noted between elementary and secondary schools. The size of the school and the school district, as well as the type of organization, would determine whether or not some of the specialists were central office personnel or regular members of the staff of a particular school. Specialists are serving today in practically all areas of the curriculum offered in the elementary and secondary schools. In addition, special personnel are found in the following categories of services on both the elementary- and secondary-school levels: nursing; library, instructional materials and media; guidance; speech; programming; technical psychology of learning; and others yet to appear. In addition, secondary schools may have department heads, roster chairmen, and attendance personnel. In schools utilizing team teaching (see Chapter VI) the following categories of personnel are found, with titles such as *team leader, senior teacher, master teacher, divisional principal,* and others.

These special personnel are all members of the principal's instructional leadership team; consequently, he must learn to work effectively with them individually and in groups. Several suggestions for the principal to follow in working with special personnel on his staff seem appropriate here:

1. Special personnel should be given the same privileges, rights, and responsibilities as regular classroom teachers. Care should be exercised that they do not appear to be a favored group.
2. Wherever possible, the principal should coordinate the work of the special personnel with the work of regular classroom teachers and the central office resource staff.
3. The principal should give the special personnel opportunity to interpret

their work to the entire staff and to learn about the work of all the other members of the staff.

4. Special services should be scheduled so that there will be a minimum of conflict with regular teachers' programs and with each other.
5. The principal should provide leadership to insure that special services that are coordinated, for example, guidance and health services, do not duplicate their efforts but rather function as a team in attacking a problem.
6. The principal should see that special personnel are involved in curriculum revision and other professional-growth programs.

The modern school today also employs a number of para-professionals carrying such titles as teacher aides, clerks, readers, etc. They assist teachers in various ways ranging from the reading of English themes to lunchroom and playground supervision. The principal also must become adept in working with these supporting members of his team.

Nonprofessional personnel. The important contributions made to the school program by the nonprofessional personnel are common knowledge. It is sufficient to emphasize here that the school secretary, custodian, bus driver, cafeteria manager, and all other nonprofessional personnel should be treated as equals and the importance of their work continually stressed. As in the case of professional staff, these persons should have the opportunity to participate in making policy decisions that affect them and their jobs. They should be invited to attend staff meetings when matters that concern them are being discussed. As part of the school team, they and their families should be welcome at social events sponsored by the school staff.

Students. The enlightened principal spends as much time as possible with students. He learns to know them and to understand their problems. Some principals who have been in a given school for a number of years try to know all their students by name. This is a valuable asset to the principal and the staff if they truly believe in democratic administration and supervision and, consequently, consider the students part of the team.

The elementary principal who assists the teacher by working with pupils when he enters the classroom and even relieves teachers occasionally, prefers to talk with pupils in the corridors rather than to shout at them, eats with them in the cafeteria instead of patrolling the lunchroom, and mingles with children on the playground rather than spying on them from a classroom window has the basis for building a strong working relationship with pupils. In addition, the example he sets may be followed by other members of the staff.

On the secondary level students are demanding the right to play on the team. In some instances they have taken over the ball game. On this level students must be treated like the mature individuals many of them have proven themselves to be. Their requests for new courses or instructional procedures, their evaluations of existing ones, and other suggestions concerning the school program should receive serious consideration by both principals and teachers. If in the past students had been treated as partners instead of being the beneficiaries of educational programs influenced too often by the whims, pet ideas, and educational philosophies of their parents, teachers, and administrators, sit-ins, lie-ins, and walk-outs might not pose such a serious threat today!

If this kind of working relationship with students has been established, they, too, can become valuable members of the instructional-leadership team. Pupils of all ages can, on their level, make a contribution to the improvement of the curriculum and the instructional program. In the past, children and youth have not been given enough opportunity to assist in these important activities. In addition to the contributions they can make, it will be a valuable learning experience for the contributors.

Lay individuals. Gone are the days when a principal could completely ignore the wishes and desires of parents in respect to the educational program. Today, education is discussed so freely on so many different fronts that in every community there are lay individuals who desire to be involved in some way in improving the educational program of their own community. This discussion is taking place even in the inner-city schools where for years principals assumed that the parents of students their schools served were indifferent to and uninterested in the kind of educational fare being served to their children. Now principals know this is no longer true (if it ever was). These silent, long-suffering parents now demand quality education that meets the needs of the children and youth who live in the inner-city. In fact, one large metropolitan district has already experienced decentralization and the election of a local board on an experimental basis. Although there are those who would like to call the experiment a failure, closer study of reports indicates that considerable success is being achieved depending upon which way you view the venture.[19]

The successful principal today most certainly is aware that lay individuals now must be considered as members of the team regardless of where he serves. He realizes that educational matters no longer are sacred. He is well aware that modern-day parents are unwilling to calmly sit by and permit decisions that affect children and youth to remain exclusively in the domain of the schools. Therefore, he will continuously involve parents in an advisory capacity in the solution of curricular and instructional problems. Some parents also can make a contribution to the actual instructional program by serving as resource persons.

[19]For example, see Mario Fantini and Marilyn Gittell, "The Ocean Hill-Brownsville Experiment," *Phi Delta Kappan*, L, no. 8 (1969), 442.

The Principal Works with the Central Office Staff

The number of central office staff personnel with whom the principal works varies considerably from school district to school district. As systems become larger, more central office personnel doubtless will be added. The personnel most likely to be found on the central office staff include the superintendent, assistant superintendent for instruction, assistant superintendent for business, school psychologist, and an array of specialists, special teachers, supervisors, and/or consultants.

The principal may find himself serving in a district where the central office continues to support an array of supervisory personnel that is no longer needed or respected by his teaching force. Here is an opportunity to provide real leadership.

Superintendent of schools. The principal is a valued and trusted member of the superintendent's team and he can contribute important consultative services in this capacity.[20]

It should be remembered that, in districts employing an assistant superintendent in charge of instruction, this official will be responsible for directing the activities of the instructional-leadership team. It is the principal's responsibility to see that the policies of the board of education and the rules and regulations handed down from the central office are carried out and the terms in negotiated contracts followed. As the responsible leader of his school, he is expected to support the superintendent and interpret policies and rules and regulations to his staff. This does not mean that he should not try to see that policies are improved and rules and regulations changed; but, as long as they are in effect, he must support them. Disloyalty to the superintendent is unprofessional and can only lead to disaster and even professional ruin.

One serious point of disagreement with the central office might be the situation mentioned above concerning over-staffing and an unwillingness of the "downtown" office to involve teachers in decision-making. If this situation prevails, the principal has a responsibility to see that, at least in his building, the central-office staff recognizes this new teacher competency and works with them accordingly. Perhaps he can make the first dent in the bureaucracy.

It, however, should be kept in mind that frequently the principal finds himself in the unenviable position of disagreeing with the superintendent or the assistant superintendent in charge of instruction. In this case he

[20]For example, see Oscar W. Knade, Jr., "Consultative Role of the Elementary School Principal in the Decision-Making Processes of Selected New Jersey School Systems" (Doctoral dissertation, Temple University, 1965); and William H. Stoutenburgh, "The Consultative Role of the Secondary School Principal in the Decision-Making Processes of Selected New York School Systems" (Doctoral dissertation, Temple University, 1968).

has only three constructive courses of action left open to him, namely, (1) he can try to change the position taken by his superior, (2) he can resign, or (3) he can support the position taken by his superior.

As a member of the administrative council, the principal is expected to help develop policies and to make recommendations for the improvement of the educational program in the district. He also is expected to utilize the talents and abilities of his staff in the solution of district-wide problems.

Assistant superintendent for instruction. The relationships of the principal to the assistant superintendent for instruction depend upon whether or not he is a line or staff official. Usually, this is a line and not a staff position. If this is the case, the principal is responsible to this assistant in all matters relating to instruction. Most of what has been said concerning the principal's relationship with the superintendent also applies here, but only in matters dealing with instruction.

Assistant superintendent for business. The relationships of principals to this official may vary tremendously from school system to school system. Under the preferred, unit-control organizational plan, the assistant superintendent for business affairs is in a subordinate position to the chief school official. The principal serving in a school system with the unit-control organizational plan should preferably not deal directly with the business manager in matters pertaining to the instructional program but instead should work through the superintendent or the assistant superintendent in charge of instruction.

Coordinators. Coordinators on either the elementary- or secondary-school level assume a line relationship with principals in respect to the instructional program. They have no authority over the principal in purely administrative matters. Working with the coordinator can prove to be one of the most difficult assignments of the principal. Because of their responsibility for the overall elementary- or secondary-school program in a district, coordinators may at times appear to be usurping some of the authority of the building principal. To prevent friction from developing, it is essential that limits of operation be drawn and understood. In most cases, if the principal is doing an effective leadership job in the improvement of the instructional program and the curriculum, the coordinator will work with and through him. However, if the principal is weak in this respect, he has only himself to blame if the coordinator takes over. K–12 subject-area coordinators, however, always work with the principalship in a staff relationship.

Resource personnel. The number of resource personnel with whom the principal must work is very large in some school districts and very small in others. Most of these resource personnel may be considered as central office staff, with the exception of those previously discussed in this chapter.

If the principal is to be successful, he must learn to work effectively with as many of these resource personnel as are made available to him. Griffiths states: "The problems that the administrator faces in working with specialists are of two varieties: (1) those involved in the *services* that the specialists bring to the school, and (2) those involved in the *limitations* of the specialists themselves."[21] In discussing these two problems, he emphasizes the difficulty of scheduling and evaluating the services of specialists and their inability to see their "own field of endeavor in proper perspective."[22] Other limitations cited by Griffiths are:

. . . the tendency of many specialists to identify with other specialists and to ignore the arguments of nonspecialists . . . to confuse the importance of their knowledge with the significance of what they recommend, . . . and the specialists' aversion to new ideas, particularly if these ideas come from outside the specialist group.[23]

Space here does not permit a discussion of the principal's relationship with each of these individuals, but a number of generalizations will be made for consideration by the principal or future principal.

1. All resource personnel should be accorded the same courtesies as regular staff members.
2. The use of the title "supervisor" should be avoided in the case of specialists in the various curriculum areas, including the special areas of music, art, and physical education. Use instead the title "coordinator" or "consultant" (see Chapter VI).
3. Coordinators preferably should have staff rather than line-authority relationships to the principal when they are working with his staff. Principals should be the instructional leaders of their schools, and coordinators should give them assistance when needed.
4. Resource personnel should attend staff meetings and be involved in making any decisions that affect their work.
5. Adequate space and materials should be provided by the principal so that resource personnel can do their most effective job.
6. The principal should be familiar enough with the work of the resource personnel so that he can support and interpret their work to the staff and the public.
7. The principal is responsible for seeing that the best possible use is being made of the special abilities of resource personnel during the times they

[21]From *Human Relations in School Administration* by Daniel E. Griffiths, p. 283. Copyright © 1956, Appleton-Century-Crofts, Inc. Reprinted by permission of Appleton-Century-Crofts.
[22]*Ibid.*, p. 284.
[23]*Ibid.*, p. 285.

are available. Failure to provide clerical assistance for the librarian, so that she spends a large segment of her time in cataloging books, is an example of uneconomical use of the librarian's time.

8. School time must be provided for resource personnel to work and plan with the teaching staff so that they may become more proficient in these areas and skills.

The following ideas summarize the relationship of the principal to the central office: All relationships of the principal to the central office staff should be clearly defined and understood. The lines of communication between the principal and the superintendent should be direct, and there also ought to be direct functional communication between the principal and all other central office services. The principal, however, must always be recognized by the central staff as the responsible head of the school he administers. Under no conditions should any member of the central staff have direct control over the employees under the principal's direct supervision. The principal is administratively responsible for the educational program in his school. However, this must not be stressed to the point where relationships become strained. Friendly and cooperative relationships between the principal and the central office staff are essential for instructional improvement. The principal does not operate alone—he is a member of a well-organized team.[24]

The Principal Works with Other Principals

Although the principal is almost autonomous in his own school, he does not work in isolation. Principals periodically are called together by the chief school official to share experiences and discuss common problems. It is during these meetings that district-wide policies concerning education are developed and their implementation discussed. The principal must be prepared to face conflicts, and he must learn to resolve differences of opinion that may arise between himself and other principals in the district. Unless he functions as a good team member, his value to the district will be lessened. This does not necessarily mean that he must compromise his beliefs, but he must learn to respect the opinions of others that may be quite different from his own.

Elementary- and secondary-school principals must learn to cooperate to a greater degree than they have in the past, because they have many problems in common.[25]

[24] Adapted from Morphet, Johns, and Reller, *Educational Administration*, pp. 285–86.

[25] For example, see Fred T. Wilhelm, "Elementary and Secondary School Principals—Partners in Pressure," *The National Elementary Principal*, XLVII, no. 6 (1968), 75.

For example, a district-wide educational philosophy is essential if children are to benefit from a continuous educational program. Curriculum development also should be pursued on a kindergarten-to-grade twelve basis. Common systems of marking, reporting, and promoting ought to be agreed upon. School evaluations might advantageously be conducted simultaneously on both the elementary- and the secondary-school level.

Another mutual problem of vital importance is that of assisting the elementary-school pupil painlessly to make the transition from the elementary to the secondary school. This requires teamwork of the highest type.

In some school districts, elementary- and secondary-school principals may be required to share common services and facilities. Here is a real opportunity for the elementary principal to demonstrate high-level leadership ability. Not only must he cooperate with the secondary-school principal, but he must insure that the elementary-school pupils do not come out second best.

The wise principal is aware of the fact that he can learn a great deal from principals outside the district, and that he has a responsibility to share his knowledge and experience with them. Consequently, he will hold membership in the local, state, and national elementary principals' associations, and he will actively participate in their meetings and the other activities sponsored by them.

Important leadership notes. Principals should become aware of the new roles and relationships that are being established. The following recommendations highlight the changes now taking place:

1. Make teachers partners in the shaping of school policies and in decisions concerning instruction and the curriculum.
2. Consider the potential in some plan of differential staffing.
3. Utilize the team concept, build the strongest possible team, and give it the kind of leadership it deserves.
4. Make the most efficient use of all special personnel who are assigned to work in your building.
5. Utilize paraprofessionals to save the teachers' and other professionals' time and energy for professional matters.
6. Utilize the talents of nonprofessional personnel to the fullest extent.
7. See that students are involved and utilize their capabilities in planning their work and in making decisions that affect them.
8. Encourage lay individuals to become part of the team for improving instruction and the curriculum, and involve them in making and keep them informed about changes and innovations.
9. Be a good player on the central-office team and support and assist other members in their efforts to improve instruction and the curriculum. In turn they will be strong allies in assisting you with your program of improvement.

10. Work with other principals in the district and in the profession at large. Everyone gains by sharing.

SUMMARY

The role of the principal as an instructional leader is changing and probably will continue to change. A number of factors concerned with the setting, the man, and the job have been influential in bringing about this change. Foremost has been the recognition that the individual school faculty is the most logical unit for improving instruction. This has been a natural consequence of greater teacher competency and the increasing realization that democracy in educational administration requires the involvement of students, parents, and teachers in the solution of educational problems. The increased importance of the principal's job has made it necessary to raise the requirements for entering the principalship. Recognition is also being given to the special needs of principals who will serve in inner-city schools.

The principal is a valuable member of a team. As a team member, he must learn to work skillfully with professional and nonprofessional staff, a host of central office personnel, pupils, lay individuals, and other principals. While working with individuals, alone and in groups, he will endeavor to use the democratic processes because he realizes that in this way he can be assured of the highest degree of success.

SUGGESTED ACTIVITIES AND PROBLEMS

1. Examine school board policies and rules and regulations that are concerned with curriculum or the improvement of instruction. Select five significant rulings of the board and discuss their implications with respect to the principal's job of instructional leadership.
2. Assume that you are the principal of an elementary or a secondary school with an enrollment of 1,000 pupils. You have been authorized to look for an assistant principal. Knowing your own capabilities and interests, for what kind of person would you look, and how would you utilize his services? Justify your choice and the division of the work load.
3. Using anecdotes freely, describe how a principal you know well works with *one* of the following groups: (a) professional staff, (b) nonprofessional staff, (c) central office staff, (d) pupils, or (e) lay persons. Confine your study to procedures affecting the instructional program. Make recommendations for the improvement of these procedures.
4. Examine one extensive negotiated contract or several short ones that contain items concerning the instructional program or the curriculum. Indicate how the role of the principal as an instructional leader is affected because these items are in the contract.

5. After reading several articles on the topic, write a paper entitled "The Changing Role of the Principalship."

SELECTED READINGS

Cooper, John E. *Elementary School Principalship*. Chaps. 6, 9, and 10. Columbus, Ohio: Charles E. Merrill Books., 1967.

English, Fenwick. "The Ailing Principalship." *Phi Delta Kappan*, L. no. 3 (1968), 159.

Jarvis, Oscar T., ed. *Elementary School Administration: Readings*. Chaps. 1, 2, and 3. Dubuque, Iowa: Wm. C. Brown Company Publishers, 1969.

Jenson, Theodore J.; Burr, James B.; Coffield, William H.; and Neagley, Ross L. *Elementary School Administration*. 2nd ed., Chaps. 4 and 12. Boston: Allyn & Bacon, Inc., 1967.

Jones,, James J.; Salisbury, C. Jackson; and Spencer, Ralph L. *Secondary School Administration*. Chaps. 9 and 11. New York: McGraw-Hill Book Company, 1969.

Laabs, Charles W. "Supervisor of Instruction—Primary Responsibilty of the Junior High School Principal." *Clearing House*, XLIII 1968), 198.

Levine, Daniel V. "Training Administrators for Inner-City Schools: A Proposal." *The National Elementary Principal*, XLVI, no. 3, (1967).

Robbins, Glaydon D. *Preparation of Elementary School Principals—Present Practices*. Washington, D.C.: Department of Elementary School Principals, NEA, 1967.

The Elementary School Principalship in 1968—A Research Study. Washington, D.C.: Department of Elementary School Principals, NEA, 1968.

Wiles, Kimball. *Supervision for Better Schools*. 3rd ed., Chaps. 9, 10, and 12. Englewood Cliffs, N.J.: Prentice-Hall, Inc., 1967.

Wilhelms, Fred T. "Elementary and Secondary School Principals—Partners in Pressure." *The National Elementary Principal*, XLVII, no. 6 (1968), 75.

chapter 6

Other Personnel Involved
in Improvement of Instruction

As suggested in Chapter IV, school systems use different titles for positions with similar job descriptions. This chapter will be concerned with a brief discussion of the roles performed by certain of these officials as they work in the areas of curriculum and instruction. Comments also will be made concerning desirable qualifications for these positions. Some of the positions described are quite familiar, others are of more recent origin. The titles used are those that appear quite frequently in the literature.

The discussion will include the following positions: K–12 Subject Coordinators, Department Heads, Team Leaders, Senior Teachers, Helping Teachers, and Specialists.

THE K–12 SUBJECT AREA COORDINATOR

This position is not as well known as the other ones discussed in this handbook; however, the authors consider it to be a very important one. With the enormous explosion of knowledge, tremendous expansion of course offerings, new curriculum programs, and the abundance of new learning resources, there is a need on the local scene for experts in each of the major disciplines or subject areas who are able to articulate instruction and curriculum on a longitudinal basis.

Serving in grades K–12, the subject area coordinator replaces the high-school department head who usually functions only on the secondary-school level. It is a rare occasion indeed when the department head makes any attempt to articulate the work of his department with the lower schools or to provide continuity in the curriculum.

There are those who might argue that this task of subject coordination should be carried on by the assistant superintendent in charge of instruction or the elementary and secondary coordinators. The rebuttal is that they are generalists; the need here is for subject-matter and discipline specialists. They are the best qualified personnel to see that provisions are made for continuity and articulation of content.

Individuals occupying this strategic position ideally should be experienced master teachers with extensive graduate preparation in their particular subject area or discipline. Preferably, they should have taught on both the elementary- and secondary-school levels and possess a knowledge of child growth, development, and psychology of learning related to children and youth of the ages found in grades K–12.

In some districts the subject coordinator will continue to teach half-time or less. In larger districts the position will require the full-time attention and efforts of the coordinator.

The following duties and responsibilities in the areas of curriculum and instruction are representative of the tasks performed by the K–12 subject-area coordinator:

1. Visits classrooms and works with teachers from K through 12 on instructional and curricular matters peculiar to his discipline or subject area.
2. Involves teachers in decision-making and change.
3. Works with the principals and coordinators of elementary and secondary education in a staff relationship and shares his particular knowledge and competence as needed.
4. Reports to the assistant superintendent and keeps him informed on the developing curriculum and new trends and research in his own area of specialization.
5. Chairs the district curriculum committees in his discipline or subject area.
6. Makes recommendations to the appropriate officials concerning instructional and curricular materials and resources.
7. Works closely with the appropriate curriculum consultants in the intermediate unit office or the regional curriculum center, and keeps current on latest research and trends in his field.
8. Conducts parent and community meetings for the lay public and interprets the latest methods and content in his subject area.
9. Prepares written materials for distribution to the lay public on topics related to his discipline.
10. Participates actively in the sessions of the curriculum council, especially when his area of concern is on the agenda.

11. Meets and works with the other subject area coordinators, under the leadership of the assistant superintendent in charge of instruction, in order that a balanced curriculum may be developed.[1]

THE DEPARTMENT HEAD

For many years the department headship has been a respected position in most of our larger secondary schools. In some schools it is a permanent appointment; in others, a department chairman is elected; and in still others, the headship is rotated. Regardless of the title of the position or the procedure used in selecting the individual to fill the post, the department head can play a valuable role in the supervisory program.

Because the department head has teaching responsibilities, it is easy for him to maintain a peer relationship with the other members of the department. Inexperienced new teachers readily come to him for counsel, advice, and assistance, and most teachers respect his ability as a teacher and leader.

In describing the role of the department head Jones *et al.* state:

The role of the department head varies considerably in secondary schools. Some department heads' functions are limited to compilation of budget requests from department members. Others may be granted a much broader role which includes supervision. Regardless of the type of role the structure of the school suggests for department heads, their purpose is the same—improvement of the instructional program.[2]

Individuals selected to serve as department heads should possess many of the same personal attributes recommended for principals (see Chapter V). The personal characteristics so necessary for success as an instructional leader should be present regardless of the title the individual bears.

The minimum professional qualifications for the headship might include the following:

1. An undergraduate major in his subject field and five years of successful teaching experience.
2. Fifty semester hours of graduate work including a Master's degree. The courses should be allocated as follows: 24 to 30 semester hours in his

---

[1]The description of the K–12 subject-area coordinator has been adapted from Ross L. Neagley and N. Dean Evans, *Handbook for Effective Curriculum Development* (Englewood Cliffs, N.J.: Prentice-Hall, Inc., © 1967), pp. 137–38. By permission of the publisher.

[2]Jones, Salisbury, and Spencer, *Secondary School Administration*, p. 298.

subject field, and 20 semester hours distributed in the areas of adolescent psychology, supervision, curriculum, and administration.

The following instructional and supervisory duties and responsibilities have been suggested for this position:

1. Sets a good example by his own teaching and on request conducts demonstration lessons.
2. Supplies information and materials that can contribute to the improvement of teaching.
3. Visits classrooms, works with teachers, and brings to their attention special resources, possible field trips, and appropriate audio-visual aids.
4. Works cooperatively with his staff in developing meaningful curriculum materials.
5. Assists in the orientation of new teachers.
6. Recommends, secures, orients, and assists substitute teachers.
7. Assists with the student teaching program, if one exists.
8. Confers with teachers on personal and professional matters that might affect their morale and teaching efficiency.
9. Recognizes, encourages, and stimulates professional growth and initiative on the part of the staff.
10. Regularly holds departmental meetings.
11. Assumes responsibility for intra-departmental communication.
12. Assists his staff in identifying and carrying out successful action research.
13. Assists in the selection, encouragement, and implementation of special informal activities, such as club activities, assembly programs, and career conferences.
14. Serves as the first recourse in assisting teachers who are having discipline problems.
15. Makes decisions concerning the placement of students in courses within his department.
16. Assists in the guidance program.
17. Provides leadership in planning the testing program.[3]

Satlow uses a unique way to characterize the activities of the department head by suggesting that he wear ten hats and then Satlow gives them the following names: (1) student, (2) dreamer, (3) innovator, (4) efficiency expert, (5) psychiatrist, (6) referee, (7) critic, (8) morale builder, (9) diplomat, and (10) clerk.[4]

Recently, changes in school organization have resulted in the appointment of department heads or area chairmen to supervise closely related

[3] Adapted from Benjamin J. Novak, "The Department Headship To-Day," *Educational Administration and Supervision*, 44, no. 2 (1958), pp. 92–95.

[4] David Satlow, "Common Gripes of Teachers About Their Chairmen," *The Journal of Business Education*, XLIV, no. 3 (1968), 110.

areas of the curriculum such as science and mathematics. This, in turn, has paved the way for a kind of divisional leadership based on groups of pupils rather than subjects.

THE TEAM LEADER

The fairly wide acceptance of some form of team teaching in the secondary school and to a degree in the elementary school has given birth to a new position—the team leader—who may be the saving grace that bridges the ever-widening chasm between administration and the teaching staff.

On the secondary level, this new role may replace that of the department head or chairman. The roles, however, are not identical. Comparison of the two roles according to an article by Goldstein would seem to favor the team leader role because of the following:

1. Performs fewer procedural functions and, consequently, does not dissipate his energy in minutiae.
2. Usually not considered as extensions of the school's administration.
3. Serves in a role that is lateral and coordinate rather than hierarchical and supervisory.
4. With the supervisory block removed, continuous, uninhibited dialogue is more likely to take place among all team members.
5. Bridges the gap between faculty and administration.
6. Functions as a manager without power—relying almost exclusively on the good will he can establish in the performance of his role as a coordinator and change agent.[5]

Although there are leadership possibilities in other types of teacher-team organization, the one that assigns a major role to the team leader will be discussed here. Anderson describes it as follows:

The essential ingredients of team teaching are not only co-operation and collaboration in the planning and presentation of the program, but also the assignment of specific leadership and responsibility (with the accompanying prestige and recognition) to career-oriented teachers of superior training and competence.[6]

Although theoretically two teachers working with the same group of pupils could constitute a team, the composition and characteristics of the

[5]William Goldstein, "Distinguishing Department Chairmen from Team Leaders," *The High School Journal*, LII, no. 1 (1968), 40–44.
[6]Robert H. Anderson, "Team Teaching," *NEA Journal*, 50, no. 3 (1961), p. 52.

Claremont Teaching Team seem to make it a desirable model to describe. The Claremont Teaching Team consists of a distinct student group, four to six faculty members with complementary talents and specializations, and certain auxiliary personnel who assist the teachers and children.

"A *Team Leader* is a mature, experienced, licensed teacher of unusual talent and extensive training who has been elected or appointed to serve as the leader of a teaching team. . . ."[7]

The role of this important functionary is further classified by Brownell in the following manner:

> The elected or appointed leader of a faculty team assumes responsibility for the general performance of his team. In order to carry out his responsibility adequately, he is given an extra period, in addition to the common conference period, to plan and to coordinate team activities. Furthermore, he is paid a stipend above his normal pay for his leadership. The primary functions of the leader are his classroom teaching and his leadership of the team in improving instruction, counseling, and the performance of other tasks required for optimum development of team students.[8]

What, then, are the specific duties and responsibilities associated with this new leadership role? Essentially, they are quite similar to many of those previously suggested for the department head on the secondary-school level or the helping teacher (to be discussed later) on the the the elementary- or secondary-school level.

Bair and Woodward list the following major tasks of a team leader:

1. Teaches approximately two-thirds of the time.
2. Serves as a member of the administrative cabinet and the instructional cabinet for the school and helps interpret cabinet decisions and plans to his team.
3. Serves as chairman for most meetings of his team, in which he places special emphasis on the planning, teaching, and evaluating cycle.
4. Initiates and coordinates daily and longer-interval schedules for teachers and pupils within the team.
5. Serves as a coordinator and supervisory agent in his field of specialization as materials of instruction, lesson plans, and/or units are developed or taught. . . .
6. Supervises instructional practices of his team members including lesson plans, teaching techniques, evaluation techniques, and reporting practices.
7. Helps plan and evaluate grouping practices and individual progress to improve learning rate of pupil members of his team.

[7]John A. Brownell and Harris A. Taylor, "Theoretical Perspectives for Teaching Teams," *Phi Delta Kappan*, XLIII, no. 4 (1962), 151.
[8]John A. Brownell and Roland P. Shutt, *The Claremont Teaching Team Program, A Research Project* (Claremont, Cal.: Claremont Graduate School, 1961), p. 11.

8. Studies, evaluates, and recommends to the principal what his team needs and reports progress in terms of personnel, curriculum, materials of instruction, and pupil supplies.

9. Plans and coordinates parent meetings to interpret the work of the school, team, and pupils.

10. Has all the duties and responsibilities of senior teachers (see below).

11. Coordinates curriculum revision with the team.

12. Plans and helps with orientation procedures for his team.[9]

A brief description of how one team leader functions will illustrate some of the advantages of this organizational plan for assisting teachers to grow professionally.

Miss X, who was chosen to head a team consisting of one senior teacher, five regular teachers, and a group of approximately 185 pupils, is an expert in subject matter as well as in educational theory. She has had over ten years of teaching experience, holds a master's degree, and has completed most of the requirements for the doctorate.

Because of large-group lessons and flexible scheduling, Miss X has one full day and several mornings free for observing her team members in action. She also has sufficient time to coordinate the team's activities by a series of conferences and memorandums.

The following are a few brief excerpts from recent notes she has circulated to team members:

Parent Conferences
Team members have been informed of the week in which to initiate parent-teacher conferences. Other team members should participate if necessary.

Think-abouts
Handwriting: Miss Y is interested in teaching handwriting—how can the schedule be changed to capitalize on her interest?

Art: Are the periods of sufficient length? Could we schedule one-hour periods?

Rainy Mornings: Can we plan better activities for pupils on rainy days when teachers have meetings?

Music: Miss Z mentioned the fact that she had conducted large music groups in camp. Can we arrange for her to take several groups to sing at one time?

Creative Writing: Miss A has shown considerable ability in helping pupils to write creatively. If she is willing, can it be arranged for her to take charge of a series of large groups instead of several other assignments?[10]

[9]Medill Bair and Richard G. Woodward, *Team Teaching in Action* (Boston: Houghton Mifflin Company, 1964), pp. 69–70.

[10]Adapted from Arthur D. Morse, *Schools of Tomorrow—Today!* (Garden City, N.Y.: Doubleday and Company, Inc., 1961), pp. 12–18.

The above illustration relates to an elementary-school teaching team and gives some insight concerning the relationship of the team leader to the members of his team.

THE SENIOR TEACHER

Next to the team leader, the *senior teacher* is the most competent professional on the teaching team. In fact he may be as well qualified as the team leader and occupy that position at some future date. Simply described, "A senior teacher is an experienced, mature master teacher with a content specialization in at least one area, who exercises coordinating and supervisory leadership for the team in that area."[11]

Bair and Woodward describe the role of the senior teacher as follows:

1. Has all the duties, functions, and responsibilities of a teacher.
2. Serves as a member of the instructional cabinet for the school and helps interpret its decisions and plans to his team.
3. Serves as a coordinator and supervisory agent in his field of specialization as materials of instruction, lesson plans, and units are developed or taught. . . .
4. Plans and conducts team meetings concerned with his area of specialization.
5. Coordinates daily and longer-interval schedules relating to his field of specialization for his team.
6. Helps develop and evaluate grouping practices and individual progress of youngsters within his special field.
7. Studies, evaluates, and recommends to his team leader and to the instructional cabinet ways of improving his team's operation.
8. Works with his team leader in planning, supervising, and coordinating his team's activities as time and ability permit.[12]

Team teaching offers many opportunities for the improvement of instruction and the curriculum. Sybouts gives the following illustrations of how team teaching can contribute to the improvement of the supervisory relationship between administrators and teachers: promotes cooperative planning; reduces teacher isolation; provides new teachers with more constant assistance and guidance; promotes peer evaluation of teaching; and relates supervision to staff-identified needs and interests.[13]

If careful appraisal should reveal that pupils learn equally well under the team teaching plan without affecting their mental health adversely,

[11]Bair and Woodward, *Team Teaching in Action*, p. 70.
[12]*Ibid.*, pp. 72–73.
[13]Ward Sybouts, "Supervision and Team Teaching," *Educational Leadership*, XXV, no. 2 (1967), 159.

an avenue will be open to attract and retain individuals of superior talent. There are doubtless many teachers who enjoy helping others to improve professionally but do not wish to leave the classroom themselves. Serving as a team leader may prove to be the solution for hundreds of individuals who are qualified for administrative and supervisory positions but cannot be placed because of insufficient demand. It also may provide teachers with the opportunity to discover whether or not they would like to prepare for a full-time supervisory position.

THE HELPING TEACHER

Many of the larger school systems have inaugurated the practice of using "helping teachers." These individuals are successful teachers who become attached to the central office staff for the purpose of helping other teachers. They have no responsibility for evaluating teacher performance but are concerned only with assisting teachers to improve in the classroom.

The following duties have been performed by "helping teachers" on the elementary-school level:

1. Holding professional conferences.
2. Helping in summer workshops.
3. Becoming "floating" teachers.
4. Giving television courses for teachers.
5. Encouraging individual schools to engage in studies.
6. Providing programs to strengthen instruction in certain subjects.
7. Offering extension courses.
8. Participating in research projects.[14]

In Santa Moncia, California, five master teachers provide materials, aids, methods, and inspiration for other teachers. Their rooms serve as distribution stations for classroom materials. If these consultant teachers see some excellent materials in one school, they may reproduce them for use in other schools.[15]

Philadelphia (Pennsylvania) selects teachers who are outstanding in a particular area to serve as curriculum collaborators. They assist teachers in interpreting curriculum guides, demonstrating methods, presenting new ideas, and suggesting instructional materials. In addition, they assist in the writing and revising of new guides and serve as group leaders in work-

[14]U.S. Office of Education, *Fourth Conference for Supervision of Elementary Education in Large Cities* (Washington, D.C.: U.S. Department of Health, Education, and Welfare, March 24–27, 1959), p. 6.

[15]American Association of School Administrators, *The Superintendent as Instructional Leader*, Thirty-fifth Yearbook (Washington, D.C.: National Education Association, 1957), p. 70.

shops or in-service courses. Curriculum collaborators must be prepared to teach any grade at any time. After serving a three-year term as a collaborator, they return to regular classroom teaching or, in some cases, are promoted to administrative and supervisory positions.

Gary (Indiana) uses "helping teachers" on the secondary-school level. These individuals serve as consultants in the various subject areas and perform many of the functions listed previously in this chapter in the section dealing with the department head.

USING SPECIALISTS IN ELEMENTARY SCHOOLS

The discussion in this section will be confined to the use of specialists in the areas of art, music, and physical education in the elementary school. Over the years, these specialists have served in the elementary school in a variety of ways which roughly fall into the following three patterns:

1. The specialist serves as a special teacher in his area of the curriculum.
2. The specialist serves as a supervisor in his area of the curriculum.
3. The specialist serves as a consultant in his area of the curriculum.

The remainder of this section will be devoted to a discussion of the advantages and disadvantages of each of these roles of the specialist.

The Specialist as a Teacher

For many years individuals specially trained in the fields of art, music, and physical education have taught their subjects one or more periods a week in each elementary classroom. Working on a regular weekly schedule, these special teachers have taken over the classes of regular elementary teachers and taught their particular specialty to the class. In some instances, the regular classroom teacher remains as an observer or an assistant teacher. In others, he uses this as a free period.

Advantages. Advocates of this role of the specialist claim the following advantages for it:

1. The specialist is much better qualified to teach his area of the curriculum than is the regular classroom teacher.
2. Having regularly scheduled periods taught by specialists insures that these areas of the curriculum will not be slighted in the programs of regular classroom teachers who feel incompetent in the special areas.
3. All pupils on a given grade level are assured of similar experiences in these areas.

4. It provides free time for the regular teacher.
5. Pupils enjoy a change from their regular teacher.
6. If at least one specialist is a male, it insures that boys will have some contact with a male teacher.

Disadvantages. Educators who are opposed to having specialists used largely as teachers of these areas maintain that it is a violation of the concept of the self-contained classroom. They give the following arguments against this role of the specialist:

1. Specialists cannot learn to know and understand the large number of pupils they are expected to teach.
2. Specialists may use different control techniques from those accepted and practiced by the regular teacher. Under this situation, the specialist may become a disturbing influence in a normally well-ordered classroom.
3. The necessity for tightly scheduling the specialist results in the disruption of the highly desirable "large block of time" approach to teaching.
4. Pupils are forced to participate in activities for which they are not ready and, in the case of a physical education class immediately after lunch, at a time that is undesirable from a health standpoint.
5. Specialists are frequently off schedule five or ten minutes and sometimes fail to show up at all. This results in the disruption of the regular teacher's program and the loss of valuable teaching time.
6. This use of the specialist makes it more difficult to relate the special areas to the other areas of the curriculum.
7. Frequently, pupils receive no experiences in the special areas other than those which they have under the guidance of the specialists.
8. Regular teachers who have a particular interest in the special area prefer to teach it themselves.

The Specialist as a Supervisor

In schools that define the role of the specialist as a supervisor, the individual also may do a considerable amount of teaching. However, in this instance the teaching is considered to be demonstration teaching, and regular teachers are expected to provide their pupils with additional experiences in the special areas.

Advantages. Defenders of this role of the specialist advance the following arguments:

1. The special areas should be a regular part of the daily curriculum experiences of children.
2. Regular classroom teachers require a lot of supervisory help in the special areas of the curriculum in order to provide these daily experiences.
3. Regularly scheduled periods for the specialist to visit each classroom and a cooperatively planned curriculum insure a balanced program in each special area.

4. Because the program is planned under the supervision of a specialist, pupils can be assured of continuity of learning in the special areas as they progress through school.

Disadvantages. Some of the disadvantages of using the specialist as a supervisor are similar to those listed in the previous section, namely, items 3, 4. and 5. The following additional arguments are also used against the practice of giving the title of "supervisor" to the specialist.

1. Because specialists are usually no better prepared in their specialty than regular classroom teachers are in theirs, considerable resentment is shown by classroom teachers when the specialists are given the title of "supervisor."
2. Even with the help of specialists, many regular classroom teachers are not competent to teach the special areas of the curriculum.
3. Although the specialists have worked out with the regular classroom teachers a teaching plan for the week, there is no guarantee that the plan will be executed.

It should be noted that in some school districts the specialist is given the title of "supervisor" but in actual practice performs as a teacher of his special subject, and in other districts a specialist might assume the role of a helping teacher and actually be performing the role discussed in the section above. Apparently, the title of a position does not define the job.

The Specialist as a Consultant

The role of the specialist as a consultant is a rather recent development. One authority in the field of supervision describes it as follows:

The new approach makes use of the specialist as a resource person, a consultant, and a helper to the teacher in his work and teaching activities; at times the specialist helps a group of teachers in some joint project of a larger nature, as with a chorus from several rooms, or in a display of children's art for parents.[16]

In the last decade, increasing support has been given to the role of the specialist as a consultant. However, as is the case in the other two roles, this one also has its strengths and weaknesses.

Advantages. The following arguments have been given for assigning to the specialist the role of a consultant in the self-contained classroom plan of organization:

[16]J. Minor Gwynn, *Theory and Practice of Supervision* (New York: Dodd, Mead and Company, 1961), p. 286.

1. The concept of the completely self-contained classroom is preserved under this plan.
2. Flexible scheduling of the special subject areas is possible because it is completely under the control of the regular classroom teacher.
3. Expert assistance is available on an "on call" basis at all times.
4. The most economical use can be made of the time and talents of the specialist, because he can devote the bulk of his energy to assisting teachers who need the most help.

Disadvantages. Opponents of this procedure for utilizing the services of the specialist point out that it has several of the same weaknesses inherent in the plan that assigns the role of supervisor to the specialist. The following weaknesses have been observed in this plan:

1. Some teachers do not recognize that they need help in the special areas and, consequently, do not ask for help.
2. Complete utilization of the services of the consultant is rarely accomplished. This is particularly true in the early stages of this arrangement.
3. The special areas may be neglected by teachers who do not consider them important and who have no desire to improve in teaching them.
4. Some teachers may monopolize the services of the specialists and thus make them unavailable for other teachers.
5. The specialists are not always available when they are needed; for example, several teachers might require the help of the art consultant at the same time.

The authors take the position that school organization serves no purpose except to facilitate learning. Regardless of whether or not the specialists serve as teachers, supervisors, or consultants, the principal must ensure that all pupils regularly have a balanced educational program including all areas of the curriculum. However, the authors believe that, under the self-contained classroom plan of organization, a balanced educational program is more likely to result if the specialists serve as consultants.

SUMMARY

The K–12 subject-area coordinator is answering a need on the local scene by providing expertness in each of the major disciplines or subject areas. Each of these coordinators articulates instruction and curriculum on a longitudinal basis in his specialty.

Although the department head may still perform an important supervisory function on the secondary-school level, imaginative kinds of staff organization and utilization are responsible for creating new posts with titles such as "area chairman," "division leader," and "team leader." These new positions hold much promise for the improvement of instruction.

Larger school districts also are releasing superior teachers from their regular classroom duties to serve as helping teachers and curriculum collaborators.

Specialists in the areas of art, music, and physical education serve in a variety of relationships to the teacher in the elementary school. Some specialists serve as teachers of their area, others as supervisors, and some as consultants. Each of the above relationships has its advantages and disadvantages. When specialists are provided to assist regular classroom teachers, they should be used in the manner that is most likely to result in a balanced educational program for each child.

SUGGESTED ACTIVITIES AND PROBLEMS

1. Interview five elementary-school teachers to determine how they would prefer the art, music, and physical education specialists to work with them. Attempt to determine to what extent each of these five teachers provides his pupils with experiences in the special fields during the days when the specialists are not available.
2. Interview an art, a music, and a physical education specialist to determine the manner in which each of them believes his services can be used most effectively in the elementary school. Ask each of them to give the reasons for his statements.
3. Compare and contrast the roles of the K–12 subject-area coordinator and the department head in the improvement of the curriculum and instruction.
4. Interview a department head in the secondary school to determine how he perceives his instructional-leadership role. Compare his perception of this role with the competencies and functions of the department head as listed in this chapter.
5. Make an intensive study of a teaching team to determine the role of the team leader. Interview the team leader to determine how he perceives his instructional-leadership role. Compare his perception of this role with the role of this position as described by experts. Attend at least one team meeting to observe the leader in action.

SELECTED READINGS

Davis, Donald E., and Nickerson, Neal C., Jr. *Critical Issues in School Personnel Administration.* Chaps. 4 and 5. Chicago: Rand McNally & Company, 1968.

Franklin, Marian Pope, ed. *School Organization: Theory and Practice.* Chaps. 8, 9, 10, and 11. Chicago: Rand McNally & Company, 1967.

Kaplan, Max, and Steiner, Francis J. *Musicianship for the Classroom Teacher.* Chicago: Rand McNally & Company, 1968.

Shaplin, Judson T. *Team Teaching*. New York: Harper & Row, Publishers, Inc., 1964.

Sybouts, Ward, "Supervision and Team Teaching." *Educational Leadership*, XXV, no. 2 (1967), 158.

Thomas, Donald, "Which Organization—Department or Division for Your School?" *The Bulletin of the National Association of Secondary-School Principals*, XLIX, no. 303 (1965), 49.

Weisgerber, Robert A., ed. *Instructional Process and Media Innovation*. Chicago: Rand McNally & Company, 1968.

chapter 7

Innovation and Factors
that Influence Change

The passwords in education today seem to be innovation and change. If, however, an honest appraisal were made of the effectiveness of many innovations purporting to improve instruction, learning, and the curriculum, the result might prove disappointing. The authors, nevertheless, are not intimating that schools should stop innovating or attempt to slow the process of change. They do, however, recommend that the preparation and planning for these processes be done more carefully and thoroughly. Developing procedures for evaluating the effectiveness of innovations as contrasted with former practices should be an important phase of the planning process.

The objectives of this chapter will be to discuss certain aspects of innovation and change in education in terms of their potential for the improvement of instruction, learning, and the curriculum.

EDUCATIONAL INNOVATION

Before discussing educational innovation, it would seem quite appropriate to define what is to be discussed. In a very comprehensive work on the subject, Miles defines educational innovation as follows:

Innovation is a species of the genus "change." Generally speaking, it seems useful to define innovation as a deliberate, novel, specific change, which is thought to be more efficacious in accomplishing the goals of a system . . . it seems helpful to consider innovations as being willed and planned for, rather than as occurring haphazardly.[1]

Although some of the reasons may be different, administrators, teachers, and lay individuals alike frequently are fearful of educational innovation. Administrators are afraid of the reactions of teachers and the lay public. Teachers fear the threat to the comfort of the *status quo*. In all fairness to them, many teachers have seen innovations come and go with little, if any, real improvement in instruction and learning for children and youth. The teachers with many years of experience also have seen some of the same innovations return under new names and prove to be no more effective on their second round than on their first.

Lay individuals frequently view educational innovations with a certain degree of alarm because of their increased cost. Then too, new instructional procedures and facilities that are advertised as being vastly superior may be considered by some as a reflection on the inadequacy of their own educational backgrounds. For these and other reasons the lay public may demand that "frills" be taken out of the school program.

Lack of understanding of what is actually meant by educational innovation itself may present a problem. Jones very succinctly makes this point when he writes:

Educational innovation is intangible because it is neither the material and paraphernalia available or proposed, nor is it the use of machines or the organizational changes or varying patterns of staff redeployment.

It is rather all of these or, more appropriately, the use of things within the context of new and different insights being brought to bear on the tasks, purposes, and philosophy of education in our society. Truly this is an intellectual concept and, as such, it cannot be measured with ordinary measuring devices. It is an attitude which cannot be felt or tasted. It is a feeling which cannot be weighed. It is an outlook which cannot be carted or crated. Nevertheless, despite the problems involved and the resistances often encountered in the profession itself, it is to our credit that schools and school systems throughout our nation are introducing a variety of educational innovations ranging from new patterns of staff utilization to the ungraded classroom, teaching machines, improved curricula, and newer methods of instruction.[2]

[1]Matthew B. Miles, "Educational Innovation the Nature of the Problem," in *Innovation in Education*, ed. Matthew B. Miles (New York: Bureau of Publications, Teachers College, Columbia University, 1964), p. 14.

[2]Clifford V. Jones, "Developing Community Understanding for Educational Innovation," *American School Board Journal*, CXLIX, no. 1 (1964), 29.

Fostering Educational Innovation

Educators and educationally-minded lay persons have long recognized that from time to time different schools throughout the nation take the lead in educational innovation. In the past, these schools have been variously designated as "lighthouse schools," "frontier schools," "schools on the growing edge," and other equally complimentary names. Other schools desiring to follow in their footsteps have often found the path to be a rocky one. The question might be raised concerning whether or not there are certain conditions and circumstances which favor innovation in education and others that actually mitigate against it.

If the school is examined as a social system (see Chapter II) operating in a larger social system (the community), then a number of agents must be considered in relation to their effects on the rate and success of educational innovation. These agents or spheres of influence are the same ones that have always determined educational progress, namely, administration, staff, students, and lay persons. It should be remembered, however, that the relative strengths of their influence vary according to time, place, and other circumstances. A very brief discussion of each of the above factors as it relates to educational innovation will follow.

The administrator and innovation. The administrator is the key to educational innovation. On whatever level he may be working, he sets the tone by providing the best possible physical environment and organizational climate. Administrators, likewise, are responsible for seeing that the necessary learning resources, equipment, and materials are made available (see Chapter XI). They also must find release time for teachers to plan, perfect, and put innovative practices into effect. If additional funds are needed, it is the administrator who must seek them.

In many instances it is the administrator who is the innovator. Regardless of who introduces the innovation, it cannot hope to succeed unless it has the approval of and encouragement from the administration. Although many of the suggestions relative to the improvement of instruction and the curriculum given elsewhere throughout this text apply equally well to the implementation of educational innovation, the suggestions given below are worthy of consideration. The reader should be aware that the suggestions are neither all inclusive or mutually exclusive.

Important leadership notes. Administrators interested in providing leadership for innovative practices in their schools should:

1. Assume some responsibility for innovation themselves.

2. Provide an *open climate* where teachers will feel free to innovate.
3. Attempt to build the best possible *organizational health*.
4. Allow teachers to make mistakes without fear of reprisal.
5. Be generous in their praise and soft pedal adverse criticism.
6. Provide the wherewithal necessary to insure success in the introduction, continuation, and evaluation of the innovation.

The teacher and innovation. Although the bulk of this chapter is concerned with the teacher and the change process, it seems appropriate here to present specific information concerning the role of the teacher in innovation.

Lippitt and colleagues emphasize the difficulty of the teachers' role when they state:

... in an applied social science field, such as education, the new invention is usually a pattern of human behavior, e.g., a new way of behaving toward a group of young learners. This cannot be passed along to others like a "thing." The adoption of the social practice or invention must be compatible with the values, attitudes and behavioral skills of the potential adopter.... Learning the new educational practice, therefore, is not a simple matter of absorbing the written transmission of information. An active learning process involving various "levels" of the person is required. To make this change effort requires more commitment, risk taking, and help from others than is true in the other fields of practice. Consequently, more apathy or resistance can be expected, and more support is needed from peers and supervisors. Further, more guidance is needed from consultants, trainers, demonstrators; and experimental opportunities are essential in the school setting.[3]

The above quotation clearly places most of the responsibility for success of educational innovation on those who serve in a supervisory capacity. This, of course, was suggested in the previous section and is actually the theme of this handbook.

The following material taken from the same source should enable the reader to grasp a better understanding of various forces that facilitate and hinder innovation.

Other staff members also can influence innovation and its use. For example, the school psychologist and guidance personnel can be either assisting and supporting allies or powerful antagonists.

Non-professional personnel also enter the picture. If the school custodian publicly criticizes the new practice it may start a wave of opposition in the community that will be difficult to stop.

The student and innovation. The success of an educational innovation

---

[3]From Ronald Lippitt and Colleagues, "The Teacher as Innovator, Seeker, and Sharer of New Practices" in *Perspectives on Educational Change*, edited by Richard I. Miller. Copyright © 1967 by Meredith Corporation, p. 308. Reprinted by permission of Appleton-Century-Crofts.

Forces Relevant to the Facilitation and Hindrance of Innovation and
Diffusion of Teaching Practices[4]

Facilitating Forces	*Hindering Forces*
1. Characteristics of the Practice	
A. Relevant to universal student problems	A. Does not meet the needs of a class
B. Can be done a little at a time	B. Requires a lot of energy
C. Consultant and peer help available, needed skills are clearly outlined	C. Requires new skills
D. Clearly aids student growth	D. Requires change in teacher values
E. A behavioral change with no new gimmicks	E. Requires new facilities
F. Built in evaluation to see progress	F. Won't work
G. Innovation has tried a new twist	G. Not new
H. Student, not subject, oriented	H. Not for my grade level or subject
I. No social practice can be duplicated exactly	I. Effectiveness reduced if practice gains general use
2. Physical and Temporal Arrangements	
A. Staff meetings used for professional growth, substitutes hired to free teacher(s) to visit other classrooms, lunchtime used for discussions, students sent home for an afternoon so teachers can all meet together	A. No time to get together
B. Extra clerical help provided	B. Too many clerical duties to have time to share ideas
C. Staff meetings for everyone to get together, occasionally; grade level or departmental meetings	C. Classrooms are isolated
D. Meetings held in classrooms	D. No rooms to meet in
3. Peer and Authority Relations	
A. Sharing sessions or staff bulletins become a matter of school routine	A. Little communication among teachers
B. Public recognition given to innovators and adopters; innovation-diffusion seen as a cooperative task	B. Competition for prestige among teachers
C. Sharing ideas is expected and rewarded; norms support asking for and giving help; regular talent search for new ideas	C. Norms enforce privatism
D. Area team liaison supports new ideas	D. Colleagues reject ideas
E. Principal or superintendent supports innovation-diffusion activity	E. Principal is not interested in new ideas
F. Principal helps create a staff atmosphere of sharing and experimentation	F. School climate doesn't support experimentation
G. Staff meetings used as two-way informing and educating sessions	G. Principal doesn't know what's going on
H. Teachers influence the sharing process	H. Teacher ideas don't matter

[4]*Ibid.*, pp. 310–11, by permission of Appleton-Century-Crofts.

Facilitating Forces	*Hindering Forces*
4. Personal Attitudes	
A. Seeking new ways	A. Resisting change
B. Seeking peer and consultant help	B. Fearing evaluation and rejecting failure
C. Always open to adapting and modifying practices	C. Dogmatism about already knowing about new practices
D. Public rewards for professional growth	D. Feeling professional growth not important
E. See groups as endemic and relevant for academic learning	E. Negative feelings about group work
F. Understand connection between mental health and academic learning	F. Mental health is "extra"
G. Optimism	G. Pessimism
H. Test ideas slowly	H. Afraid to experiment
I. Suiting and changing practice to fit one's own style and class	I. Resistance to imitating others

can depend to a great extent upon the cooperation of the students. After all, schools exist for the education of children and youth. It is their future that we are affecting when we innovate.

On the secondary-school level, students are demanding a role in determining their future and many of their demands are being met.

The cooperation of elementary-school pupils also should be sought. We have talked about teacher-pupil planning for years, but many schools have done little more than render lip service to the idea.

Students in both the elementary and secondary schools possess creative talent that should be released. They can make contributions to the planning, execution, and evaluation of innovative practices, and they should be given the opportunity to do so.

Finally, students are excellent public relations agents. If they enthusiastically carry home favorable reports concerning the success of an educational innovation, a big step has been made in securing public support. Conversely, if students believe the new practice is inferior to a former one, the innovation may be doomed when they report this to their parents.

The lay public and innovation. Earlier in this chapter the point was made that educational innovation is intangible and thus difficult to understand. This is particularly true in the case of the lay public. It therefore is extremely important that an effective program of school-community relations is in effect when educational innovation is contemplated.

An adequate school-community relations program would involve representatives of the lay public in an advisory capacity when decisions are being made concerning the trial and adoption of any particular educational innovation.

The chief school administrator and his administrative team are responsible for developing community understanding of the schools. In the same manner that the state of *organizational health* in a school district or within a particular school facilitates or hinders educational innovation, the community climate affects the chances for its success.

Important leadership notes. In order to secure community support for educational innovation, individuals responsible for introducing new instructional and curricular practices might profitably consider the following additional suggestions:

1. Keep all channels of communication open between the school and all segments of the community. See that regular progress reports are made available to the lay public concerning the innovation.
2. Remember that students and staff members are high-powered channels of communication. Learn to cultivate and use these channels wisely.
3. Do not make claims for the new practice that cannot be supported by evidence. Never oversell the innovation to the lay public.
4. Help the community to understand that educational innovation is a slow process; that it takes time to plan, prepare, carry out, and evaluate new practices.
5. Prepare the lay public for possible failure of the innovative practice and its subsequent discontinuance.
6. Make an honest assessment of comparative costs of the educational innovation and report these figures to the public.

THE PROCESS OF CHANGE

The first part of this chapter dealt with educational innovation which was acknowledged to be a type of change. An effort was made to present the roles of certain agents or agencies influencing or hindering educational innovation. The remainder of the chapter will be concerned with the change process itself, factors that influence change, and suggestions for helping teachers to change. For any supervisory technique or device to accomplish its purposes, change must be brought about in the understandings, attitudes, appreciations, and practices of individuals. Too frequently we concentrate on the device or the technique for effecting change and pay little or no attention to change itself and the factors that influence it.

Before the factors that influence change can be understood, it is essential that certain misconceptions about the phenomenon of change be corrected and a positive approach adopted. The following suggestions should prove helpful to the supervisor in this respect:

1. Approach change with an attitude of "let's see."
2. Realize that the most fundamental change is a gradual steady growth.

3. Recognize that change is natural.
4. View change not as a threat, but as an opportunity for growth.
5. Recognize that acceptance of change is not vacillation.
6. Realize that understanding and accepting change requires more than factual knowledge.[5]

Change is everywhere about us. It is, perhaps, like birth and death, one of the few certainties in life. Because of its complexities, it would seem appropriate to briefly discuss here some of the elements of change in respect to changes in the educational process.

THINKING VERSUS DOING

In educational circles the argument over which comes first, thinking or doing, is as bitter as the long-debated question concerning which came first, the chicken or the egg. Do teachers change their instructional practices because their thinking has been changed by a vicarious educational experience, or does their thinking change only after they have actually used an educational procedure or technique successfully?

Reeder labels this as a false dichotomy when he writes:

It seems obvious that when in asking whether one should change the doing of teachers by changing their thinking, or change their thinking by changing their doing, one has created another of the false dichotomies which has been the curse of our educational thinking. The only sensible answer is that one should change both. But when one has said that, it does not follow that the analysis made above is futile. On the contrary, it shows that in the case of producing change in any significant area of behavior, thinking and doing are inextricably interwoven. Progress in the two must proceed not only simultaneously but in close relationship to each other.[6]

It should, therefore, be apparent that anyone concerned with improving instruction must take into account both the thinking and the doing of the members of the staff.

Translating Thinking Into Doing

It is not too difficult to understand how doing may be translated into thinking, since the eating is the proof of the pudding; but the factors that prevent the translation of thinking into doing are frequently subtle and

---

[5]Department of Elementary School Principals, *The Flexible School* (Washington, D.C.: National Education Association, 1957), pp. 14–16.

[6]Edwin H. Reeder, *Supervision in the Elementary School* (Boston: Houghton Mifflin Company, 1953), p. 19.

obscure. In the first place, the thinking of individuals concerning a particular educational practice may be on several different levels. To illustrate the point, on the same faculty Teacher A might reject the concept of team teaching with little or a great amount of knowledge concerning it, Teacher B might passively accept it on a verbal level, Teacher C might actively accept it on a verbal level, and Teacher D might believe in it implicitly as a superior way to organize for instruction. If the school had been reorganized for team teaching, you would expect four distinct types of performances from the above staff members. Teacher A, if he remained in the district, would begrudgingly comply but he would be likely to use every opportunity to criticize and, perhaps, jeopardize the success of the new procedure. Teacher B would respond with little enthusiasm and probably attain only mediocre success in team teaching. Teacher C might be so occupied with selling the idea to other staff members that he would never develop much proficiency in the procedure himself. Teacher D you would expect to be eminently successful from the start. How does an individual working in a supervisory capacity help teachers to bring about changes in themselves that will result in more of them reacting in the same manner as Teacher D? Perhaps the biggest step is the one from the position of Teacher C to that of Teacher D.

Whether or not thinking comes before or after doing, it is a widely accepted psychological fact that human beings tend to find time for and learn to do those things which they understand, believe in, and value as important. The task of the supervisor, then, is to assist teachers in the examination of their present beliefs and of the values they hold, and to assist them to modify those beliefs and values in light of the changing needs of children and society and the findings of research in child growth, development, motivation, and learning.

FACTORS INFLUENCING CHANGE

An essential prerequisite to success in helping teachers to bring about changes in their thinking and doing is an awareness and understanding of some of the forces that encourage or obstruct change in beliefs and values that teachers hold. Knowledge and understanding of these forces and factors enable the supervisor to bring about change more readily. Cognizance of these facts helps him to maintain a more sympathetic attitude toward staff members who are struggling with change and consequently are slow in showing signs of improvement. In addition, he will be more tolerant of individuals who reject change in a completely similar fashion to the case of Teacher A previously cited.

No claim is being made here that the following list of factors influencing change is all-inclusive, but rather that it is representative. The following factors will be discussed briefly: individual differences, insecurity, shadows of the past, fear of the new, resistance to change, lack of understanding, lack of skill, too much work, too much time required, different philosophies of education, adult impatience, desire for approval, sense of accomplishment, and discontent.

Examination of the above list gives the reader the impression that most of the factors impede change rather than encourage it; however, the discussion which follows will emphasize both aspects where applicable.

Individual Differences

School administrators for years have been insisting that teachers must make provisions for individual differences in children; then they have treated teachers as if they were all alike. *Readiness* is another term that is applied to children and seldom, if ever, thought of in connection with teachers. However, there are great differences in teachers' readiness for change, owing to factors such as age, health, energy, motivation, and educational background and experiences. The wise supervisor knows all staff members well, understands their individual differences, and gauges the growth of each teacher in terms of his own peculiar growth pattern rather than by comparing it with that of the group or with an ideal held by the supervisor. This is what good teachers are expected to do with children. Why should we ignore individual differences when we work with adults?

Insecurity

Security is one of the basic needs of mankind. We know that too much insecurity in childhood can result in poor mental health and even neurosis in adult life. Much of our striving in life is for security now and in our old age. Billions are being spent for defense in order that we may feel more secure as a nation. Teachers are fearful of giving up practices with which they are familiar. This is true particularly if they have felt secure in using these practices for many years.

Individuals who serve in a supervisory capacity must do everything possible to assist teachers to feel secure in the new situation. Each case will be different, but taking steps similar to the following should prove helpful.

1. Encourage the teacher to change procedures gradually, taking one step at a time.

2. Help the teacher to evaluate each step taken before moving to the next one.
3. Assist the teacher to discover the similarity of the old and new procedures.
4. Sincerely praise each accomplishment.
5. Be readily available to render assistance when needed.
6. Let the teacher know that he is not alone in his feeling of insecurity.

Shadows of the Past

Very often the longer a teacher has taught, the more he is swayed by the influence of the past. The supervisor must recognize that it is difficult for a teacher who, for example, has successfully taught arithmetic to seventh-grade youngsters for thirty years to admit that the team teaching approach might be superior. In the mind of the teacher (perhaps at a subconscious level), this is tantamount to admitting that his work for the past thirty years has been inferior.

The supervisor has all around him examples of progress in other professions and areas of living to use in helping teachers to understand that one's past performance is not to be condemned when newer and better ways are found to accomplish an objective. Present-day automation does not mean that the millions who are now being replaced by machines have labored in vain.

Fear of the New

Basically man, except for the adventurous few, is fearful of something new and different. Part of this fear, of course, has to do with his sense of insecurity previously discussed. In addition to the steps suggested in that section, supervisors should encourage the pioneering spirit. Education needs more adventurous people. Teachers should be encouraged to experiment—to try new things. Too many teachers with twenty-five years of teaching experience have in reality taught one year twenty-five times. If this spirit of inquiry, investigation, and experimentation is to prevail, teachers must not be penalized for making mistakes. Thomas Edison performed hundreds of experiments before he developed the incandescent light bulb. Teachers must learn that success usually comes as the result of a number of failures.

Resistance to Change

Man is a creature of his habits. The daily routine of the average individual changes little during a lifetime. Many teachers day by day, month by month, and year by year go through the same motions. As one observes them teach, the impression is received that much of their teaching has become automatic. These teachers are "in a rut" instead of being "in the groove." How does the supervisor help teachers to overcome these old habits? The simplest answer is to form new and more desirable habits to replace the old ones. The suggestions given under the two areas discussed immediately above also may be applied effectively in this case. In fact, all three factors are closely interrelated.

Lack of Understanding

Too frequently, supervisors assume that teachers understand a certain procedure or process and later on find out that there is considerable misunderstanding. An example of this occurred some years ago when one of the writers was a supervisor in a school district that was attempting to move to a "less regimented" program of instruction. One day he visited a second-grade class that resembled a three-ring circus. During the conference which followed the observation, it soon became apparent that the teacher believed that she was successfully conducting a "less regimented" program. Upon further analysis of the learning situation based on criteria that previously had been developed, the teacher was shocked to discover that, instead of the desired freedom, she was encouraging license in the classroom.

What is the cue for the supervisor when lack of understanding prevents a teacher from following a new technique or procedure? The answer to this question is obvious. The good supervisor does everything possible to see that all teachers understand the change that is to be effected. One way to ensure that this happens is to move slowly. Evolution is preferable to revolution, even though it takes a considerably longer period of time. Teachers should be discouraged from trying a new procedure until they thoroughly understand the purpose of what they are attempting to do as well as the correct manner in which it is to be done. For example, teachers should not be encouraged to employ such child-study techniques as the keeping of anecdotal records or the using of sociometric techniques until they have had considerable competent instruction in these areas.

Lack of Skill

It is quite possible for a teacher to thoroughly understand a process and its purposes and at the same time lack the necessary skill to use the process effectively. Here again the individual differences found in teachers must be given consideration. These differences in teachers were quite evident in one school district which was attempting to change from a basal reading system to an experience approach. It soon became apparent to the supervisor that some teachers made the transition easily, that others made the move with varying degrees of success, and that a few teachers were unable to make this change at all. In this particular instance, the district continued to supply sets of up-to-date basal and co-basal readers if teachers desired to use them. However, teachers were encouraged to employ the experience approach to the degree in which they felt comfortable in using it.

Too Much Work

Many of the new procedures being advocated today require the additional expenditure of energy. The already overburdened teacher is reluctant to try new techniques if it requires a heavier load than he is now carrying. The trend of the times is toward less work and more leisure. Teachers should not be expected to willingly increase their work loads when everyone else is lightening theirs.

In attempting to counteract this impediment to change, the supervisor must look for ways of reducing the clerical and supervisory duties of teachers before the instructional load is increased. There are many duties performed by teachers that can be done equally well by less-qualified personnel.

Too Much Time Required

Quite frequently teachers equate work and time, but these are actually of different dimensions. One of the most serious points of conflict has to do with the definition of a teacher's day. For some reason boards of education and school administrators have been unwilling to designate what constitutes a teacher's day. As a consequence, a teacher's work day varies considerably from school district to school district. Because there has been no common agreement, most teachers and the general lay public assume that a teacher's day consists of the hours during which the pupils are in school. Any demands made by the school on the teacher's time after the pupils leave is resented by many teachers. For years, secondary-school teachers have expected additional remuneration for certain services performed after school hours and, more recently, elementary teachers also have received extra pay for similar assignments.

One school district that introduced team teaching on the elementary-school level has received considerable opposition from the teachers because team meetings are held after school several evenings a week. With this attitude on the part of teachers, great success in the new type of organization can hardly be expected.

As was suggested in the previous section, if teachers are expected to carry additional responsibilities because of the changes desired, they must be relieved of part of their work load. In this instance, the essential element is time. In the case just cited, unless teachers are willing to define their day as extending beyond the time when pupils are present, time for team meetings will have to be found during the pupil-attendance day. This may necessitate the employment of additional personnel.

Different Philosophies of Education

Many teachers hold strong beliefs about educational procedures and cannot honestly support practices which are contrary to what they believe. For example, a secondary-school teacher who strongly believes in the merits of team teaching combined with individualized instruction may find himself in a situation where a decision has been made to return to a completely departmentalized plan of school organization. Instead of responsibilities that include working on a team with three other teachers and a group of 100 students, his new assignment under the departmentalized organization would consist of teaching English to five sections of seventh-grade pupils. He honestly believes that it is essential for a teacher to know his pupils well and that English can be taught best by relating it to other areas of the curriculum. Under the team-teaching plan of organization he has 100 different pupils to work with each day, while under the departmentalized plan his pupil load will be 150 pupils each day.

Under the above circumstances, could the teacher be blamed for resisting the change and giving the departmentalized organization only half-hearted support? What procedures can the supervisor follow in situations similar to the one cited above? Should teachers be required to work under conditions that make it necessary for them to engage in practices that are in conflict with their philosophy of education? The authors believe that generally it is not good educational practice to require teachers to change under these circumstances. If there is reliable research to prove the superiority of the new procedure, the supervisor should do everything possible to help the teacher to "see the light." If he fails, the teacher should be given the opportunity to accept within the district another assignment that does not conflict with his philosophy. If this is not possible, the administration should assist the teacher in locating elsewhere a position that is consistent with his beliefs.

Unfortunately, too frequently these changes are an administrative expediency or a "band wagon" tactic, neither of which can be justified under any circumstances. Consequently, if the supervisor meets strong resistance to change because of differences in philosophy, it might be a cue for him to examine more carefully the contemplated change and the procedures used to arrive at the decision to make the change.

Adult Impatience

This characteristic of the adult which may result in resistance to change is described as follows in an authoritative publication:

The typical adult learner is an *impatient learner*. After he has worked a few years and acquired the normal number of adult responsibilities—a home, a family, a lawn to mow, household bills to pay, a monthly bank statement to check—he has less time to be patient. With so many tasks competing for his limited supply of time, he has the least patience with those things he does not have to do. Usually an out-of-school project can be classified as one of the things he is not forced to do. He may feel compelled to attend the meeting but he cannot be forced to produce in a discussion.[7]

The adult learner shows his impatience in other ways. If he can't learn quickly, he may stop trying. Because of his status, he often considers it a reflection on his ability if suggestions for improvement are made. He violently defends the *status quo*.

In dealing with this trait of the adult learner, the supervisor must react to impatience with patience. He must help the teacher to realize that new patterns of action are not easy to acquire. Every small gain must be consolidated. The motto must be, "the less haste, the greater the speed."

Desire for Approval

Another strong basic human need is the desire for approval. This basic need can influence change both positively and negatively. Teachers will change their practices in order that they may receive the approval of their peers, parents, pupils, and supervisors. They also may resist change if they find that their friends are not in favor of the innovation. Many a principal has wondered why a teacher who in private conversation spoke enthusiastically in support of a contemplated change voted against it with the majority in a subsequent staff meeting. If one of these bewildered principals could have followed that teacher in the interim, he would have noted the strong influence of friends as they rejected the new idea.

The enlightened supervisor capitalizes on this desire for approval by

[7]American Association of School Administrators, *Staff Relations in School Administration,* Thirty-third Yearbook (Washington, D.C.: National Education Association, 1955), pp. 91–92.

working with groups to arrive at group decisions. In addition, as previously suggested, approval and recognition are sincerely given for every little achievement.

Sense of Accomplishment

A sense of accomplishment spurs the doer on to even greater efforts. Each step upward widens the horizon of the climber and urges him on to greater heights. Conversely, there is very little motivation for the climber who tries to reach the second floor by using a "down" escalator.

Successful supervisors know that teachers must be urged regularly to evaluate their accomplishments. They must be encouraged to aim high but often should be satisfied with small gains. Sometimes teachers are so close to their jobs that they do not recognize the progress that they have made. They welcome the assistance of the supervisor in assessing their accomplishments.

Discontent

Discontent is one of the most valuable allies that a supervisor can enlist to bring about change.

Any conscious change in an individual's method of teaching or his selection and use of instructional materials starts when he becomes discontented with what he is doing. Discontent is the first phase of the process of change and improvement, and discontent results from the more or less continuous assessment every professional person makes of the effects of what he is doing. When these effects indicate too great a difference between what he sees happening and what he believes should happen, he becomes uneasy. He is moved to begin to change his practice in order to bring the *is* and the *ought* closer together.[8]

The authority quoted above believes that, when the dissatisfaction is great enough, the teacher will search for new procedures that will reduce the gap between present and desired practices. Eventually new practices will be selected (sometimes unwisely), a design worked out, the procedures tried, and finally an evaluation made.[9]

It should be evident to the reader that the supervisor has an important role to play in each one of the above steps. One of the most difficult tasks is to help teachers to overcome their complacency. The supervisor can

[8]American Association of School Administrators, *The Superintendent as Instructional Leader*, Thirty-fifth Yearbook (Washington, D.C.: National Education Association, 1957), pp. 30–31.
[9]*Ibid.*, p. 31.

encourage continuous assessment, which is prerequisite to discontent, but how can he be certain that teachers will be displeased with what they find? The real leadership role here is to assist teachers to set their sights high enough so that they are never completely satisfied.

Chapters VIII and IX are concerned with individual and group techniques that the reader can use in assisting teachers in the assessment, search, selection, design, trial, and evaluation steps.

SUMMARY

Innovation and change are closely related, in fact, innovation is planned change. Because educational innovation is intangible it is frequently misunderstood. Some schools are more successful in innovating than others. This may be due to good organizational health, an open climate, and, consequently, the cooperation and support of administrators, staff members, students, and laymen in planning, initiating, and adopting the educational innovation.

The supervisor who wishes to develop competency in producing educational change must know and understand the factors that influence change. As his knowledge and experience increase, he will learn that, among others, the following elements encourage or impede change: individual differences, insecurity, shadows of the past, fear of the new, resistance to change, lack of understanding, lack of skill, too much work, too much time required, different philosophies of education, adult impatience, desire for approval, sense of accomplishment, and discontent.

As he works with teachers, the supervisor will become increasingly more skillfull in eliminating or ameliorating the factors that retard change and more adept at utilizing those elements that are favorable to change.

SUGGESTED ACTIVITIES AND PROBLEMS

1. Select a school system that has been successful in introducing one or more educational innovations in the areas of curriculum or instruction. Interview a member of the central office staff and several teachers, students, and lay persons to determine how one of these innovations was planned and introduced. Ascertain what plans, if any, have been made to evaluate the new practice.
2. Select one innovation that you believe might improve instruction and learning in your school. Outline the procedures you would follow to plan for and adopt the innovation if you were serving in a supervisory capacity.
3. Interview five teachers who have been in positions where it was necessary for them to adopt new teaching procedures. Keeping in mind the factors discussed in this chapter, attempt to find out which of them influenced

each of the teachers for or against the innovations. Write a paper in which you report the findings from the interviews and the conclusions you have drawn.

4. Compare and contrast change as it operates in the teaching profession with the way it takes place in medicine, government, and industry.

5. Agree to make a radical change (for the better) in the area of your job in which you are the least proficient. During a minimum period of six weeks, keep a record of your trials, tribulations, and successes in effecting this change. Write a final report in which you recount your experiences and relate them to the information in this chapter.

SELECTED READINGS

Abbott, Max G., and Lowell, John T., eds. *Change Perspectives in Educational Administration.* Auburn, Ala.: The School of Education, Auburn University in co-operation with The University Council for Educational Administration, 1965.

Bennis, Warren G.; Beune, Kenneth D.; and Chin, Robert, eds. *The Planning of Change.* 2nd ed. New York: Holt, Rinehart & Winston, Inc., 1969.

Carlson, Richard O.; Gallagher, Art, Jr.; Miles, Matthew B.; Pellegrin, Roland J.; and Rogers, Everett M. *Change Processes in the Public Schools.* Eugene, Oregon: The Center for Advanced Study of Educational Administration, University of Oregon, 1965.

Goodlad, John I., "Educational Change: A Strategy for Study and Action." *The National Elementary Principal,* XLVIII, no. 3 (1969), 7.

Lucio, William H., and McNeil, John D. *Supervision—A Synthesis of Thought and Action.* 2nd ed., Chap. 8. New York: McGraw-Hill Book Company, Inc., 1969.

Miles, Matthew B., ed. *Innovation in Education.* New York: Bureau of Publications, Teachers College, Columbia University, 1964.

Ovard, Glen. *Change and Secondary School Administration: A Book of Readings.* New York: The Macmillan Company, 1968.

Raths, James, and Leeper, Robert R., eds. *The Supervisor: Agent for Change in Teaching.* Washington, D.C.: Association for Supervision and Curriculum Development, NEA, 1966.

chapter 8

Working with Individuals
to Improve Instruction

The improvement of the instructional program in a school results from changes that take place within each individual staff member. Some of these changes take place as a result of group experiences and others, as an outcome of individual experiences; moreover, individual and group techniques are not mutually exclusive. In fact, operationally they reinforce each other. In addition, there are some techniques that could be placed in either category, depending upon whether the emphasis is on the individual or the group. For example, if a teaching demonstration is conducted in a given teacher's classroom to assist him in the solution of an instructional problem, this type of demonstration lesson would belong in the category of individual techniques. On the other hand, if a demonstration lesson is taught before a group of teachers to introduce a new teaching procedure—for example, teaching the new mathematics—it would be considered a group technique. Therefore, for the purpose of discussion, the authors have arbitrarily assigned the various supervisory techniques to one or the other of the two categories. Tradition supports a majority of the assignments, but in several cases the writers have departed from it. The individual techniques will be discussed in this chapter and the group techniques in Chapter IX. In addition to a discussion of devices to be used in working with individuals, this chapter will deal with creative teachers, problem teachers, and teachers who have personal problems.

INDIVIDUAL TECHNIQUES

For convenience of discussion, the following devices or techniques will be classified as supervisory procedures to be used largely in working with individuals: assignment of teachers, classroom visitation and observation, classroom experimentation, college courses, conferences (individual), demonstration teaching, microteaching, evaluation, activities and conferences of professional organizations, professional reading, professional writing, selection of instructional materials, selection of professional staff, supervisory bulletins, informal contacts, and other experiences contributing to personal and professional growth.

Assignment of Teachers

Many school administrators would not consider the assignment of teachers a supervisory function, but in reality it can be the one supervisory move that affects not only the immediate success but the entire career of the teacher. If a teacher is given an assignment for which he is not qualified emotionally as well as academically, he may be a complete misfit and beyond any real supervisory help.

Here, again, administrators should take a cue from their own educational clichés. "Place a child in the situation in which he has the greatest opportunity for success," they say. However, in the assignment of teachers, they frequently give inexperienced and other teachers new to the district the worst teaching situations. The best assignments are awarded to staff members on a seniority basis or, in some cases, as a reward for conforming (*cooperating* is the term most frequently used). On the other hand, rarely do the senior citizens (those within five years of retirement) receive the consideration they should have. Certainly, teachers who are approaching retirement should be permitted to ease up gradually rather than be expected to run full steam ahead until the very end and then come to a full stop.

As a supervisory technique, then, the qualifications of each teacher should be carefully studied before an assignment is made. Teachers should be placed, with their consent, in positions for which they are best qualified, taking into consideration all their characteristics as well as their education and years of teaching experience. In making assignments, the concept that all teachers must be treated in an identical manner should be discarded. In its place the belief that individuals should be treated in terms of their needs should be substituted in order that an effective teaching force may be developed.

Classroom Visitation and Observation

Probably no area of supervision has been discussed in greater detail, with more conflicting opinions, than the conditions under which observations are to be made and the procedures that are to be used. Early texts in supervision gave the supervisor a blueprint for entering the classroom and conducting the observation. Later texts advised against the use of this unpopular technique, and present-day writings emphasize that classroom observations should be made only after the supervisor has established rapport with the teacher, and then largely on an "on call" basis.

Beliefs held about visitation. Currently there are a number of beliefs concerning procedures to be followed in classroom visitation that are rather commonly held by authorities in the field of supervision. There are, of course, those who take exception to one or more of the statements. It will become clear later that the authors will have to be placed in this group of dissenters. The following list is representative of these beliefs and not a complete list:

1. Good rapport should exist between the teacher and the supervisor.
2. Visitation should be largely on an "on call" basis and teachers should determine the purpose of the visits.
3. The supervisor should carefully prepare for each classroom visit.
4. The visitor should enter the classroom as unobtrusively as possible.
5. The supervisor should not participate in the activity in progress.
6. A conference should precede the visit.
7. A conference should follow the visit.
8. Notes for use in the conference should be kept of each extended classroom observation, but they should not be made during the visit without the approval of the teacher.
9. The observer should concentrate on the total learning situation.
10. The supervisor should attempt to discover the strong points in the learning situation.
11. Suggestions for the improvement of the lesson should not be made unless the teacher asks for them.
12. The supervisor should not remain in the classroom if his presence is disturbing either the pupils or the teacher.
13. There is no established minimum and maximum time for a visit.
14. Details of room management are important to observe.
15. Records of supervisory visits should be kept.
16. During the visit, the supervisor should not in any way show disapproval of what is happening in the classroom.
17. The supervisor should make a complimentary remark before leaving the classroom.
18. Supervisory visits and classroom observations made for the purpose of teacher evaluation should never be mixed.

Although each of the above suggestions has merit under certain conditions, they must be followed intelligently in respect to a particular set of circumstances. Perhaps the first suggestion has the most universal application. The authors concur with those authorities who stress the importance of rapport between supervisor and teacher. However, they believe that, after rapport has been established, there is no single set of classroom visitation procedures that is applicable under all circumstances. They agree with Jordan when he writes: "Actually teachers differ so much, classrooms differ so much, and methods differ so much that it is almost impossible to determine the protocols of visiting."[1] Therefore, it would seem logical to suggest that it is no longer possible to generalize concerning the correct procedures to use under all circumstances in classroom visitation and observation. The visitor, the purpose of the visit, the teacher visited, and the type of activity observed condition the procedures to be used. It would be impossible in a work of this dimension to demonstrate all the variables, but several illustrations will be given to clarify the point made above.

Assisting an inexperienced teacher. Miss Willing is in her first month of teaching English to a tenth-grade class of general students. She has been having difficulty in getting her students interested in Shakespeare's *Twelfth Night.* Miss Willing had an unusually good relationship with her critic teacher during her practice teaching; consequently, she has no fear of the supervisor but looks upon him as someone who can assist her in solving her problems. Miss Willing has informed the supervisor of her problem and invited him to drop in at any time and as often as it is possible for him to come. In this favorable climate, which of the above suggestions apply?

Assisting an experienced teacher. Mr. Oldster has been teaching general science to eighth-grade pupils for thirty years. During that period his instructional procedures and the content of his science curriculum have changed very little. With the new emphasis on science in the elementary school, much of the material which Mr. Oldster presents is now learned in the elementary school. As a consequence, pupils are bored in his classes and refuse to cooperate. A constant stream of pupils are sent to the office. Mr. Oldster has always resented classroom visitation by any school official. If you were a new principal in this situation, which of the above suggestions would you consider important to observe in attempting to improve this learning situation?

Assisting non-certificated teaching personnel. Because of a short supply of certificated teachers, Mr. Smart, a graduate of a liberal arts

[1]William C. Jordan, *Elementary School Leadership* (New York: McGraw-Hill Book Company, Inc., 1959), p. 195.

curriculum, has been engaged to teach a self-contained classroom of fifth-grade youngsters. Although he seems to enjoy working with pupils in this age group, Mr. Smart has some decided opinions concerning instructional procedures. By the end of the second week of school, you have received several reports from parents that Mr. Smart is conducting his classes largely by the lecture method. You know that he needs help. Which of the suggestions would be pertinent in this situation?

Implementing a group study project. An elementary-school staff has undertaken an in-service education project concerned with the use of pro-grammed instruction in the teaching of arithmetic in grades four, five, and six. The principal has taken a summer workshop dealing with this topic and is serving as the consultant for the project. Classroom visitation and observation are necessary to the success of the project. Which of the suggestions would apply in this situation?

Purposes of classroom visitation. The above anecdotes illustrate four different classroom situations in which visitation and observation may be used as one procedure for improving instruction. It should be noted that, in the first three anecdotes mentioned above, teacher status is the most crucial variable that must be considered. In the fourth one, this is not an important factor.

Although the list is not complete, the following additional purposes are worthy of note: (1) to observe a substitute teacher in action, (2) to hear a resource person make a presentation, (3) to view small- and large-group instruction under the team teaching plan of organization, (4) to observe an outstanding lesson by invitation of the teacher, and (5) to assist in the evaluation of an audio-visual presentation.

It should be apparent to the reader that the four purposes included in the anecdotes and the five purposes listed above roughly fall into the following two (although not mutually exclusive) categories: (1) observations made to obtain an overall picture of the instructional program and (2) observations performed to acquire information that can be used in the solution of instructional problems. Most writers on the subject emphasize the second category almost to the exclusion of the first. The authors believe that the first category is equally important. They support this belief with the ensuing discussion of the necessity for individuals in a supervisory capacity to have an accurate over-all picture of the learners, the learning environment, and the instructional program.

Observation as a basic supervisory technique. It is impossible for the principal or other staff personnel to serve effectively in a supervisory capacity without seeing the pupils in action. If the objective of super-vision is to improve the learning situation, the supervisor must spend a great deal of time in the places where the learning is taking place. If he is to assist in the development of a curriculum that will meet the needs of the children or youth in the particular building or school district in which he serves, he must observe these youngsters—all of them—at work and play. He must be aware of their activities in the classroom, library and instructional materials center, auditorium, gymnasium, and cafeteria, and on the playground and athletic field. He must see them in study halls, in co-curricular activities as participants and spectators, and at social events. No activity should escape his notice.

As he observes his charges, the supervisor gathers a lot of information about them. He learns something about their homes and their state of health from the way they look, act, and speak. He acquires a good understanding of the learning situation. He notes whether or not they are enthusiastic or disinterested, unchallenged or over-extended, cooperative or overly competitive, active or passive, independent or overly dependent, secure or insecure, and happy or unhappy.

He checks to see whether or not they are improving in their work habits, growing in their ability to think critically and creatively, becoming more proficient in using research techniques, and learning how to get along better wth each other. These things and others the supervisor learns about the pupils through visitation and observation.

Although his attention is on the children and the learning situation, the supervisor gets some cues from the teacher as part of the learning environment. He soon knows whether or not the pupils like and respect the teacher, how the teacher feels about the pupils, and something about the effects of the teacher's personality on the pupils. He learns how the teacher feels about the area of the curriculum being taught and the extent to which the teacher is providing for individual differences. He notes the teacher's skill in classroom management, and he soon becomes aware of the more obvious strengths and weaknesses in the instructional program.

The supervisor who spends sufficient time in the classroom also learns much about the curriculum. Crosby makes this point clear when she writes:

Observation throws new light upon the quality of the learning experiences present in a teaching situation. The kinds of experiences provided, the relationships between and among the various experiences, the roles of the teacher and children in planning and evaluating their experiences, and the quality of planning revealed are factors which must be analyzed when teacher and supervisor work together to help the teacher provide for more effective curriculum building with children.[2]

[2] Muriel Crosby, *Supervision as Co-operative Action* (New York: Appleton-Century-Crofts, Inc., 1957), p. 52.

Through classroom visitation the supervisor learns how effectively the teaching tools are being utilized. Are pupils using reference materials other than the basic text? How effectively are workbooks being employed? To what extent and how effectively is programmed learning being used? Are audio-visual materials being utilized to the greatest advantage? What is the quality and quantity of homework that is being assigned? Complete answers to these and other similar questions cannot be obtained except through classroom visitation and observation.

Finally, classroom visitation is necessary to determine the physical learning environment in which pupils and teachers are working. In recent years much research has been conducted in order to discover the effect of the physical environment on learning. The effects of the thermal, visual, and sonic environments on learning have all been the subject of investigation. In spite of the findings of research in these areas, hundreds of thousands of children and youth attend classes in rooms that violate all known principles of a good learning environment. During the past few years the authors visited several hundred elementary- and secondary-school classrooms in buildings ranging in age from some that were 100 years old to others that were being used for the first school term. In classrooms old and new, children were working in thermal environments ranging from 60 to 90 degrees, in visual environments varying in light intensity from 20 foot-candles to 200 foot-candles, and in sonic environments that ranged from rooms that were adequately sound-conditioned to those in which sounds within the room and outside reverberated at a distracting level.

In addition to the above, the furnishings of the room and their arrangement influence the learning of pupils. Whether or not desks are too large or too small, in straight lines or grouped, light- or dark-colored, defaced or unmarred, screwed to the floor or movable, all tell their story about the learning environment.

In the case of the physical environment, the authors are not suggesting that, just because the supervisor is aware of any undesirable situations, these can be improved immediately. However, they are stating that, unless the supervisor visits all classrooms frequently, these conditions may not be discovered. Unfortunately, teachers are prone to continue year after year in classroom environments that are undesirable for learning. In fact, they frequently are responsible for this undesirable physical environment. By their own poor classroom management and through unreasonable requests to the custodian, teachers keep their classrooms too hot or too cold, too light or too dark, and too neat or too untidy. They place movable furniture in straight lines and keep it there, or they are constantly shuffling their furniture. Yes, teachers must accept some responsibility for the physical environment of their classrooms.

Visitorial and observational procedures. It has been the thesis of this section that the individual who serves in a supervisory capacity must spend a great deal of time in classroom observation under many different conditions and sets of circumstances. It also has been suggested that, because of the variety of circumstances, no hard-and-fast set of rules and regulations for classroom visitation can be drawn up and followed on every occasion. However, the remainder of this section will offer suggestions that show how the visitorial and observational patterns of the supervisor might vary, depending upon whether he is observing to obtain an over-all picture or to assist in the solution of a problem.

There are at least three different types of observational visits that the supervisor might use in obtaining an over-all view of the educational program. One of these is the classroom visit made in the morning before the teachers and pupils arrive or in the late afternoon when they have departed. Much can be learned about the educational program from an empty classroom, particularly on the elementary level. The observer should note whether or not the classroom is neat and attractive and at the same time has the earmarks of a workshop. The use that is being made of the bulletin boards also should be observed. Is there any evidence that special projects are being carried on in the classroom? Projects and displays are quite revealing. Other pupils' work may be in evidence for examination. Writing on the blackboard or on charts may be quite informative. If an elementary classroom (self-contained) is visited, the observer should note whether or not the room has work centers and if it is homelike in appearance. He should also pay particular attention to the arrangement of the furniture. This often gives clues concerning the extent to which informality is encouraged in the learning environment. Finally, the observer should check to determine whether or not the classroom is well equipped with supplies, books, maps, charts, pictures, and other audio-visual materials.

A second and somewhat similar procedure is to make a series of short visits during the school day. Five- or ten-minute visits to a large number of classrooms during a span of several days will make it possible not only to get answers to the above questions but also to gather a considerable amount of information concerning teacher-pupil relationships and the general climate of learning.

A third type of observation in this category, applicable largely in the elementary school, consists of visiting a number of classrooms on different grade levels and becoming a participant in the activities in progress. Some authorities frown upon this procedure, maintaining that it is very poor visitation etiquette. The authors disagree with this attitude. They firmly believe that individuals who work in a supervisory capacity (particularly principals) are not visitors, but part of the instructional team. For years they have entered classrooms and pitched right in, working with pupils at their seats or in work groups while the teacher was conducting some other small-group activity. One of the authors gauged his rapport in a given classroom in terms of whether or not pupils approached him for assistance when the teacher was otherwise occupied. To hear one of the following salutations as soon as you enter the classroom is music to the ears of a supervisor: "Mr. Jones, we are writing an original play; please come over and help our group." "Miss Smith, our group is trying to set up an original experiment to prove how evaporation takes place—please, won't you give us some guidance?" A supervisor then is no longer an outsider in that classroom.

On other occasions, the supervisor may assist the teacher in correcting papers or workbooks, help pupils who are working on a frieze, make suggestions to pupils who are working on a social studies project, join in the singing, participate in playground activities, and engage in numerous other activities which demonstrate to pupils and teachers that the supervisor is there to help. This is not only one of the best procedures to keep in touch with the total program, but it is more likely to insure a welcome for the supervisor at other times when problems arise that need to be solved cooperatively. The principal or a general supervisor must be careful not to pose as an expert in all areas of the curriculum. In this day of rapidly expanding knowledge and constantly changing instructional techniques, the generalist can not be a specialist in all areas.

The reader will note that the authors have not suggested that the supervisor under any circumstances should take over the class. The *teacher is in charge* of the class at all times. The supervisor is merely assisting pupils who need and desire help which the teacher cannot give at the moment because he is working with other pupils. It is important to emphasize again that the rapport between the supervisor and the teacher must be excellent for this type of visitation to take place.

Observations made for the purpose of gathering information to use in the solution of a problem may be of the "on call" type or they may be scheduled by the supervisor in cases where the teacher is not aware of the problem, unable to accept the problem, or unwilling to admit that it exists. Observational visits made for this purpose would have to take place at a time when the activity to be studied was in progress or the condition to be observed was present in the classroom.

Careful preparation is required for this type of visit, including a conference with the teacher before the visit in some instances. The supervisor under these circumstances would be likely to work most efficiently as a passive observer, at least at first. In some instances it may be highly desirable to take notes, if it is agreeable to the teacher. The teacher may even be willing to have parts of the activity recorded on tape. Doubtless, in the future, both sight and sound reproduction will be employed as an aid in the solution of classroom problems, as equipment becomes less expensive and more readily available.

A number of visits of varying length, followed by conferences, may be necessary before a plan for a solution to the problem can be cooperatively agreed upon. It may take a long time to improve some situations. The supervisor who expects speedy improvement in all instances is doomed to disappointment.

Throughout the years, authorities in the field of school administration and supervision have developed various types of check lists, observation forms,[3] and observational procedures to assist the observer in appraising the teaching-learning situation. The opponents of these devices frequently have been as loud in their condemnation as the exponents have been in their praise. The authors maintain that any device that assists the observer to improve his observation techniques can be of value at certain times and under certain conditions. If the use of such a device destroys the rapport between the teacher and the supervisor, it should not be used.

One very promising procedure, the Flanders system of interaction-analysis observation,

. . . has been found to be an effective way to supply to the teacher objective and reliable information about his role in the classroom. It is a procedure which may be used by observers who may collect data systematically in his classroom, or it may be used by the teacher himself as a method of analyzing tape recordings of his own teaching. It is a method of summarizing what he actually does in the classroom where he is free to make his own judgments of value about it.[4]

The following brief description of the Flanders System written by Amidon *et al.*, should be enough to interest the reader sufficiently that he will desire to learn more about the procedure:

Flanders classifies classroom verbal interaction in ten categories, seven of which identify teacher talk. Categories 1, accepting and clarifying student feeling; 2, praising or encouraging student behavior; 3, accepting and clarifying student ideas; and 4, asking questions, are considered indirect teacher talk. Categories 5, lecturing, giving information or opinion; 6, giving directions; and 7, criticizing or justifying teacher authority, are considered direct

[3]Dwight E. Beecher, *The Teaching Evaluation Record* (Buffalo, N.Y.: Educators Publishing Co., 1956).

[4]Edmund J. Amidon and Ned A. Flanders, *The Role of the Teacher in the Classroom, A Manual for Understanding and Improving Teachers' Classroom Behavior* (Philadelphia: Temple University, College of Education, Group Dynamics Center, June 1962), p. 4.

teacher talk. Student categories 8, response to the teacher; and 9, student initiated talk, classify student talk. Category 10 is used to identify silence or confusion.

The observer, who may be present in the classroom or listen to a tape, records in sequence every three seconds the appropriate category numbers. When the lesson is over, the observer enters the numbers in the form of tallies in a 10-row by 10-column grid, called a matrix. The matrix reveals both quantification and patterns of verbal interaction.

Data which are related to quantification include the percentage of time consumed 1) by teacher talk, 2) by student talk, and 3) in silence or confusion. The percentages of time spent in each of the seven categories of teacher talk may be computed.

The matrix, while summarizing the data found by the observer, also maintains some of the sequence. The teacher can see the patterns of his reactions to student response, to silence, or to student initiation. He may find answers to such questions as, "Which of my verbal behaviors seem to elicit student response?" and "At what point in the interaction do I find it necessary to criticize?"

The Flanders System of interaction analysis does yield descriptive information about the teacher-pupil dialogue, but this information is *in no way* an evaluation of teaching. If any kind of value judgment about teaching is to be made, it is done by the teacher himself after studying his own interaction patterns.[5]

In a study comparing the effectiveness of the Flanders System of inter-action-analysis observation with other types of feedback Wright found that:

The combination of *training* in the Flanders System of *interaction analysis* and feedback through a supervisor produces a greater change toward a more *indirect* pattern of verbal behavior than does any other combination of inter-action analysis or conventional *training* and *feedback* through a supervisor or through a teacher's self-analysis of tape recordings of his teaching.[6]

The implications here are that if an indirect pattern of verbal behavior is desirable in teaching, then teachers will show the greatest improvement if they are trained in the use of interaction analysis before receiving feedback through the supervisor.

Benjamin suggests that supervisory programs might be conducted on the basis of an inventory of all that is generally known about teaching and learning. Although he presents in his article a partial list of psycho-

---

[5]Edmund J. Amidon, Kathleen M. Kies, and Anthony T. Palisi, "Group Supervision," *The National Elementary Principal*, XLV, no. 5 (1966), 55. Copyright 1966 Department of Elementary School Principals, National Education Association. All rights reserved.

[6]Donald L. Wright, "A Study of the Effect of Selected Types of Training and Feedback on the Verbal Behavior and Attitudes of Teachers" (Doctoral dissertation, Temple University, 1967), pp. 84–85.

logical supports for good learning activities, accompanying classroom behaviors, and a list of suggestions to the principal for follow-up supervisory activities, Benjamin believes teachers should assist cooperatively with the conduct of the supervisory program and, consequently, in the preparation of the list.

The following items taken from his list illustrate the procedure:

Support No. I. Interest. A learning experience becomes more productive and is retained longer when there is a real interest in the activity.

Classroom behaviors. Do students appear at ease and attentive or do they squirm in their seats and keep looking out the window? In their oral recitations, do they relate personal experience to the matter under discussion or do they seem to be speaking from rote memory? Do they make comparisons with something they learned in the past? Does a single question from the teacher elicit several responses? Can you see a light in their eyes?

Principal's follow-up. 1) Devote a faculty meeting to the general topic of interest and ask teachers to share ideas. 2) Present teachers with a dittoed sheet showing developmental tasks of youngsters and indicate the general interests of youngsters at various age and grade levels. 3) Invite someone from the community to speak to the faculty and tell what types of neighborhoods the youngsters come from, and what children do in their spare time that interests them. 4) Subscribe to the local paper and share with your teachers any news articles that relate what is going on in the children's neighborhood that might be of interest to them. 5) Have teachers analyze cumulative records to learn of hobbies and other special interests of each individual. 6) If your school has a document called "guide to parent-teacher conferences," include an item in which teachers ask parents about each child's interests.

Support No. II. Motivation. Very little learning takes place without some urge to learn, whether it be inborn drive, a need for self-satisfaction, fear, anxiety, peer approval, or some other motivating force.

Classroom behaviors. 1) Do students show a "love of learning" or are they working mostly for stars or grades? When a student receives his homework paper from the teacher, does it have personal notes giving constructive criticism or is the entire emphasis on the grade? 2) Do students volunteer to do extra work? 3) Does the teacher have a positive attitude of praise or one of negative criticism? 4) Do students share in making some of the decisions? 5) Is the spelling in the daily written work of the same quality as it is during the spelling period?

Principal's follow-up. 1) Invite a psychologist or a professor from a nearby college to come and speak to the faculty on the topic of intrinsic vs. extrinsic motivation. 2) Have a committee of teachers lead a discussion on motivation for immediate reward and for delayed reward.[7]

[7]Dayton Benjamin, "A Psychological Approach," *The National Elementary Principal*, XLVII, no. 4 (1968), 33–34. Copyright 1968 Department of Elementary School Principals, National Education Association. All rights reserved.

These examples of several different kinds of visitorial behavior, together with the other discussion provided, should be sufficient to convince the supervisor or prospective supervisor that each individual must determine his own pattern of classroom visitation in keeping with his unique situation. Finally, the authors hope that they have convinced the reader that this is a very important technique if it is used properly.

Classroom Experimentation

Although innovation and change are presented in Chapter VII and action research in Chapter IX, the general area is of sufficient import to discuss a phase of it in this chapter.

Teachers should be encouraged to originate new approaches, new techniques, and new materials for teaching. For years schools have been reluctant to experiment because they were fearful of unfavorable public reaction. The answers received in opinion polls in three rather diverse areas involving respectively, 2,201, 1,253, and 769 parents indicated that from 75 to 80 per cent of the parents favored experimentation in the teaching of arithmetic and reading.[8] This should give us some encouragement to experiment.

Experimentation may vary from small changes in teaching practices to large-scale research projects that include the use of control groups. One third-grade teacher with whom the writer worked as a supervisor actually had her class write a third-level reader, claiming that adults could not write books for children. Another teacher experimented with *individualized reading* ten years before it became a popular topic in the literature in the field. A third teacher taught eighth-grade science on an individual basis with every pupil working in areas of his own interests.

However, experimentation also has its dangers. Gwynn suggests the following cautions in using classroom experimentation as a supervisory technique:

1. The new method that is tried out should be judged to be as good and as effective as the old method and should not harm the pupil or hinder his learning.
2. Both children and parents should be made aware of the experimentation and the reasons for it, and their co-operation should be secured in carrying it out.

[8]Educational Service Bureau, Temple University, *A Survey of the Neshaminy Joint Schools, An Evaluation of the Easton-Forks Elementary Schools,* and *A Survey of the Cornwall-Lebanon Schools* (Philadelphia: The Bureau, 1962) (Mimeographed).

3. The teacher should not be blamed if the experiment is not as successful as was hoped. Not all experiments succeed.[9]

College Courses

If they are going to prove helpful to the teacher in his present teaching situation, supervisors should assume a more active role in assisting teachers to select courses offered on campus and in extension centers. The writer has advised hundreds of students in planning their graduate programs, and he has found only a small number of students who actually recognize their strengths and weaknesses. This awareness seems to increase somewhat with experience. Too many teachers (particularly men) take graduate work to prepare for another type of educational position instead of to improve themselves for their present assignment.

Another manner in which supervisors can help in this respect is to sponsor college or university extension classes in their school buildings or districts. Quite frequently the educational institution can be persuaded to offer a course especially tailored to fit the needs of a particular faculty if sufficient registration can be assured.

Conferences with Teachers

Next to classroom visitation and observation, the supervisory conference is the most direct procedure to assist the individual teacher. Because conferences frequently precede and almost always follow all but general classroom observations, they are commonly thought of as companion techniques.

As was the case in the discussion of classroom visitation and observation, the authors are reluctant to prescribe hard-and-fast rules for conferencing. Here, again, the situation to a great extent determines the course of action.

Reasons for a conference. Various reasons have been given for holding conferences with teachers. After teachers have been observed, they naturally are anxious to know how the supervisor feels about what he saw and heard. If a conference is not held, the teacher frequently begins to worry and is fearful that the supervisor was not pleased. On the other hand, some teachers know that the lesson observed was a good one, and they are eager for words of praise. However, the basic reason for holding a conference is that it is a valuable technique for improving instruction. Observations to assist inexperienced teachers, non-certificated teachers,

[9]J. Minor Gwynn, *Theory and Practice of Supervision* (New York: Dodd, Mead & Company, 1961), pp. 339–40.

and experienced teachers with problems would not prove very helpful unless one or more conferences were held to plan a program for improving the situation.

Suggestions for conferencing. In keeping with the philosophy that the supervisor-teacher relationship should no longer be a superior-inferior relationship but instead a peer relationship, Burton and Brueckner define a conference in the following manner:

An individual conference is (or should be) a meeting between two persons equally interested in improving a situation. The views and facts of each party are necessary to complete the picture. Exchange of facts and ideas is focused on problem-solving and not on one of the persons in the conference.[10]

Wiles stressed the importance of mutual understanding as the reason for the conference when he wrote:

The purpose of an interview should be clear to the supervised. A man kept in the dark is afraid and insecure. He plays his cards cautiously, until he knows where the conference is going and what is expected of him. If the supervisor does not want to waste time, he should state the purpose early in the conference or announce it beforehand. Of course, if the conference is requested by the teacher, the supervisor has an equal right to know the purpose. In either case, the person invited to the conference has a right to ask what it is to accomplish.[11]

If the reader keeps in mind the fact that each conference is unique, and follows or adapts the suggestions that fit his situation, the following list should prove helpful.

1. The individual supervisory conference should be looked upon as part of a problem-solving technique.
2. Conferences should be thoroughly prepared for by both the supervisor and the teacher.
3. The conference should be held as soon after the classroom observation as possible.
4. The conference should be held on school time, or within the teacher-day as defined by district policy.
5. The conference should be as informal as possible and held in a place where both the teacher and the supervisor feel at ease.
6. The discussion must be in light of a common, district-wide philosophy of education understood and accepted by both parties.

[10]From *Supervision: A Social Process*, by William H. Burton and Leo J. Brueckner (New York: Appleton-Century-Crofts, Inc., 1955), p. 168. Copyright © 1955, Appleton-Century-Crofts, Inc.

[11]Kimball Wiles, *Supervision for Better Schools*, 3rd ed. (Englewood Cliffs, N.J.: Prentice-Hall, Inc., © 1967), p. 80.

7. A plan of action should be drawn up in writing, including a summary of points agreed upon by both parties and the assignment of responsibilities.
8. A written summary should be kept of all conferences, and copies should be given to both participants.
9. The conference should be evaluated by both participants with the idea in mind of improving the conferencing technique.

Important leadership notes. As a result of research by Blumberg and Amidon, the following additional suggestions seem warranted:

1. Supervisory conferences might be more productive if at the beginning the supervisor engaged the teacher in a discussion of how the teacher perceives the supervisor-teacher relationship.
2. Supervisors should pay more attention to the inter-active nature of their supervisory confrontations.
3. During the conference the supervisor should emphasize indirect behavior and de-emphasize direct behavior.
4. Supervisors should work with teachers in such a manner that defensiveness, where it exists, is replaced by supportiveness.[12]

Demonstration Teaching

As was indicated in the introduction to this chapter, demonstration teaching may be used as an individual or a group supervisory technique. Although it is true that, under the modern concept of supervision, a supervisor would not take over a teacher's class unless he requested it, demonstration teaching has an important place in a supervisory program. Spears highlights its role when he writes:

There is nothing old-fashioned about demonstration teaching in a supervisory program. From the point of view of the one receiving the help it is observation, and the observation of the good work of other teachers is a sound practice in teacher training that begins in the undergraduate school and continues throughout the professional career of a teacher.[13]

In fact, the results of at least one research project conducted at the University of Texas by Harris reveal that demonstration teaching is quite modern and highly effective as a procedure for improving instruction. The following conclusions may be drawn from the study:

[12]See Arthur Blumberg and Edmund Amidon, "Teacher Perceptions of Supervisor-Teacher Interaction," in *Administrators' Notebook*, XIV, no. 1 (Midwest Administration Center, The University of Chicago 1965), pp. 3–4.

[13]Harold Spears, *Improving the Supervision of Instruction* (Englewood Cliffs, N.J.: Prentice-Hall, Inc., 1953), p. 273.

1. Formal demonstrations do promote changes in teacher and student behavior of specific kinds at a very significant level.
2. A contagion appears to function within schools where experimental subjects are making substantial changes in their practices.
3. The initial level of teaching practice seems to be a very critical factor in determining the amount of change in teacher behavior that can be anticipated.
4. Behavior changes resulting from quality demonstrations tend to persist for at least a year.
5. Attitudes toward teaching practices are influenced significantly by the various interventions accompanying the demonstrations while classroom practices are not.
6. A serious reversal of practices effect seems to be induced in teacher subjects who are initially exhibiting the desired practices to a high degree, but are nonetheless subjected to a strong array of interventions.[14]

The procedures for planning and conducting teaching demonstrations as part of a supervisory program should be adapted to the particular situation. If the reader keeps this in mind, the following list of suggestions should prove helpful when they are used with discretion:

1. Careful preparations should be made for the demonstration by the demonstrator and the observer(s).
2. Demonstrations are more effective if they are conducted in the classroom of the participating pupils.
3. The demonstration should be as similar to a normal classroom situation as possible.
4. During the demonstration, emphasis should be placed on the particular skill or procedure in which the observer(s) desire(s) help.
5. Demonstration teaching should be largely, if not entirely, on an "on call" basis.
6. If the demonstration is conducted by individuals other than supervisory personnel, these persons should not be imposed upon too frequently.
7. The same group of pupils must not be used so often for demonstration purposes that it interferes with their regular planned learning program.
8. A conference including the demonstrating teacher should be held as soon after the demonstration as possible to raise questions and to clarify procedures.
9. The demonstration should be evaluated by observers and participants.

If a school is organized for team teaching, supervisors should capitalize on the possibilities of using large-group instruction as a form of demonstration teaching. As the other team members observe the large-group presentation, they should be learning and benefiting from the material

[14]Ben M. Harris, *A Research Study of the Effects of Demonstration Teaching Upon Experienced and Inexperienced Teachers* (Austin, Texas: The University of Texas, Projects S-384. USOE, Project No. 5-8237), pp. 220–23.

presented and the techniques used. One of the strong arguments for team teaching is the many opportunities for professional growth that can be inherent in this plan of organization.

Demonstration teaching is a form of modeling whether it is live, video-taped, kinescoped, or audio-taped. In relation to modeling as a procedure for improving instruction, the following statements by Young are a result of research on this topic:

1. Modeling as a training variable has been demonstrated effective in modifying teaching behavior.
2. Video-taped models are most effective when a supervisor provides discrimination training while a teacher is viewing or when such discrimination training is provided by the addition of auditory and visual cues on the tape.
3. Models featuring only positive instances of teaching behavior have been demonstrated to have a greater transfer to teaching situations other than the one in which training occurred.
4. Listening to an audio-taped model with a typescript and subsequently verbalizing the model teacher's indirect verbal behavior effected significant behavior changes in the predicted direction.[15]

It should be evident to the reader that there is a natural relationship between demonstration teaching and microteaching in that they both are a form of modeling. The next section will discuss microteaching in some detail.

Microteaching

Although microteaching is rather widely known as a pre-service and research technique for improving teaching, it has been somewhat less widely applied as a supervisory procedure in the improvement of instruction. The writers of this handbook believe that it holds great promise as a supervisory technique.

The following description of a session on microteaching attended by the authors should help the reader to understand the process.

The teacher observed worked for approximately eight minutes with a group of five pupils. The purpose of the lesson was to assist the teacher to improve her ability to ask leading questions. The topic in economic geography dealt with the relationships of· products to environmental factors. In this instance an observer was present who took notes. The lesson was video-taped. At the close of the session the observer discussed the lesson with the teacher. The video-tape was then played back so the

[15]David B. Young, "The Modification of Teacher Behavior Using Audio Video-Taped Models in a Micro-Teaching Sequence," *Educational Leadership*, XXVI, no. 4 (1969), 402.

teacher could see and hear herself in action. The observer raised questions concerning aspects of the lesson as the video-tape was played back.

The teacher then taught the same lesson to a different group of five pupils. The second time some improvement was noted in the teacher's ability to ask leading questions. The lesson was again video-taped, replayed, and discussed with the observer.

The above cycle could have been repeated as many times as would be necessary for the teacher to perfect the technique. The students also could have been used for feedback in addition to the observer, the playback of the video-tape, and the teacher's own reflections.

Allen and Ryan in their pioneer work on microteaching characterize it as follows:

First, microteaching is real teaching. Although the teaching situation is a constructed one in the sense that teacher and students work together in a practice situation, nevertheless, bona fide teaching does take place.

Second, microteaching lessens the complexities of normal classroom teaching. Class size, scope of content, and time are all reduced.

Third, microteaching focuses on training for the accomplishment of specific tasks. These tasks may be the practice of instructional skills, the practice of techniques of teaching, the mastery of certain curricular materials, or the demonstration of teaching methods.

Fourth, microteaching allows for the increased control of practice. In the practice setting of microteaching, the rituals of time, students, methods of feedback and supervision, and many other factors can be manipulated. As a result, a high degree of control can be built into the training program.

Fifth, microteaching greatly expands the normal knowledge-of-results or feedback dimension in teaching. Immediately after teaching a brief micro-lesson, the trainee engages in a critique of his performance. To give him a maximum insight into his performance, several sources of feedback are at his disposal. With the guidance of a supervisor or colleague, he analyzes aspects of his own performance in light of his goals. The trainee and the supervisor go over student response forms that are designed to elicit students' reactions to specific aspects of his teaching. When the supervisor has videotape available, he can use videotape playbacks to help show the teacher how he performs and how he can improve. All this feedback can be immediately translated into practice when the trainee reteaches shortly after the critique conference.[16]

In a discussion of the utilization of microteaching as a research tool, Gage mentions the following technical skills that may be learned by using this technique: (1) "establishing set" (*rapport*), (2) "establishing appropriate frames of reference," (3) "achieving closure," (4) "using questions," (5) "recognizing and obtaining attending behavior," (6)

[16]Dwight Allen and Kevin Ryan, *Microteaching* (Reading, Mass.: Addison-Wesley Publishing Company, Inc., 1969), pp. 2–3.

"controlling participation," (7) "providing feedback," (8) "employing rewards and punishments," and (9) "setting a model."[17]

Important leadership note. Because of its ease of utilization, great flexibility, and potential for both the improvement of teaching and research in instruction, individuals serving in a supervisory capacity should become familiar with microteaching and at least experiment with it on a limited scale.

Evaluation

Evaluation is an essential process in the improvement of the learning situation. Self-evaluation,[18] evaluation by peers, evaluation by supervisory personnel (which actually should be a peer relationship), and evaluation by pupils should all be encouraged. Evaluation of the administrative and supervisory activities by other professional staff members also should be invited. (See Chapter XII.) Individuals serving in a supervisory capacity should attempt to create an atmosphere in which everyone is constantly on the alert to improve himself, to assist others to grow professionally to enrich the curriculum, to upgrade the materials of instruction, to better the physical facilities, and to enlarge the scope of the special services. This is not to imply that evaluation is only negative. To evaluate and acknowledge that something is good may result in greater improvement in the learning situation than to concentrate on the weaknesses. This idea is not new; authorities for a number of years have suggested that a good supervisory program emphasizes strengths rather than weaknesses.

No attempt will be made here to discuss all aspects of evaluation as it relates to the improvement of instruction; however, several less evident aspects will be highlighted.

Evaluation by pupils and teachers. The authors have found that the evaluation of the instructional program by the pupils can be quite revealing and at the same time stimulates teachers to improve their programs. Administrative and supervisory personnel also benefit greatly from having their effectiveness evaluated by the staff. These procedures are more likely to be of value if the instruments to be used in evaluation are cooperatively formulated and then anonymously filled out by the evaluators. It is asking too much to expect pupils to identfy themselves when they are evaluating

[17]N. L. Gage, "An Analytical Approach to Research on Instructional Methods," *Phi Delta Kappan*, XLIX, no. 10 (1968), 602.

[18]For example, see Herbert F. A. Smith, "A Self-Analysis of Classroom Teaching," *The Bulletin of the National Association of Secondary-School Principals*, 42, no. 236 (1958), 182–84, and Richard P. McLean, "Teacher, How Do You Rate Yourself?" *New York State Education*, 47, no. 4 (1960), 32.

their learning experiences. If their honest opinions are desired concerning their teacher(s) and other aspects of the school program, they must have the protection of anonymity. The same protection should be given teachers when they are asked to evaluate the administrative and supervisory services. It is somehow easier to be frank in making evaluations when you know that your future relationships with the individuals whose services are being evaluated are not likely to be affected.

Participation in total evaluations. Too frequently the diagnostic aspects of evaluation are considered to be the end results. As a technique for improving instruction, the evaluation process itself is a valuable professional growth experience. For approximately forty years, many secondary-school personnel have periodically participated in the self-evaluation of their education units. In this process, standardized evaluative criteria have been used which provide check lists for each aspect of the educational enterprise.[19] During that period, a number of evaluative criteria have been developed for use in elementary schools.[20] In keeping with the trend that views the educational process as a continuous K to 12 enterprise, the authors recommend that the application of evaluative criteria be made on a K to 12 basis. Committees for the various areas to be evaluated should include membership from both the elementary- and secondary-school faculties.

Any staff that spends six months to a year (longer if necessary) in an exhaustive evaluation of all aspects of their educational enterprise is bound to grow professionally. Individuals who see only accreditation as an objective in overall school evaluation are short-sighted indeed.

Many school personnel will have the opportunity to serve on a visitation committee to another school as part of a total evaluation process. Although this necessitates making provisions for the absent teachers' classes, principals and other supervisory personnel should encourage teachers to serve on visitation committees. In fact, the principal should contact the proper authorities to see that his school is represented from time to time on visitation committees. Many teachers who have had this experience place it high on the list of activities that have contributed to their professional growth.

[19]*Evaluative Criteria* (Washington: National Study of Secondary School Evaluation, 1970).

[20]James F. Baker, *Elementary Evaluative Criteria* (Boston: School of Education, Boston University, 1953); *Faculty Self-Study in Elementary School*, 2nd ed. (Harrisburg, Pa.: Department of Public Instruction, Bureau of Curriculum Development, Commonwealth of Pennsylvania, 1965); and for research pertaining to elementary-school evaluations see Francis Raymond Deitrich, "Procedures and Results of Elementary School Evaluations Conducted in Twenty-five Public School Systems in the Commonwealth of Pennsylvania Between 1955 and 1962" (Doctoral dissertation, Temple University, 1965).

Professional Activities and Conferences

Teachers should be encouraged, but not forced, to engage in activities, meetings, and conferences sponsored by the various national, state, and local educational groups. In recent years the quality of programs presented at these meetings has steadily increased and so has the caliber of their publications. By maintaining a liberal travel budget, administrators should make it possible for staff members to attend these meetings. This is usually accomplished by sending representatives to the meetings of the various organizations on a rotating basis. These representatives should be encouraged to share their experiences with the staff by making an oral or written report. In some instances, both types of reports may be desirable. Supervisors should follow similar procedures when they attend professional meetings.

Some school districts have considered it desirable to have their entire staffs attend certain educational meetings. Typical of this were the Annual Schoolmen's Week Meetings held in Philadelphia, Pennsylvania for many years and sponsored by the School of Education, University of Pennsylvania. Most of the Philadelphia suburban schools closed for one or two days so that their staffs might attend these excellent educational meetings.

Professional Reading

One of the best ways to keep abreast of the profession is regularly to read several professional magazines and representative books in the field of education as they are published. However, so much is being written that it is impossible for any one person to be thoroughly acquainted with even the literature of his special interest. How, then, can the supervisor make professional reading serve as an individual supervisory technique? First, every school should subscribe to several good professional publications. Second, a strong professional library should be organized in every building. Third, procedures should be cooperatively formulated that will encourage extensive use of these books and magazines. The routing of articles and books to staff members who might benefit from reading them, brief reports on books at staff meetings, and book circles organized for the purpose of discussing current works on education have all proved helpful under certain circumstances. If the supervisor reads widely, he can, during a conference, for example, recommend certain books or articles that have a bearing on the problem to be solved.

Staff members should also be encouraged to build up their own professional libraries and to share books with each other. The supervisor might set the example in this respect. At least one book club for educators is in existence.[21]

Professional Writing

The self-discipline required to write for publication results in a kind of professional growth that is not a by-product of any other educational experience. To encourage a teacher to read widely on a topic, to investigate it further through observation and, if necessary, experimentation, and then to organize the findings into a lucid, written discussion that may prove helpful to others is a valuable individual supervisory technique. Supervisors, therefore, have the responsibility to encourage teachers to write for publication. The writer has read many fine research papers that are worth publishing, but unfortunately most of them never appear in print.

Not only does the writer benefit from his experiences, but through publication individuals who read the article share the fruits of the author's labors.

Here, again, the supervisor can set the example by submitting articles for publication or even engaging in a more ambitious undertaking. An excellent way to interest teachers in writing is to invite them to collaborate in a writing project. One acquaintance of the writer, while serving as a supervisor in a suburban school district, involved a number of teachers in writing an elementary language series.

Selection of Textbooks and Other Instructional Materials

It should be apparent to the supervisor and prospective supervisor that textbook selection offers many opportunities for the professional growth of teachers and other participants. Determining need, developing criteria, examining sample copies, attending textbook exhibits, applying score cards, and conferring with book-company consultants all can be made to contribute greatly to the in-service growth of the staff. However, this will necessitate wise leadership by the supervisory personnel. At each step of the way, as many teachers as possible should be involved in the selection process. This means that time must be provided. If the main objective is to select one or more series as rapidly as possible so that the textbook order will meet the deadline set by the central office, little opportunity will be provided for professional growth. The search for new textbooks and other teaching materials should be a continuing one. As the curricu-

[21]Educator's Book Club, Englewood Cliffs, N.J.

lum is under constant scrutiny in its entirety, and as areas of it are up for revision periodically, concurrent studies should be conducted to find the necessary texts and other instructional materials that seem to fit the needs of the pupils best. If this procedure is followed, not only will better text-book selection result, but the entire staff will benefit immeasurably as a result of their involvement in the process.

Representatives of publishing companies are always ready and willing to discuss their publications with principals, supervisors, textbook com-mittees, and individual teachers. They are usually familiar with competing books in the field and, consequently, they are in a position to point out the strengths and weaknesses of their textbooks as well as those of com-peting series. This is usually a valuable educational experience.

School authorities and publishers have a common purpose in studying the problem of textbook selection: to determine those procedures which best assure a fair and objective evaluation of every textbook under consideration. This means an understanding not only of what each book contributes to good teach-ing, but also of how well it meets the school's objectives for the grade and subject. Obviously such an understanding benefits both children and schools; it also works for better textbooks by making the publisher an active partner in the teaching profession.[22]

Although, as has been suggested, it is possible to involve an entire faculty in certain phases of textbook selection, the actual selection com-mittee might profitably consist of five or six teachers together with ad-ministrative and supervisory personnel. Members of the committee should be selected because of their experience, proven teaching competence, indi-vidual judgment, and resourcefulness. Other desirable attributes are the ability to recognize imaginative teaching and to appreciate the contribu-tion that good textbooks can make to the learning process when they are used properly.[23]

The following policies concerning the work of the textbook committee are worthy of serious consideration:

1. The membership of the committee should be announced.
2. The membership should be small.
3. The committee's assignment should be reasonable.
4. Adequate free time should be made available.
5. The selection period should be long enough.
6. Publishers should be informed of pending adoptions.
7. Time for interviews with textbook representatives should be provided.

[22]The American Textbook Publishers Institute, *Textbooks Are Indispensable* (New York: American Book-Stratford Press, Inc.), p. 65.
[23]*Ibid.*, p. 66.

8. Textbook hearings should be arranged if necessary.

9. Opportunities for prudent consultation with other staff members should be provided.

10. All aspects of the publisher's program should be studied.

11. The selection of textbooks and the development of a course of study should be coordinated.

12. Individual subjective judgment should be stressed in selection.[24]

If the informal method of selection is followed, some of the above policies also apply, and these should be observed in the selection process.

When the field finally has been narrowed to two or three basal series, the assistance of the publishing companies can be solicited once more. These firms all employ educational consultants who will be glad to work with your staff in appropriate ways.

Developing criteria for selection. A continuous program of textbook evaluation based on a set of written criteria developed locally and a subjective appraisal as books are used day by day make the task of selecting new textbooks a less complicated one. Too frequently, textbooks are examined critically only at adoption time. All materials of instructions, as well as methods of instruction, should be under constant scrutiny at all times. Evaluation is a continuous process.

Criteria for selection are of both a quantitative and a qualitative nature. Some of the most commonly used quantitative measures are: vocabulary counts, number of illustrations, length of sentences and paragraphs, number of exercises included, number of teaching aids, and so forth.

The qualitative judgments, naturally, are of a subjective nature. Criteria concerned with format, quality of paper and illustrations, and general attractiveness are not too difficult to apply. However, the more important subjective judgments, such as the way ideas are developed, appropriateness of content material for the curriculum area and the age level for which they are selected, and program balance are much more difficult to determine. These, however, may be the crucial ones. The old adage, "You can never tell a book by its cover," applies here.

If used in the correct manner, score cards can be of some value in textbook selection. A well-organized score card calls attention to the important elements to be considered in comparing several series of textbooks. It is quite common for publishers to make score cards available for evaluating a particular text series of theirs, such as, for example, a reading, arithmetic, or language series.

If a publisher's score card is used to evaluate, for example, several series of language texts, the score card may favor the series for which it was designed. This, of course, is to be expected, but it must be kept in

[24]*Ibid.*, pp. 67–70.

Figure 11. Textbook Score Card.

LANSDOWNE-ALDAN JOINT SCHOOL SYSTEM
ELEMENTARY SCHOOL TEXTBOOK EVALUATION SCORE CARD
LANGUAGE TEXTBOOKS OR WORKBOOK TEXTS

Rating of Book

Title _____ Superior _____

Author _____ Good _____

Publisher _____ Average _____

Copyright date _____ Price _____ Poor _____

Scale for rating each item: 3-Superior; 2-Acceptable; 1-Not acceptable; 0- Not included

ITEM   RATING

3 2 1 0

A. Authorship and Point of View
1. Are the authors well qualified in training and experience?
2. How acceptable is the underlying philosophy of the series?
3. Is the philosophy clearly and consistently demonstrated in the presentation and use of the contents?
4. Does the textbook follow and interpret the objectives of the course of study?
5. Is the series based on important research?

B. Content
1. Does the material arouse the interest of the children?
2. Is it related to the children's experiences in speaking, writing, reading, and spelling?
3. Is there adequate emphasis on fundamental English skills? Is enough functional grammar provided?
4. Are stories, poems, and children's literature appropriate and of high quality?
5. Is there correlation with the other subject areas of the curriculum?
6. Is there proper balance between oral and written expression and listening experiences?
7. Are the vocabulary and sentence structure well adapted to the grade level?
8. Are ideas developed skillfully?
9. Is the development of social competence emphasized? Are the social amenities taught in due perspective to the communicative skills?
10. Is there provision for creative work in language?

C. Presentation of Material and Organization
1. Is readiness developed for each new topic?
2. Are skills developed in natural settings and with purposeful practice?
3. Is the presentation clear, understandable, and stimulating?
4. Is the organization flexible?
5. Is the development of content easy to follow by pupils and teacher?

D. Practice and Drill Material
1. Is practice preceded by careful development?
2. Is the book adequately equipped with practice material?
3. Is sufficient practice provided for initial mastery of new processes or understandings?

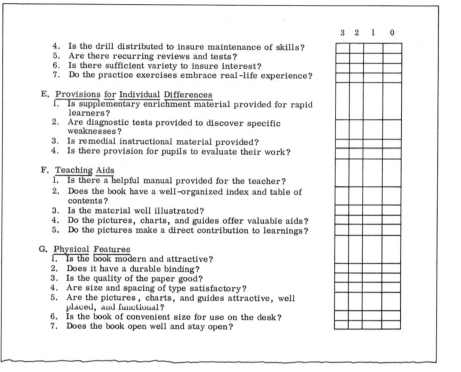

	3	2	1	0
4. Is the drill distributed to insure maintenance of skills?				
5. Are there recurring reviews and tests?				
6. Is there sufficient variety to insure interest?				
7. Do the practice exercises embrace real-life experience?				
E. Provisions for Individual Differences				
1. Is supplementary enrichment material provided for rapid learners?				
2. Are diagnostic tests provided to discover specific weaknesses?				
3. Is remedial instructional material provided?				
4. Is there provision for pupils to evaluate their work?				
F. Teaching Aids				
1. Is there a helpful manual provided for the teacher?				
2. Does the book have a well-organized index and table of contents?				
3. Is the material well illustrated?				
4. Do the pictures, charts, and guides offer valuable aids?				
5. Do the pictures make a direct contribution to learnings?				
G. Physical Features				
1. Is the book modern and attractive?				
2. Does it have a durable binding?				
3. Is the quality of the paper good?				
4. Are size and spacing of type satisfactory?				
5. Are the pictures, charts, and guides attractive, well placed, and functional?				
6. Is the book of convenient size for use on the desk?				
7. Does the book open well and stay open?				

mind when the scores are being compared. For this reason, some schools have developed their own score cards. Under the proper leadership, this exercise can prove to be a valuable learning experience for the participants. A facsimile of a locally developed score card for evaluating language textbooks and workbook texts may be found on pages 182 and 183.

Sharing in the selection of other instructional materials can be equally valuable as part of the professional-growth program of teachers. Teachers should be given opportunity to attend educational exhibits during the various educational meetings.

Distributors can frequently be prevailed upon to demonstrate the use of supplies and equipment in the local school system. Demonstrations on the use of handwriting materials and workshops on the use of art media are frequently run by companies that supply these materials. The same is true in respect to the newer teaching materials in arithmetic and science. Distributors of devices for use in programmed learning also are eager to demonstrate, and purveyors of foreign-language teaching materials will gladly give demonstrations. See Chapter XI for an extended discussion on learning resources.

Selection of Professional Staff

The selection of the professional staff is related to the improvement of instruction in several ways. In the first place, a well-qualified staff will render a higher level of professional services than will a less-qualified corps of teachers. Some teachers also are capable of infinitely greater professional growth than others.

In the second place, if present staff members have a part in setting up the qualifications desired for teaching positions and if teachers are actually involved in the selection of co-workers who have these qualifications, then a great potential exists for professional growth on the part of these faculty members who participate. As faculty members draw up these qualifications and search for individuals who meet them, a process of self-examination is certain to take place. This should result in some professional growth on the part of each staff member involved.

Supervisory Bulletins

The supervisory bulletin can be made a valuable aid in the improvement of instruction if it is a well-written document that is used properly.

Types of supervisory bulletins. Usually the supervisory bulletin assumes one of three different forms. In certain instances it is a device used to prepare staff members for another type of activity, as, for example, a field trip or a demonstration lesson. The second form of supervisory bulletin is the summary, supplementary, or follow-up type. This form of bulletin may be concerned with generalizations resulting from many classroom observations, conclusions, and recommendations reached at a staff or in-service meeting, the summary of the highlights of a school-visitation program, or the significant conclusions drawn from a demonstration lesson.

The third category includes bulletins, handbooks, and guides, preferably prepared by a group of teachers working with the principal, other supervisory personnel, or a specialist. For example, a bulletin on child study would require the assistance of a guidance specialist and/or the school psychologist. Bulletins of this nature may be only several pages in length if they deal with a subject as specific in nature as the one on Bulletin Boards, excerpts of which appear on page 185; or they may be quite long, representing weeks and even months of research and study. Among others, the authors have seen excellent examples of supervisory bulletins on the following subjects: audio-visual aids, child study, disci-

IDEAS For Your Classroom

A BULLETIN FOR TEACHERS,
PRINCIPALS AND SUPERINTENDENTS

PUBLISHED BY THE PHILADELPHIA AREA SCHOOL STUDY COUNCIL, SOUTHERN NEW JERSEY GROUP

EFFECTIVE BULLETIN BOARDS
HERE'S WHY THEY'RE IMPORTANT!!!!!

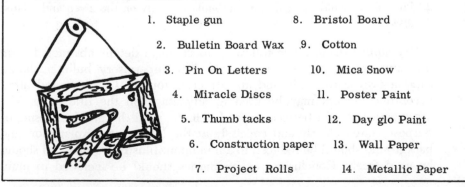

1. Arouse interest and curiosity

2. Emphasize important ideas

3. Bring out relationships

4. Introduce a unit

5. Make abstract ideas more concrete

6. Encourage extra student activity

7. Sharpen the sense of observation

HERE'S WHAT THEY DO!!!!!

1. Show contrast and comparison

2. Show central idea

3. Show development of events

4. Show relationships

5. Show sequence

6. Show progress in student work

HERE ARE YOUR TOOLS!!!!!

1. Staple gun
2. Bulletin Board Wax
3. Pin On Letters
4. Miracle Discs
5. Thumb tacks
6. Construction paper
7. Project Rolls
8. Bristol Board
9. Cotton
10. Mica Snow
11. Poster Paint
12. Day glo Paint
13. Wall Paper
14. Metallic Paper

Figure 12. Effective Bulletin Boards.

pline, field trips, guidance, instructional-materials center, parent-teacher conferences, programmed instruction, school library services, team teaching, ungraded primary organization, and the unit method. Bulletins of this type are also issued on all phases of the curriculum, but they are distinguished from the regular curriculum bulletins by the fact that they emphasize new approaches and specific techniques.

Teachers' handbooks may also be considered in the category of supervisory bulletins in view of the fact that they frequently include much valuable information that enables the teacher to do a more effective job. For example, the section on evaluation in a teachers' handbook may be so complete that it serves the same purpose as a separate guide on the topic.

The writing and illustrating of a good supervisory bulletin require skill and practice. The following suggestions should prove helpful in perfecting this technique:

1. A sharp distinction should be made between educational bulletins and notices, summaries of regulations, routine announcements, news notes, and the like.
2. A supervisory bulletin should be written to meet a specific need.
3. The scope of a bulletin should, preferably, be confined to one problem, issue, or item.
4. Supervisory bulletins may result from individual action but, preferably, they should be issued as an outcome of cooperative group study, discussion, and summary.
5. Supervisory bulletins should be used only when their unique values serve better than any other technique.
6. Bulletins should be dynamic in tone, stimulating both thought and action. (They should include questions, suggested activities and procedures, study guides, and references.)
7. The vocabulary, style, and tone of the bulletin should be lively and interesting.
8. Provisions should be made for individual and group actions.
9. Provisions should be made for continuity of study on the given and related problems.[25]

Mechanical details. The following mechanical details abstracted from the same source are worthy of note. The supervisory bulletin should carry a provocative title and an attractive format. Cartoons and other decorative devices may be used to advantage on the title page. The organization should be clearcut and definite, with the problem, issue, or purpose stated clearly and concisely at the beginning. Explanation and background should be reduced to a minimum. Illustrative material should be used freely. Conclusions or summaries should be included in num-

[25]Adapted from *Supervision: A Social Process*, by William H. Burton and Leo J. Brueckner (New York: Appleton-Century-Crofts, Inc., 1955), p. 159. Copyright © 1955, Appleton-Century-Crofts, Inc.

bered, outline form. Credit for quotations and contributions from staff members should be properly acknowledged.[26]

Informal Contacts

Supervision is a continuous process. The supervisor must realize that he is never free of his responsibility for improving instruction. By the same token, his being on the job at all times offers many opportunities to assist teachers to grow professionally. Supervisors should never forget that a valuable part of their college education was obtained in "bull sessions," "kaffee-klatches," and heart-to-heart talks with individual students or faculty members. Opportunities for supervision, then, are presented each time the supervisor comes in contact with a teacher. In fact, this influence is felt each time that the teacher observes the supervisor, even though the supervisor may not see the teacher. For example, the writer vividly recalls the time that a teacher came to her mailbox for her keys a few minutes late and went to her classroom in tears when the writer (at that time her supervisor) failed to say "Good morning" because he did not see her. Even after an explanation and an apology, this sensitive teacher believed she had been snubbed because she was late.

Another supervisor, who is very congenial when he interviews teachers for positions but rarely notices them during informal contacts after they are appointed to the staff, quickly destroys the illusion that his is a friendly school. He thus loses many opportunities to assist teachers. It is unfortunate when individuals spend years learning and perfecting the formal techniques of supervision and ignore completely the informal contacts.

Particularly on the elementary level, informal contacts with pupils also can prove valuable in a supervisory program. The writer regularly ate lunch with different groups of pupils, mingled with children on the playground, and talked with them before and after school. During classroom visitation, the supervisor is encouraged to focus his attention on the pupil. He sometimes learns more about the program by observing pupils during informal contacts than he does in more formal situations. He can observe how they conduct themselves and hear what they say when they are free to discuss the topics they choose to talk about. If interest in a classroom activity spills over into the lunch or play period, the supervisor knows that good things are happening to these children. If they appear eager before school to attack the day's work, he is aware that they have been highly motivated in some way.

One word of caution seems appropriate. Although the supervisor should

26*Ibid.*, p. 159.

be a good listener, he must not interrogate pupils for the purpose of obtaining derogatory information about their teachers. This is an un-ethical practice that can place the entire supervisory program in jeopardy.

Other Experiences

There are many different kinds of experiences usually not discussed in a work of this nature that can contribute to the personal and professional growth of teachers. Some years ago the writer had the privilege of serving on a state committee to recommend procedures for the renewal of teaching and administrative certificates. The committee began with the premise that any activity that contributed to the personal and/or professional growth of an individual ultimately contributed to the improvement of the instructional program. As a result of this committee's work, the following procedures for certificate renewal, in addition to the usual ones, were recommended to the State Council on Education, approved by this body, and kept in effect for a number of years:

Complete Special Methods for Renewal, to be undertaken only after careful counseling and the approval of the teacher's immediate supervisor and the State Department Special Committee to be appointed by the State Super-intendent, of which the following are suggestions:

1. Active participation in self-evaluation in preparing for accrediting by a recognized educational agency.
2. Participation in a curriculum revision of major proportions.
3. Participation in an in-service program of recognized importance whether connected with a college or university or independently conducted by the local school.
4. Courses in Human Relations.
5. Courses in Personal Grooming, Social Usage, and Personality.
6. Extended critical attendance and evaluation of musical or art events, movies, or theatrical performances.
7. Extended independent critical evaluation of current printed matter.
8. Acquisition and consistent pursuit of new avocational interests.[27]

Some of the above suggestions may appear bizarre to the reader; however, thoughtful examination of each of them should convince the supervisor that they have a great deal of merit. How many times have teachers been accused of being dull, uninteresting individuals with one-track minds? How many teachers has the reader known who could benefit greatly from a few sessions on personal grooming and/or personality development? What would learning to bowl, swim, or play golf do for

[27]*Certification Rules and Regulations* (Dover: State of Delaware, Department of Public Instruction, Bulletin No. 5–52, February, 1952), p. 22.

Mr. Stout or Miss Plump? How much more interesting might Mr. Flat's elementary-school music program become if he attended a few operas, orchestral concerts, recitals, or even "jam sessions"? What enthusiasm, new ideas, and information can teachers bring back from a tour of Europe or visits to historical landmarks in our own great country?

Working with the Creative Teacher

Interest in the creative individual is a comparatively recent phenomenon. For years the creative child has been ignored and the creative teacher misunderstood. Important recent research and a review of past research indicate that creativity can be discovered and measured. The individual in a supervisory capacity must learn to work with creative teachers and to assist all teachers to work with creative children. In order to do this effectively, he first must learn to recognize the creative individuals. The following characteristics have been attributed to them:

1. They are highly sensitive individuals with a great amount of resourcefulness, flexibility, and willingness to explore new fields.
2. They have unusual capacity to establish rapport with their creative students.
3. They like to tackle difficult tasks, some of which may be beyond their capacity, and, consequently, they may fail at times.
4. They may possess some odd characteristics, refuse to conform, and at times display childish tendencies.
5. They at times may seem discourteous, uncultured, primitive, unsophisticated, and naïve.
6. They are not concerned with being sociable or socially skilled because of their absorption in assisting children to grow and develop.
7. They outwardly may appear bashful, withdrawn, and quiet.
8. They are accustomed to having others laugh at their ideas and, consequently, question the genuineness of the friendly advances of other teachers.
9. They at times may seem haughty and self-satisfied because of their independence in thinking.
10. They frequently appear to be discontented and critical of the *status quo* as a result of their ability to recognize problems and defects. However, they may readily be distinguished from the malcontents because creative teachers always have constructive suggestions for improving the situation.[28]

Because a number of the above characteristics are objectionable to the average individual, the supervisor must assist the creative teacher so that he does not become obnoxious but at the same time retains his creativity.

[28]Adapted from E. Paul Torrance, *Guiding Creative Talent,* © 1962 by Prentice-Hall, Inc., Englewood Cliffs, N.J., pp. 195–96.

The following suggestions given by Stein to creative research chemists so that they would be less obnoxious should prove equally valid for creative teachers:

1. Maintain assertiveness without showing hostility or too much aggressiveness.
2. Become more aware of superiors, peers, and subordinates as persons. Adopt the human touch.
3. Work alone at times, but do not become isolated, withdrawn, or uncommunicative.
4. In school, be congenial but not sociable; outside of school, be sociable but not intimate.
5. "Know your place," but don't appear timid, submissive, or acquiescent, and give your opinions without being domineering.
6. In making a point, be subtle without being cunning or manipulative.
7. In all human relationships, be sincere, honest, purposeful, and diplomatic.
8. Intellectually, be broad without spreading yourself too thin, deep without seeming "bookish" or "too pedagogical," and "sharp" without being overcritical.[29]

In addition to the suggestions that may be given to creative teachers to assist them to become better members of the professional team, the individual who serves in a supervisory position takes the following steps in guiding creative talent:

1. Lets teachers know that he respects creativity and creative teaching.
2. Uses some regular system for obtaining teachers' ideas.
3. Tolerates disagreement with his own ideas.
4. Encourages experimentation.
5. Avoids loading teachers with too many extra duties.
6. Makes it possible to try out new ideas without failure being "fatal."
7. Makes school atmosphere an exciting, adventurous one.
8. Avoids *overemphasis* on teamwork.
9. Holds meetings in which ideas are evaluated honestly.
10. Helps develop sound but exciting ideas from failure experiences.
11. Exposes teachers to the creative work of other teachers.
12. Makes it easy for new teachers to generate new ideas and stimulate the staff.
13. Facilitates communication between teachers in his school and teachers elsewhere working on related problems.
14. Occasionally questions established concepts and practices.
15. Carries on a continuous program of long-range planning.

[29]M. I. Stein, "A Transactional Approach to Creativity," in Calvin W. Taylor (ed.), *The 1955 University of Utah Research Conference on the Identification of Creative Scientific Talent* (Salt Lake City: University of Utah Press, 1956), pp. 176–77, and in Calvin W. Taylor and Frank Barron (eds.), *Scientific Creativity: Its Recognition and Development* (New York: John Wiley & Sons, 1963), p. 224.

16. Recognizes and tries to relieve tension when frustration becomes too severe.
17. Maintains frequent communication with individual teachers but lets them make most decisions alone.[30]

In assisting teachers to improve their procedures for working with creative pupils, the supervisor can help them to adapt many of the procedures suggested for helping creative teachers to the operational level of creative pupils. However, as was true in the case of the supervisor, teachers must be given assistance in learning to recognize and identify pupils with creative talent. Through study they will learn that creative pupils manifest characteristics similar to those mentioned earlier in this section. Consequently, these pupils may be just as obnoxious as creative teachers. Unfortunately, not only do creative pupils offend their peers but, if misunderstood, they annoy their teachers and are rejected by them. Thus, the creative pupil may become a bored, unchallenged student, a discipline problem, or a withdrawn, ineffectual individual. In these days of struggle for our very survival, schools dare not fail to develop the creative talent of our children and youth. To assist teachers in developing creative talent effectively may prove to be one of the supervisor's most important tasks.

Much of the supervisor's time is spent working with problem teachers and assisting teachers with problems. The remainder of this chapter will be devoted to these topics.

Working with Problem Teachers

Teachers, like children, come in assorted sizes, dispositions, personalities, and physiques. They vary greatly in ambition, motivation, state of health, vitality, interest, voice, and any other characteristic you choose to name. There is even a considerable range in their intelligence. The supervisors must recognize these differences and understand each teacher so well that he can help him individually to capitalize on his assets, overcome many of his liabilities, and minimize the remaining ones.

In a fairly comprehensive discussion of teacher personality, Bartky writes:

There are sick teachers and their illnesses do influence their teaching behavior. There are also a very few nonintelligent teachers who make the efforts of

[30]E. Paul Torrance, *Guiding Creative Talent*, p. 206. As adapted from E. Paul Torrance, "The Creative Teacher and the School Team: Problems and Pleasures of the Principal," in *Professional Growth for Principals*, April 1961 (Arthur C. Croft Publications).

their supervisors seem almost futile. There are lonely teachers. There are queer teachers of all types, seclusive, hardboiled, artistic, grouchy, radical, or suspicious. There are frustrated teachers with neurotic doubts, fears, anxieties, obsessions, or compulsions. There are moody teachers, some highly optimistic and some always pessimistic; there are perverse teachers, sadists, masochists, sexual perverts, all suffering from antisocial drives. These teacher personalities each demanding its own therapeutics are the responsibility of the supervisor.[31]

It would be presumptuous to suggest procedures for dealing with the diversified personalities mentioned above; however, there are several types of individuals that a supervisor most certainly will have to work with many times during his professional career. Wiles includes the following teachers in this category: (1) the "lazy" teacher, (2) the "colorless" teacher, (3) the older teacher, (4) the "undemocratic" teacher, and (5) the "disagreeing" teacher.[32]

The "lazy" teacher. The "lazy" teacher has lost the zest for teaching. His satisfactions are being derived from activities outside of his job. The task of the supervisor is to assist this teacher to rediscover the joys and rewards of teaching. The following suggestions for accomplishing this end should prove helpful:

1. Attempt to build the teacher's confidence in himself and pride in his profession through the enlistment of staff members in a total school evaluation program.
2. Include the "lazy" teacher in a professional reading program.
3. Involve "lazy" teachers in the work of the teacher-welfare, self-evaluation, or program-planning committees.
4. Try to interest this type of teacher in some new procedure or action research, as, for example, programmed learning, team teaching, aero-space education, or new trends in his own field. (A summer workshop in the area of the teacher's assignment might do the trick.)

The "colorless" teacher. This type of individual is found teaching on every academic level. Strangely enough, there is something about teaching that attracts the person with the colorless personality. This teacher is drab in appearance and speaks in a monotonous voice. He lacks a sense of humor and is overly conscientious about his work. He follows the school's rules and regulations meticulously. Socially he is withdrawn, and

[31]John A. Bartky, *Supervision as Human Relations* (Boston: D. C. Heath and Company, 1953), pp. 68–69.

[32]The five teacher categories and many of the ideas in this section on "Problem Teachers" have been adapted from Kimball Wiles, *Supervision for Better Schools* 3rd ed. (Englewood Cliffs, N.J.: Prentice-Hall, Inc., © 1967), pp. 124–31. By permission of the publisher.

he is unable to be friendly with his pupils or colleagues. He is a loner.

Assisting this individual to develop a more colorful personality is a difficult assignment. Prerequisite to any personality change is the recognition by the individual of a need for the change. How can a supervisor help this teacher to face the facts of life? The following suggestions have proved to be of value in helping the "colorless" teacher:

1. Involve him in a program of faculty social activities. (Square dances, masquerade parties, and glee clubs are excellent means of releasing participants from their inhibitions.)
2. Assist the teacher in developing an interest in a recreational activity involving groups of individuals. (One school found a faculty dramatics club helpful in this respect.)
3. Encourage the "colorless" teacher to participate in workshop experiences. (A group dynamics or human relations workshop would be particularly valuable.)
4. Encourage the teacher to make tape recordings of his voice and assist him in working out a program of voice culture.
5. Courses in personal grooming and personality development would be valuable here but difficult to recommend to the individual.
6. Assist the teacher in grasping a better understanding of the fact that it is possible to have informality in the classroom without losing the pupils' respect.
7. Encourage the teacher to bring humor into the classroom.

The older teacher. The problem of the older teacher was discussed briefly in this chapter in the section dealing with teacher assignment. However, the authors consider the topic of sufficient importance to elaborate here on other aspects of the problem.

The older teacher is not always an individual who is old in years. Old age comes not only as a result of living but from the way one lives. Some teachers are old at fifty; others remain young after retirement and begin new careers. The discussion here is concerned with teachers who retire on the job. Wiles describes them in this manner:

Some seem to be seeking the easiest way to complete the last few years. They have reached maximum salary and make no attempts to improve their teaching. They have not attended any in-service course or read any of the newer publications in education. Others seem to want to prevent change. They have commitments to certain values which keep them from adapting their courses of study to meet the broad range of abilities present in the modern school. They try to keep the rest of the staff on the right path by attempting to dictate on the basis of seniority.[33]

[33]Wiles, *Supervision for Better Schools,* p. 126.

The following suggestions have been made for dealing with the older teacher:

1. Capitalize on the experience of the older teacher by using his leadership.
2. Provide opportunities for him to share his skills, information, and abilities with the other staff members.
3. Stress the fact that progress results from different types of contributions.
4. Emphasize that the child's needs should be the criteria for judging ideas, not their source.
5. Provide opportunities for younger teachers to work with older teachers but discourage domination by the latter group.
6. Encourage the older teacher to experiment and share his findings with the staff.
7. Fit the teaching schedule to the physical condition of the older teacher.

The reader will recognize that some of the suggestions given for helping the "lazy" teacher also apply here.

The "undemocratic" teacher. It is a strange coincidence that in a democratic society the agency that shapes and is shaped by society is frequently one of our most undemocratic institutions. Although administrators and supervisors must assume some of the blame for this situation, many teachers do not hold democratic values or believe in democracy in educational practice. There are also educators and lay persons who would like to see schools become even less democratic than they are by making them more teacher-centered.

Individuals in a supervisory capacity, then, must be prepared to deal with "undemocratic" teachers. In order to work with them, it is necessary to identify them by their patterns of behavior, which are as follows: The "undemocratic" teacher dominates the classroom completely, and the pupils have no opportunities to participate in classroom management, express their opinions, or plan learning activities. This teacher is the fount of all wisdom and believes that education is the acquisition of knowledge rather than the development of democratic attitudes, skills, and values. In this teacher's classroom, pupils are not given the opportunity to learn to discuss issues and to think for themselves.

In his relationship with the administration, he may expect undemocratic leadership, and he opposes democratic participation of the staff in school administration. On the other hand, he may, through undemocratic procedures, attempt to dominate the decision-making. He frequently becomes the leader of the vociferous minority.

The following suggestions have proved to be helpful in dealing with the "undemocratic" teacher:

1. Examine your own pattern of behavior to ascertain whether or not you are truly democratic in your actions, and encourage others to do likewise.
2. Recognize that some individuals were raised in autocratic homes and were educated in autocratic schools. As a consequence, they do not understand or feel comfortable in democratic situations.
3. Begin "where teachers are" in using the democratic processes. Develop a readiness on their part and encourage small beginnings.
4. Encourage the "undemocratic" teacher to visit (preferably in another school) the classroom of a teacher who is skillful in using democratic procedures.
5. Bring to the staff materials that emphasize democratic practices and individuals who stress democratic values.

The "disagreeing" teacher. In every group of people you find individuals who seem to enjoy disagreeing with others. Irrespective of the point of view expressed, they take the opposite one, regardless of how untenable their position may be. They thrive on argument.

The following suggestions should receive consideration in working with the teacher who disagrees:

1. Recognize that disagreement can be healthy. Without disagreement there would be little discussion, and issues would be decided without sufficient study and consideration.
2. Do not take disagreement as a personal affront. Work as closely with those who disagree as will those who agree.
3. In dealing with the teacher who disagrees, place the professional growth of the teacher above winning an argument.
4. Remember that the teacher might be correct in his viewpoint. Many of the great advances in all fields of knowledge were made because an individual or small minority opposed the majority.

In dealing with problem teachers, the supervisor must remember that each individual is unique. The suggestions that have been made may work in some situations and be ineffective in others. As a student of human nature, the supervisor knows that there are no pat formulas that fit all situations. Much of the time he will be "playing by ear."

Assisting Teachers with Personal Problems

There are only a few problem teachers in each school, but all teachers have problems. Like all other human beings, teachers have financial problems, marital difficulties, and worries about their offspring. They become ill, lose loved ones, run afoul of the law, and suffer from disasters of various types. Any of the vicissitudes of life are bound in some way to affect the quality of teaching. Some few individuals become stronger and better individuals as a result of these experiences; others may be defeated by them. Although some supervisors may be reluctant to become involved in the solution of teachers' personal problems, those who do know that the results are infinitely rewarding. Some of the best supervision may be done through these channels.

Teachers want a supervisor who cares. The writer learned this fact early in his career as a supervisor. When he requested teachers to make an anonymous rating of the supervisory services, a number of them suggested that the supervisor should show more interest in the personal lives of teachers. They accused him of never discussing anything but educational matters with them. One teacher expressed the sentiment of the group when he wrote: "Make conferences pleasant occasions in which pleasant topics are discussed. Learn to know the teacher as a friend at such times. Forget school once in a while."

As a result of experience, the authors believe that good personnel administration and supervision require that administrators and supervisors show interest in teachers' personal problems and assist in their solutions whenever it is possible. However, good rapport must exist between the supervisor or administrator and the teacher before this type of assistance is welcome or even approved. After rapport has been established, some teachers will come to the supervisor for help with personal problems. If a feeling of mutual respect does not exist, any assistance offered to the teacher may be misconstrued as meddling in affairs that are of no concern to the supervisor.

Supervisors who believe that helping teachers with their personal problems is an important part of their job have assisted in many different ways. In the experience of the writers, the following situations have arisen and some assistance has been rendered: helping teachers out of debt, matchmaking, testifying for a teacher wrongly accused, arranging for funerals of loved ones, locating living quarters, comforting them in time of grief or illness, and assisting them with problems concerning their children or spouse.

Sometimes all that teachers need is the sympathetic ear of someone who is interested in them personally and can be depended upon to keep in confidence what he has heard.

SUMMARY

In their efforts to improve instruction, individuals serving in a supervisory capacity spend a large segment of their time working with individuals. In order to do this most effectively, they utilize the following techniques to assist teachers in their personal and professional growth: assignment of teachers, classroom visitation and observation, classroom experimentation, enrollment in college courses, conferences with teachers, demonstration teaching, microteaching, evaluation, professional activities and conferences, professional reading, professional writing, selection of textbooks and other instructional materials, selection of professional staff, supervisory bulletins, informal contacts, and other experiences that may in any way contribute to the improvement of the teacher as a person.

In working with individuals, the supervisor becomes more sensitive to the fact that teachers differ from each other in many ways. He is particularly anxious to assist creative teachers to realize their greatest potential. He also realizes how important it is to assist all teachers to work more effectively with creative children. Finally, he learns to work with problem teachers and to become interested in the problems of teachers. As a result, these individuals benefit greatly from their association with him.

SUGGESTED ACTIVITIES AND PROBLEMS

1. Secure permission to visit three classrooms when the teachers and pupils are not present. Carefully examine the physical environment and look for signs of learning activities as suggested in this chapter. Write a description of the learning environment and indicate the kinds of learning that you believe take place in each classroom, giving the reasons for your tentative conclusions. Check your tentative conclusions by observing the teacher in action or interviewing the teacher, or both.
2. Secure permission to observe a teacher make a large-group presentation under the team teaching plan of organization. Interview the teacher to find out his objectives and purposes for the lesson and the procedures he used in preparing for it. Interview three pupils and secure their reactions to the lesson. On the basis of this information, make recommendations for improving the lesson.
3. Collect five supervisory bulletins and evaluate them on the basis of the nine criteria and suggestions concerning mechanical details given in this chapter. Select the poorest of the five bulletins and rewrite it so that it meets the criteria and suggestions for mechanical details.
4. Write a detailed case study of a "lazy," "colorless," or "undemocratic" teacher, illustrating the forces, experiences, and circumstances that may have contributed to developing this type of teacher. Using dialogue freely, describe how you would assist this individual to grow personally and professionally.
5. Interview several teachers to determine whether or not they are aware of creative talent in their pupils. Try to find out what procedures they use in working with these creative pupils.
6. Read several references on microteaching and then prepare a ten minute

lesson on any topic to present to a group of five students. The purpose of the lesson should be to perfect one of the nine technical skills listed in the section on microteaching. Video-tape or audio-tape the lesson and criticize the playback. Repeat the cycle with a different group of students. Write up your reaction to the experience.

SELECTED READINGS

Allen, Dwight, and Ryan, Kevin. *Microteaching*. Reading, Mass.: Addison-Wesley Publishing Company, Inc., 1969.

Amidon, Edmund J., and Flanders, Ned A. *The Role of the Teacher in the Classroom*. Minneapolis, Minn.: Paul S. Amidon and Associates, 1963.

Bartky, John A. *Supervision as Human Relations*. Chaps. 4, 5, 6, 8, 10, and 12. Boston: D. C. Heath and Company, 1953.

Bradford, Luther E. *Supervision for Modern Elementary Schools*. Chap. 2. Columbus, Ohio: Charles E. Merrill Books, Inc., 1964.

Curtin, James. *Supervision in Today's Elementary Schools*. Chaps. 4 and 5. New York: The Macmillan Company, 1964.

Guidelines for Textbook Selection. Report of the Joint Committee of the National Education Association and the American Textbook Publishers Institute. Washington, D.C.: NEA, 1967.

Gwynn, J. Minor. *Theory and Practice of Supervision*. Chaps. 3, 14, and 16. New York: Dodd, Mead and Company, 1961.

Hicks, Hanne J. *Educational Supervision in Principle and Practice*. Chaps. 3, 4, 5, 6, and 7. New York: The Ronald Press Company, 1960.

Stoops, Emery, and Marks, James R. *Elementary School Supervision*. Chaps. 11 and 12. Boston, Mass.: Allyn & Bacon, Inc., 1965.

Torrance, E. Paul. *Guiding Creative Talent*. Chap. 10. Englewood Cliffs, N.J.: Prentice-Hall, Inc., 1962.

Wiles, Kimball. *Supervision for Better Schools*. 3rd ed., Chap. 7. Englewood Cliffs, N.J.: Prentice-Hall, Inc., 1967.

chapter 9

Working with Groups to Improve Instruction

It is the purpose of this chapter to identify ways of working with professional groups to improve the instructional program. By definition, *group supervisory techniques* are those which involve the administrators and supervisors with a number of staff members, ranging from a grade-level committee of two teachers to the total teaching staff at times. Certain procedures aimed at the improvement of instruction can best be initiated and carried out through group interaction which involves the sharing of experiences, ideas, and the findings of educational research. Dynamic, democratic leadership and effective human relations, as discussed in Chapter I, are prerequisites to success in group techniques. Each staff member must be encouraged to play a significant and cooperative role in the evaluation and improvement of the teaching-learning situations in the school district.

GROUP TECHNIQUES

As discussed in Chapter VIII, some supervisory methods may be considered either individual or group. The following have been identified by the authors as group techniques and are discussed in this chapter: orientation of new teachers, action research, development of professional libraries, visiting other teachers, coordination of student teaching, cooperative development of the testing program, implementing new organizational patterns, conducting effective faculty meetings, and interpretation of the instructional program to the public.

Since in-service education often includes many of the techniques listed above and is usually a group-oriented activity, a discussion of the organization of in-service programs of various types is included in this chapter.

Important leadership notes. The following suggestions are offered to supervisors who desire to be most effective in the implementation of group supervisory techniques.

1. Be sensitive to the importance of group dynamics and interaction. The successful supervisor will have had several courses and considerable experience in the group approach to problem solving and cooperative action.
2. Always help the group to identify with reasonable and attainable goals.
3. Be honest, open, and straightforward in working with fellow staff members.

Orientation of New Teachers

Every school district needs a comprehensive, continuing program for the orientation of new staff. There are several compelling reasons for this:

1. The turnover of teachers in most school systems is substantial.
2. Any person, and especially a teacher, identifies more easily and confidently with his role expectation if he has the opportunity to learn a great deal about the position and its setting.
3. Evaluation of successful teacher-orientation programs attests to their ultimate value in helping to develop a strong, competent professional staff.

The following basic topics and guiding principles have been suggested for program planners:

1. *Approach*—Orientation programs should use an *individualized* and *flexible* approach, keeping in mind both the characteristics and needs of new and beginning teachers and the school district's local conditions.

2. *Scope*—Orientation programs should be *comprehensive* in terms of needs and involve the cooperation and participation of a wide variety of persons and agencies.

3. *Timing*—Orientation programs should begin with the *first contact,* have a high degree of *continuity* over an extended period of time, and be a permanent part of the *in-service training program.*

4. *Evaluation*—Orientation programs should be *evaluated* annually for effectiveness and *revised.*[1]

In the planning of orientation programs it is essential to recognize that there are several categories of new teachers:

[1]*Orientation Programs for Teachers,* Research Memo 1964–24, NEA Research Division (Washington, D.C.: National Education Association of the United States, July 1964), p. 2.

(a) the beginning or inexperienced teacher who has never taught on a full-time basis before.

(b) the experienced teacher who is either new to the school district, having served elsewhere, or returning to teaching after a break in career. Other teachers in need of various phases of the orientation program are the experienced teacher reassigned to another school in the same system or reassigned to a new department or level of teaching.[2]

Obviously, teachers in these categories have varying needs. The orientation program, therefore, does need to be individualized and flexible. The following planning principles may help:

1. Human relations, as always, are most important. It is necessary for supervisors and administrators to be understanding, sympathetic, cooperative, and friendly.
2. Experienced teachers should be involved in planning, but should be compensated if they return early in the school term to participate in the orientation sessions.
3. Orientation is a continuous process, not a "one shot" program. However, the early emphasis will be on adjustment to the problems and concerns which the teacher must face immediately.
4. The orientation plan should be comprehensive but not overwhelming. If the new teacher gets too many regulations, booklets, and suggestions, for example, she will remember very little.
5. Each principal should have the new teachers in his building evaluate the orientation program by the end of the first semester. Many helpful suggestions for improvement will be forthcoming.
6. As indicated later in this chapter, special in-service programs for new teachers should be arranged.

A comprehensive list of planning suggestions has been compiled by the American Association of School Administrators. The superintendent or the supervisor designated by him to coordinate the teacher-orientation program can select activities from this list which meet the needs of the new teachers in his district.

Understanding Terms and Conditions of Employment
1. Include full description of job with announcement of vacancy and application forms.
2. Take time for complete and honest discussion of job during interview.
3. Give full explanation of salary, certification, benefits, assignment (as nearly as can be determined), and other terms of employment at time contract is offered.
4. Review regulations governing rights, privileges, and restrictions at time of reporting and later as questions arise.

[2] *Ibid.*

Becoming Acquainted with the Community

1. Enclose description of community with announcements and application forms.

2. Take time for more information and questions during interview.

3. Arrange for visit to community before hiring or between employment and reporting time.

4. Acquaint teacher with facilities for transportation, banking, shopping, and medical, dental, and other personal services.

5. Prepare and put in teachers' hands listings of housing, with descriptive information.

6. Arrange tours of the community to become acquainted with its business, cultural, and educational activities, for personal reasons and for teaching background.

7. See that invitations are extended to attend and take part in civic, religious, social, cultural, and recreational activities.

8. Enlist the help of organizations in arranging special events for introducing new teachers.

Getting to Know School System, Its People, and Its Organization

1. Provide information about organization of school system at time application is made and during interviews.

2. Furnish copies of rules and regulations, statements about policies, philosophy, and practices. (A number of school systems incorporate this and other information into a handbook for distribution.)

3. Describe help available, such as teaching materials, supervisory assistance, and special services.

4. Place copies of courses of study, textbook lists, and similar materials in hands of incoming teacher.

5. Put new teacher on mailing list for all bulletins, newsletters, and other publications sent to teachers.

6. Arrange for correspondence by superintendent, principal, supervisors, and fellow teachers prior to reporting.

7. See that new teachers meet and talk with superintendent.

8. Schedule conferences with supervisors and other staff personnel responsible for services to teachers prior to opening of school.

Learning About the School to Which Assigned

1. Take teacher on tour of building for becoming acquainted with layout and facilities.

2. Arrange meetings with building principal to learn about obtaining supplies and equipment, keeping records, making reports, handling problems of classroom management and organization, and the other details of school operation.

3. Assign an experienced teacher as a personal counselor and adviser.

4. See that there is time for getting acquainted with other members of the faculty and staff.

5. Allot time to work professionally with faculty in meetings before school opens.

6. Acquaint the new teacher with her professional organizations.

Adjusting to the Teaching Job

1. Set aside time of principal and supervisors to help in planning work,

locating sources of materials, handling problems of classroom organization and management, making pupil evaluations, and preparing reports.

2. Make time freely available for talking over problems as they arise in private conferences with principal, supervisors, and others, as often as either party feels the need.

3. Assist the new teacher in getting to know pupils and parents.

4. Arrange opportunities for viewing demonstrations and observing experienced teachers at work.

5. Schedule meetings of new teachers for discussion of their own special problems.

6. See that the new teacher is given a reasonable and fair teaching load, commensurate with her training, skills, and experience.

7. Provide opportunities for continuing and expanding professional preparation begun in college, by offering in-service education activities specially designed to help new teachers.[3]

Additional suggestions for organizing and carrying out orientation programs may be found in the following publication: *Orientation Programs for Teachers*, Research Memo 1964–24, NEA Research Division, National Education Association of the United States, 1201 Sixteenth Street, Northwest, Washington, D.C.

Action Research

This term has been subject to many definitions in the literature. To some writers, a teacher who tries out new programmed learning materials with a group of pupils is conducting action research. To others, an experiment must be carefully set up and controlled, involving equated groups of pupils and an adequate sample, in order for it to qualify as action research.

There is considerable agreement that much more research should be conducted in the public school classroom, since here is the crucible where the findings of laboratory experimentation should meet the practical situations of the classroom teacher. Several obstacles, however, have retarded the development of significant research projects in many of the nation's schools.

1. Many administrators and supervisors, because of their limited training, experience, or vision, fail to appreciate the gains to education that can result from properly conducted studies. Some are afraid to have teachers engage in activities that might upset the *status quo*.

2. Teachers often lack the time, the interest, or the specialized abilities required for research in the classroom.

3. The loose concepts of action research held by some educators have resulted in a negative reaction by others.

[3]American Association of School Administrators, *Off To A Good Start: Teacher Orientation* (Washington, D.C.: National Education Association, 1956), pp. 11–15.

Definition of the term. Corey says,

Probably the most important characteristic that differentiates action research from more casual inquiry is that evidence is systematically sought, recorded, and interpreted. This is done to find out more definitely just what the problem is as well as to learn what happens when certain procedures are used to deal with it. Every kind of research involves accumulating and interpreting evidence, but action research focuses on evidence that helps answer the question, Did a particular action result in the desirable consequences that were anticipated?[4]

According to Franseth,

In action research in education, the researchers are usually teachers, curriculum workers, principals, supervisors, directors of instruction, or others whose main function is to help provide good learning experiences for pupils. The hypotheses or theories are tested by the teacher in the classroom, the consultant in a curriculum study group, or some other educator in a practical situation. If, however, an on-the-job research project is not conducted under carefully controlled conditions, or if it is conducted only in a single classroom, the findings must be applied to other situations with extreme caution. . . . All types of research—basic, pure applied, or action—have one characteristic in common: all imply studious inquiry, systematic investigation, and a careful search for truth.

The scientific principles of research are the same for all kinds of research: a problem is defined; a systematic method of collecting, organizing, and analyzing data is adopted; generalizations are made on the basis of the evidence collected; the results are used to guide future action or to improve practice.[5]

Action research, then, is carefully planned and controlled research in the classroom, which can be one of the best laboratories for the discovery of means to improve instruction.

Procedures for initiating and carrying out action research. If the administrator or supervisor is convinced of the possibilities of research in school situations, the following steps are suggested:

1. Using the techniques discussed in Chapters I and VII of this handbook, continue to develop a climate that will free staff members to participate actively in group projects and to consider change.
2. Through group processes, decide on tentative areas for research, for example: "A Study of Certain Programmed Learning Materials in Modern Elementary Arithmetic." At this stage, an educational research professor

[4]Stephen M. Corey, *Action Research to Improve School Practices* (New York: Bureau of Publications, Teachers College, Columbia University, 1953), p. 26.
[5]Jane Franseth, "Improving the Curriculum and Teaching Through Action Research," *School Life*, XLII, no. 4 (December, 1959), 8–9.

from a nearby college or university could be helpful in selecting areas for study.

3. Seek professional help in structuring the research project according to approved methods. All interested teachers and supervisors should be involved.

Davison has outlined the following steps in action research and the methods of accomplishing them.

Steps in Action Research	*Methods of Accomplishing These Steps*
1. There must be a clear need for the proposed research activity so that the staff involved can see why and how the study may directly help them.	1. The research coordinator must do some pre-study but must not act like an expert. A series of definite examples of the school problems should be presented for review by the school staff so that the participants can grasp the need for the study and then focus on the most essential elements to be included in their study. If there are no crisis problems a survey of the teachers' problems can give a starting point. The staff must know that the research will be sincere, and that they will have the opportunity to evaluate the whole outcome and make their contributions willingly rather than on the basis of pressure.
2. The problem and subordinate problems must be clearly defined with realistic limitations of such a nature that the research becomes actually feasible in that situation.	2. There must be review and restatements of the problems periodically. This enables the staff to look at the need and the stated problem to see if these are in harmony so that they will personally defend the choice of research problem.
3. The literature on the subject should be reviewed to help set the design of the proposed study. What methods have a chance for success? What curricular units are teachable? What do other current and prior research findings tell us that will assist us?	3. Assignments to review the literature and make group reports should be based on the individual interests of the staff members. School planning time, and if possible paid travel and materials, should be provided. The work should not be hurried, but there should be periodic checks on reading progress and staff morale. Reassignments may be necessary and deadlines may be required. The reports should be properly received and respected by all participants.
4. The procedure of the study requires initial and final evaluation so that effect or progress can be determined.	4. The instruments of evaluation can have many forms: Pupil rating scales, teacher rating scales, achievement

Steps in Action Research	*Methods of Accomplishing These Steps*
The measures used must be designed to enable the acceptance or rejection of hypotheses at the end of the study.	tests, judged projects with score cards, problem check sheets, inventories, projective techniques, internal and external criteria, case studies and follow-ups. The instruments used must be checked against the objectives of the hypotheses investigated with evaluation as to the procedure's effectiveness.
5. Part of the procedure will include progress reports so that the whole group of investigators can keep in touch with the study. Incorrect or misunderstood procedures that might lead to confusion at a later date should be cleared up.	5. This, with the design of the instruments above, is one of the difficult parts of the research. The administration needs to be alert to the need for group meetings. It is better for the research group to have many short meetings which clear the air immediately than to expose the teachers with the content and frustrations of long meetings.
6. Record keeping is the history of the evidence. The data and the notes from the meetings are both gathered. Materials are distributed and a schedule of events maintained. Diaries and classroom journals may be needed. All things issued to the participants should be ample so that steps can be retraced and all activities can be gathered into the retelling of the study.	6. One person should be delegated to keep track of where the study is and where it is going. In order to do this, ample clerical help and time are necessities.
7. Data analysis is the process of discovering possible meaning and principles in the evidence gathered. The interpretation of the data should be absolutely clear and should arrive after much reflection by the participants.	7. Graphs, flow charts, statistical comparisons, verbal evidence organized by some logic, and thoughts checked against criteria may form the basis for analysis. Data can be classified by logical groupings. Age, ability, interest, and experience groupings often point up the sense or usefulness of the data.
8. Conclusions for the research should accept or reject the hypotheses set up. The major problem of the study should be answered. A written and an oral report of the study should be given by the research group to the public or the school board.	8. There will need to be review and writing sessions on the part of the research team.
9. The written recommendations of such a report should have the unqualified endorsement of the research team. The recommendations should be put into operation in the school system according to a schedule agreed upon by the research staff and the school administration.	9. Conferences will be needed between the administration and the research team. It is possible that the board will require a private hearing before a public announcement of the results.

Davison concluded:

If there is to be a revolution in educational research, it should come from the classroom teacher and the curriculum specialist. There are several reasons for this. The professional personnel have the basic tools for research: the children, the materials, and a large accumulation of experience with children in a school setting.[6]

Important leadership notes. Administrators and supervisors will have increasing opportunities for their schools and teachers to participate in research projects initiated by the large, regional educational laboratories that have been established with Title IV, ESEA funds. Almost every school in the nation is located in an area served by one of these research labs. Pilot schools, teachers, and classrooms are often sought to carry out the action part of research projects. The supervisor in charge of such activities in a school district should visit the headquarters of the regional laboratory serving his area to learn about current research and the opportunities to become a participant.

Colleges of education in universities are increasingly interested in joining with schools to plan and carry out research in various areas of the curriculum and teaching methods. Someone often has to take the initiative to get such joint efforts underway. The school supervisor might plan a conference with the dean or some other appropriate official at a nearby college or university, to explore the possibilities of action research projects.

Development of Professional Libraries

A most important supervisory technique is the establishment and maintenance of extensive professional libraries. Teachers should have readily available at both the building and the district level a wide selection of up-to-date books.

Certain books, because of the need for frequent referral, will be much more effective if they are available in the building library. General education books and those which would be of interest on occasion to individuals and groups will normally be housed in the district professional library.

Some districts will have full-time librarians to handle the curriculum center and main professional library. In any event, it is essential that

[6]Used by permission of Dr. Hugh M. Davison, Professor of Educational Research, Pennsylvania State University. From address to Department of Supervision and Curriculum Development, Pennsylvania State Education Association, November, 1961.

responsibility for the maintenance and distribution of these books be assigned to one of the district librarians. All staff members should be made aware of the volumes available and the procedures for using them.

At the building level, the school librarian, if there is one, should have charge of the professional books.

The coordinators of elementary and secondary education, the supervisors of special subject areas, and department heads may want to build up their own collections of specialized books in addition to the district and building libraries.

The following suggestions are designed to help the supervisor in establishing and maintaining professional libraries.

1. A general administrator or supervisor should be given responsibility for the central district library.
2. Each principal should coordinate with his staff and librarian, if any, the acquisition, placement, and distribution of the books in his building.
3. All staff members should be urged to suggest new titles for the several collections, and to join in the evaluation of new books.
4. A substantial sum must be budgeted each year to allow for the addition of current titles.
5. Potential usage of a book should determine its placement in the district.
6. A section of the district professional library could be set aside for certain types of curriculum materials.

Visiting Other Teachers

Intervisitation is one of the most neglected yet promising techniques for improving instruction. All teachers can profit from observing master teachers at work. The beginner can learn how to organize a classroom, how to manage a group of pupils, and how to plan effectively. The weak teacher can often be helped through observation of class management, good methods, and utilization of resources in his field. Even the master teacher can share ideas with another outstanding colleague, and through this experience the classes of both will be enriched.

Careful planning must precede any visitation program. The district administrative council should develop, through its regular democratic procedures, a visitation policy. Such questions as these must be answered:

1. What are the purposes of staff intervisitation?
2. Should one or two days per year be established in the calendar for visitation by all professional personnel? Or should substitute teachers be hired during the year to permit flexibility in visits? (Some districts hire permanent substitutes for this purpose and for regular substitute teaching.)
3. Should all staff members participate in the program, or only certain persons, such as new teachers and those with special problems?

4. Should visitation be planned inside and outside the district?
5. Where can skillful teachers in the various subject areas and at all grade levels be found? Each principal will, of course, be able to identify some of his own teachers for a district list. All administrative and supervisory personnel must use considerable discretion in the preparation and execution of a plan for visiting within the district. Some experienced teachers will feel hurt or rejected if they are omitted.

Important leadership notes. The following ideas may help in building up a file of outstanding teachers in other districts.

1. All administrators and supervisors should use their contacts in principals' associations, curriculum study groups, and other organizations to identify master teachers in various fields.
2. The principals or the coordinators of elementary and secondary education can write to their counterparts in good school districts, requesting the names of teachers with certain identifiable skills. Don't ask for "your best teachers." Rather, make a specific request, for example, "a teacher who excels in social studies unit work at the intermediate level," or "one who uses the CHEMS course in senior high school chemistry."
3. A card file can be maintained in each principal's or coordinator's office, listing superior teachers skilled in various techniques and subjects, both inside and outside the district.

Other suggestions on implementing a plan for intervisitation are:

1. Administrators and supervisors should plan to join their teachers on some classroom visits. Then follow-up discussions can be held back at school.
2. Standards and procedures for visiting should be established.
   A. Visitors should not interrupt class activities or speak to pupils without consent of the teacher.
   B. All classroom visits should be a full period or lesson in duration.[7]
   C. Visitors usually see the principal for orientation before entering the classrooms.
3. Experienced teachers should be encouraged to visit levels other than the ones they teach. It is most important that elementary teachers observe high school classes, and vice versa.

Many positive outcomes of intervisitation both inside and outside a district have been reported.[8]

1. Ideas for new teaching methods are shared.
2. Greater appreciation and understanding of other teachers and children result, especially when visiting a different level.

[7]Audrey M. Borth, George K. McGuire, Illa E. Podendorf, and James P. Rose, "Visiting Other Teachers in Your School: A Basis for Communication," *Elementary School Journal*, LVIII, no. 6 (March, 1958), 331–34.
[8]*Ibid.*

3. Specific goals may be achieved, such as learning the methods of handling pupils in team teaching.
4. Visiting staff members gain a broader understanding of the whole learning process in going beyond their own classrooms and schools. Too many professional educators get into a comfortable rut. Intervisitation raises sights and expands horizons in a healthy way if the program is carefully planned.

Coordination of Student or Intern Teaching in a District

It is the responsibility of schools located near a teacher-training institution to take student teachers or interns, if asked to do so. An increasing number of good classroom experiences must be made available to students as they move from educational theory into the practicalities of teaching a group of pupils. Prospective teachers should have opportunities to observe in their first and second college years, and should engage in real teaching experiences through the third and fourth years.

The alert supervisor realizes that a student teaching program is not a one-way street. Many advantages accrue to the receiving district that reflect themselves in an improved instructional program.

1. First of all, master teachers who agree to serve as student supervisors usually do an even better job in the classroom. They are often eager to assist a novice in the profession and to share their experiences.
2. The entire climate of the school can be enhanced by the freshness and vitality of the interns. Their knowledge of current theory and their earnest desire to succeed in the profession can often stimulate average teachers more successfully than a number of techniques employed by the principal or coordinator. Enthusiasm is contagious.
3. While they will not always admit it, experienced teachers often learn new methods and approaches from students who have had the benefit of the latest research at college.
4. The district becomes known as a development center for the profession, as the interns leave to enter successful careers in teaching.

Procedures for accepting and training student teachers must be carefully developed. A handbook or duplicated pamphlet is suggested to summarize all important aspects of the intern program. The administrative council should prepare guidelines to be followed by all schools. Teachers would be consulted as the policy evolves. The following areas need clarification:

1. Are supervising teachers to be paid, and by whom? The trend is toward payment by the college, and at times by the receiving district.

2. By what criteria are supervising teachers to be selected? Here are some suggestions:
   A. Must be an above-average teacher with at least three years' experience in the public schools, one of which has been in the present district.
   B. Only volunteers should be accepted; no one should be asked to take a student against his will.
   C. The building principal has final authority in approving supervising teachers.

To implement the program, principals and coordinators should meet with the designated officials from the teacher education institution to work out cooperatively the assignment of students to supervising teachers.

The principal and teachers of a school should welcome interns as fellow staff members. In every sense they are regarded as a part of the team. Gone are the days when student teachers were considered clerical aides and servants in the classroom. As quickly as possible, the interns are encouraged to become familiar with the school and their specific teaching-learning situations. The skillful master teachers then lead them steadily into more and more responsibility with classes of pupils. From the beginning, student teachers should be peers of the supervising teachers in the eyes of the pupils.

The principal will sometimes be confronted with the lazy teacher who likes to have an intern so he can loaf on the job. Of course, there will be other evidences of such an attitude. Needless to say, teachers who do not want to make the necessary effort to become good supervisors should not be given student teachers.

On occasion, older teachers will resent student interns in the school much as they are irritated by the new young teacher on the staff. The reason is usually jealousy, insecurity, or fear of change. The skillful principal will handle these situations through the practice of sensible human relations. The confidence of the older teacher must be maintained while the student teacher is given every opportunity to become a member of the team while he is there.

Cooperative Evaluation and Development of the Testing Program

Since tests represent one means of measuring the impact of the instructional program on pupils, they are a legitimate concern of the supervisor in the modern school. Testing programs today often are nonexistent, chaotic, or overburdening to students. In some districts, no attempt has been made to develop logical series of tests in the various areas of the curriculum. The result often is confusion, with each principal or teacher following his own program. Some pupils may receive no standardized tests; others may have a reasonable number. In other systems, test has been piled upon test over the years until pupils and teachers alike stagger under the weight of an unwieldy, inefficient, and overlapping program. Many school districts, of course, have tried to control the growth of their tests patterns, keeping pace with the findings of research and curriculum development.

Here is a step-by-step process to enable administrators and supervisors to evaluate their present achievement testing programs and to formulate balanced and effective plans for the future.

1. The suggestion to examine the present testing program is placed on the agenda of the district administrative council for discussion.

2. Each principal then works with his own staff to identify the standardized and teacher-made tests now in general use throughout the district. If this compilation has not been done recently, the length and variety of the list will be surprising.

3. The district or county school psychologist or a testing expert from a nearby college or university should now be involved for consultation. Outdated, unreliable, or invalid tests should be eliminated immediately.

4. Considering the present curriculum in each subject area, the psychologist, supervisors, and teachers can begin to look for those standardized tests which most nearly measure the objectives of the courses of study. Some of those presently used will be retained as suitable. The programs from the various test producers can now be examined in light of the desired pupil outcomes.

Important leadership note. Tests should always be selected after the curriculum has been developed. Otherwise, there is a tendency to conform the course of study to the tests.

5. The achievement testing program must be planned in relation to the other tests administered in the district, such as those in aptitude and ability. Standardized testing should be spaced throughout the school year and be well balanced from kindergarten through high school. Above all, there should not be too many tests. Other methods of evaluation are just as important.

6. There should be many opportunities for teacher-made tests. Some of these may be adapted for use by more than one teacher. Others would be used once for a particular group of pupils. All available instruments should be listed if they might be helpful to a number of teachers.

7. The final list of tests should be continually revised as the curriculum changes from year to year. Pupil learning patterns are never static, and a testing program must always measure as accurately as possible desired pupil behavior. In this statement we see the danger of overemphasis on

tests. Learning is a highly individual and complex matter. Any attempt to measure it will be grossly inaccurate. Our best tests merely sample the body of knowledge they purport to cover. In the proper perspective, achievement testing can add to our knowledge of the pupil and his progress. Tests, therefore, should be used but not abused as a supervisory technique.

Important leadership note. An overemphasis on the results of standardized tests and their relationship to teacher effectiveness can adversely affect teacher morale. It cannot be assumed that Miss Jones is not teaching arithmetic well just because her class median is below the national norm. Supervisors who look over test scores as an indicator of teaching success should be cognizant of the many other elements that must be considered, such as pupil ability, previous achievement, and other evidences of progress in learning.

Two research studies on elementary and secondary standardized testing programs offer additional guidance to the supervisor.[9]

Initiating and Carrying Out New Organizational Patterns

While mainly administrative in nature, the newer plans of organization, such as the nongraded school and team teaching, are being adopted to facilitate instruction. Consequently, they are of vital concern to the supervisor who is primarily interested in the improvement of learning opportunities in the instructional environment.

Supervisory personnel should be involved in each planning step as new organizational plans are introduced. For example, if the decision to inaugurate team teaching has been made in a district, the following steps are indicated to insure success of the instructional program.

1. The assistant superintendent in charge of instruction or the coordinator of elementary or secondary education usually would coordinate the planning. In the small district, the chief school official probably would direct the change.
2. The supervisory responsibilities of the following persons must be determined so that line organization is clear: the team teaching coordinator, the principal, and the team leader.

[9]William F. Nye, "A Study of Standardized Test Programs in Selected Public Secondary Schools of Pennsylvania and the Attitudes of Secondary Classroom Teachers of Selected Subjects Toward Standardized Test Practices" (Doctoral dissertation, Temple University, 1962); John W. O'Brien, "Standard Test Programs of Selected Public Elementary Schools in Pennsylvania and the Attitudes of Elementary Classroom Teachers Toward Certain Standardized Test Practices" (Doctoral dissertation, Temple University, 1962).

3. Team leaders and master teachers are identified and trained for their roles.
4. Each teaching team must be well balanced, considering the experience and major preparation of every teacher.
5. As the teams are organized and begin to plan, it is essential that some supervisory official attend every team meeting.
6. The principal works with all team leaders in his school to integrate the evolving instructional program. Experiments have shown that teams of teachers planning together actually evaluate and develop the curriculum as they proceed through the school year. It is imperative that the principal be a part of this supervisory activity.
7. If team teaching is being introduced at the same level in more than one school in a district, then the assistant superintendent or the general supervisor or coordinator must work with all principals and team leaders simultaneously.

In the introduction of any new organizational pattern, job descriptions must be outlined by the chief school official and the district administrative council to guide the staff and to assure continuity in the supervision of the instructional program. The table of organization should be clear in its designation of line authority and yet flexible enough to permit the most cooperative working relationships among staff members. As indicated in Chapter I, these are the most important ingredients in an effective supervisory program.

Conducting Effective Faculty Meetings

Teachers in several large cities, dissatisfied with the length and format of their faculty meetings, have demanded in recent years that their union negotiate conditions under which the principal may schedule and conduct meetings with the faculty. One school board-union contract even specified that principals may not read notices to the teachers during meetings.

Research has shown that teacher dissatisfaction with faculty meetings is no new phenomenon. Blumberg and Amidon reported the following research findings in 1962:

1. That teachers take a rather dim view of their faculty meetings as a use of time and energy.
2. That attitudes toward faculty meetings tend to parallel more general feelings about the school and its faculty; that is, the more negative the attitude toward the faculty meeting, the more negative the feelings about school as a whole, and *vice versa.*
3. That the critical variable accounting for differences in teacher attitudes from school to school seems to be the principal's behavior as reflected in the pattern of faculty meeting interaction, as that is perceived by the teacher. More positive attitudes are associated with faculty-centered interaction (the locus of responsibility and control being with the faculty); more negative

attitudes are related to principal-centered interaction (the locus of responsibility and control resting with the principal).[10]

Further research by Blumberg and Amidon indicated that teachers and principals have very different views about the value of faculty meetings. For example, in a survey of teachers and their principals, the following question was asked, "What is your general reaction to faculty meetings in your school?" Teachers saw them as being close to a "waste of time." On the other hand, the satisfaction of principals with faculty meetings was rather high. They viewed the meetings as an "effective use of time and energy."[11]

This research study and others show the need for more effective communication and interaction between the principal and his teachers. Faculty members must know that their views are sought and respected, or they will not take a meaningful part in meetings. A principal who espouses free discussion, but is then critical or defensive in his faculty meeting, will discourage real honest participation by teachers.

The implications are clear for the principal who would use the faculty meeting as an effective supervisory technique.

1. Teachers should be involved in planning the agenda and in preparing items for discussion.
2. Leadership should be rotated in the group.
3. A time limit must be set and adhered to strictly. Meetings of course are to be scheduled within the "teacher day" as defined by district policy.
4. The contributions of all faculty members are viewed as worthy of consideration. The principal and teachers need to understand and practice the basic principles of group dynamics and effective interaction.
5. If the group members lack training and experience in real interaction, the principal might invite an expert from a nearby university to conduct several sessions on the techniques of working together, sharing leadership, respecting the views of others, etc.
6. Topics of vital concern to the faculty, such as proposed new curriculums, nongrading in the high school, or summer workshop planning, should be given priority. Routine matters ought to be eliminated from the agenda; these can be handled by administrative bulletin.

In planning for effective faculty meetings, the principal is the key figure. His attitude, personality, and leadership ability will make the difference between dull, unproductive sessions and scintillating meetings that release the potential of all willing participants.

[10]Arthur Blumberg and Edmund Amidon, "A Comparison of Teacher and Principal Attitudes Toward Faculty Meetings," *The Bulletin of the National Association of Secondary School Principals*, XLVIII, no. 290 (1964), 45.
[11]*Ibid.*, p. 49.

Interpretation of the Instructional Program to the Public

Without public acceptance of a school district's philosophy and curriculum, the finest supervisory program will be of little value. Therefore, all administrators and supervisors need to be vitally concerned with public relations as an aspect of the improvement of instruction.

The coordinator of secondary education and his teachers may be convinced that a new approach to mathematics is highly desirable in the senior high school. The superintendent may be prepared to recommend new courses and materials of instruction to the board of education. But the parent and other interested citizens of the community must also be prepared for this change. Indeed, they should be involved in it to some extent. Through P.T.A. discussions, citizens' council meetings, news releases, educational television programs, and service club talks, to mention a few, the newer research in high school mathematics could be presented in language that lay persons can understand. In other words, through an effective public relations program, improvements in the curriculum and funds to support them are made possible.

Several excellent guides to successful public relations are available, and the reader is ferred to them for specific and detailed assistance in this vital area.[12]

IN-SERVICE EDUCATION

Many of the group supervisory techniques described above are often used as in-service training activities. When a definite program is organized, involving faculty members and utilizing group techniques, it is commonly designated "in-service education." Some researchers define any effort to improve instruction with the staff as in-service. For the purposes of this discussion, however, programs which involve the staff conference, workshop, or study-group approach are considered in-service by definition. The purpose always is to provide experiences for staff members which will enable them to work together and grow professionally in areas of common concern. The list of possible in-service programs is almost

[12]Leslie W. Kindred, *How to Tell the School Story* (Englewood Cliffs, N.J.: Prentice-Hall, Inc., 1960); Leslie W. Kindred, *School Public Relations* (Englewood Cliffs, N.J.: Prentice-Hall, Inc., 1957); American Association of School Administrators, "School-Community Relations That Promote Better Instruction," *The Superintendent as Instructional Leader,* Thirty-fifth Yearbook (Washington, D.C.: National Education Association, 1957); publications of the National School Public Relations Association, National Education Association, Washington, D.C.

infinite, since actual planning will be based on a number of factors, such as staff experience and training, nature of the pupil population and community, and the status of curriculum development in the district. However, some common group in-service activities are:

1. Curriculum study and development.
2. Self-evaluation by staff, using available evaluative criteria.
3. Workshops or institutes on various aspects of child study, the nature of the learning process, identification of pupil problems and needs, and the changing nature of society and the community.
4. Evaluation of school-district philosophy and general objectives.
5. Special programs or workshops for teachers new to the district.
6. Study of trends in reporting pupil progress.
7. Research project on grouping of pupils.
8. Study of newer organizational patterns, such as team teaching and the nongraded school.
9. Workshops on use of aids to instruction, including programmed instructional materials, single concept films, and other learning resources.
10. Workshops on instructional techniques and new content in the subject areas.

How to Plan In-service Programs

Poor planning can ruin any in-service project before it is launched. Supervisors should be aware of significant research results to avoid mistakes. Burton and Brueckner reported a study by C. A. Weber which lists the most serious obstacles encountered in programs of in-service education:

1. Lack of time, heavy teaching loads, heavy extracurricular loads, no suitable time of day.
2. Unprofessional attitudes of teachers.
3. Lack of money for providing professional books and magazines and suitable library facilities for staff.
4. Lack of planning.

In analyzing the second obstacle, "unprofessional attitudes of teachers," Weber found the following types of poor teacher attitudes:

1. Older teachers who have little interest in any kind of in-service education. [See Chapter VIII for suggestions.]
2. Indifference, inertia, complacency of teachers.[13]

[13]William H. Burton and Leo J. Brueckner, *Supervision: A Social Process* (New York: Appleton-Century-Crofts, Inc., 1955), p. 525. Original source: C. A. Weber, "Obstacles to Be Overcome in a Program of Educating Teachers in Service," *Educational Administration and Supervision* (December, 1942). Copyright © 1955, Appleton-Century-Crofts, Inc.

Some of Dreisbach's conclusions in his study of the opinions of principals and teachers regarding their in-service programs are pertinent:

1. ... although the majority of respondents expressed their belief in democratic participation, there was evidence that democratic participation was invited and exercised in very few of the in-service programs held. ...

2. The majority of respondents expressed satisfaction with the problem areas selected for study, but few of them could agree as to why those areas had been selected.

3. Although nearly all of the principals expressed the belief that the in-service programs had benefited the instructional program, there was no evidence to indicate that a majority of the teachers interviewed shared this belief.

4. Only in those school systems where teachers helped to plan the programs did the majority of teachers feel that any improvement in the instructional program had resulted. ...

5. The lack of coordination in the curriculum ... was not solved by most of the in-service programs.

6. Although nearly all of the respondents felt that the in-service programs could be improved, many of the teachers were interested in improving the programs through cooperative planning, whereas most of the principals were interested in devoting more time to the programs and in engaging the services of consultants.

7. There seemed to be a lack of communication between those who planned the programs and those who attended them. Many teachers did not know why the topics had been selected, nor did they know what to expect from the programs before they were presented.

8. Although the teachers reported that they enjoyed the in-service meetings, the programs apparently made no lasting impression on the majority of them.

9. The fact that a large majority of respondents felt that attendance at in-service programs should be compulsory and that teachers need not be reimbursed for time spent in in-service programs indicated that a majority of principals and teachers view in-service programs as being important professional obligations.[14]

Since a cooperatively planned in-service program will attract the interest and vital participation of more staff members, the following steps for action are suggested.

1. The district administrative council tentatively identifies areas for in-service study.
2. Building principals and supervisors discuss suggested ideas with all staff members informally. A part of a school faculty meeting agenda can be

[14]Dodson E. Dreisbach, "A Survey of the Opinions of the Supervising Principals, Elementary Principals, and Elementary Teachers Concerning the In-Service Programs Conducted in the Joint School Systems of Berks County, Pennsylvania" (Doctoral dissertation, Temple University, 1959), pp. 198–201.

devoted to consideration of in-service projects. Everyone should have an opportunity to take part in the initial planning, since this will help to insure success of the program.

3. The administrative council spells out objectives for the in-service work and decides on the topics for the year. These conclusions are made known to all staff members for their reactions.

4. The scope of the program is finalized by the administrative council and the following decisions are reached:

   A. Format of the project—workshop, group discussion, total staff conference, or combination.

   B. Time allotments and scheduling. For example, will the in-service program include curriculum study and development? (Details in Chapter X.) In-service projects are scheduled as summer workshops, as preschool conferences in late August, and on early-dismissal days or full days throughout the year. Adequate time is essential to the success of any program. Teachers cannot be expected to react favorably to in-service work scheduled after a full teaching day. Furthermore, teachers should be paid for full in-service days placed in the calendar if these extend the total contract year.

   C. Adequate funds must be budgeted by the district as recommended by the administrative council for such purposes as consultant fees, purchase of research materials, and compensation of staff.

   D. All staff members are notified of the final plans for the year's in-service program, and each person has an opportunity to join a phase of the study which is of primary concern to him.

Important leadership notes.

1. Each workshop session must be carefully structured to insure maximum staff participation and interest.

2. Consultants should not be employed indiscriminately but only when a specific purpose is identified. For example, in a workshop on "The adolescent learner," a psychologist with considerable experience in adolescent behavior might be engaged to present current research findings on learning to the total secondary staff. He might then be used as a resource person in a small discussion group to follow.

3. Different programs should be planned for new and experienced teachers.

4. Imaginative supervisors can arrange after-school in-service programs on one of the local television stations. Educational channels are most often available for this purpose. The same careful planning is necessary, of course, and other interested districts should be involved.

5. Chief school officials in small districts can often pool their in-service resources by planning regional workshops, institutes, or cooperative projects through study councils. Administrative assistance is often available from the office of the county superintendent or the intermediate unit.

6. Principals, as the educational leaders of their schools, can plan periodic staff meetings on some phase of supervision. These can be scheduled within the district program planned by the administrative council. For example, an elementary staff might plan one or two sessions on techniques of

teacher-parent conferencing. An outside consultant or the coordinator of elementary education in the district could direct this program. At the secondary level, the county reading supervisor might be asked to a faculty meeting to help all teachers become more aware of reading problems and their solution.

In-service Programs in Selected School Districts

Representative in-service activities in an intermediate and large city district are described to indicate the variety of programming that is possible.

Moorestown Township Public Schools, Moorestown, N.J. A comprehensive in-service program is planned each year for the staff of this intermediate-size school system. During a recent school year the following meetings, workshops, and special programs were planned:

1. A drugs and narcotics workshop
2. In-service day on human relations
3. School building meetings twice monthly with varied topics
4. Departmental meetings and district committee meetings, involving many teachers, scheduled twice monthly
5. A district-wide curriculum committee organized to study priority of needs in curriculum development
6. Two-year program on personal growth (sex education) inaugurated
7. Intervisitation program with Moorestown industry planned and carried out
8. District-wide human relations committee organized to sensitize staff and to motivate revision and enrichment of materials in human relations
9. Staff members employed for summer curriculum revision

In Moorestown, all in-service programs are planned by representative committees, often chaired by classroom teachers. The school district budget includes a substantial amount for in-service work, reflecting the importance attached to these programs by Superintendent Arthur G. Martin and his staff.

The intervisitation with Moorestown industry is conducted monthly, with fifteen teachers visiting community businesses and industries each month. The purpose of this program is to develop better mutual understanding between the school and the companies. Substitute teachers are hired by the district to enable these visits.

During the summer, teachers are employed for three-week terms to assist with evaluation of the instructional program and curriculum development. Most department chairmen and some elementary and secondary teachers are already employed on twelve-month contracts, and lead the curriculum teams in the summer months.

As shown on the following program, there were 58 participants in the drugs and narcotics workshop. Substitute teachers were employed so that professional personnel might participate. By planning workshops in this manner it is not necessary to close school for the day.

Moorestown Township Public Schools, Moorestown, New Jersey,
Drugs and Narcotics Workshop

Schedule of the Day

8:30 a.m.	Arthur G. Martin, Orientation
8:45 a.m.	Dr. Gerald Edwards, Adelphi University "Need for Concern and Involvement—Communication Gap and Haight Ashbury"
9:45 a.m.	Coffee and . . . . .
10:15 a.m.	Dr. Gerald Edwards—Role of teacher, administrator, nurse, guidance, social worker, parents, community
11:15 a.m.	Discussion
12:15 p.m.	Lunch
1:15 p.m.	What is being done in Moorestown schools Elementary—Virginia Austermuhl Junior High—Paula Barnosky Senior High—Jack Welch
2:00 p.m.	Discussion
2:30 p.m.	Film preview and evaluation—Dr. Gerald Edwards
3:30 p.m.	Adjournment

    (4)—Nurses
    (1)—Arthur G. Martin, Superintendent of Schools
    (6)—Principals
    (13)—Health and Physical Education Teachers
    (4)—Science (2—Junior High, 2—Senior High)
    (2)—English (1—Junior High, 1—Senior High)
    (2)—Social Studies (1—Junior High, 1—Senior High)
    (4)—Child Study Team
    (5)—Elementary Teachers (1 from each school)
    (1)—Mrs. Louise Bechtel, Executive Assistant
    (6)—Guidance
    (4)—Librarians
    (1)—Mrs. Margaret Werber,
        Acting Multi-media Coordinator
    (1)—Dr. Gerald Edwards
    (2)—P.T.A. Representatives
    (2)—Board of Education members
    58   participants

Presiding: Mrs. Paula Barnosky, Coordinator of Workshop

In the words of Superintendent Martin, "A good in-service program costs money, and a district must be able to see the value of the expenditure. I believe that our in-service activities are worth every cent we spend on them. The benefits are found in pupil and teacher growth."

San Diego City Schools, San Diego, Calif. The following excerpts from a report by William H. Stegeman, Assistant Superintendent, indicate the extent of in-service programming, including curriculum production, during a recent school year.

The responsibility for in-service education is carried out by the administrator of in-service education programs, assisted by one coordinator. This responsibility includes participation in the planning of professional improvement programs; arranging for personnel to conduct workshops, conferences, college courses, and special in-service programs; scheduling and providing facilities for these activities; serving as liaison between the district and institutions providing in-service education; arranging for professional consultants; and serving as liaison with other divisions in in-service planning. Curriculum production is administered by a supervisor, assisted by a permanent clerical staff; this staff is augmented during peak periods as necessary.

In-service activities during a recent school year included the following:

—— Planning was completed for approximately 220 district-college classes, 250 demonstration lessons, and a wide variety of workshops and meetings. Arrangements were also made for a variety of special programs and for selected instructional staff members to attend local conferences.

—— Special emphasis was given to the Inner City Project, narcotics and dangerous drugs, human relations and intergroup relations, a new language arts program, and special programs related to the handicapped, substitute teachers, new teacher orientation, para-professionals, and others.

—— Nineteen summer in-service education classes, enrolling 633 members of the instructional staff, were completed.

—— More than 80 in-service education courses were begun in the fall semester.

—— Fourteen different types of area workshops in critical instructional areas were developed for regional and area presentations. Many have been given and numerous others have been requested and scheduled.

—— The summer curriculum writing workshop was planned, involving subject area specialists, teacher-writers, and both teachers and field administrators serving as members of advisory committees. As a result of summer writing workshop projects and other projects completed during the year, 150 publications were produced.

New Directions in In-service Education

Two promising developments in in-service education are being utilized by some school districts. The first is the use of simulation and the second is packaged in-service training.

Simulation. One of the problems in any in-service education program is to make it as interesting and realistic as possible. Cruickshank evidently believes simulation fills this requirement when he writes:

Currently the technique of simulation is being tested to meet the criterion of realism as well as to provide a setting wherein trainees or teachers in service may practice a wide range of teaching behavior without fear of censure or failure.[15]

Quoting from another one of his writings he describes the process as follows:

Simulation may be defined as the creation of realistic games to be played by participants in order to provide them with lifelike problem-solving experiences related to their present or future work. Such game situations require each player to make decisions based upon previous training and available information. After the player encounters an incident and makes a subsequent decision, he is provided with opportunities to see and/or discuss one or more possible consequences that may result.[16]

It should not be necessary to give any illustrations of simulation here because the reader can examine those found in Appendix VI. The episodes written for teachers would, of course, deal with actual classroom and other school situations which require some action on the part of teachers.

Packaged in-service training. For a number of years now, it has been possible for a school district to choose a packaged program in almost any curriculum area and either to use the entire program, or to modify it to meet the school's peculiar needs. As a natural sequence, it is now possible to purchase packaged programs for in-service training. *Starting Tomorrow* is the imaginative name for this equally imaginative and exciting program.

Winslow describes a social studies workshop for elementary teachers in which a packaged program was used:

The teachers watched a short film that showed children in Kansas City mapping their classroom and their downtown neighborhood. Then the teachers did a bit of what they saw the Kansas City children doing: they formed themselves into teams of four and began some map making on their own. This led to a lively discussion on the value of such highly visual lessons for "turning on" their own classrooms with materials that related so directly to the here-and-now of their city neighborhoods.[17]

[15]Donald R. Cruickshank, "Simulation: New Direction in Teacher Preparation," *Phi Delta Kappan*, XLVIII, no. 1 (1966), 23.
[16]Donald R. Cruickshank and Frank W. Broadbent, *The Simulation and Analysis of Problems of Beginning Teachers*. University of Tennessee and State University College at Brockport, New York: U.S. Office of Education Cooperative Research Project 5-0798, p. 2.
[17]Richard K. Winslow, "Conduct Your Own Faculty In-service Workshop—Starting Tomorrow," *Today's Catholic Teacher* (February 7, 1969), p. 28.

It would seem that the immediate involvement of teachers in the same activity observed in the demonstration film, and then an early opportunity to try it out in their own classes are the strong points in this technique. The materials also are flexible. Although a limited number of topics are available at the present time, it is safe to predict that new ones will be published as quickly as the demand warrants.

SUMMARY

There are many ways of working with professional groups to improve the instructional program. Certain supervisory techniques can best be carried out through group interaction involving the sharing of experiences, ideas, and the findings of educational research. Dynamic, democratic leadership and effective human relations are essential to success in group supervisory activities.

The following have been identified as group techniques.

1. With the current large turnover of teachers in many school districts, it is essential that a comprehensive program be developed for the *orientation of new teachers.*

2. *Action research*, while subject to many definitions, is on-the-job practical research in the public school classroom. It is carefully planned and controlled, requiring definite steps in execution. Since the pupils, materials of instruction, and experienced teachers are available in the schools, more research should be conducted there.

3. An important supervisory technique is the *maintenance of professional libraries.* These should be established both in the school buildings and at the district level.

4. *Intervisitation* is one of the most promising group techniques for improving instruction. All teachers can profit in some way from observing a master teacher at work, either inside or outside the district.

5. A good *student teaching* plan in a district can help to improve the entire instructional program and make a significant contribution to the profession at the same time. Teachers usually perform even better when they have interns in their classrooms.

6. Since tests are one means of measuring the impact of classroom instruction on pupils, supervisors should evaluate their present *testing programs* to see if they are really measuring what is being taught. The achievement tests must be planned in relation to other tests, such as those in aptitude and ability.

7. The supervisor is concerned with any *new organizational plan*, such as team teaching, that might be introduced into the district. Indeed, the initial decision should be made on the basis of definite possibilities for improved instruction. It is important that supervisory personnel be involved in each planning step as new organizational patterns develop.

8. Since research shows much teacher dissatisfaction with *faculty meetings*, supervisors and principals are well advised to practice group dynamics and interaction in planning and conducting effective meetings.

9. All administrators and supervisors need to be vitally concerned with *public relations* as an aspect of the improvement of instruction. The people of a community must feel that they have a part in the school program if curriculum advances and the funds to support them are to be forthcoming.

In-service education has been defined as any planned program involving supervisors and teachers in the improvement of classroom instruction. Included are staff conferences, workshops, study groups, and curriculum-development projects. The list of possible programs is almost infinite. Supervisors should work with teachers in planning, so that in-service activities will result in more real participation and lasting results.

SUGGESTED ACTIVITIES AND PROBLEMS

1. Develop a detailed plan for the orientation of new teachers in a school district with which you are familiar.
2. Initiate an action research project, and report your progress.
3. Interview a supervisor to determine the plan for teacher intervisitation in his school district. Critically evaluate the program and make suggestions for improvement.
4. Develop a comprehensive policy for accepting and training intern teachers in a school system.
5. Investigate a new plan of organization in a school district. Write a paper describing the process by which the plan was conceived and implemented. Evaluate the results to date.
6. By interviewing the assistant superintendent in charge of instruction, make a study of the in-service program for one year in an intermediate or large school system. Discuss the program in light of the principles presented in this chapter.

SELECTED READINGS

Blumberg, Arthur, and Amidon, Edmund. "A Comparison of Teacher and Principal Attitudes Toward Faculty Meetings." *The Bulletin of the National*

Association of Secondary School Principals, XLVIII, no. 290 (1964), 45–55.

Bradfield, Luther E. *Supervision for Modern Elementary Schools.* Chaps. 2 and 3. Columbus, Ohio: Charles E. Merrill Books, Inc., 1964.

Graves, John W., and Hixon, Lawrence B. "How to Keep New Teachers Happy." *Nation's Schools*, LXXXI, no. 4 (1968), 76–78.

Harris, Ben M. *Supervisory Behavior in Education.* Chaps. 3 and 9. Englewood Cliffs, N.J.: Prentice-Hall, Inc., 1963.

Harris, Ben M., and Bessent, Wailand, in collaboration with McIntyre, Kenneth E. *In-Service Education: A Guide to Better Practice.* Englewood Cliffs, N.J.: Prentice-Hall, Inc., 1969.

Kindred, Leslie W., and Associates. *How To Tell the School Story.* Englewood Cliffs, N.J.: Prentice-Hall, Inc., 1960.

Neagley, Ross L., and Evans, N. Dean. *Handbook for Effective Curriculum Development.* Chaps. 4 and 9. Englewood Cliffs, N.J.: Prentice-Hall, Inc., 1967.

Orientation Programs for Teachers. Research Memo 1964–24, NEA Research Division. Washington, D.C.: National Education Association of the United States, 1964.

Wiles, Kimball. *Supervision for Better Schools.* 3rd ed., Chaps. 7 and 14. Englewood Cliffs, N.J.: Prentice-Hall, Inc., 1967.

chapter 10

How to Organize
and Carry Out a Program
of Curriculum Study
and Development

It is difficult to exaggerate the importance of curriculum study when the sum total of man's knowledge is doubling each decade. Constant societal changes, shifts in man's cultural patterns, and the continuing explosion of knowledge are all interacting forces which increase the rate of obsolescence of school curricula. In an age of unprecedented change and tremendous challenges that threaten to rock the foundations of Western civilization, the nation's schools must direct their attention to a thorough evaluation of what they are teaching and how they are teaching it. No longer can the gap between research and classroom practice be tolerated. The newer trends in each subject field and discipline must be carefully examined for possible additions to the school program. At the same time, obsolete or less important topics must be dropped.

BASIC CONSIDERATIONS AND PRINCIPLES
IN CURRICULUM STUDY AND DEVELOPMENT

The *curriculum* has been defined as "all of the planned experiences provided by the school to assist pupils in attaining the designated learning outcomes to the best of their abilities."[1]

[1]Ross L. Neagley and N. Dean Evans, *Handbook for Effective Curriculum Development* (Englewood Cliffs, N.J.: Prentice-Hall, Inc., 1967), p. 2.

Supervisors who are involved in curriculum development projects should be familiar with developing theories of the curriculum. Although in the embryonic stages, a dialogue in curriculum theory has been joined, with the fields of educational administration and leadership providing some basic theoretical positions.[2]

The newer patterns of school organization definitely affect and possibly determine to some extent the shape of the curriculum. There are a variety of vertical organizational schemes, including grading, multigrading, and non-grading. Horizontal plans encompass departmentalization, the self-contained classroom, ability grouping, individualization of instruction, and team teaching.[3] While no organizational plan in itself will significantly improve instruction, some of the newer designs do show potential for the facilitation of teaching and learning. The total professional staff may want to consider possible changes in school organization either before or during a curriculum development project.

Other basic considerations are the time and money that must be provided for an effective program of curriculum study. Time for full staff participation and money for resource persons, research materials, summer curriculum staff, and additional teachers to reduce instructional loads are all essential to the success of such a study.

Teachers cannot be expected to work productively for several hours in the late afternoon after a full day of teaching. Consequently, release time or extra calendar days should be provided for curriculum work. At the very minimum, five or six full days or their equivalent per school year are needed to carry out any significant project. At least ten days per year or weekly released time is recommended. Also, if teachers are to have time for needed reading and research between regularly scheduled curriculum days, teacher-pupil ratios and class loads must be reasonable.

School districts with experience in curriculum study have found that it is most important to hire administrators and teachers during the summer months to collate, edit, and further develop material which has been prepared by staff committees during the school term. In this way, no time is lost, continuity is established, and teacher interest can be maintained from year to year. Summer regression in curriculum work can be as disastrous as pupil regression in some areas.

A substantial sum should be provided in the budget for initial resource persons and curriculum study materials. This amount should be increased for each additional subject area to be studied. The need for funds will vary according to the amount of current curriculum materials already on hand and the availability of resource persons from the county super-

[2]*Ibid.*, pp. 15–22.
[3]*Ibid.*, Chap. 4.

intendent's or intermediate unit office, the state department, or local colleges and universities.

It should be evident from the foregoing discussion that time and money are indeed vital ingredients in any program of curriculum development. If they cannot be provided as indicated, then the outcomes will be limited accordingly.

Basic principles of curriculum development have been evolved through research and are summarized here as a foundation for local district study. (For detailed discussions, see selected readings at the end of this chapter.)

1. Dynamic leadership from the chief school administrator and his assistants is essential.
2. All professional staff members should be involved to some extent in curriculum development. Therefore, projects should be sensible in scope and not too burdensome to any individual.
3. The values, attitudes, and prevailing opinions of the citizens of the community must be ascertained through lay advisory committees or similar groups.
4. All effective curriculum work will evolve from actual teaching situations and problems, and will continually be related to classroom experiences. Any study should begin with the existing curriculum of the district.
5. Curriculum development must be continuous; the job is never finished. Proceeding from year to year, modern curriculum revision is no "one shot" effort.
6. The "bandwagon" philosophy is shunned. New programs are considered only when they can be justified in terms of the needs of the community and society and have been proven valuable through sound educational research and experimentation.
7. Time and money in sufficient quantities must be available.
8. The program must be well-planned, logically organized, and crisply launched.
9. District-wide coordination of the curriculum is essential.
10. Evaluation must be continuous and comprehensive.

THE PROCESS OF CURRICULUM DEVELOPMENT

Some critics of local school district curriculum development state that "starting from scratch" is an inefficient and even impossible task. However, as the ensuing discussion emphasizes, many resources can be mobilized for effective curriculum design. A well-planned project never "starts from scratch" but takes advantage of previous work by national organizations, state departments of education, and other school districts, to name a few sources.

As Alexander has stated, "Undoubtedly each of our . . . local school systems will not be able to do all of its own programing, but each should at least be able to make intelligent selections by its own criteria, among those programs to become available. . . . Each district, perhaps in concert with its neighbors, must as a minimum, it is believed, draw up its own design of the curriculum, including overall goals and expected areas of content, and some specifications for its pupil population of the alternative scopes and sequences of content needed and the instructional resources thereby required."[4]

There are those who believe that local curriculum development is impossible, and that the job should be turned over to (1) the federal government; (2) a national curriculum commission; or (3) the giant "learning" corporations which have organized to design and market both hardware and software. The arguments for and against local district responsibility for curriculum development have been cogently expressed elsewhere.[5] *The authors here simply state their firm belief that curriculum determination and/or design is the legitimate and necessary function of a strong, well-staffed local school district.* We agree with the following statement prepared for the United States Senate Subcommittee on Education in April, 1967, by William M. Alexander:

Strengthening of local curriculum development—Any fundamental efforts at improvement of the curriculum of . . . school districts in the United States must place high priority on improvement of the leadership and the processes of curriculum development in these districts. The alternative is to abandon local responsibility, turning over curriculum development to State and National agencies, and this is not considered a satisfactory alternative. Improve State leadership, utilize National resources better—yes. But eliminate the opportunity for local school people to make decisions regarding the programs they must direct—no. The need is to enable local leadership to make intelligent decisions based on full knowledge of available curriculum possibilities.[6]

Figure 13 depicts the logical sequence of curriculum development, culminating in the instructional program or the learning opportunities offered to students. Moving from identification of values to actual instruction is

[4]William M. Alexander, "Curriculum Development," *Notes and Working Papers Concerning the Administration of Programs Authorized under Title III of Public Law 89–10, E.S.E.A. of 1965,* as amended by Public Law 89–750. Prepared for the Subcommittee on Education of the Committee on Labor and Public Welfare, United States Senate (Washington, D.C.: Government Printing Office, April, 1967), pp. 103–4.

[5]Ross L. Neagley and N. Dean Evans, *Handbook for Effective Curriculum Development* (Englewood Cliffs, N.J.: Prentice-Hall, Inc., 1967), Chaps. 2, 3.

[6]Alexander, "Curriculum Development," *Notes and Working Papers Concerning the Administration of Programs Authorized under Title III of Public Law 89–10, E.S.E.A. of 1965,* p. 104.

a complex and scientific procedure, requiring proper staff organization followed by definite sequential steps. Let us examine a workable structure for curriculum development in a school district and then refer back to Figure 13 to trace the process of curriculum design.

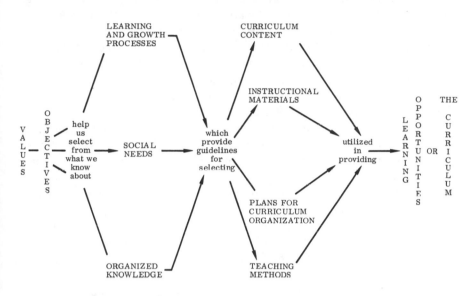

Figure 13. The Process of Curriculum Development.[7]

Organizing for Effective Curriculum Development

The basic administrative unit should be the district curriculum council or steering committee. All administrators with some responsibility for supervision of instruction are logically members, including the assistant superintendent in charge of instruction, the subject area curriculum coordinators, the coordinator of learning resources, and principals. In very large districts not all administrators and supervisory personnel will be able to serve on the curriculum council. However, each group should be adequately represented. The chief school administrator will meet with the council on occasion. Also, it is imperative that teachers representing all levels of instruction are members of the district curriculum council. In addition, a school psychologist, the director of guidance services, and

[7]Robert S. Fox, "Curriculum Development with a Purpose," *Theory Into Practice*, I, no. 4 (1962), 204.

the librarian in charge of the professional collection can be valuable members of this council.

The district curriculum council's main responsibility is to coordinate all curriculum and instructional programs in the district, and to recommend basic policy changes to the chief school administrator. The council also organizes, under direction of the assistant superintendent in charge of instruction, the various subject area committees which carry out the continuing work in curriculum evaluation and change.

District-wide subject area curriculum committees are the key to effective curriculum development. They should be chaired by the subject-area curriculum coordinator and should include in their membership teachers from all levels, a principal, the coordinator of learning resources, and the assistant superintendent in charge of instruction. If they are really expected to function in a meaningful way, these committees need time during the school day and year to work. Key personnel need to be employed for continuing curriculum work during the summer, and adequate professional resource materials must be available. For example, a subject area committee studying newer objectives and courses in mathematics cannot proceed very far unless the dozen or so major programs currently used in the field are available for analysis. Finally, expert resource consultant help is required at key points throughout the process of curriculum evaluation and design. The math committee needs to have available the services of a top-level consultant to help analyze, for example, the common elements of content found in the major math programs on the market. Then the committee will be in a position to adopt, adapt, or re-write a curriculum.

The Process of Curriculum Design

It is the responsibility of the district curriculum council under the leadership of the assistant superintendent in charge of instruction to initiate or maintain action on the broad front of curricular change. Only this group can keep in focus the various forces that tend to affect the curriculum in a school district. The curriculum council is charged, therefore, with the task of maintaining balance in the instructional program, through constant review of priorities.

As depicted in Figure 13, the initial concern is identification of values, which are basic determinants of the remainder of the process. The curriculum council, the administrative staff, and ultimately the board of education, need to agree on those individual and societal values that the school feels committed to uphold through the learning experiences made available to the students. Such value determination will then lead to a statement or re-statement of the philosophy of the school district—the fundamental concerns that should occupy the attention of the teaching and administrative staff and the learners.

The specific goals which the school aims to attain are then derived from the statement of philosophy, and these become the objectives. At this point many schools publish the philosophy and objectives in the faculty handbook, file them mentally away, and get on with the "real business" of curriculum making. This is a fatal step, and if taken, can doom the entire project. To be meaningful, objectives must be refined further until they can be stated as *learning or behavioral outcomes*. Only when the curriculum worker indicates how the behavior of a learner will be changed in the accomplishment of a certain objective does the process of goal identification take on real meaning.

REQUIRED READING

Robert F. Mager, *Preparing Instructional Objectives* (Palo Alto, Calif.: Fearon Publishers, 1962).

Taxonomy of Educational Objectives, The Classification of Educational Goals (New York: David McKay Co., Inc., 1956–1964), Handbook I: *Cognitive Domain*, and Handbook II: *Affective Domain*.

Careful specification of the general educational objectives for the school system in terms of learning outcomes will lead the curriculum council (see Figure 13) to three major sources of curriculum content: learning and growth processes, and the resulting needs of each learner; social needs, or the demands of society on the school; and the sum total of man's organized knowledge. At this point the curriculum council should be able to identify the major categories or organizing points around which the curriculum can be built. Historically, we have organized by discipline: history, mathematics, physics, theology, and music, for example. But what about cybernetics, sex education, and biochemistry? Do they deserve a place in the already cluttered elementary and secondary school curriculum? The district curriculum council is the logical group to consider these fundamental questions and to identify or revise the basic sets of learning experiences to be offered by the school. By referring again to Figure 13 the reader will see that the process outlined above leads to *plans for curriculum organization*, or subject areas to be taught in the school system. These become the basic groupings of curriculum content.

The subject-area curriculum committee now picks up the process of curriculum development, and begins to consider objectives for the subject field. In its first few meetings the science committee, for example, identifies goals for the total curriculum, elementary and secondary. This process leads to the organization of content for the various levels of instruction. The result at the upper secondary level may be a decision to organize an interdisciplinary seminar and laboratory course to enable advanced students to explore the interrelationships that are being discovered among the traditional disciplines of chemistry, physics, and biology.

Considerable work then is necessary to specify instructional objectives in behavioral or performance terms. According to Robert F. Mager,

> An objective is an *intent* communicated by a statement describing a proposed change in a learner—a statement of what the learner is to be like when he has successfully completed a learning experience. It is a description of a pattern of behavior (performance) we want the learner to be able to demonstrate.
>
> When clearly defined goals are lacking, it is impossible to evaluate a course or program efficiently, and there is no sound basis for selecting appropriate materials, content, or instructional methods.[8]

In his book, which should be in the hands of all curriculum workers, Mager describes how to write objectives that will explain the desired terminal behavior of the learner:

> *First*, identify the terminal behavior by name; you can specify the kind of behavior that will be accepted as evidence that the learner has achieved the objective.
>
> *Second*, try to define the desired behavior further by describing the important conditions under which the behavior will be expected to occur.
>
> *Third*, specify the criteria of acceptable performance by describing how well the learner must perform to be considered acceptable.[9]

As the subject area curriculum committee develops the behavioral objectives and subsequent learning sequences for the various units of content to be taught, the members must certainly be aware of the voluminous research in learning[10] which points to one significant conclusion:

---

[8]Robert F. Mager, *Preparing Instructional Objectives* (Palo Alto, Calif.: Fearon Publishers, 1962), p. 3.

[9]*Ibid.*, p. 12.

[10]Ronald C. Doll, *Curriculum Improvement: Decision-Making and Process* (Boston: Allyn & Bacon, Inc., 1964), Chap. 2.

John D. McNeil, *Curriculum Administration, Principles and Techniques of Curriculum Development* (New York: The Macmillan Company, 1965), Chap. 1.

Percival M. Symonds, *What Education Has to Learn from Psychology* (New York: Teachers College Press, Teachers College, Columbia University, 1964).

Goodwin Watson, *What Psychology Can We Trust?* (New York: Teachers College Press, Teachers College, Columbia University, 1961).

True learning involves much more than the simple acquisition of factual knowledge. In fact the modern curriculum worker who would adopt such a narrow definition of learning is lost before he starts. He would be immediately inundated with the exploding mass of new facts in any subject area, which could not possibly be taught even if the entire school day were devoted to the single discipline in question.

Real learning involves the processes of inquiry and discovery, where the student is led to explore, to experiment, to question, to debate. In building any curriculum sequence, it is imperative to include opportunities for observation, reflection, and problem solving. Learners become more self-motivated as they discover opportunities to form their own concepts, generalizations and insights, and as they are led to relate new ideas to old ones in the constant search for meaningful identity as human beings. This is the stuff that real learning is made of—not the dull routine of recitation, memorization, and repetition that so often marked the drive for excellence in American schools of the 1950s and 1960s. Thousands of students never tasted the thrill of learning for its own sake, and dropped out along the way. Countless other thousands discovered how to "beat the system" and stuck it out until graduation. No such sterile curriculum will suffice for the 1970s and 1980s. In an age of space exploration, color television, and globe-girdling jets, the curriculum must be as exciting as the world of the learner.

The Role of Media and Method

It is important to emphasize that *only at this point in the process of curriculum development are we prepared to consider instructional materials and teaching methods.* (See Chapter XI.) It is imperative that learning resources and techniques of instruction be designed to aid in accomplishing the objectives of the learning sequence. For instance, even the best documentary film on Adolf Hitler and the Third Reich must be related to the behavioral outcomes and content of the appropriate unit in modern world history before the film becomes relevant as a learning resource.

Also, modern concepts of the nature of the learning process, which were capsulated in the preceding discussion, require considerable imagination and flexibility in the use of instructional materials and methods. (1) For example, if students are really to have the opportunity to inquire, to exchange ideas with their teacher and with each other, and to debate various issues, there must be ample opportunity for confrontation in small groups of ten to fifteen. Perhaps the only learning aid required here would be a chalkboard. The method obviously is group discussion.

(2) To meet other learning objectives students can study on their own in carrels, using materials previously prepared and stored electronically. In this way true individualization of the learning process can be achieved. (3) The two preceding methods can often be supplemented by large-group instruction, where major concepts introducing a unit of instruction can be presented to several hundred learners at one time. Through the selective use of overhead transparencies, 16mm film clips, closed circuit television, and various student response systems, a skilled lecturer can effectively teach 200 students instead of the 40 he might have in a regular classroom.[11]

The supervisor who is interested in organizing a comprehensive program of curriculum development may want to examine a companion work by the authors: *Handbook for Effective Curriculum Development*, by Ross L. Neagley and N. Dean Evans.

The next part of this chapter is a brief outline for action in curriculum development designed for small- or intermediate-size districts. The outline is flexible and is designed to assist the supervisor who can initiate curriculum work in only a few subject areas at one time.

Large city systems often have full-time curriculum staffs which carry on continuous review of all major fields simultaneously. The supervisor from the larger district will find some useful suggestions in the step-by-step program that follows. These ideas may be helpful in building or sub-district level work in the city.

Many variations of the ensuing steps are possible and desirable in certain situations, according to the needs, facilities, staff talents, and resources of particular districts. If curriculum work has been inaugurated before, some of the preliminary steps may be omitted or modified. The format and suggested procedures are designed to be helpful at any stage of curriculum study. The best time for beginning Step 1 is the spring of the year, when the initial phases of the district program can be organized. In this way the first four steps can be completed before the close of school, and the calendar can be set for the following year.

OUTLINE FOR ACTION IN CURRICULUM DEVELOPMENT

Step 1

At a meeting of the administrative and supervisory staff, or district administrative council, curriculum needs and problems are explored. The

---

[11]*Note:* Pages 230–36 are quoted with minor revisions from Ross L. Neagley, N. Dean Evans, and Clarence A. Lynn, Jr., *The School Administrator and Learning Resources: A Handbook for Effective Action* (Englewood Cliffs, N.J.: Prentice-Hall, Inc., 1969), pp. 39–45.

state of the existing program of studies is discussed, as well as possible starting points in identification of subject areas that need evaluation.

If the district is just beginning a planned curriculum study, a good speaker could be invited at this point to address the total staff on such a topic as "A Dynamic Curriculum for a Changing Society."

Step 2

Through classroom observation, informal supervisor-teacher conferences, and building meetings held by the various principals, problem areas in the curriculum begin to be revealed. Gradually priorities emerge as the total elementary and secondary staff takes a problem census and begins to think seriously about curricular needs in terms of the district philosophy of education.

During this stage, the chief school administrator should make available the current thinking of his citizens' advisory committee or other interested lay groups, if any, regarding the adequacy of the present curriculum and course offerings.

Important leadership note. If little or no initial interest or need is felt by the teachers, it is the responsibility of the chief school official and the supervisory staff to create a climate in which proper attitudes toward curriculum development have a chance to flourish. Teachers are stimulated most by supervisors who are vitally interested in current curriculum trends, materials, and techniques. The reader is referred again to the characteristics of modern supervision in Chapter I, which must be somewhat in evidence if a staff expects to work cooperatively in the improvement of the instructional program.

Step 3

A curriculum council or steering committee is organized. Districts with a functioning administrative council may decide to expand this group into the steering committee. In any event, membership includes the chief school official; assistant superintendent in charge of instruction and all general supervisors or coordinators, if any; building principals; the subject-area curriculum coordinators; the coordinator of learning resources; and classroom teachers as follows: one or two teachers each from the primary and intermediate levels, selected by the elementary teaching staff; department heads (if any) at the high school level, or representatives from the subject areas, selected by the secondary staff. The junior high or middle school and senior high school levels each should be represented. In addition, a resource person or consultant from the county, state, or a nearby university might be secured.

It may be desirable to establish minimum requirements for the teacher representatives on the steering committee. These might include a Master's degree, at least three years' teaching experience, and demonstration of leadership qualities.

The chairmanship of the curriculum council may be rotated periodically. The most likely initial chairman would be the chief school official or assistant superintendent in charge of instruction. However, any other qualified administrator or classroom teacher could be elected chairman by the group.

Step 4

The curriculum council meets and accomplishes the following:

1. Curriculum areas that seem to exhibit the most crucial need for study, kindergarten through high school, are tentatively selected. It is difficult to study all or most of the major areas simultaneously, except in large districts where permanent committees are established for each main curriculum area. An effective working committee should number from four to eight classroom teachers plus a leader or resource person from the administrative level. Therefore, the size of the total teaching and supervisory staff will be one factor in determining the number of subject areas that it is feasible to study at one time.

2. The time schedule for a year's program is set up and recommended to the school calendar committee. Five to ten full days or more should be planned for curriculum study throughout the year. Some districts plan for two or three days before school opens, and then block out the other days during the term. If full days are not always available, then a number of partial days could be provided.

Important leadership note. There must be enough time between full curriculum work days to permit necessary committee research and consultation. Teachers are very busy, and some of the tasks suggested in this chapter will require out-of-school time. In this connection, many districts are defining the teacher-day in their professional contracts to include time before and after the pupil-day for planning, conferences, and curriculum research.

3. Several resource persons are suggested for each of the subject areas considered. Such consultants are most likely to be found in the state department of education, college and university departments, offices of county school superintendents, or the curriculum offices of larger school districts.

4. A budget for the entire program must be prepared. Items such as the following should be included:

   A. Fees for curriculum consultants.

    B. Funds for developing the district curriculum center. (See Step 6.)

    C. Summer salaries for selected staff members. (See Step 16.)

    D. Clerical and postal costs.

    5. *Curriculum Bulletin No. 1* should be issued to each professional staff member announcing the date of the first general meeting in Step 5 and outlining the tentative conclusions reached in Step 4. This is the first of a series of bulletins to be issued by the curriculum council to keep the staff fully informed during the curriculum study.

Step 5

    A general staff meeting is convened for the purpose of discussing progress to date; reporting in detail the tentative plans made by the curriculum council; reaching agreement on the over-all structure of the curriculum project; and obtaining staff preferences for their participation in the year's work. The chief school official or the chairman of the curriculum council presides, and his agenda could include the following:

    1. Outline the scope of the proposed curriculum study as planned by the curriculum council. This would include a general overview of district curriculum development to date and a presentation of the areas proposed for study at this time.

    2. In small- or intermediate-size districts, a general discussion of plans would be in order. Consensus could be reached on curriculum areas to be studied and teachers then asked to list their preferences for the year's project.

    In larger districts, general discussion would not be possible because of the total staff size. Decisions on the subject areas to be examined could be made in building meetings and the conclusions sent to the assistant superintendent in charge of instruction. Or mimeographed sheets such as the following could be distributed, on which teachers could indicate their choices for the year's work.

UNION SCHOOL DISTRICT #1

Please check two.

Of the curriculum areas presented by the curriculum council, I believe that these two are most important for district study this year, kindergarten through twelfth grade.

_____ Social Studies

_____ Science

_____ Foreign Languages

             (Including consideration of instruction at primary and intermediate grade levels.)

Please indicate first, second, and third choices by numerals 1, 2, and 3.
This year I would like to take part in the following program:
Curriculum development
——————— Social Studies
——————— Science
——————— Foreign Languages
Other in-service programs
——————— Research on team teaching
——————— The psychology of learning
——————— Trends in reporting pupil progress
Note: All first-year teachers will participate in a special workshop series.

3. This general staff meeting might be concluded with these announcements and information items:
   A. First choices for curriculum or other in-service participation will be granted wherever possible, but second and third choices will be used to balance the committees. Also, two of the three subject areas will be finally selected from the tabulation of staff responses above.
   B. The completed sheets should be handed to building principals in two or three days. [Give the due date.]
   C. [The time schedule for the year's curriculum and in-service work is reviewed.]
   D. The next curriculum bulletin will list the subject areas to be studied and the final committee assignments.

Step 6

After the staff responses are tabulated, a district curriculum center or laboratory is established or expanded. It is imperative that a qualified teacher or supervisor be given responsibility and time to organize or upgrade this materials center. This is one of the most important steps in curriculum development. Effective progress cannot be made without resources and research findings. According to Wiles,

Any faculty needs to be sure that in its work procedures time is provided for the collection of evidence on which to base decisions. A decision made on the spur of the moment without taking the time or making the effort to collect sufficient data to make an intelligent decision may result in a deterioration rather than an improvement in the school program.[12]

It should be apparent that an abundance of material is needed for the various committees to maintain staff interest and to insure profitable results.

[12]Kimball Wiles, "Does Faculty Participation Produce Curriculum Improvement?" *Educational Leadership*, XV, no. 6 (March 1958), 349.

The curriculum council and the designated person in charge of the curriculum center will have to locate an accessible room in the district and see that shelves are available. Then the following sources should prove helpful in stocking the laboratory.

1. The personal files of the chief school official, assistant superintendent in charge of instruction, the coordinators or supervisors, and principals should contain a wealth of material that can be catalogued and filed in the curriculum lab.
2. Current written courses of study can be obtained from state departments of education, county offices, college and university curriculum libraries, and from other school districts. The resource consultants suggested in Step 4 will often have many guides and courses of study available or will know where they can be procured.
3. General reference works and bibliographies should be studied to identify the latest research findings in the subject areas on the agenda for the year. Such sources include *Education Index, Encyclopedia of Educational Research, Readers' Guide to Periodical Literature, Vertical File Index,* and *Doctoral Dissertations: Index to American Doctoral Dissertations.* Copies of pertinent studies should then be ordered.
4. The United States Office of Education publishes numerous pamphlets, booklets, and research studies in all of the subject areas and in general curriculum development. A complete bibliography is available on request.
5. The National Education Association *Publication Index* lists a wide variety of printed materials from the Association for Supervision and Curriculum Development and the other departments and commissions of the N.E.A.
6. Current issues of educational periodicals can be checked for appropriate articles. The subject-area magazines are very helpful, as well as journals like *Review of Educational Research* and *Educational Leadership.*
7. State departments of education will often be able to send bibliographies of curriculum research publications and suggested state curriculum guides in the various areas.
8. There are a number of school study councils throughout the country. Some of these make significant contributions to local curriculum development. A list of recent publications should be available from nearby study councils.

Important leadership note. Following is a list of major sources of curriculum and learning resource information.[13]

*Educational Products Information Exchange (EPIE), 527 Lexington Avenue, New York, N.Y. 10017. An independent, non-governmental, non-industry source of information regarding the availability and performance of instructional materials and equipment. The EPIE Institute publishes *The EPIE Forum,* a product information service which is issued nine times yearly from September through May.

[13]Ross L. Neagley, N. Dean Evans, and Clarence A. Lynn, Jr., *The School Administrator and Learning Resources: A Handbook for Effective Action,* pp. 46–47.

*National Information Center for Educational Media, McGraw-Hill Films, 330 West 42nd Street, New York, N.Y. 10036. Center established in 1967 at the University of Southern California to research new methods of auto- mated cataloging and to compile information about instructional materials, to be stored in a master computer file.
Two publications available, $29.50 each: *Index to 16mm Educational Films,* and *Index to 35mm Educational Filmstrips.* Order from McGraw-Hill Films.
*Educators' Progress Service, Randolph, Wisconsin. Annually revised guides to a variety of instructional materials: *Educators' Guide to Free Films,* $9.50; *Educators' Guide to Free Film Strips,* $7.00; *Educators' Guide to Free Tapes, Scripts, and Transcriptions,* $6.75.
New Educational Materials, Citation Press, Scholastic Magazines, Inc., 904 Sylvan Ave., Englewood Cliffs, N.J. 07632, $2.75. A book which evaluates approximately 300 instructional aids and over 300 books in all major cur- riculum areas. Evaluations by teachers, librarians, administrators, and cur- riculum specialists.
Free and Inexpensive Learning Materials, Division of Surveys and Field Services, George Peabody College for Teachers, Nashville, Tennessee 37203, $3.00. Comprehensive listing of 3,500 different media items, arranged under 120 categories. Completely revised every two years. All entries evaluated by staff of Division of Surveys and Field Services. Indexed and cross-referenced.
Textbooks in Print, published annually by R. R. Bowker Co., New York, N.Y., $3.00. Listing of elementary and secondary textbooks, supplementary books, and professional texts, classified by subject. Other Bowker publica- tions on encyclopedias and other reference works may be additional valuable sources.
Sources of Information on Educational Media, U.S. Department of Health, Education and Welfare, Office of Education. Available from Superintendent of Documents, U.S. Government Printing Office, Washington, D.C. 20402, $.20. A comprehensive little booklet listing many sources of motion pictures, filmstrips, records, tapes, transcriptions, and audio-visual equipment. Also included are listings of selected catalogs of elementary and secondary school books; a selected list of journals concerned with educational media; a selected list of periodicals concerned with new educational media; sources of information regarding the planning of facilities for use of new media; and selected summaries of research studies including new educational media. Somewhat dated but a good 20¢ worth!

Step 7

The curriculum council sets up work committees based on staff interest as indicated by the questionnaires. Depending on the number of cur- riculum areas to be studied at one time, teachers are assigned to subject- area or in-service groups, using first choices where possible. Curriculum development committees should be limited to about eight teachers in order to allow maximum participation. These may be organized K-12, with equal representation from the primary, intermediate, and junior-

and senior-high levels. Or the committees may be basically elementary or secondary, with teacher representatives from the other area.

Here are several possible plans for organizing a staff of 100 in an intermediate-size district. There are many options, depending on variables in any given district.

Plan A Two subject areas, social studies and science, have been selected for K-12 review and development of curriculum guides. Five work days have been placed in the calendar; school will be closed and all staff members have expressed preferences for committee assignments.

Social studies—2 primary-level teachers

2 intermediate-level teachers

2 junior high school teachers

2 senior high school teachers, including the head of the social studies department

1 elementary principal

Science—1 primary-level teacher

2 intermediate-level teachers

2 junior high school teachers, including the head of the science department

3 senior high school teachers, 1 each in biology, chemistry, and physics

1 secondary principal

Other in-service programs (Groups include elementary and secondary teachers and administrators)

Workshop for first-year teachers   —   16

Psychology of learning   —   37

Trends in reporting pupil progress   —   27

Note: The superintendent and the assistant superintendent are not assigned.

Important leadership note. As the year's work progresses, the science and social studies committees may decide to set up subcommittees to pursue specific subjects after general objectives, scope, and sequence have been identified. For example, it might be desirable to organize work groups in biology, chemistry, and physics. This means that staff members taking part in the initial in-service programs would have a later opportunity to participate in the curriculum study or to take another in-service unit. To permit this flexibility, the first two or three curriculum days in the calendar should be used to complete the first in-service series. Then new programs could be set up for those staff members not ultimately involved in the expanded curriculum study.

Plan B—Assume that two subject areas, arithmetic and reading, have been identified for study at the elementary level and three, English, social studies, and foreign languages, at the secondary level. School will be closed for five curriculum days. Committee assignments might be broken down as follows.

Elementary arithmetic—6 primary-level teachers
6 intermediate-level teachers
2 junior high school teachers
2 senior high school teachers
1 elementary principal
1 coordinator of elementary education
All buildings and grade levels should be represented if possible. There would be two committees, one operating at the primary and one at the intermediate level. There would be some joint meetings during the year. These comments also apply to:

Elementary reading—6 primary-level teachers
6 intermediate-level teachers
3 junior high school teachers
1 senior high school teacher
2 elementary principals
1 secondary principal (junior high)

Secondary English—4 senior high school teachers, including the head of the English department
4 junior high school teachers, including the head of the English department
2 intermediate-level teachers
2 primary-level teachers
1 secondary principal (senior high)

Practically all secondary English and reading teachers are on this committee. Exceptions are those who chose other assignments at the elementary level or in another field. While this group would meet together initially, it would divide into two subcommittees at the junior high and senior high school levels.

Secondary social studies—5 senior high school teachers, including the head of the social studies department
4 junior high school teachers, including the head of the social studies department
3 intermediate-level teachers
2 primary-level teachers
1 elementary principal

Virtually the entire membership of the secondary social studies departments is included on this committee, which possibly will break up into three subcommittees, perhaps on American history, world cultures, and government. Each of the smaller groups would consider the coordinated program from Grades 7 through 12, with attention to the foundations provided by the elementary-school social studies. The elementary teachers would provide valuable help in articulation.

Secondary foreign languages—4 senior high school teachers, including the head of the modern foreign language department
3 junior high school teachers
1 primary-level teacher
2 intermediate-level teachers
1 elementary principal
1 elementary French teacher

After initial work on the scope of the new foreign language program, possible new languages to be offered, and establishment of elementary grade levels for introduction of a foreign tongue, this group might divide into French, Spanish, and German subcommittees.

Additional in-service program. The 16 first-year teachers will be involved in a special workshop.

Note: The superintendent and assistant superintendent will provide the general supervision of all committees. The five district specialists in art, music, and physical education are not assigned above, and, of course, should be included in one of the scheduled programs. At other times, curriculum work in the special fields would proceed as outlined above.

Important leadership note. If curriculum days are scheduled in the school calendar, then provision must be made for all members of the staff. An infinite number of organizational patterns are available to the curriculum council. Those outlined immediately above serve only as examples. It is obvious, however, that all personnel must have a meaningful assignment on each work day. This will often mean an additional in-service program running concurrently with curriculum development. A district experienced in curriculum study can involve all or most of the professional staff on curriculum committees because teacher and supervisory leadership have been developed.

The alternative to full staff involvement on a given day is the provision of substitute teachers at staggered times throughout the year so that committees can meet during the school day. If there is a lack of sufficient administrative and supervisory personnel for committee assignments, this plan enables the chief school official or the assistant superintendent to meet with each curriculum study group.

Step 8

The curriculum council takes care of these administrative matters:

1. A curriculum bulletin is issued, listing all committee assignments for the first work day and including a reminder of the date. Teachers are urged to bring all available course outlines (if any), state guides, and lists of instructional materials presently used in the district in the subject area and grade levels assigned. (See Step 9.)

2. Considering individual talents, at least one administrator or supervisor is appointed to each curriculum committee and in-service program.

3. Outside resource persons are secured immediately, if any are needed at this time.

4. A format for the first day's work is developed, and a copy is sent to all staff members. In addition, a number of these sheets are duplicated for use during Step 9. (See Appendix I, page 304 for a suggested outline.)

Step 9

The first full-day session convenes for the purpose of examining the present state of the district curriculum in the areas that have been selected for study. These procedures might be followed.

1. In a brief general meeting, review the scope of the day's work. Using the suggested format, discuss the main objective for the day: to outline in some detail the existing curriculum for each subject area under study. In other words, "What are we teaching now?" The following should be listed on the outline sheets provided to each committee:

A. Subject-matter units or topics with specific objectives.

B. Concepts, generalizations, attitudes, and skills to be developed.

C. Suggested teaching techniques and pupil experiences.

D. Teacher-pupil resources and instructional materials.

2. The staff divides into the various committees, which proceed as follows:

A. If group process has been developed in the district, a chairman and a recorder are elected. Otherwise, the administrator might lead the committee initially, with the chairmanship changing as the leadership role emerges from the group.

B. Following the format, the existing curriculum for the subject area is summarized.

The subcommittees may be formed at this time. Staff members will be working individually or in two's and three's. The chairman makes sure that everyone understands his assignment and that all grade or instructional levels are covered. For example, if Miss Jones and Miss Smith are the two primary-level representatives on the social studies committee, it is their responsibility to list the existing curriculum in that area from grades kindergarten through third.

Note: All units or topics that are taught by at least one teacher are a part of the current course of study and should be included.

3. At the close of the day's work, the curriculum council members collect the curriculum outlines from the various chairmen.

Important leadership note. Some individuals will need more time to complete this project. The chairman of the curriculum council should ask for all outlines to be completed by a reasonable date—for example, two weeks later.

Step 10

The curriculum council compiles and duplicates the summaries of the existing curriculum in the areas under study. Copies are sent to all staff members with a request that they examine the outlines for omissions, overlapping, and inconsistencies. Reactions should feed back to the council through its members, through the chairmen of all committees, and through the principals in particular. One or two building-staff meetings might be devoted to this purpose.

The next curriculum council meeting includes all curriculum-committee chairmen. The suggested agenda would include the following:

1. An evaluation of the first day's work and the present state of the district's curricular offerings would be the first item. "Where are the gaps?" "How much overlapping and repetition do we have?"

2. A final check is made on research and resource materials in the district curriculum center to be sure that all groups have adequate supplies for the next work day. The person in charge of the center will arrange these materials by subject areas and have them ready for the committees. It may be necessary at this point to send for additional books, pamphlets, or research reports.

3. The purpose of the next full-day session (Step 11) is clearly stated: To begin to examine current philosophy, theory, research, and trends in each area, and to compare the findings with present practice in the district.

4. The general staff meeting for Step 11 is planned.

Step 11

The next curriculum day begins with a general staff session in which the total project to date is summarized. The chief school official or the chairman of the curriculum council presides, and each committee chairman gives a brief report on staff reactions to the existing curriculum as outlined. Any problem areas that have been identified are presented at this time. Vertical overlapping is stressed particularly, along with any obvious gaps in the program. In some subject areas, a shortage of up-to-date instructional materials might be noted.

The remainder of the day is allotted for curriculum committee meetings. In these sessions, readings can be assigned to each member from the resources that have been compiled. Lively, open discussions should then enable all participants to begin to share the current theory, research, and practices in the area under study. Broad cultural and societal goals can be tentatively identified in relation to the needs of pupils and the present curriculum. Committee members are encouraged to borrow books, research materials, and other available items at the end of this day so that they can continue to develop ideas on objectives and general philosophy.

Important leadership note. This day should not be spent in examining sample textbooks or courses of study in detail, although these are on hand for future reference. The temptation is great at this point, especially with the inexperienced curriculum worker, to select a particularly attractive text and to suggest that this might form a good basis for the revised course. Equally dangerous is the common practice of "borrowing" a course of study from another district. Some committee members will be ready to accept almost word for word a well-bound and impressive curriculum outline already prepared by another school staff. Since much of the value of curriculum work is found in the process, the two quick solutions suggested above should be rejected. Textbooks as instructional aids will be selected near the end of the study when objectives, units, concepts, generalizations, attitudes, and skills have been developed. Then, and only then, will it be possible to determine intelligently the necessary materials of instruction for the course.

Obviously, work should not be duplicated unnecessarily, and committees may want to use or adapt portions of several courses of study from other districts. However, this is not the time to narrow the method in this manner. Rather, the chairman must make sure that the study proceeds in depth through all the research and resource materials that are available.

Step 12

The curriculum council convenes immediately after the work session to check the progress of all groups. Some committees may require a resource person or additional research materials. Generally, good working relationships should be established by now.

From this date, the curriculum council will meet at the discretion of its chairman and always at the end of each curriculum day. Continuing functions are to guide, support, and coordinate the various studies.

Step 13

On the next work day, the committees continue to discuss and investigate further the research findings, courses of study from outside districts, and other pertinent materials. Basic questions must be raised and answered:

1. What are we now teaching that is outmoded or that does not agree with our philosophy and objectives?

2. In what ways should our course objectives be changed, if any? Should we specify all instructional objectives in behavioral or performance terms? (Review discussion on pages 232–33.)

3. What are the big ideas in this field today?

4. What does educational research say about scope and sequence for today's curriculum?

5. What are the current trends in this subject area, and why? Are they valid?

6. In terms of the needs of our boys and girls in this community, nation, and world, what are the concepts, generalizations, attitudes, and skills that should be stressed in this subject field?

According to Goodlad,

In curriculum planning, disciplined choice must replace the leisurely, often whimsical, cumulative processes of the past. The selection of most significant bits of content no longer is difficult; it is impossible. Consequently, teachers and pupils must seek out those fundamental concepts, principles, and methods that appear to be most useful for ordering and interpreting man's inquiries.[14]

Step 14

The next curriculum day is a continuation of the last, as all committees continue to plumb their research materials under the direction of the chairmen or outside resource consultants. After the questions in Step 13 have been reasonably answered and tentative objectives identified for the broad subject areas, the task of curriculum construction or revision begins. This work will continue for the remainder of the school year. Depending on their over-all teaching loads, committee members will assume

[14]John I. Goodlad, *Some Propositions in Search of Schools* (Washington, D.C.: Department of Elementary School Principals, National Education Association, 1962), p. 29.

certain responsibilities between work days, as decided by their group and chairman.

It is recommended that an outline similar to the sample on page 304 of the Appendix be used by districts during the early stages of formal curriculum development. More experienced staffs may want to add additional headings or detail.

In any event, the immediate task is identification of subject-matter units or topics for the course under consideration. Following the sample outline, the suggested units with specific objectives are written in some detail in the first column. Then decisions are reached on concepts, generalizations, attitudes, and skills to be developed for each unit, and these are detailed in the second column. Goodlad has made some positive suggestions for this phase of the project:

> The school curriculum should be planned to reveal continuing threads—ideas, generalizations, principles, concepts, methods—by means of which specific learnings might be related effectively one to another. These threads are derived from at least three sources: the developing characteristics of children, the subject-matter disciplines, and the nature of society. . . . However, schools have tended to stress specific bits and pieces of knowledge, in part because these can be packaged attractively for instructional occasions and in part because more basic methods and principles were thought to be beyond the grasp of the young. Research into the alarming rate at which youngsters forget information they have not organized or related and recent experimentation with children's ability to comprehend fundamental methods and principles force a new look at the variables and constants of the . . . curriculum. In the past, specific content has tended to be the constant. Teachers and pupils alike have been left to find unifying principles where and when they could. . . . In the future, specific content must be recognized as dispensable data in the effort to understand things more fundamental and constant.[15]

Behavioral objectives, concepts, principles, and generalizations, then, are most important. In a world where man's knowledge is doubling each generation, a curriculum based on factual content alone is obsolete before it is published.

As curriculum construction proceeds, all members need to think of learning experiences continuing from level to level. There is no room in the modern curriculum guide for rigid grade content. Rather, units are introduced at recommended levels to avoid overlapping, but pupils are encouraged to progress as rapidly as they can. A good outline will enable a teacher to review when necessary—to know which concepts have been introduced and which are yet to come.

Continuing with the suggested format, the third column is used for

---

[15]Goodlad, *Some Propositions in Search of Schools*, pp. 23–24.

teaching techniques or methods and pupil experiences recommended to achieve the objectives. In the last column, teacher-pupil resources and instructional materials are listed. (See Step 15.)

Important leadership note.

1. The evolving written courses of study should not be overemphasized. While these are important, since they reflect the overall framework of the district curriculum, important values of curriculum revision are to be found in the actual participation by staff members. This cannot be emphasized too strongly. Throughout the study, research is evaluated, goals are examined, and attitudes are challenged and sometimes modified or changed; a healthy group interaction takes place. In other words, changes emerge in people and in their classrooms which cannot be measured merely by the final written course of study.

2. It is imperative that all staff members be informed by curriculum bulletin and in meetings of the deliberations of the study committees. Constant intercommunication must take place if, for example, fifty elementary teachers are to accept and begin to teach a new curriculum in social studies prepared by eight of their colleagues.

Building meetings must be held throughout the year to discuss the curriculum work. Administrators and supervisors should take advantage of every opportunity to talk about philosophy, objectives, or contemplated changes at the various levels. Informal discussions between teachers and administrators will reveal any areas in need of clarification, further study, or integration.

It is the responsibility of the committee chairmen and the curriculum council to make sure that sufficient communication takes place among all concerned groups. On a given curriculum day, for example, the elementary reading and the secondary English committees might profitably plan a joint session to share findings to date and to discuss correlation of their work. Of particular interest would be the programs in the sixth and seventh grades, if the elementary-junior high break occurs here.

At the secondary level, several departments will meet together on occasion to coordinate efforts. For example, groups working in mathematics and science will have reason to discuss common areas, and possible interdisciplinary approaches.

Step 15

The selection of instructional materials—an important step in curriculum development—is discussed in Chapters VIII and XI. Only after the units, concepts, generalizations, attitudes, and skills have been structured are the committee members ready to assemble suggested techniques and aids to instruction. This is a continuous process that is never complete. Many good sources of materials are available; some of the following list should be included for each unit. The "Resources" column on the curriculum outline should be as complete as possible—including, for example, titles of films, tapes, and programmed learning devices.

List of teacher-pupil resources and instructional materials.
Textbooks (Basic and supplementary)
Trade and library books
16mm motion picture films
Filmstrips
Commercial and teacher-made slides
Educational television programs (UHF, VHF, and closed circuit)
Programmed learning materials, including teaching machines and programmed textbooks
Tape recordings and transcriptions
Phonograph records
Picture collections (for bulletin board and opaque projector)
Exhibits
Charts
Displays
Community resource persons
Field trips
Projects
Dramatization
Maps and Globes
Flannelboards
Free and inexpensive materials

Note: An excellent booklet from the Pennsylvania Department of Public Instruction, entitled "The School Instructional Materials Center and the Curriculum," describes ways to set up a center for many of the instructional materials listed above.[16] (See also Chapter XI.)

Step 16

The curriculum council makes a final editing of the year's work as written courses of study and progress reports are submitted. Any completed courses are duplicated to be presented for full staff approval or modification early in the fall. Loose-leaf binding is best for this purpose so that the curriculum guides can be kept current. The chairman of the curriculum council makes sure that all completed materials are collected from the various chairmen before school closes for the summer.

[16]Commonwealth of Pennsylvania, *The School Instructional Materials Center and the Curriculum,* Curriculum Development Series No. 5 (Harrisburg, Pa.: Department of Public Instruction, 1962).

Important leadership note. Many districts are hiring interested and qualified teachers, administrators, and supervisors to work during the summer in compiling and editing the work of curriculum committees. Indeed, this is often the only feasible way to complete the work in a reasonable time. The persons assigned to this task should be good writers and experts in the techniques described in this chapter. The summer teams work hand in hand with the regular staff committees. Total involvement in curriculum is desirable, but it is most difficult to complete the entire job during the school year. Thus, a combination of summer work and the procedures described herein is best.

Step 17

The first general staff meeting in the fall should provide opportunity for a review of curriculum development to date, including any work done over the summer. Copies of completed or tentative course outlines should be distributed. In the small or intermediate-size district, discussion can be invited.

Step 18—Continuing Curriculum Study

Continuous evaluation of the ongoing curriculum work is essential. The curriculum council will make sure that a reasonable amount of curriculum development is proceeding at all times. Classroom teachers are usually involved in no more than one committee assignment at a time. Administrators and supervisors often will have multiple responsibilities and assignments as resource persons and group leaders.

The chief school official and the chairman of the curriculum council must always be aware of the total program so that current needs and problems can be assessed.

Each year the cycle of curriculum study will lead the curriculum council back to Step 4. The personnel of this group can change as more staff members develop interest and ability in curriculum development. In this way there will be a widening circle of staff leadership in this vital area.

Important leadership notes. As a district gains experience in curriculum work, additional procedures such as the following may be used:

1. Curriculum guides will contain blank spaces or pages on which classroom teachers may make suggestions for changes, additions to the curriculum materials list, and other comments.

2. Separate sequences may be prepared to cope with the great diversity among learners in all subject areas and at all grade or unit levels. Appropriate instructional materials and techniques can be suggested for the

varying learning abilities of the pupils. Thus, well-developed courses and units will list experiences geared to the potential of a wide variety of students. Individualization of instruction remains a worthy goal.

Curriculum development, then, is seen as a continuous process which is never completed. In an ever-changing society, the curriculum cannot be static. It is always in process, and this means continual evaluation. A written course of study in earth and space science, for example, may represent the best staff thinking at the moment of its completion. However, under classroom use and evaluation, it may prove defective or incomplete, in some respects, within a year. Or it may prove to be basically sound for several years. Only constant evaluation will indicate the appropriate time for complete revision of a course or learning sequence.

A staff trained in curriculum study is always alert to the changing needs of the school and community. Curriculum development is one of the most vital supervisory functions. It must be done thoroughly if subject matter is to come alive in the classroom. Teachers who have a role in democratic curriculum work are more apt to know what they are teaching and why they are teaching it.

CURRICULUM DEVELOPMENT IN ACTION— SOME EXAMPLES

Simon Gratz High School, Philadelphia, Pennsylvania

"Many of the pressing and persistent social problems of students attending a pocket of poverty school—education, poverty, housing, employment, discrimination, consumer education, etc.—have been described many times before. However, it is the intention of the participants in this [program] to involve students and parents in defining, describing, and evaluating the seriousness of these and other social problems in the North Philadelphia area. By linking these problems directly to conditions faced daily by Gratz High students along with the ways students can identify and meet them, the committee can take its work out of the realm of the academic and make it purposeful."

The above quotation from a Curriculum Writing Project typifies the approach to curriculum development at Simon Gratz High School. Principal Marcus A. Foster and his staff work continually to relate the instructional programs of the school to the needs, interests, and aptitudes of the four thousand students. The curriculum is always undergoing dynamic change at Gratz, as evidenced by the following examples.

Curriculum Writing Project. Recently the faculty and administrators concluded that the current curriculum was in many ways outmoded and not really relevant to student and community needs. They asked and received approval from the Philadelphia Board of Education to launch a curriculum writing project that would permit more meaningful content and instructional materials to be developed.

Under the leadership of Marcus Foster, teams of teachers were organized to work under the leadership of vice principals and department heads on Saturdays during the school year. All of the major subject areas were studied, dialogue with many persons in the community was initiated or continued, and the various curricular sequences were dissected and restructured.

Adopting the Brunerian concept of identifying the underlying principles that give structure to a subject or discipline, the Gratz staff agreed that isolated teaching units were undesirable. For example, the diffusion approach to Afro-American history was accepted, in which all aspects of Negro life and history were woven into every subject of the curriculum. It was agreed that racial contributions are so pervasive in every facet of American life that they should not be treated as an isolated unit or course. The basic school curriculum was restructured in order to emphasize the positive role black people have played, and can play, in the building of American society.

"Survival Kit." Several units have been prepared to better enable the learner to exist in the city. Drawing on English, social sciences, and mathematics, these curriculum sequences deal with such practical problems as these:

1. What do you do when the landlord won't fix the house?
2. How do you organize for political change?
3. What do you do when you're gypped on an installment plan?

The "survival kit" is an experience-based curriculum that deals with real issues and solutions. Math takes on meaning when it helps you to figure true interest on an installment contract.

Industry Councils for relevant curriculums. Department heads and teachers have organized industry councils involving unions and employers to advise the school staff on practical courses. Current instructional programs at Simon Gratz High School that reflect such industry-union-teacher cooperation are printing, sign shop, drafting, power sawing, upholstery, tailoring, and building maintenance. The school also has an agreement with the telephone company to train linesmen and telephone repairmen.

The 15 Point School Improvement Program. As can be seen in the Appendix, page 305, this innovative program serves a number of critical needs in the school and community. For example, the first effort described is the health careers program. Gratz students have been placed in over sixty research laboratories in hospitals, industries, and other institutions. Here they serve as student assistants, working under experts in the fields of medicine and biochemistry.

It is obvious that Principal Marcus Foster, vice principals, the department heads, teachers, parents, and students at Simon Gratz High School are jointly developing learning experiences that are literally raising the sights and educational level of the entire community. Here curriculum development is no "ivory tower" operation. Rather, the instructional program is continually tested on the crucible of the inner city—its problems, frustrations, and challenges. What doesn't work is modified or discarded. New paths are constantly charted as the Simon Gratz staff strives to offer ever more relevant learning experiences for their four thousand students.

Clark County School District, Las Vegas, Nevada

The following Curriculum Development Procedure was initiated by the Clark County School District. The step-by-step procedure is charted in Figure 14.

Step by step procedure.

1. The identification of curriculum problems and needs will be determined by the Curriculum Commission.
2. The administrative staff of the Division of Instruction will develop a plan to solve the problems identified by the Curriculum Commission.
3. The administrative staff submits a plan of action to the Advisory Council requesting that they review the feasibility of implementing the proposed plan.
4. The Division of Instruction will submit the recommended plan to the Cabinet, Superintendent, and Board for their information.
5. The Division of Instruction will organize a Task Force from qualified Clark County School District personnel who will write a curriculum publication.
6. The Task Force will submit a working copy to the Instructional Communication Commission and the Research and Development Department.
7. The revised plan will be submitted to the Reaction Committee and the Cabinet for changes.
8. The Curriculum Commission receives the final form of the curriculum publication as an information item.
9. The Instructional Communications Commission and the Research and Development Department submits adoptions and descriptions of evaluative techniques to the Curriculum Task Force.
10. The Curriculum Task Force will prepare the continuative document for publication.

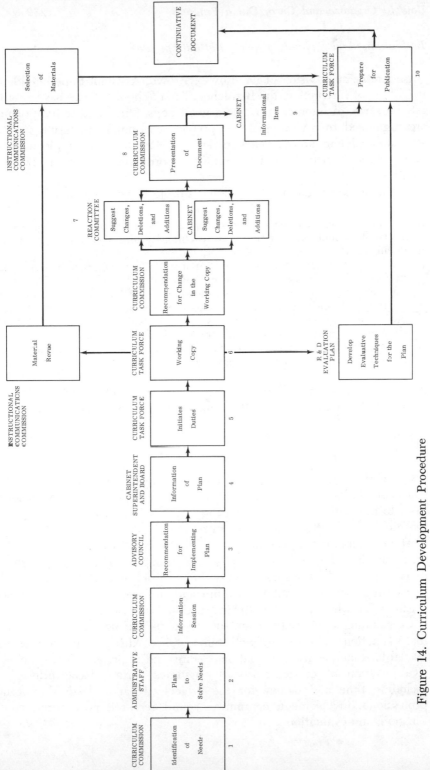

Figure 14. Curriculum Development Procedure

Bethlehem Area School District, Bethlehem, Pa.

Under the supervision of Dr. Roy A. Brown, Assistant Superintendent in Charge of Instruction, the Bethlehem Area School District has inaugurated a series of summer curriculum workshops. Study and writing teams are organized to review, plan, or prepare curriculum materials in the several academic areas. Teachers are employed on a supplementary basis, while principals and curriculum coordinators serve on twelve-month contracts.

During a recent summer, the following projects were scheduled:

1. A team of four mathematics teachers identified, selected, and correlated multi-media materials for the basic teaching-learning concepts of geometry in the junior and senior high schools.
2. Six elementary teachers developed an instructional program in the social studies and the sciences, focusing on new materials and media. This team was supervised by an elementary principal and a curriculum coordinator.
3. A group of junior high English teachers continued a curriculum materials project in reading. The objectives were to organize all reading materials in sequence, and to proceed with the development of a program in three areas of reading: corrective, developmental, and enrichment. A curriculum coordinator supervised the project.

Note: A summary of recent curriculum development efforts in the Bethlehem Area School District may be found in the Appendix, page 311.

SUMMARY

Curriculum study is one of the most significant tasks challenging the supervisor today. In an age of unprecedented change, the nation's schools need to direct their attention to a thorough evaluation of what they are teaching and how they are teaching it.

The curriculum has been defined as all of the planned experiences provided by the school to assist pupils in attaining the designated learning outcomes to the best of their abilities. Supervisors should be familiar with developing theories of the curriculum and the newer patterns of school organization which can affect the instructional program.

Curriculum determination and/or design is the necessary and legitimate function of a strong, well-staffed school district, which uses all available resources from the national, state, and regional levels. An effective program of curriculum study assumes certain basic principles, including time and money for the project, dynamic leadership, total professional involvement, continuity, sound research procedures, coordination, and evaluation.

In planning for effective curriculum development in the school district, the basic administrative unit is the curriculum council or steering committee. All administrators with some responsibility for supervision of instruction are logically members, except in very large systems. It is imperative that teachers are included in the membership of this council. The district curriculum council's main responsibilities are to coordinate all curriculum and instructional programs in the district and to recommend basic policy changes to the chief school administrator. The council also organizes, under direction of the assistant superintendent in charge of instruction, the various subject-area committees which carry out the continuing work in curriculum evaluation and change.

The process of curriculum design is concerned, initially, with the identification of values. Next is a statement of the philosophy of the school district followed by specification of the goals which the school hopes to attain. Further refinement will lead to the statement of objectives in behavioral or performance terms. Then the basic groupings of curriculum content, or the subject areas to be taught, are identified, revised, or refined.

Next, the subject-area curriculum committee picks up the process of curriculum development, and begins to consider objectives for the subject field. This is followed by specification of instructional objectives in behavioral terms. As various learning sequences are then developed, the curriculum workers go beyond simple factual content to include the processes of inquiry and discovery, experimentation, and debate. Opportunities are included in each sequence for observation, reflection and problem solving. In every case the learner is given many chances to form his own concepts, generalizations, and insights. Appropriate learning resources and teaching methods are then incorporated into the developing curriculum guide.

A comprehensive step-by-step outline for action is often useful in launching a program of curriculum development.

In an ever-changing society, the school's instructional program cannot be static. It is always in process, with most subject areas under careful study and evaluation at all times. Curriculum development is a continuous function which is never completed.

SUGGESTED ACTIVITIES AND PROBLEMS

1. Read several sources on developing theories of the curriculum. Write up a viable curriculum theory.
2. Interview a chief school administrator or assistant superintendent in charge of instruction to determine the status of curriculum development in the school district. Write up your findings and give a critique.
3. Select a school system which has organized a district curriculum council

or its equivalent. Summarize the activities of this group for the past year.
4. Write a critical analysis of Robert F. Mager's book, *Preparing Instructional Objectives.*
5. Interview the chairman of a subject area curriculum committee to discover the nature of his responsibilities and duties. Report your findings.
6. Set up an appropriate time schedule for a year of curriculum study in a district of your choice. Include plans for summer work by selected staff members.

SELECTED READINGS

Conner, Forrest, and Ellena, William J., eds. *Curriculum Handbook for School Administrators.* Washington, D.C.: American Association of School Administrators, 1967.

Frost, Joe L., and Rowland, G. Thomas. *Curricula for the Seventies, Early Childhood Through Early Adolescence.* Boston: Houghton Mifflin Company, 1969.

Goodlad, John I.; Von Stoephasius, Renata; and Klein, M. Frances. *The Changing School Curriculum.* New York: The Fund for the Advancement of Education, 1966.

Gwynn, J. Minor, and Chase, John B., Jr. *Curriculum Principles and Social Trends.* 4th ed. New York: The Macmillan Company, 1969.

Hass, Glen, and Wiles, Kimball, eds. *Readings in Curriculum.* Boston: Allyn & Bacon, Inc., 1965.

Inlow, Gail M. *The Emergent in Curriculum.* New York: John Wiley & Sons, Inc., 1966.

King, Arthur R., Jr., and Brownell, John A. *The Curriculum and the Disciplines of Knowledge.* New York: John Wiley & Sons, Inc., 1966.

McNeil, John D. *Curriculum Administration, Principles and Techniques of Curriculum Development.* New York: The Macmillan Company, 1965.

Rational Planning in Curriculum and Instruction. Washington, D.C.: National Education Association Center for the Study of Instruction, 1967.

Saylor, J. Galen, and Alexander, William M. *Curriculum Planning for Modern Schools.* New York: Holt, Rinehart & Winston, Inc., 1966.

Silva, Dolores, ed. *Samplings.* Future Schools Study Project—Albuquerque Public Schools in co-operation with Temple University, Department of Curriculum Theory and Development, I, no. 3 (1967).

Wiles, Kimball. *Supervision for Better Schools.* 3rd ed., Chap. 6. Englewood Cliffs, N.J.: Prentice-Hall, Inc., 1967.

chapter 11

Selecting and Using Effective Learning Resources and Techniques[1]

John Bright, the assistant superintendent for instruction in Midvale School District, was both pensive and troubled as he closed his office door at the end of a particularly hectic day. Among his many appointments and activties throughout the district that day, he remembered the following especially:

8:30 A.M.—The parent of a junior high school student questioned the content and propriety of a 16mm film shown in her daughter's health class tho provious day.

8:50 A.M.—The director of the county regional instructional materials center called to request the assignment of a teacher to the film preview committee in science.

9:30 A.M.—A senior high school social studies teacher stopped in to discuss the possibility of converting a basement storage room into six individual study carrels. Of course, dial access equipment would be needed to enable students to select and study video-tapes stored at the district master studio.

10:15 A.M.—The first salesman of the day arrived with a set of 3,000 master color diazo transparencies that "every district needs to be up to date in all subject areas."

11:05 A.M.—The superintendent of schools called to ask Mr. Bright if Midvale was considering computer-assisted instruction. "After all, Shadeland District is seriously studying this CAI, or whatever it's called, and they're only 12 miles away!"

[1]Pages 261–71 are quoted and adapted from Ross L. Neagley and N. Dean Evans, *Handbook for Effective Curriculum Development* (Englewood Cliffs, N.J.: Prentice-Hall, Inc., 1967), Chapter Eight. Reprinted with permission of the publisher.

12:10 P.M.—During lunch in one of the elementary schools, the principal asked Mr. Bright if the board had approved district membership in the newly forming tri-state educational television council. It seems that the local PTA had already agreed to purchase the necessary TV sets.

2:00 P.M.—Returning to his office, Mr. Bright found three visitors waiting. One was a textbook salesman with a "new math series you just have to see." The next was an educational representative from a large manufacturing company in the area who had some free booklets on patriotism sprinkled with a specific philosophy of economics. "Your high school seniors ought to study these." The last visitor of the day was a salesman with several "brand new" programmed texts in algebra, English grammer, and chess.

John Bright had just cause to be troubled that evening. He knew that he was expected to be competent in the field of learning resources and newer instructional techniques and media. After all he was the assistant superintendent in charge of instruction. And yet he felt inadequate to cope with many of the pressures and demands.

There is little wonder that John Bright and his fellow curriculum workers across the nation feel such frustration. As the knowledge explosion continues apace in all fields, an avalanche of teaching materials and resources threatens to inundate even the hardiest supervisor or classroom teacher. And yet this threat is offset by the promise that some of the newer devices and instructional materials can substantially help educators to achieve that most elusive of all goals—the individualization of the learning process.

But how do the local district and its curriculum personnel make sense out of the jungle of new textbooks, supplementary books, open and closed circuit TV, 8 and 16mm sound films, tapes, maps and globes, programmed learning devices, and all the rest? There is, of course, no magic formula. However, it is the purpose of this chapter to suggest guidelines that should enable the curriculum worker to select and properly use effective learning resources in each subject area. The reader will first note the position of this chapter in the handbook. It is no accident that selection of learning resources and techniques of instruction *follows* the curriculum development processes presented in Chapter X. *Only after the curriculum has been thoroughly studied and revised in terms of objectives and content should learning techniques and resources be chosen.* Instructional materials should never determine content to be taught, as they will do if they are introduced into the curriculum haphazardly or prematurely.

The remainder of this chapter will deal with: (1) effective organization of educational agencies to efficiently provide learning resources, and

(2) examples of modern instructional aids and their possible contribution to the curriculum. In every context it must be remembered that no matter how advanced or sophisticated the device or technique, it will be fully successful as a learning aid only when used under the direction of a skillful teacher who knows the objectives and content of the curriculum.

HOW TO ORGANIZE FOR ADMINISTRATION OF LEARNING RESOURCE SERVICES

Adequate organizational structure for the selection and utilization of resources for the curriculum involves at least four levels of administration and service: the state, the region, the school district, and the school building. The curriculum worker should be aware of the unique functions of each level as he seeks the best possible instructional materials and services to help implement the curriculum in the classroom.

Available State Facilities

A number of state departments of education are assuming leadership roles in the production and distribution of certain instructional materials, as follows:

1. Master audio tape libraries have been established to serve the entire state. In some cases where central facilities are adequate, teachers or supervisors may send blank tapes directly to the state center and have recorded on them selections from a catalog which is available in all schools.[2] In other states blank tapes are submitted through the regional curriculum or instructional materials centers.
2. Educational motion picture films and video-taped programs are produced. Prints are then offered to regional educational television councils and instructional materials centers for distribution.
3. Various curriculum publications are issued, listing pertinent instructional resources for particular units and subject areas. For example, one state department has published a complete bibliography on Intergroup Relations including books, 16mm films, records, tapes, and filmstrips.[3]
4. Standards and specifications for equipment such as television sets, projectors, language laboratories, record players, screens, and tape recorders are often established to insure basic quality. These standards are only suggested, but they are often enforced by the provisions for the purchase of this equipment under the National Defense Education Act.

[2]*Tapes for Teaching Catalog* (Harrisburg, Pa.: Bureau of Instructional Materials and Services, Department of Public Instruction, Commonwealth of Pennsylvania, 1964).

[3]*Insight, A Bibliography on Intergroup Relations for Pennsylvania Schools*, Department of Public Instruction, Commonwealth of Pennsylvania, I, no. 7 (1966).

Regional or Intermediate Unit Services

It has been determined that many learning resources can be most efficiently provided by regional curriculum or instructional materials centers. These centers can be organized with the leadership of the county superintendent, the intermediate unit of administration, or by agreement of school districts covering a larger regional area.

In any geographic area there are services that are almost impossible to render efficiently or economically at the state or local district level. One of these is the 16mm sound film service. With the high initial cost of prints and the accelerating rate of obsolescence as prime considerations, all but the very largest school districts will find it most impractical to attempt to build up their own libraries of 16mm offerings. By joining together in forming a county or multi-county center, however, schools can cooperatively purchase and distribute films to each building. With modern and simplified booking procedures and with delivery provided by the center's own trucks, classroom teachers can usually be assured of instructional films when they need them. At the very least, the percentage of bookings will be considerably higher than would be possible from a statewide or university rental library. Also, experience shows that the cost per delivered film will be much lower from a regional center, and the time periods for film loans can be shortened. Large rental libraries must use the mails, and this results in longer booking periods and fewer bookings per print per year.

In addition to the 16mm film service, regional centers can offer the following for the curriculum worker and classroom teacher:

1. Audio taping service can be made available directly to member schools, or can be provided in cooperation with the state master tape library, if any.
2. Through joint action with an area educational TV council or broadcasting station, video-tapes of instructional programs can be stored and catalogued for replay on video-tape recorders in local schools. Tapes would be booked as needed by classroom teachers. Also, through a 2500 megacycle outlet or closed-circuit cable network, the regional center could replay tapes as requested.
3. Regional centers often produce certain instructional materials such as master transparencies for the overhead projector. Copies can then be made from the masters for schools requesting them.
4. The director of the center and his assistants are in a position to offer professional advice to curriculum committees on the selection of appropriate learning resources. In addition, they are available to conduct in-service programs for supervisors and teachers on the best ways of using audio-visual and other resources.

Organizing District and School Centers

Many instructional materials should be available at the school district or building level. These would usually include texts and supplementary books, library books, filmstrips, slides, programmed learning materials, exhibits, maps, globes, and picture collections. To encourage the effective use of various learning resources in the instructional program, the curriculum worker and supervisor must see that the maximum number of such materials are directly available to the classroom teacher, either in his school or from a nearby district center.

It is difficult in a general discussion to identify those resources that might best be provided in the individual buildings, and those which should be collected and disseminated from a central district depository. Many variables will have to be considered as these centers are established in a particular school system. For example, if the entire educational plant, K–12, is located on a single site in an educational park, then one resource center might be adequate for all levels, but if the district is large and the buildings are scattered geographically, then the major emphasis would probably be on separate centers in each school, with expensive and rarely used resources being maintained in the district center.

The district curriculum council should have a primary role in determining the placement and function of instructional materials centers in the district. The goal should always be to provide the necessary resources to the classroom teacher as efficiently as possible, and at a cost that can be justified. The district council and supervisory staff will usually need to seek consultant help in organizing the various local centers. The district library staff should be helpful, since there will be many areas of joint concern. Assistance also can be provided by the director of the regional curriculum or instructional materials center, or by a staff member from the intermediate unit. The Pennsylvania Department of Public Instruction published a very helpful booklet outlining ways of organizing such centers at the district level.[4]

The previous discussion has merely outlined the four levels at which instructional resources can be provided: the state, the region, the school district, and the individual building. Typical functions and services were listed for the various levels, but we merely scratched the surface of possible learning materials and services that may be provided by each agency. The ultimate decisions on resources to be provided will grow

[4] *The School Instructional Materials Center and the Curriculum*, Curriculum Development Series No. 5 (Harrisburg, Pa.: Department of Public Instruction, Commonwealth of Pennsylvania, 1962).

out of the need to find the best possible techniques and materials to implement the curriculums which have been developed by the local subject area committees.

HOW TO PLAN FOR THE SELECTION AND USE OF MODERN INSTRUCTIONAL MATERIALS AND TECHNIQUES

The curriculum worker and the subject-area committee are most concerned at the district level with the selection of appropriate learning resources to help achieve the objectives of the curriculum. The following guidelines are designed to aid local personnel in the selection and classroom use of the best modern instructional techniques and materials.

Important leadership note.

1. Each subject-area committee should maintain an up-to-date file of the latest learning resources in the field. Such sources as those listed in Chapter X, pages 241–42, should be available and regularly used. . . .

2. Refer all suggestions for inclusion of new learning resources or deletion of present materials to the appropriate subject area committee for consideration. This is a policy which can be made clear to all salesmen, parents, representatives of commercial interests, and pressure groups of various kinds. Never make any "snap" decisions on new instructional materials.

3. Appoint a director (or coordinator) of learning resources for the school district. This may be a part-time position, but in larger systems it should be full-time. The director can meet with subject-area committees to assist them in the selection of instructional materials. He also will plan in-service programs to train teachers in the use of new media and resources.

4. See that the subject-area coordinators and all supervisory personnel are well informed on the services offered by the state and regional curriculum or instructional materials centers. Local district personnel should have a part to play in determining the kinds of materials to be purchased by the regional center. The subject-area coordinator in social studies, for example, will assign a member of his committee to the social studies film preview committee at the center. Also, each coordinator should be thoroughly familiar with the services provided by the state in his field, and it is hoped that he will have opportunities to help develop policy for the selection and distribution of instructional materials at all levels.

5. The district curriculum council should recommend policy on the consideration and adoption of all learning resources. This policy then becomes the framework within which each subject-area committee operates.

By following the above recommendations a school district will have a fighting chance to keep abreast of the growing numbers and kinds of instructional resources that are flooding every subject field. Decentralization is the key, so that subject matter experts will be studying the latest developments in their fields, calling in resource personnel and consultants to assist when necessary, and making decisions based on the developing curriculum.

The subject-area committee will have the continuous job of collecting and analyzing the current learning resources, and then identifying appropriate materials and techniques for use with the developing curriculum. This is a task that is never finished as the committee and ultimately the classroom teacher seek to achieve the objectives of the curriculum through effective learning experiences.

In the following discussion modern instructional resources and techniques are considered. The curriculum worker will select from these and many others the methodology, hardware, and learning materials necessary to implement all facets of the changing curriculum.

The New Role of the Textbook

The most traditional of all learning aids, the textbook, occupies a different position in the modern curriculum. Historically it has been the basic resource in the classroom, containing most of what was to be taught. Today it is impossible to conceive of any one book encompassing the varied learning experiences demanded by a comprehensive curriculum. Modern methods of inquiry demand that many sources be consulted so that the student can compare concepts and their interpretation, differing points of view, and the conclusions of various researchers.

What, then, is the new role of the textbook? While a comprehensive, balanced text may be selected as one of the basic resources for a course or segment of the curriculum, it is usually much more desirable to examine and select several texts that cover the objectives and content. By having copies of various basic and supplementary books available in the classroom, the students can engage in real study and research. The same is true of encyclopedias. Learners should have access to several of the leading sets at any level, so that comparative ideas and facts may be explored.

Printed resources are still important aids to instruction. But the student must not get the idea that all or most of the learnings on a particular topic can be found between the pages of a book. As emphasized earlier in this handbook, true learning is far more than this.

Procedures for effective textbook selection have been detailed in Chapter VIII of this handbook.

The Educational Motion Picture

Sixteen millimeter sound films, many of them in color, can provide classroom experiences that are quite realistic. Increasing numbers are available in all of the subject areas so that curriculum committees can select those which best fit the objectives of the learning sequence. Previewing can be done at the district or regional center level, but it is imperative that the content and techniques of a particular film be known before it is listed in the curriculum guide as a resource for a specific unit.

Eight millimeter sound and silent films are being used in more curriculums because of their low cost and availability at the building or district level. With the expanded "Super-8" frame and improved projection equipment, it is possible to throw a large, clear picture on the typical classroom screen. The 8mm silent film cartridges are designed to teach or reinforce single concepts in a learning sequence. For example, these short, inexpensive films can be purchased for such units as the planets, dinosaurs, shape of the earth, and structure of the United Nations.

The Overhead Projection Transparency

One of the most exciting modern media for the curriculum worker and teacher is the large transparency. This technique requires a relatively inexpensive projector and a large screen for the classroom. The teacher may then project prepared transparencies or may draw figures, charts or other data directly on a piece of film as the class progresses.

Increasing numbers of commercially prepared transparencies, many with intricate overlays, are appearing on the market. As usual, the curriculum committee in any subject field will want to examine carefully what is available, and then list in the curriculum guide those sets which seem appropriate. Or the committee may recommend that special transparencies be prepared locally or in the regional center to meet the objectives and content needs of a particular learning unit.

Instructional Television

Despite a number of promising experiments throughout the country, the medium of television has proven difficult to harness as an effective classroom resource. There are several reasons for this problem. Many programs have been broadcast over educational TV stations to large school audiences, and it is virutally impossible to assure that lessons involving direct instruction on the air will fit the curriculums developed in hundreds of schools within the viewing range. Also, scheduling of TV programs has been a big problem, particularly in secondary schools. The advent of low cost video-tape recorders, however, has improved this situation.

Curriculum committees considering television as a potential resource should take the following steps:

1. See that the school district affiliates with the regional educational television council or station so that the district's voice may be heard in planning the programs.
2. Insist that most instructional TV programs be developed as supplementary or enrichment experiences rather than as direct teaching courses, for the latter tend to remove curriculum decision-making from the local district to the TV council. Or worse, it is impossible for all viewing districts to agree on the basic objectives and content of courses to be taught.
3. Consider video-tapes and kinescopes of TV programs that are available through regional broadcasting councils and commercial sources.
4. Purchase video-tape recorders for each school building and hire enough technicians to operate them. A trend of the future may be twenty-four-hour-a-day broadcasting by educational television stations. This will mean that a number of video-taped instructional programs can be aired during the night and recorded at the school for rebroadcast at a time selected by the teacher.
5. Consider a closed-circuit cable network or 2500 megacycle outlet for a group of school districts or counties. This would make much more flexibility and control of programs possible.

In any event, do not let the television "dog" wag the curriculum "tail." Remember, TV is or can be a valuable resource, but it should not determine the curriculum.

Programmed Learning

Although much more research is needed, programmed textbooks or units and programmed materials prepared for teaching machines have demonstrated their ability to help individualize instruction. Since most programs present their content in small portions or frames, arranged in sequence from simple to advanced concepts, the student is able to progress at his own rate. Programmed materials demand an immediate response from the learner, who is then told whether he is right or wrong. Thus the powerful stimulant of reinforcement motivates the student to further effort. Well developed programs lead to continuous correct responses and learning proceeds accordingly.

Most programs have been developed in factual subjects, although research in programming of creative areas is progressing. Programmed learning materials, properly selected and used, can help with many of the routine aspects of instruction, thus freeing the teacher for the major learning activities in which teacher-pupil interaction is vital.

As with other instructional resources, the curriculum worker must carefully examine the content of programmed learning materials to determine their applicability to the portion of the curriculum under study. The psychologist should be helpful at this point in evaluating the learning processes involved in particular programs.

Electronic Push-Button Instruction

The age of electronics has arrived in the nation's classrooms. Teachers in specially equipped teaching centers can dial audio- or video-tape programs or motion pictures as they are needed in the instructional program. Or, through pushing several buttons, a series of colored slides can be projected on the screen from a control center. Student carrels with TV screens and headsets provide dial-access equipment for individualized study, utilizing video-tapes, microfilmed materials, and motion pictures. Teachers with individual terminals on their desks or at home can dial computer centers for research and resource information on units they are planning to initiate.

It is easy to become enamored with all of this marvelous technology. But the curriculum worker must keep his feet on the ground and insist that such hardware be used for one main purpose: to enhance the learning experiences of students in accordance with the objectives and content of the curriculum.

Computer-Assisted Instruction

In recent years the computer has been developed as a teaching device which, according to its advocates, has a real capability of adapting the instructional environment to the needs and characteristics of the individual learner. There seems to be little doubt that computers hold great promise for individualizing instruction at any level. In the usual installation, terminals are connected to a central computer in which the curriculum content is stored on magnetic disks or tapes. There is really no limit to the number of courses or units which can be programmed and stored. Modified "typewriters" are used for two-way communication between the student and the computer.

The curriculum worker will, of course, be concerned with the basic data which is originally stored in the computer. He must make sure that course development always proceeds from the values identified by the community, and the purposes and objectives of the curriculum. The computer will "think" and respond, not only according to the needs, questions and responses of the student, but mainly on the basis of the content originally "fed" into it. The human mind of the curriculum worker must still determine ultimate objectives on which the computer program will be based.

Important leadership note. Many of the techniques and learning resources summarized briefly in this chapter will quickly become obsolete as the new technology continues to develop at a fantastic pace. It is, therefore, difficult to visualize with any degree of certainty the typical classroom or learning center of 1980. And yet the determination of learning experiences to be introduced into the instructional program will always be a main concern of the curriculum worker. The task ahead, then, is to keep oneself informed and open-minded regarding the changes in learning resources and techniques of instruction that will continue to occur in every field of man's endeavor. By constantly focusing on the evolving goals of instruction and the content necessary to achieve them, the curriculum worker will best be able to select appropriate methods and resources for the total learning environment.

THE ROLES OF SUPERVISORY PERSONNEL IN SELECTING AND USING LEARNING RESOURCES

An effective learning resources program is dependent upon the leadership of those supervisors responsible for improvement of instruction. The following is a summary of the roles of key persons in the process.[5]

The Chief School Administrator

A dynamic, alert, intelligent superintendent of schools is the key to a successful learning resources program. Although he will have little time to participate directly in media selection, production, or use, his attitudes and actions profoundly influence teaching methods and resources. In all respects he sets the tone for district philosophy and practice.

The chief administrator can provide leadership in the following ways.

1. Analyze the budget to determine total funds expended for various instructional media in the several subject areas; amounts spent in the various

---

[5]Pages 271–75 are quoted and adapted from Ross L. Neagley, N. Dean Evans, and Clarence A. Lynn, Jr., *The School Administrator and Learning Resources: A Handbook for Effective Action* (Englewood Cliffs, N.J.: Prentice-Hall, Inc., 1969), pp. 54–64 and 76–77.

schools; and totals for the elementary and secondary levels. The superintendent will then know exactly what his media dollars are buying.
2. Read as much as possible in the field of new instructional media and route pertinent articles and books to other members of the staff.
3. See that the agendas of the district administrative council or curriculum council provide for periodic discussions on learning resources.
4. Support budget requirements for various media recommended by the assistant superintendent in charge of instruction, and growing out of current curriculum studies in the district.
5. Work with other chief administrators and the local intermediate unit staff to provide or expand needed cooperative services in learning resources.
6. Visit innovative schools and learning resource centers at least two or three times a year.
7. Spend considerable time in the schools, classrooms, and other learning centers of the district to observe the role of media in many teaching-learning situations. Confer with teachers, coordinators, and principals.
8. See that the board of education receives periodic reports on the learning resources program and its contribution to the fulfillment of curriculum objectives.
9. Make sure that professional contracts provide released time for participation of all staff members in the program of curriculum development, including the selection of appropriate instructional media.

In summary, the chief administrator's main task is to provide top-level support for the learning resources program. This is evidenced by his enthusiasm, his expanding knowledge of the field, and by his coordination of all curriculum activities in the school district. His most important personnel decision concerns the administrator to whom he delegates the responsibility and authority for the development of the curriculum and supporting media.

The Assistant Superintendent in Charge of Instruction

The responsibilities of the assistant superintendent encompass supervision and coordination of the entire instructional process, including curriculum development. In every sense he is the team leader for instruction (see Chapter IV). In developing the instructional media program, he performs the following leadership tasks.

1. He keeps up-to-date on the latest research and technical developments in the field of learning resources. He relies on the director of learning resources and the curriculum coordinators to keep him abreast of new trends, but he also reads as widely as he can.
2. The assistant superintendent meets regularly with all those administrators who report directly to him: the principals, the director of learning resources, and the subject-area curriculum coordinators. This group forms

the nucleus of the district curriculum council, which makes all major decisions regarding the instructional program and its supporting media. The assistant superintendent usually is the catalytic agent of the council, coordinating the group action that emerges.

3. He delegates considerable responsibility and authority to the director of learning resources, and expects him to work cooperatively with the principals and subject-area curriculum coordinators in exploring new thrusts or changes in instructional aids. In the media field, the director of learning resources is obviously the right arm of the assistant superintendent, who relies heavily on him for guidance in making the ultimate decisions regarding introduction or modification of media systems and resources in the district.

4. The assistant superintendent spends at least two days a week in the schools talking with principals, curriculum coordinators, and teachers, and participating in the instructional program as an observer and resource person.

5. He participates, whenever possible, in the meetings of the subject-area committees and knows the current status of each curriculum study. He relies on the curriculum coordinators to keep him informed of progress in each area.

6. The assistant superintendent keeps the chief school administrator informed on all major instructional projects, especially possible changes being considered by the curriculum council or the subject-area committees. This is particularly important if there are budget considerations involved, for instance, in the introduction of new educational technology.

7. Beyond the school district, the assistant superintendent in charge of instruction has a major responsibility, with the director of learning resources, for determining the extent of district participation in county, regional, state, and federal programs for learning resources.

In some intermediate and larger school districts, the positions of coordinator of elementary or secondary education are found (see Chapter IV). Usually these administrators report directly to the assistant superintendent in charge of instruction, serving as assistant administrators for elementary or secondary education. They are therefore delegated certain responsibilities in the learning resources program.

The Principal

The comprehensive supervisory role of the principal is discussed in Chapter V of this handbook. As a phase of his leadership in improving instruction, he assists in the administration of the learning resources program in several significant ways.

1. Within the framework of cooperatively-developed district curriculum guides, he encourages his staff members to experiment with new media that show promise in realizing the stated goals of instruction.

2. The principal serves as a member of the district curriculum council and is able to present his own views on learning resources, as well as reflecting the ideas of his staff. From his classroom visits and other supervisory activities, the principal brings a wealth of helpful data to any problem on the council agenda.
3. He confers on a regular basis with the director of learning resources and the subject-area curriculum coordinators to deepen his own understanding of instructional media and their relationship to the evolving curriculum.
4. While his desk is usually piled higher with unread periodicals than those of other administrators, the principal tries to keep himself generally abreast of new developments in learning resources through his professional reading.
5. At the request of the assistant superintendent in charge of instruction and the subject-area curriculum coordinators, the principal recommends master teachers to serve on various curriculum committees and to participate in extra-contractual summer work. The principal is best qualified to know the strengths of his own staff members.
6. The principal plans faculty meetings around curricular themes that seem to grow out of the deep concerns of his staff. While not guaranteed to keep a tired teacher alert after 4:00 P.M., such topics as: "The computer and instruction" or "Anyone for wet carrels in the classroom?" will provide livelier discussion than "Improving playground supervision."
7. Principals should visit each other's schools often and have lunch with one another occasionally, just to explore common goals, aspirations, and problems, without emphasizing the latter. They should also visit exemplary schools to get ideas for improving their own curriculum and learning resources.

The Subject-Area Curriculum Coordinator

The curriculum coordinator's role has grown from that of the high-school department head, and in advancing districts is now a full-time position, with responsibilities for the elementary and secondary curriculum (see Chapters VI and X). Basically, the subject-area coordinator is the local expert in his field, working cooperatively with principals, teachers, and the director of learning resources.

The main functions of the typical subject-area curriculum coordinator which pertain to learning resources can be described as follows.

1. He serves as chairman of the district-wide curriculum committee in his field, which ultimately decides on the instructional resources to be recommended for a particular learning sequence.
2. The subject-area curriculum coordinator meets often with the director of learning resources to make sure that he is up-to-date on the latest media in his area. For example, the language arts coordinator would want to know about the new filmstrips in linguistics, the latest video-tape series on great English poets, and the experimental computer program in beginning reading.

3. He regularly visits schools and classrooms to observe, participate, and confer. By knowing teachers and principals well, the subject coordinator is in a better position to evaluate cooperatively the learning resources now in use.
4. The subject-area curriculum coordinator keeps his superior, the assistant superintendent in charge of instruction, fully informed on the latest curricular trends in his particular field and is a constant resource regarding the feasibility of using various instructional media.

The Director (or Coordinator) of Learning Resources

This administrator is responsible for the supervision of the entire learning resources program of the school district. Reporting to the assistant superintendent in charge of instruction, he is expected to maintain close contact with all district administrators, curriculum coordinators, and teachers.

His specific leadership activities include the following.

1. The director of learning resources meets with all subject-area curriculum committees to assist in the identification of criteria for the selection of learning materials, and in the acquisition of the appropriate resources.
2. He works closely with the subject-area curriculum coordinators to help keep them up-to-date on the latest learning resources in their respective fields.
3. He organizes in-service programs to enable effective utilization of all types of learning resources.
4. The director of learning resources continually develops effective procedures for the evaluation and selection of all learning materials and equipment.
5. He prepares the learning resources budget to be submitted to the assistant superintendent. This budget is the outgrowth of many identified needs in the district, flowing mainly from the principals and the various curriculum committees.
6. The director plans a program to train technicians, clerks, and student aides in the production of certain learning resources and the operation of instructional equipment.
7. He provides for the continuous evaluation of the learning resources program based on the philosophy and objectives of the instructional program.

SUMMARY

Individuals serving in a supervisory capacity can easily become bewildered by the great array of learning resources and techniques that are now available for the improvement of instruction. It is difficult, if not impossible, to keep current on these aids to the curriculum and instruction.

Supervisory personnel must be certain that the selection and use of new learning resources and procedures are a consequence of a thorough study of the curriculum in terms of both objectives and content.

Supervisors likewise must become aware of the unique functions that may be performed by the state, the region, the school district, and the individual school unit in respect to the selection, storage, distribution, and use of learning resources.

The new role of the textbook in learning, various types of educational motion pictures, overhead projection transparencies, instructional television, programmed learning, electronic push-button instruction, and computer-assisted instruction are among the avalanche of learning resources and techniques with which the supervisor must become familiar.

An effective learning resources program is dependent upon the leadership of the following supervisory personnel, whose roles must be carefully defined: the chief school administrator, the assistant superintendent in charge of instruction, the principal, the subject-area curriculum coordinator, and the director (or coordinator) of learning resources.

SUGGESTED ACTIVITIES AND PROBLEMS

1. Select the curriculum area with which you are the most familiar and list a minimum of ten objectives for this area. Demonstrate how these objectives would influence the selection of specific learning resources and techniques.
2. Write to three state departments of education and request a list of services they provide to local school districts. Compare and contrast these services and evaluate your findings in terms of their potential value to a school district.
3. On the basis of the material in this chapter prepare an interview guide to be used in interviewing the director of either a regional or local learning resources center. Using the guide, conduct an interview with an official serving in either of these positions, and report your findings.
4. Prepare a questionnaire that will discover teachers' knowledge concerning several of the newer instructional resources. Ask ten or more teachers to complete the instrument and write a report on your findings.
5. Interview an administrator in one of the leadership positions described in this chapter. Analyze the extent of his contributions to the learning resources program of the district.

SELECTED READINGS

Brown, James W., and Norberg, Kenneth. *Administering Educational Media.* New York: McGraw-Hill Book Company, 1965.
Carlson, Mildred A., and Tillman, Rodney. "Selection and Evaluation of

Learning Materials." *Childhood Education,* XLIII, no. 5 (1967), 266–70.

Coulson, John E. "Automation, Electronic Computers, and Education." *Phi Delta Kappan,* XLVII, no. 7 (1966), 340–44.

Erickson, Carlton W. H. *Fundamentals of Teaching With Audiovisual Technology.* New York: The Macmillan Company, 1965.

Joyce, Bruce R. *The Teacher and His Staff: Man, Media, and Machines.* Washington, D.C.: National Commission on Teacher Education and Professional Standards and Center for the Study of Instruction, National Education Association of the United States, 1967.

Neagley, Ross L.; Evans, N. Dean; and Lynn, Clarence A., Jr. *The School Administrator and Learning Resources: A Handbook for Effective Action.* Englewood Cliffs, N.J.: Prentice-Hall, Inc., 1969.

Schultz, Morton J. *The Teacher and Overhead Projection.* Englewood Cliffs, N.J.: Prentice-Hall, Inc., 1965.

Wyman, Raymond. *Mediaware: Selection, Operation and Maintenance.* Dubuque, Iowa: Wm. C. Brown Company Publishers, 1969.

chapter *12*

The Evaluation of
Supervisory Programs

The evaluation of supervision is somewhat like the weather; everyone talks about it, but hardly anyone has really done anything about it. Research is lacking on the means for assessing the effectiveness of a comprehensive supervisory program.

Consequently, in many school districts today, supervision is evaluated very informally and grossly, if at all. It is apparently assumed that all persons engaed in coordinating or directing the improvement of instruction must be making a contribution to the education of pupils. The very existence of the supervisory positions and the increased activity in curriculum work and other in-service programs, for example, are often taken as evidence of real progress.

We need a total or comprehensive approach to the difficult and involved problem of evaluating supervisory programs. Just as the entire teaching-learning situation is evaluated today, and not the teacher alone, so must we seek to appraise not only the supervisor but also the whole school program of which he is an integral part. Since all evaluation involves human relationships and personalities to a great extent, subjective judgment will always play an important role. For this reason some say it is impossible to assess the contributions of teachers, administrators, and supervisors fairly. However, competent, well-trained, and experienced professional educators have repeatedly demonstrated that they can work together cooperatively in the development and evaluation of educational experiences for pupils. Again we refer the reader to Chapter I and a consideration of the characteristics of modern supervision. If these are valid for the development of a supervisory program, they are no less so for the evaluation of it. In fact, fundamental human relations and real democracy in administrative functions are prerequisites to the suggestions outlined below.

PROCEDURES FOR EVALUATING SUPERVISION

Two approaches are suggested for the comprehensive evaluation of the supervisory program in a school district. First, the various elements of the total instructional program must be appraised, including pupil progress toward the goals of instruction, and the effectiveness of various supervisory techniques. Second, plans need to be developed for the evaluation of supervisory personnel, considering the role that each person is expected to play in the improvement of instruction.

Evaluation of the Total Program

In considering the various aspects of the instructional program listed below, the following basic questions should be constantly raised as an aid to evaluation.

1. What is most effective in this situation?
2. What is least effective in light of our goals?
3. Where problems are evident, what are we doing about them?
4. Who is responsible for the present situation?
5. Who should be stimulating action for improvement?
6. Is the latest educational research being considered?
7. Are we good enough in this area? Can we be satisfied with what we are doing?
8. Where are our pupils encountering difficulties? Why?

These and other important questions can be discussed in the district administrative council, in staff meetings, and in supervisory conferences. By continuous probing in this manner, weak areas in the program of instruction are bound to be identified. Some specific facets are detailed below, with suggested questions. It is essential that evaluation check lists using these and other questions be prepared cooperatively by teachers, administrators ,and supervisors.

Pupil progress and achievement. If measured by the best instruments available against the goals of the curriculum, then real pupil achievement should give an important clue to the quality of the educational program.

1. How clearly are the philosophy and goals of the curriculum defined? Have teachers and supervisors jointly developed them?
2. How closely are teacher-made and standardized tests, formal and informal, related to behavioral objectives in each learning sequence?
3. In terms of their abilities, home and cultural backgrounds, and other limiting factors, how are our pupils achieving? Do principals and teachers recognize each child and his profile—not merely the median test scores of a group?
4. Are the limitations of all tests—intelligence, achievement, and aptitude— recognized by staff members?
5. Are national medians considered in their proper perspective in interpreting the performance of local pupils?
6. Do teachers and supervisors have many opportunities to discuss pupil progress, from one group to another, and from one grade or level to the next?
7. Is the teacher's professional judgment given adequate weight in the measurement of pupil progress?

Curriculum study and development. The status of the curriculum in a district must weigh heavily in any assessment of the effectiveness of supervision.

1. Is there evidence of curriculum coordination, kindergarten through high school? Or are there great gaps, say, between the elementary and junior high school grades?
2. Is a comprehensive program of curriculum development (such as that outlined in Chapter X) carried out in the district? If not, why not? Who is responsible for coordination of the instructional program?
3. Have all subject areas been studied in the last five years?
4. Are courses of study available to all staff members?
5. Are teaching materials and methods up-to-date or obsolete?

Pupil needs and the curriculum. To be truly successful, the instructional program must meet the needs of *all* pupils in the district.

1. What percentage of those taking the academic curriculum actually enter institutions of higher learning? How many of the others elect this course because there is none to really satisfy their needs?
2. What happens to non-college-bound graduates? Have they been prepared for the fields they enter? Is there a lack of high-level technical education in the secondary school?
3. What is the drop-out rate? How many of these pupils quit because there is little to hold them in the existing curriculum? Is there a sufficient variety of courses in the high school?
4. Are adequate provisions made for the slow learner, the child with creative talent, and the gifted pupil in both elementary and high school?

Supervisory techniques employed in the district. Evaluation of the various techniques used to improve instruction will help to indicate their effectiveness. Chapters VIII and IX discuss a number of widely used individual and group procedures.

1. Do teachers feel that the in-service programs are helping them to improve classroom instruction? Do they have a part in planning them?
2. How often do principals and supervisors visit classrooms? Are follow-up conferences held, and do teachers feel that the visits are valuable?
3. What procedures have been established for the selection and orientation of new staff members? Is the district securing and keeping good teachers?
4. Is there a carefully developed plan for teacher intervisitation? Do benefits accrue from this program?

Important leadership note. Check list questions like the above can be made up from the main sections of Chapters VIII, IX, and X. These should be structured according to the organizational and supervisory patterns of the district. The main aims are: (1) to determine the most successful supervisory techniques as an aid to the overall evaluation of the instructional program; (2) to identify those practices which should be eliminated.

Evaluation through outside committees. Such evaluation should be welcomed by all schools. Some good criteria have been developed by accrediting commissions, state departments of education, and other groups at both the elementary and secondary levels. Many secondary schools are now evaluated by a visiting team at least every ten years. There is a growing movement for similar evaluation of elementary schools. Any district can profitably engage in a self-evaluation, using one of the available criteria. Then a team of administrators, supervisors, and teachers can be invited to the district for a detailed appraisal. The result should be a better understanding of the strengths and weaknesses of the current instructional program, if the evaluators are objective and decisive.

Moorer developed an instrument that should be valuable for self-analysis of the supervisory program.[1] (See Appendix IV, pages 314–25.)

Evaluation of the Supervisory Personnel

The second approach to comprehensive assessment of the value of supervision in a district involves complete evaluation of the work of each supervisor, both by himself and by other professional personnel. Again, the difficulties that will be encountered should not be allowed to scuttle this effort.

Self-evaluation. This is the real key to effective analysis of one's contribution to the improvement of instruction. It cannot be assumed that

[1] Sam H. Moorer, "How Good Is Your Supervisory Program?" (An Instrument for Self-Analysis, Florida State Department of Education, 1950).

individuals will regularly engage in this practice unless the administrative council develops some criteria and check lists. The superintendent must set the example by helping to develop an instrument for his own self-appraisal.

Wiles outlined a number of self-evaluation procedures for supervisors. In the following list, the supervisor asks himself questions that examine the way he works.

1. Do I set up a schedule of activities for each week? for each day?
2. Am I flexible in my schedule without becoming disturbed?
3. Do I get upset when my plans don't go as I hoped?
4. Do I check off the things I've accomplished?
5. Do my feelings get hurt?
6. Am I able to take criticism?
7. Am I able to put myself in the other person's position?
8. Am I making a sincere effort to learn more about the staff?
9. Do I consult those who will be affected by an action before I take it?
10. Do I live up to commitments?[2]

Wiles further pointed out that "the measure of a supervisor's success lies in the worth-while change he is able to effect. . . . These are important questions in judging the effectiveness of a supervisor."

1. How many more teachers are experimenting?
2. Has there been an increase in the calls for help in thinking through problems?
3. Has there been a change in the nature of the problems presented?
4. Is there an increased demand in the staff for professional materials?
5. Is there more sharing of materials among members of the staff?
6. Is the faculty identifying the problems it has to face farther ahead, so that it isn't confronted with so many emergencies?
7. Is there a greater use of evidence in deciding issues?
8. Is there within the faculty a greater acceptance of difference?
9. How many more parents are involved in the school?
10. How many more rooms are more attractive?
11. How many more teachers are active in professional organizations?
12. How many more teachers are seeking in-service experience?
13. How many more teachers are planning with other teachers?
14. How many more pupils are being included in planning and evaluating?
15. Is a larger percentage of the staff assuming responsibility for the improvement of the program?
16. Are staff meetings becoming more faculty-directed?
17. How many more teachers are using a wider range of materials?
18. How are students scoring on achievement tests?[3]

[2]Kimball Wiles, *Supervision for Better Schools*, 3rd ed. (Englewood Cliffs, N.J.: Prentice-Hall, Inc., 1967) pp. 291–94.
[3]*Ibid.*, pp. 295–301.

Wiles discussed each of these questions in some depth as a guide to evaluation of the supervisory process (see footnote 2).

Such check lists can be developed for each position according to the job descriptions and the working relationships and responsibilities exist-ent in the district. This suggestion, of course, assumes that line and staff functions have been defined according to the modern democratic principles of supervision outlined in Chapter I. The check list items would vary somewhat from one position to another. It is essential, how-ever, that all supervisors participate: the superintendent, assistant super-intendent in charge of instruction, coordinators of elementary and secondary education, principals, and special supervisors or coordinators.

Evaluation by others. In 1968, the Educational Research Service re-ported procedures for evaluating administrative personnel in sixty-two of the larger school districts throughout the nation.[4] From a check list on the survey instrument, the main purposes of such evaluations were indi-cated as follows: (1) "To identify areas in which improvement is needed. (2) To assess evaluatee's present performance in accordance with pre-scribed standards. (3) To help evaluatee establish relevant performance objectives and work systematically toward their achievement."[5]

In the majority of the sixty-two districts, each administrator is evaluated annually by his superior. While procedures used to evaluate administra-tive and supervisory personnel in the districts vary considerably, they tend to fall into two different types: (1) procedures that stress rating re-lated to *job standards*, and (2) procedures that rate the extent to which the evaluatee has accomplished *job targets* or performance objectives tailored to his needs. Table 1 summarizes characteristics of the sixty-two evaluative procedures.

The reader will find this entire publication useful in developing pro-cedures for the evaluation of supervisory personnel. As an example, the forms for appraisal of administrative and supervisory performance in the Cincinnati, Ohio, Public Schools are shown in Appendix V, pages 326–27.

To illustrate a more simple device, the following is a check list devel-oped by an elementary-school principal, which enabled teacher evaluation of the supervisor. The form was distributed to all teachers, and their anonymous reactions were sought. Following the check list is a descrip-tion of the procedures followed in this evaluation and the subsequent steps taken by the principal to improve his effectiveness with the staff.

---

[4]*Evaluating Administrative Performance*, ERS Circular No. 7 (Washington, D.C.: Educational Research Service, American Association of School Administrators and Research Division, National Education Association, 1968). 56 pages, $1.50.
[5]*Ibid.*, p. 1.

Table 1. Summary: Characteristics of 62 evaluative procedures

Characteristics	Frequency
Self-evaluation required	16
Use different evaluation form for self-evaluation	3
Format of evaluation form:	
Rating on prescribed scale only	21
Rating by narrative comments only	12
Rating scale and narrative comments	25
Summary evaluation included	18
Space for recommendation regarding future employment	10
Different forms for each position	13
No forms used	4
Rating of probationary and permanent administrators differ:	
In forms used	2
In method used	4
In frequency of evaluation	19
Evaluatee is informed of his rating:	
Post-evaluation conference is held	55
Evaluatee signs evaluation form	43
Evaluatee is given a copy of form	40
Evaluatee may request a copy of form	2
Automatic review by individual or group other than original evaluator	33
Evaluatee may appeal rating:	
By comments entered on form	10
By filing dissenting statement	33
By requesting review by third party	4

TEACHER EVALUATION OF PRINCIPAL

(Please number according to principal's areas of best performance: #1 best, #2 next, etc., with weakest area indicated as #4.)
(   )   Supervision and Improvement of Instruction
(   )   Leadership in Personnel Relations
(   )   Development of Community and Public Relations
(   )   Maintenance of School Plant

Please use this scale in evaluating the following characteristics:
5—Superior
4—Very Good
3—Average
2—Below Average
1—Unsatisfactory

Personal
(   )   Personal appearance.
(   )   Resourcefulness.

(   )   Initiative; drive.
(   )   Dependability.
(   )   Enthusiasm.

Supervision and Improvement of Instruction
(   )   Curriculum guidance
(   )   Help in getting the professional and classroom materials needed.
(   )   Classroom visitation.

Personnel Relations
Relationships with:
(   )   Teachers.
(   )   Pupils.
(   )   Parents.
(   )   Custodians.
(   )   Secretary.

(   )   Ability to deal with individual staff problems.
(   )   Cooperation with staff members; group participation in school policy-making encouraged.
(   )   Democracy in philosophy and procedures.
(   )   Conduct of staff meetings.
(   )   Administration of routine duties, such as administrative procedures, handling of materials and supplies, and keeping of school records.

Please use back of sheet to complete the following: (Be specific.)

Areas of greatest strength.
Needs for improvement.
How can the new teacher be helped more effectively? (First-year teachers please complete this item.)

How teachers helped a principal to evaluate his effectiveness. An important phase in the evaluation of the elementary school is the assessment of the effectiveness of the principal. Teachers can and should play a role in helping the elementary principal to evaluate his work and relationships with the staff.

The value of such total staff involvement in evaluation of the administrative and supervisory functions can be found in experiments like the one conducted by the writer with his 14-teacher staff at the close of the school year.

First of all, the form printed above was developed from research on the role of the principal. Copies were distributed to members of the teaching staff, and they were urged to complete the items according to the indicated scale and to make further subjective comments on the sheet. The purpose was explained as one of attempting to improve the role of the principal in instruction and in dealing with his staff. Personal as well as professional relationships are explored on the evaluation sheet.

The results were quite interesting and helpful. It was possible to identify the areas that were in need of improvement, both from the point scores and from the subjective comments. The main areas of weakness may be summarized as follows:

1. Classroom visitation was felt to be inadequate, both in the number of visits and in the constructive help offered to the teachers. It was suggested that more specific curriculum aids be provided after the visitations and follow-up conferences.
2. It was proposed that the principal develop a more thorough knowledge of the primary-grade children and their needs, as well as more extensive understanding of the techniques of instruction in the lower grades.
3. The staff felt that there was good group participation in policy formation. However, it was made clear that the principal should be more firm in carrying out and administering group decisions. It is his major responsibility to see that staff members cooperate within the framework of the school policies. In this connection it was pointed out that some teachers who do not see their responsibility as part of the staff should receive firmer guidance from the principal.
4. Many excellent suggestions were made by the first-year teachers regarding items to be included in the new-teacher orientation at the start of the fall term. There apparently had been some deficiencies in this area.

It is not enough to make such an evaluation. The principal must combine the results with his own self-evaluation and that of his superiors. Then he should be in a position to constructively improve his staff leadership.

Acting on the above conclusions, reported by his staff and verified in his own thinking, the writer took the following steps toward improvement, and noted the indicated progress.

1. Schedule-wise, more time was set aside for classroom visitation and conferencing with teachers. The curriculum and professional libraries were expanded and more of the principal's time was spent in bringing techniques and materials of instruction to the classroom situation.
2. The principal, whose teaching experience extended down to fifth grade only, began to do some substitute teaching from first grade on up. This, of course, required extensive study and preparation in the principles of primary-grade education. Much was learned through classroom observation. Much more was learned through the exciting experience of teaching. As a result, the principal developed a much greater understanding of the growth patterns of six-, seven-, and eight-year-olds, and was in a better position to help primary teachers in the classroom situation.
3. Steps were taken to see that policies decided by group decision were properly administered.
4. The orientation program for new teachers was improved through the suggestions of the first-year teachers.

The elementary principal who is seriously interested in improving his effectiveness will find an instrument such as this a valuable aid in the total program of evaluation.

It is imperative that all persons with supervisory roles be evaluated by each other and by the classroom teachers. The check lists may be used annually, but evaluation can and should take place at any time, as indicated above. If the proper climate of personal relationships and group interaction exists, staff members learn to share successes as well as failures. Each person, as he matures in this type of environment, faces up to his own problems and does not blame someone else. On the other hand, credit is given where it is due. Evaluation then becomes an honest and fair assessment of the contribution of each individual to the instructional goals. With a number of persons involved, the total result should be helpful to the teachers and supervisors and to the program of instruction.

Much research is needed in the development of more precise methods of evaluation. Probably, there will never be perfection in the measurement of relationships among human beings, but we should be able to discover more effective ways of assessing the contribution of each to the goal of better pupil learning experiences.

SUMMARY

While some check lists have been devised for the evaluation of supervisors and their work, in many school districts today the process of supervision is evaluated very informally and grossly, if at all.

Two approaches are indicated for comprehensive appraisal of the supervisory function in a district. First, the total instructional program should be evaluated, including the areas of pupil progress and achievement, curriculum study and development, provision for pupil needs, and the supervisory techniques employed. Second, each supervisor must be evaluated, both by himself and by other professional personnel.

Additional research is needed to develop more exact methods of evaluation.

SUGGESTED ACTIVITIES AND PROBLEMS

1. Select a supervisory position and design an appraisal form for the evaluation of a person in that position.
2. Critically assess the publication, *Evaluating Administrative Performance*, which is discussed in this chapter.

3. Using one of Wiles' check lists, evaluate yourself or another professional as a supervisor.
4. Develop a comprehensive program for the evaluation of the supervisory process in a school district.

SELECTED READINGS

Bradfield, Luther E. *Supervision for Modern Elementary Schools.* Chap. 8. Columbus: Charles E. Merrill Books, Inc., 1964.

Evaluating Administrative Performance, ERS Circular No. 7. Washington, D.C.: Educational Research Service, American Association of School Administrators and Research Division, National Education Association, 1968.

Franseth, Jane. *Supervision as Leadership.* Chaps. 16 and 17. Evanston, Illinois: Row, Peterson and Company, 1961.

Moorer, Sam H. *How Good Is Your Supervisory Program?* Tallahassee: Florida State Department of Education, 1950. (See Appendix 4, pages 314–25.)

Neagley, Ross L., and Evans, N. Dean. *Handbook for Effective Curriculum Development.* Chap. 11. Englewood Cliffs, N.J.: Prentice-Hall, Inc., 1967.

Wiles, Kimball. *Supervision for Better Schools.* 3rd ed., Chap. 15. Englewood Cliffs, N.J.: Prentice-Hall, Inc., 1967.

chapter 13

A Look Ahead

How will supervision change in the next decade or so? Why will it change, and what are some of the contributing factors?

Although no one can foretell accurately the future in this rapidly changing world, certain trends are discernible that may give us some hints concerning the directions in which education and, consequently supervision might move.

This chapter will be concerned with some of the factors that are producing changes in education, a description of some of the probable changes, and a few of the implications for supervision.

FACTORS THAT ARE PRODUCING CHANGES

It would be impossible to enumerate here all the factors that will likely affect education in the future. Some are so subtle in their influence that relationships are difficult to establish. Others, as yet, have not made their appearance upon the scene. The following list, though far from complete, will be discussed in this chapter: population increase and urban renewal, technological revolution, scientific discovery and invention, demand for quality education, increase in leisure time, child development and learning, decentralization of large school systems, and shifting of decision-making power.

Population Increase and Urban Renewal

Some years ago, population forecasters warned us that our population would level off soon and that we would become a nation of old people. Instead, our population has been growing at a steady pace. Providing for this population increase has become one of the major problems in this country, as well as in many other parts of the world.

As our population has expanded, people who could afford to leave the city have moved into the suburbs. Overproduction on the farm resulting from the use of machinery and improved agricultural procedures has made it necessary for the younger generation to leave the farm and move to the city and suburbs to seek other employment. The time is rapidly approaching in many areas, and has arrived on the East Coast, where the suburbs of one city have reached those of another to form one gigantic sprawling megalopolis.

When the economically more fortunate families moved out of the cities, slums developed as the less economically- and socially-favored families moved into the city. Although these slums have been tolerated for many years, our great cities are at last awakening, and urban renewal is on the way.

Implications for education and supervision. The population increase has created and will continue to create problems in the areas of staffing and school buildings. These factors, in turn, will affect class size. Hand in hand with population increase comes the resulting mobility of population, which usually means a high rate of teacher and pupil turnover.

With urban renewal proceeding at a rapid pace, providing decent new housing for the culturally disadvantaged masses is not enough. Adults must be re-educated to a new way of life, and their children must receive a kind of education different from that given to those who have been raised in more favorable home environments.

These, together with other factors to be mentioned later, will make it desirable to place greater emphasis on learning than on teaching. Supervisory programs must be geared to assist teachers to acquire know-how in helping children to become independent learners. The superior teacher of the future will be the one who enables the child to become a self-dependent, self-motivated learner. This new breed of teacher works himself out of a job. In fact, if Shane and Shane have made accurate predictions the title of the teacher will change. They anticipate that the basic role of the teacher will change noticeably when they state:

Ten years hence it should be more accurate to term him a "learning clinician." This title is intended to convey the idea that schools are becoming "clinics" whose purpose is to provide individualized psychosocial "treatment" for the student, thus increasing his value both to himself and to society.[1]

Prudent and expeditious use of instructional media, programmed learning, computer-assisted and individually-prescribed instruction, teacher aides, interns, clerks, paraprofessionals, and large-group instruction will enable master teachers to have a much wider sphere of influence.

Increase in the school population requires more professional personnel. To meet this demand many individuals will enter the profession well qualified in respect to subject matter but lacking in professional education. Teachers who have been absent from the profession to raise a family will return to the ranks in large numbers. In addition, the knowledge explosion and rapid changes in instructional procedures and technology will result in professional obsolescence rather quickly. As a result, many new problems face the supervisor. The spread in professional know-how on some faculties will be so great that several levels of in-service education will have to be operating simultaneously. Ingenious techniques and procedures must be developed to prepare teachers on the job and new types of relationships must be formed with colleges having teacher-education programs.

Not only will the shortage of professionally prepared teachers persist, but space for teaching and learning will continue to be at a premium. The school of the future will have to become a learning center for six days a week and twelve months a year. More and more secondary-school buildings will need to be used during the evening hours. The twelve-hours-a-day, six-days-a-week, twelve-months-a-year schedule will create numerous supervisory problems. Supervisory personnel may find themselves working in shifts or even in an "on call" status. Unless supervisors are assigned to teaching platoons, they may be working with a larger number of individuals. The use of the same physical facilities and instructional materials by several different groups of teachers also may present some morale problems for the supervisor.

On the other hand schools might grow smaller according to Goodlad's gaze into the future. He writes as follows:

... there is no reason at all why we could not plan an educational program that requires a school building only half the usual size, with the balance of the money going for trips, special projects, and individualized activities supervised by the staff or even programed by a computer.[2]

[1]Harold G. Shane and June Grant Shane, "Forecasts for the 70's," *Today's Education*, LVIII, no. 1 (1969), 31.
[2]John I. Goodlad, "Learning and Teaching in the Future," *NEA Journal*, LVII, no. 2 (1968), 50.

It might be inferred from the above that the supervisor more and more will be involved in planning if many of the learning activities are to be carried on outside the school building as we know it today.

Finally, supervisors must become much more creative and imaginative in developing instructional materials and procedures for the thousands of culturally disadvantaged children and youth found in our large cities. It is unrealistic to expect to meet their needs by subjecting them to the same middle-class educational fare served today in the majority of the classrooms throughout our land.

Technological Revolution

Research in the field of automation is progressing so rapidly that a machine can scarcely be built and put into use before it is obsolete. In every line of work we find machines taking over the tasks formerly done by human beings. What American is not thrilled as he views on television the intricate computers and numerous gadgets located in the control room of a space center during a rocket launching and during the subsequent monitoring of the space flight. The computer has invaded every walk of life and daily touches the life of each individual in some way. According to the experts, its potential is limited only by man himself. In many areas of use the "hardware" is far in advance of the "software."

Will automation be a boon and a blessing to our society, or will it prove to be a woe and a calamity? Only time will tell; but, if schools will accept the challenge, the machine can be made to serve man—otherwise, man may succumb to his own creation.

Implications for education and supervision. It is safe to predict that advancing technology and automation will affect education in a number of ways. Not only will the content of the curriculum be changed, but the purposes, program, techniques, procedures, and the entire scope of education will be affected. The day is fast arriving when adult education at public expense will become a big business.

It is safe to predict that the following changes affecting education may be expected as a result of the technological revolution:

1. Individuals will become lifelong learners and they may expect to be trained for three or more jobs during the course of their lives.
2. Industry and business will increasingly assume more responsibility for training and retraining their employees.
3. Hundreds of new jobs will be "born" each year requiring different skills and knowledge from those in existence.
4. Graduation from high school will become a prerequisite for nearly all occupations.

5. Vocational education will be upgraded to keep pace with technological change.
6. Adult education will become an important phase of all educational programs.

Several direct effects of this move toward automation are being felt in the public schools. One important result will be a great reduction in the amount of clerical work that needs to be done by teachers and administrators. Among other things, data-processing machines are now handling pupil schedules, conflict sheets (schedule errors), attendance lists, athletic lists, class lists, book and equipment inventories, report cards, grading papers, payroll checks, payroll registers, building construction schedules, transportation assignments, and testing programs.[3]

The implications here for supervision are quite apparent. As teachers and supervisor are freed from routine clerical duties, they will have more time to improve the curriculum and perfect their teaching and supervisory techniques.

Although the above uses of electronic data-processing are impressive, the greatest impact of the computer on education is yet to come. Computer-assisted instruction and individually-prescribed instruction are in their infancy; however, the use of the computer in instruction is proceeding at a rapid pace. The use of the computer in knowledge retrieval is growing in leaps and bounds. University planners are talking about automated libraries with certain resource materials stored on tapes for rapid print out. The computer is also entering the field of administrative decision-making.

Electronic data-processing also is becoming a valuable aid in the curriculum revision process and in the development of curriculum theory. In the field of educational research the computer has become indispensable. By its use the entire process of research can be accelerated greatly.

The continued improvement in the technology of other electronic learning and instructional aids will increase their impact on education.[4]

The video-tape recorder with its instant playback feature gives both the teacher and the supervisor a very versatile tool. Educational TV may take a new lease on life particularly in areas where school districts form agreements with Cable TV companies.

What then are some of the implications of technology in the classroom

[3]For example, see AASA Committee on Electronic Data Processing, *EDP and the School Administrator* (Washington, D.C.: American Association of School Administrators, 1967).

[4]See Ross L. Neagley, N. Dean Evans, and Clarence A. Lynn, Jr., *The School Administrator and Learning Resources: A Handbook for Effective Action* (Englewood Cliffs, N.J.: Prentice-Hall, Inc., 1969).

for the supervisory program? It would seem that, among others, the following are likely to occur:

1. Differentiated staffing will become the rule rather than the exception.
2. Supervisors will be working with teams of professionals and paraprofessionals who have the responsibility for the education of several hundred children. The professionals on the team will have specialities in guidance and counseling, child growth and development or adolescent psychology, learning theory, instructional media, engineering, evaluation, simulation, systems analysis, game theory, and others yet to appear.
3. Instructional leadership will consist of coordinating and directing the specialists and their assistants.
4. Since a large part of the supervisor's time will be spent in working with groups, he must become highly skilled in the use of the group processes.
5. To counteract possible undesirable effects on students of too much individualized instruction and association with "hardware" and gadgetry, individuals in a supervisory position must make every attempt to humanize and socialize learning and instruction. The very best human values must be emphasized in the curriculum and in the teaching-learning environment.

There may be those who wonder how computerized instruction is supervised. The authors agree with Van Til's solution when he suggests the following model:

The . . . model may conceive psychologists, curriculum specialists, and computer technologists not as all-knowing authorities, yet as more than consultants. It may conceive teachers not as completely autonomous, yet as far more than robots. It may conceive supervisors not as taskmasters, yet as more than just facilitators. . . .

The supervisor should have a leadership role in solving problems, in injecting ideas, and in humanizing and enriching the process of education both in relationship to teachers and in relationship to the developers of the new technology.[5]

Scientific Discovery and Invention

Man has discovered many of the secrets of nature, and daily he is creating and producing new foodstuffs, household appliances and products, building materials, fuels, wearing apparel, and drugs. He has invented machines and gadgets to amuse himself and to perform many onerous tasks. He has harnessed the atom, and he is now fathoming the mysteries of the universe. He has conquered the earth and the moon and is now reaching for the stars. Yesterday's dreams are today's realities; today's visions will become tomorrow's actualities.

[5]William Van Til, "Supervising Computerized Instruction," *Educational Leadership*, XXVI, no. 1 (1968), 45.

Man has also turned the x-ray and the microscope on himself. The use of miracle drugs, the transplanting of human tissue and organs, and the substitutions of man-made materials for human tissues have prolonged the life of man appreciably and wiped out many dreaded diseases.

Psychiatry, psychology, and surgery are slowly revealing to man some of the mysteries of the human mind. Sociology, social psychology, and group dynamics are assisting us to understand better group interaction and behavior.

Implications for education and supervision. Just as the marvelous discoveries of science are revolutionizing other areas of living, they will continue to affect education. Through the use of new building materials, improved lighting, air-conditioning, and acoustical treatment, the learning environment of students will be greatly improved.

New gadgets in the field of audio-visual education will greatly increase the repertoire of teaching and learning aids. Telstar and its successors will bring to the classroom history as it is being made any place on the earth, and from outer space as well.

New drugs are being experimented with that will assist in learning and memory, subliminal learning will be employed, and auto-conditioning and hypnosis may some day be utilized as aids to learning.

As transportation becomes swifter and cheaper, field trips to any point in our nation and to other continents as well will become as common as the class excursion by bus is today.

With this brief look at the probable effects of scientific discovery and invention on instruction and learning, let us hypothesize what they will be on the curriculum. Certainly, more and more science will be taught and current events will play an increasingly more important role in the social studies program. However, the language arts and foreign languages may be in for a surprise treatment. Because of inventions now being perfected, the English language will have to become completely phonetic in structure.[6] Electric typewriters which automatically type out dictated material will place greater emphasis on the learning of correct oral English. Other gadgets, as yet unnamed, will translate any spoken language into any other language by the flick of a switch. What will happen to shorthand classes and foreign language laboratories when these things come to pass?

If TV dinners, frozen soups, pies, cakes, and what have you continue to increase in popularity, and ready-made clothes (including disposable paper garments) are available at prices that are competitive with home-

---

[6]For example, see John R. Malone, "The Larger Aspects of Spelling Reform," *Elementary English*, XXXIX, no. 5 (1962), 435.

made garments, the content of the home economics courses will have to change drastically.

Finally, how will the widespread use of computers and data-processing machines affect the mathematics and commercial education curriculum?

It should be apparent to the reader that all the implications for supervision mentioned in the previous section also apply here to a certain degree. In addition, the following questions might be raised:

1. Should we continue to teach children and youth skills that have been made obsolete by machines?
2. What emphasis should aerospace education receive in the instructional program?
3. What responsibility has the school for instruction concerning the effects of psychedelic drugs?
4. What should be the attitude of the school in respect to scientific discoveries and inventions that destroy life?
5. How may spiritual values be introduced to counteract the increasing materialistic trend so common in the world today?

Demand for Quality Education

At last our nation is beginning to clamor for quality education. It may mean different things to different persons but individuals regardless of where they live are demanding it. From the ghetto to the most privileged suburb and from the farm to the village hamlet, the cry for more and better education is heard.

It also is being accepted that quality education for all does not necessarily mean identical education for everyone. But rather, it suggests an education for each individual that is in keeping with his needs, interests, and abilities.

In addition to the demand for quality education, cries are being heard for all subjects that traditionally have been taught plus many new ones. In the past decade or so beginning with science we have strengthened all areas of the curriculum. In some cases, as for example mathematics, we are working on the third generation of revision.

Subjects and subject matter have been moved downward so that elementary school pupils are studying topics formerly placed in the secondary school and secondary students are tackling courses formerly offered in college.

Subjects like economics, anthropology, and social psychology have appeared in the secondary school. The conventional foreign languages are being taught on both the elementary- and secondary-school levels.

Russian, Chinese, Hebrew, and Swahili have made their appearance on the educational scene.

Programs in vocational and special education have received tremendous impetus in terms of personnel, plant facilities, and financial support.

Great demands are now being made for black studies programs. To this segment of the population quality education must include an understanding of its history and heritage. For children and youth in the ghetto, compensatory education will continue to be a great need for some time to come.

Implications for education and supervision. The demand for quality education, that is, education that is appropriate for each individual, will tax the ingenuity and creativity of teachers and supervisors alike for years to come. New concepts concerning the purposes of education will need to be examined. Old ideas about content and method may have to be changed. Grades, written reports, Carnegie units, rigid schedules, school terms, and even diplomas as we now know them may disappear. Variability will become a key word as each student follows a truly individually prescribed instructional schedule.

In our evaluation of the educational programs of the future, answers to questions similar to the following ones raised by Goodlad must be sought.

1. To what extent are our young people coming into possession of their culture?
2. To what extent is each child being provided with unique opportunities to develop his potentialities to the maximum?
3. To what extent is each child developing a deep sense of personal worth, the sense of selfhood that is a prerequisite for self-transcendence?
4. To what extent are our people developing universal values, values that transcend all men in all times and in all places?
5. What kinds of human beings do we wish to produce?[7]

Increase in Leisure Time

The trade unions are already predicting a five-hour work day and a twenty-hour work week. As man finds more and more free time on his hands, he must be equipped to engage in a variety of worthwhile leisure-time activities. Boredom will become one of the greatest enemies of mankind unless individuals are prepared adequately to participate actively in stimulating experiences during their free time.

Implications for education and supervision. The school of the future

[7]Goodlad, "Learning and Teaching in the Future," p. 51.

along with other agencies must assume responsibility for insuring that this leisure time is wisely and constructively spent. Adult education experiences of both a vocational and avocational nature must be made available without cost. School facilities such as shops, home economics rooms, typing rooms, cafeterias, auditoriums, music rooms, art rooms, libraries and instructional materials centers, gymnasiums, swimming pools, tennis courts, and playing fields must be available for community use.

It is not enough just to make the above facilities available. Most of the responsibility must be assumed by the school for seeing that health clubs, music ensembles, dramatics groups, art groups, and others are organized and maintained. Much of the supervision and instruction will be carried on by school personnel.

Child Development and Learning

Whether imagined or real, the common belief held by many persons today is that children now mature sooner than they did formerly. This, of course, is a relative judgment. Certainly no one would claim that the twelve-year-old should earn his living as his great-grandfather did in the days when "sweatshops" existed before adequate child labor laws were passed. On the other hand, it would be foolish to deny that children of today are healthier, better informed, and socially more mature than their counterparts of the late nineteenth and early twentieth centuries.

Experimentation, research, and experience have shown that children can profit from formal learning situations at a much earlier age than originally believed. Children of three years of age have learned to read by use of the talking typewriter without creating emotional problems.

The importance of the early years (birth to four or five) in terms of language use and the development of adequate self-concepts has been emphasized greatly in recent years.

The accumulation of a considerable amount of knowledge about how children learn and, in particular, the fact that learning is an individual matter has had and will continue to have considerable influence on the educational program.

Implications for education and supervision. Universal schooling at an earlier age seems to be a certainty in the future. Schools will provide the opportunity for all children at the age of two or three to enter nursery-school programs and others similar to Head Start and to progress at their own rate through kindergarten, pre-primary, primary, and intermediate programs. For the culturally disadvantaged child born into an educationally sterile environment, some communities will give serious consideration to providing five-day boarding schools for children whose parents desire this advantage for them. The child living in a more favored home environment may begin his early education seated before a console in a home learning center. In fact, much of his individually-prescribed instruction throughout his school career might take place right there.[8]

The school of tomorrow will give due recognition to the fact that the maturation of girls is more rapid than that of boys. Perhaps we will eventually develop achievement norms based on sex as well as grade level. Grouping by sex may be used particularly in the early school years. Due to the same uneven maturation of the sexes, social activities will have to be arranged so that they cross school organization lines.

Because we believe each child's learning pattern is unique, individually-prescribed instruction will improve and increase in popularity with the computer playing an important role.

Due to the fact that the years from birth to five are so important and, likewise, the prenatal months, at least in respect to the effect of the mother's health on the child, schools of the future must assume some responsibility for parent education. Parents also should be directly involved in the early schooling. Unless the mother can see her child among others and learn how a professional works with small children, there is little chance of the home environment being improved.

There will be a demand in the school of the future for supervisors of early childhood education. Since these are extremely crucial years for children in terms of their future learning and adjustment, good instructional and supervisory programs are paramount. The supervisor working on this level must have a good background in child growth and development and a good understanding of the psychology of learning. He also must be prepared to coordinate and direct the work of a team of specialists who understand the early years. Principals serving in a supervisory capacity who have not had teaching experience at least on the primary level may find themselves at a disadvantage.

Decentralization of Large School Systems

This topic and the remaining one will not be discussed in the same detail as the others not only because they are interrelated, but also because they have been referred to in Chapters III to VI inclusive.

It is fairly safe to predict that the school systems in our largest cities will eventually decentralize in the hope that the control of education will be brought closer to the people and, consequently, the administration made more responsive to their wishes.

[8]For a more detailed description see Neagley, Evans, and Lynn, *The School Administrator and Learning Resources*, Chap. 1.

Exponents of decentralization hope that more realistic education will result. All other things being equal (and they are not), the quality of education in the big city could equal that found in suburban areas. In terms of supervision the bureaucracy in the central administration will be broken down. The individual school will become more influential and thus without the red tape more educational progress should take place.

Shifting Decision-Making Power

The future of education in the United States hangs on the balance in terms of whether or not teachers, parents, administrators, and school boards can finally agree on their authority, responsibilities, and relationships. Teachers are taking the initiative all over the nation. In their negotiations they have bypassed supervisory and other administrative officials including the superintendent of schools. Parents also have gone straight to the board of education with their complaints and demands. Even students prefer to deal with the highest authority who will listen to their gripes and requests.

Under this new arrangement what will be the role of the supervisor and the administration in general? Can the principal continue to be an instructional leader or will teachers seek their own leaders and consultants?

Redfern gives excellent advice for the future in answer to questions like those above. He states:

Wishing that the stirrings in the ranks of teachers might go away is unrealistic. Reality dictates that principals and other administrators would be wiser to accommodate themselves to changes in working relationships. The reallocation of power in educational decision making more properly means a more effective division of responsibility and authority among teachers, principals, other administrators, and supervisors. It is the application of the best expertise available to a given problem. Sometimes teachers will be in the best position to supply that expert knowledge and skill. On other occasions, it may be the principal or the supervisor who can provide the most information and expertness in making the necessary determination. The allocation of more power to teachers does not necessarily mean a surrender of a like amount to the other components in the decision-making process.[9]

It may be too simple a conclusion, but it seems to the authors that if an individual in a supervisory capacity has some expertise to share and he is the right kind of individual with leadership ability, there will be a demand for his services. If this is not true, he will find himself out of a job.

[9]George B. Redfern, "Negotiation Changes Principal-Teacher Relationships," *The National Elementary Principal*, XLVII, no. 5 (1968), 25.

The supervisor in the school of the future must develop much greater skill in working with parents than formerly. He must learn to communicate with them on their level. If he is not "tuned in" to their wave length, the picture will not be clear and no communication, or even worse, distorted communication will result.

CURRICULUM REVISION AND THE FUTURE

In addition to the factors previously discussed, the following developments may affect drastically the procedures used in curriculum revision in the schools of the future: (1) large school districts, (2) more state control of education, (3) greater influence of the federal government, and (4) accelerated research in the various areas of the curriculum. Although schools that are assuming a leadership role will be searching for original solutions to problems, curriculum revision in most schools no longer will be a "start from scratch" procedure. Instead, it will be a matter of selection and adaptation from the giant smorgasbord which is adding "new dishes" of educational fare almost daily.

The curriculum leader of the future must know how to work with staff members so that they improve in their ability to pick and choose wisely from the large selection that will be available. After the selection has been made, they must develop skill in adopting and adapting their choices so that the local school curriculum becomes a meaningful whole. Otherwise, hodgepodge learning will result.

Opportunities must be provided for teachers to travel, so that they may observe at first hand the new programs that later may be adopted *in toto* or in part. Teachers and supervisors also must acquire greater skill in evaluation, with particular emphasis on outcomes.

The curriculum maker of the future also must be prepared to push back the frontiers of learning by participating in research and by sharing his findings with others. (See Chapter X for additional trends.)

SUMMARY

Civilization is on the move and society is ever changing. Many of the factors producing change affect education and in turn are influenced by it. Population increase and urban renewal, the technological revolution, and scientific discovery and invention have all left deep imprints on education and may be expected to continue to do so. The demand for quality education, the increase in leisure time, the finding of research in child development and learning will all continue to play an influential role in shaping our educational program. The effects of decentralization and shifting of decision-making power are not too easily predicted.

As education changes, supervision also will change. Individuals serving in supervisory roles in the schools of the future will have at their command many new instructional techniques and procedures. Continuous curriculum development will be one of the most important supervisory tasks, as patterns of cultural change evolve in the world community.

SUGGESTED ACTIVITIES AND PROBLEMS

1. Write a brief case study (hypothetical or real) of a school district that has experienced a sudden population explosion. In your case study indicate the supervisory problems that the district faced as a result of the rapid increase in population.
2. Discuss the instructional problems faced by an elementary-school staff in a culturally disadvantaged area. If you were serving in a supervisory position in this school, how would you proceed in the solution of these problems?
3. Describe a school in the year 2000 that has an instructional program and curriculum based on several of the predictions made in this chapter. Depict what you believe the job of the supervisor would be like in this fictitious school.
4. Locate and read some recent research on sex differences in maturation, motivation, and learning. Outline an educational program that takes these differences into account.
5. What implications for the instructional program are there in recent research on creativity?
6. Read several references on individually-prescribed instruction. Write a paper indicating how you would contribute to the improvement of this type of program if you were serving in a supervisory capacity.

SELECTED READINGS

Eye, Glen G., and Netzer, Lanore A. *Supervision of Instruction: A Phase of Administration.* Chap. 22. New York: Harper & Row, Publishers, 1965.

Jenson, Theodore J.; Burr, James B.; Coffield, William H.; and Neagley, Ross L. *Elementary School Administration.* 2nd ed., Chap. 15. Boston: Allyn & Bacon, Inc., 1967.

Klohr, Paul R. "Looking Ahead in a Climate of Change," in *Role of Supervisor and Curriculum Director in a Climate of Change,* ed. Robert R. Leeper. Washington D.C.: Association for Supervision and Curriculum Development, 1965.

McMurrin, Sterling M., Project Director. *Innovation in Education: New Directions for the American School.* Washington, D.C.: Research and Policy Committee of the Committee for Economic Development, 1968.

McNally, Harold J. "The American Principal Tomorrow." *The National Elementary Principal*, XLVII, no. 6 (1968), 90.

Neagley, Ross L., and Evans, N. Dean. *Handbook for Effective Curriculum Development*. Chap. 12. Englewood Cliffs, N.J.: Prentice-Hall, Inc., 1967.

Neagley, Ross L.; Evans, N. Dean; and Lynn, Clarence A., Jr. *The School Administrator and Learning Resources: A Handbook for Effective Action*. Chap. 1. Englewood Cliffs, N.J.: Prentice-Hall, Inc., 1969.

Shane, Harold G., and Shane, June Grant. "Forecast for the 70's." *Today's Education*, LVIII, no. 1 (1969), 29–32.

Wiens, John L.; Whitney, Stephen C.; and Haviland, David S. *Schools and Innovations: A Prologue to Planning*. Troy, N.Y.: Rensselaer Polytechnic Institute, 1965.

Format for Course
of Study Outline

Subject Area:
  Level: Course Objectives:

Subject-matter units or topics with specific objectives	Concepts, generalizations, attitudes, and skills to be developed	Suggested teaching techniques and pupil experiences	Teacher-pupil resources and instructional materials

appendix 2

The 15 Point School Improvement Program, Simon Gratz High School, Philadelphia, Pennsylvania

1. Medical Committee on Human Rights Health Careers Program
2. Coordinated Programs with Local Industries
3. Program Research and Development
4. Women's Medical Hospital Nursing Program
5. Center for Personal Adjustment
6. Communications Skills Laboratory
7. Curriculum and Staff Development Programs
8. Gratz High School Scholarship Support Fund
9. Students Revolving Loan Program
10. Athletes Tutorial Program
11. Human Resources Center
12. Simon Gratz High School Literary Magazine
13. Simon Gratz High School Film Library
14. Fiscal Control Expenses
15. Gratz Extension School

15 POINT PROGRAM TO IMPROVE THE EDUCATIONAL CONDITIONS AT GRATZ HIGH SCHOOL

It is apparent that the wide variety of needs and the multiplicity of problems presented by the student body of Gratz High School require the resources of other facilities and institutions in addition to the work of the school. We believe that the activities listed below will assist us in reaching answers to these problems.

The School District Office of the Director of Research and Evaluation has given its consent to the evaluation of the objectives and the structuring of the data which will be assembled for research purposes.

The entire program would be under the supervision of Marcus A. Foster, Principal of Gratz High School. The administration would be headed by Martin Rugg, Vice Principal for Curriculum and Innovative Programs; the financial comptroller would be Robert Hoffman, Vice Principal in charge of Organization; and program leaders would be John Glenn, Vice Principal; and Norman Cohen, David Cucler, Leonard Laskin, Herman Steinberg, and Harold Zeitz, Department Heads.

1. Gratz High School Medical Committee on Human Rights Health Careers Program

From the beginning of the current semester until now, over sixty research laboratories in hospitals, industries, and institutions have Gratz students engaging in experimentation under the guidance of experts in the fields of medicine and biochemistry. This activity could well become the prototype of an upgrading of our students into the constantly expanding field of public health. It is our hope to make Gratz High a magnet school in Health Careers. In our advisory role, we expect to study the impact of the total experience in order to discover areas of agreement and reenforce the work of the school with our students.

Health Careers Program, 83 students working as student assistants with practicing professionals until June 1970.

2. Coordinated Programs with Local Industries

Gratz High School has a series of student work programs involving Acme Markets, Western Saving Fund Society, Philadelphia Navy Yard and other employing organizations. Several local industries have indicated an interest in cooperating with us. One out of town group, Boeing-Vertol, is anxious to explore the possibilities of a closer relationship, that of "adopting" Gratz High, with all that it implies. As stated elsewhere, we are interested in the advisory role of the school in these programs and in seeing the relationship between work and school activities.

3. Program Research and Development

With the proliferation of work programs throughout Gratz High School (in addition to those described in these proposals), it is becoming more and more necessary to foster closer coordination between the school and cooperating organizations. There is need for a full-time professional employee to devote his energies to planning, research, and developing all the potentials that exist in all of our programs.

In our advisory role, we expect to study the impact of the total experiences on our students in order to reinforce the work of the school with our student in their new roles.

4. Gratz High–Women's Medical Hospital Nursing Program

A program designed to enroll thirty of our students in the three year Nursing Program at Women's Medical Hospital has been in operation since September, 1968 without any financial support. The staffs of the Hospital and Gratz High have been operating without reimbursement in the hope that funding might become available. If this program is to be continued through June, 1969, it will be necessary to secure a grant now. If this program should be finally supported by the state, then any previous grant would be refunded.

5. Center for Personal Adjustment

The Center for Personal Adjustment, which was funded by the Black Coalition in the amount of $20,000.00 has continued to render invaluable service to the students. However, with the increasing enrollment and the growth in magnitude and intensity of the problems which plague our students, it is absolutely necessary to expand the Center.

6. Communications Skills Laboratory

Before Gratz High students can realize their full potential, they must improve their reading skills. To do this more effectively, we would want to establish a Communications Skills Laboratory. It would be supervised by personnel trained in the use of individualized reading materials and listening-recording equipment. Teachers from all subject matter areas will be able to send small groups or individuals to work with reading materials in their content area. Within this laboratory, which will also be concerned with listening and speaking skills, several small cubicles will be available for individual students to use tape recorders, projectors, (loop films, film strips, slides, movies), recording machines, and other devices especially designed for the improvement of reading and listening skills. The laboratory will also serve as reading teacher-training center. Laboratory supervisors will train other teachers in the availability and use of materials and equipment for the classroom.

7. Curriculum and Staff Development Programs

Last year, Gratz High School received a grant of $35,000.00 to revise its curriculum. The process of examining the present practices with a view to improving them was in itself beneficial. However, the valuable program that was created must continue replenishing itself if it is to remain at all viable. In several areas (Pressing and Urgent Problems of the Inner City, Diffusion and Dissemination of Afro-American History, the mathematics, art, sociology, and other subject matter fields) material must be updated and completed. It is also necessary to employ the services of the skilled department heads—beyond their usual school day—to help prepare this material with other teachers and prepare experimental programs that will implement all that has been done.

8. *Gratz High School Scholarship Support Fund*

One of the major thrusts at Gratz High School has been to get students into post high school educational programs. It is significant to note that in the past three years, the number of students has risen from eighteen, with one scholarship, to 170 receiving scholarship aid to the value of $166,000.00. Many of our students require some financial assistance to take advantage of the scholarship opportunities open to them. This assistance would be in terms of fees for college applications, College Entrance Examination Board tests, deposits, travel expenses, books, clothing, etc.

9. *Students Revolving Loan Program*

Many of our students are frequently in desperate need of a few dollars or more to buy school supplies, athletic and street clothing, food, school tokens, and the like. Frequently, a family financial crisis forces a student to quit school to take on a job to augment family income, or makes it impossible to give a student pocket money he needs for everyday expenses. The money which is requested will be made available to students in need. It will be repaid, wherever and whenever possible, by the student-borrower in order to make this a revolving loan program.

10. *Athletes Tutorial Program*

Almost twenty Gratz High athletes a year are offered athletic scholarships provided that they can meet college requirements such as fulfilling academic course requirements and passing College Entrance Examination Board Tests. While another program—Scholarship Support Fund—meets some of the needs of these students, extra services are required. These services would include tutorial assistance at night, after school, summers, and holidays. Some provision would have to be made for small stipends in order to free them from having to drop from school or taking on jobs at times when they could be getting tutorial help.

11. Human Resources Center

The Human Resources Center, under the direction of a Coordinator, would serve the entire student body of Gratz High School. The purpose of the Center would be to broaden the educational and vocational sights of the students through utilization of human resources in the community in the following ways:

1. Arranging visits for small groups of students to the homes or offices of outstanding individuals who represent a wide variety of occupational areas.
2. Providing first hand on-the-job experiences for students in a wide selection of occupations and professions.
3. Bringing in lecturers or other resource persons to enrich lessons, speak to assemblies, inspire or motivate student groups and parent meetings.

12. Simon Gratz High School Literary Magazine

There is great interest among students to publish original work in poetry, drama, short stories, and art. A faculty sponsor for this magazine has been secured, material has been submitted, and a format chosen that is imaginative and orginal. There would be 36 to 40 pages in a single issue with two issues being published during the school year.

13. Simon Gratz High School Film Library

The importance of the multi-media approach to teaching in all subject natter areas is becoming greater all the time. Many of our students have gained a great deal from films properly presented and discussed. Many teachers would like to engage in such a program but are unable to because of the cost of purchasing or renting films for a short time. The films that would be purchased would include those of literary and historical value and which could also be used in a successful Film Study Humanities Course.

14. Fiscal Control Expenses

A program of this type that has fourteen different activities requires close accounting in order to ensure that the project administrators report and record their financial transactions in such a way as to satisfy an outside audit. For that reason, a sum of about 1% of the total budget is being asked to pay for the uniform bookkeeping systems that would be used, the services of a bookkeeper on an hourly or a per diem basis, and for such equipment as might be necessary to do a thorough job.

15. Simon Gratz High Extension School

An unstructured, informally organized learning experience conducted in the Nicetown Boys Club building for 75 students who had been "turned off" by regular school and were dropping out.

Current Developments
and Programs,
Bethlehem Area School District,
Bethlehem, Pennsylvania

The guiding view that the system exists to provide educational experiences for children is paramount. Innovations which are being attempted are keys to helping children becoming productive learners.

Listed below are several ideas which have been implemented.

ORGANIZATIONAL CHANGE

This is the second year for two councils. The District Curriculum Council reflects civic interests and social judgments of education. Its specific responsibilities are to provide an opportunity for all facets of the community to react to the instructional program, and to keep the community informed of curriculum plans and achievements. The membership includes representatives from the Chamber of Commerce, service clubs, P.T.A., Council School Board, professional associations, professional staff, and student body. A news item related to the February 28 meeting is attached. The Curriculum Coordinating Council recommends for the instructional program and coordinates all curriculum activity. Its task is large for it inaugurates workshop ideas, curriculum projects for summer study and action, and approves new courses. In short, its central task is to come to grips with how our schools can best serve the interests of our youth.

INSTRUCTIONAL PROGRAMS

1. Project AVID. This project was developed to refine the "saturation" concept in an elementary school situation. During the summer six elementary teachers, teams from grades 1, 3, and 6, worked together in

planning and designing audio-vsual resources so that during the ensuing term classroom arrangements could be created for independent self-selection activities according to the development, needs, and interests of the individual or the group.

The summer project permitted teachers to familiarize themselves with educational hardware and, more importantly, to develop broad guidelines for utilizing material during the school year.

Items which were new on the market were tested and tried out. If the material fitted the needs of the program, it was purchased.

The program as developed allows pupils to preplan their day within broad blocks of time. If children are working in social studies, they select the particular area they will work in, the materials to be used and the length of time they'll stay, before moving on to another area. They choose from a wide selection of media, the one best suited to meet the needs.

If children encounter difficulty, the teacher or a peer may assist. The teacher as the program is designed is a resource agent—a diagnostician and a stimulator for learning.

Multi-media in the classroom ranges from book resources to tape, slide, film, and overhead transparencies.

At this point, Project AVID is making a change for both children and teachers. Plans are being developed for a second summer project and a subsequent amplification in the following school term.

2. Independent Study. The Bethlehem Area Schools are witnessing a change in facilities which will permit flexible teaching, scheduling, and grouping. New facilities have opened opportunities to move away from the dominant rectangular classroom and the "lecture" presentation. Groups of twenty-five to hundreds can receive one-way communication through the electronic system.

Primarily, the schools in Bethlehem propose to set the model for curriculum change through (1) independent study, (2) an extended school-year program, and (3) the communications system approach.

In all of this endeavor, it is realized that the key to success in an independent study program is the teacher. Through summer study programs for curriculum re-design the district will want its staff to achieve a new role in counseling, diagnosing, and programing.

3. Curriculum Workshops. In its commitment for improvement the school system is setting a course to (1) involve teaching staff in curriculum re-design and (2) create a change oriented supervisory and consultative staff. The renewal efforts are scheduled for the summer. Summer study or writing teams are scheduled to review, plan, or prepare curric-

ulum materials in the several academic areas. Such activity is essential if an independent study and communications system is to achieve its maximum usefulness.

The administrative and supervisory staff assembled itself during a summer seminar to re-study some of the major curriculum areas. A follow-up of the seminar has been a program of studies (K–12) committee which is a committee of faculty to (1) review the program of studies (K–12) as it exists, (2) advise and set priorities for study-writing teams, and (3) suggest dates for fulfillment of activity.

Plans which are being developed for next summer intend to focus on innovative changes in teaching.

How Good Is Your Supervisory Program?

AN INSTRUMENT FOR SELF-ANALYSIS
by SAM H. MOORER, FLORIDA STATE
DEPARTMENT OF EDUCATION

A good supervisor is constantly seeking to narrow the gap between *what is* and *what might be* in the county supervisory program. This means that the supervisor often takes stock of *what is* and looks at the present program in the light of *what might be*. It is important to know where the program stands along the line of development from an *inferior program* to a *superior program*.

Progress along this line is possible only when *thinking* has *run ahead* of *realization*. You dream of a better program of supervision, and as time goes on you discover the means of bringing it about and become more proficient in the ways of working which will bring the program closer to realization of your dreams.

In case your dreams are to some extent vague and nebulous, this instrument is designed to give substance to them with respect to *what might be*. Study of the best writers and most successful practitioners in the field of supervision reveals certain principles and purposes upon which nearly all agree. These agreed-upon principles and purposes provide the clue to *what might be*. Here they are:

Reliance Upon Democratic Leadership	Development of Educational Leadership	Total Program of Education	Materials and Resources

Long-Range Plans		Research and Experimentation	
Purposes of Education	Human Growth and Learning	Coordination of Effort	Cooperation with Other Agencies

Every supervisory program makes use of these principles to some extent. It is important to know how far the county program has advanced along the line of progress from an *inferior program* to a *superior program*. To help you find out, this instrument presents a sharp *contrast* between some of the more important elements of an *inferior program* and a *superior program* of county supervision. You can approximate the status of the present program on a *scale*. In most instances it is likely that the program of supervision in your county will fall somewhere *between* the two extreme points on this scale. That is the problem for *you* to decide. Here is the scale:

1	2	3	4	5
Inferior Program	Moving Toward	Average Program	Moving Toward	Superior Program

The marking of the scale is simple. If you circle the number four (4) for *Materials and Resources*, for example, this means that in your best judgment the supervisory program in your county is above average and moving toward a superior program.

Place your faith in the step-by-step progress. Nobody expects you to achieve the finest possible supervisory program by next year. But the children of Florida and their parents have a right to expect *some* improvement. This instrument is designed to challenge the alert supervisor. If you can get the folks in the schools and communities in which you work pulling together; and if a program for the improvement of instruction can be worked out in terms of commonly accepted, long-range goals; and if it can be decided who is going to do what and how; things are bound to happen!

The Aims of Supervision

The ultimate purpose of a county program of supervision of instruction is to make the maximum contribution to the realization of the purposes of education in a democracy. The immediate purpose is to improve the conditions which surround the growth and learning of teachers and pupils.

Reliance upon democratic leadership. The supervisory program should rely upon democratic leadership for the achievement of its purposes.

Inferior Program	*Superior Program*
1. The supervisor assumes that he or she knows what is best for teachers to do and proceeds to tell them what they should do and how they should do it.	1. The supervisor realizes that working together in pursuit of improvement is at the same time a challenging adventure and the best procedure.
2. Teachers who do not respond readily to new ideas are scolded, criticized, reported to the superintendent as recalcitrant and otherwise rejected.	2. Slowness to respond to new ideas which break sharply with old traditions is recognized as a trait common to most people. The supervisor realizes that only through providing stimulating learning experience for teachers can progress be made.
3. Relationships with teachers are impersonal and authoritative. No attempt is made to develop good human relationships. Communication with teachers is usually in the form of orders, directives, and regulations issued from the central office.	3. Relationships with teachers are cordial. There is high quality of human relationships between supervisors and teachers. Communication with teachers is on a personal basis. The supervisor spends much of the time working with teachers individually and in groups.
4. The supervisor relies mainly upon criticisms of shortcomings of teachers to secure results.	4. The supervisor seeks out the strong points of teachers and builds upon these.
5. The supervisor rejects contributions made by teachers which do not measure up to the highest professional standards.	5. The supervisor realizes that every teacher is capable of making some unique contribution to the improvement of education. Each contribution, no matter how small or insignificant, is graciously sought and accepted as an evidence of growth.
6. The supervisor assumes that the ways of democracy can be learned through imposition and coercion and that democratic practices can be *required*.	6. The supervisor knows that growth in understanding and practice of democratic ideals cannot flourish in an authoritarian atmosphere.

1	2	3	4	5
Inferior Program	Moving Toward	Average Program	Moving Toward	Superior Program

Development of educational leadership. The supervisory program should develop educational leadership in schools and communities.

Inferior Program

1. It is assumed that teachers, pupils, and parents are not capable of contributing to the development of plans for the improvement of education.

2. The supervisor does not give teachers, pupils, and parents an opportunity to grow by living through experiences in taking responsibility for doing those things in which their help could make a definite contribution to improvement.

3. Leadership on the part of pupils, teachers, and parents in educational matters is looked upon as a threat to the authority of the supervisory staff.

4. The supervisor has a few trusted cronies among the teaching staff who can be depended upon to assist in carrying out plans which the supervisor has made.

Superior Program

1. The supervisor knows that a sound program of democratic education cannot be developed without participation of all groups concerned.

2. The program provides experiences for teachers in accepting responsibilities and in making decisions in matters which are of concern to them because it is recognized that understanding and support will be gained and growth in doing these things better in the future can be expected to occur.

3. Growing leadership on the part of pupils, teachers, and parents is recognized as the only way to achieve genuine and permanent progress.

4. The supervisor seeks diligently to discover and develop leadership on the part of the largest number of individuals in the school and community. The supervisor knows that the more people who feel a personal responsibility for the program, the more successful it is likely to be.

1	2	3	4	5
Inferior Program	Moving Toward	Average Program	Moving Toward	Superior Program

Total program of education. The supervisory program should be concerned with developing a total program of education at all grade levels and in all areas of human experience.

Inferior Program

1. The supervisory staff is highly specialized. Instruction services are sharply divided into separate units which operate independently. Spe-

Superior Program

1. General supervision, with provision for expert consultative service in special subjects, is the prevailing pattern. There is provision for co-

cial subject-matter supervision is stressed, to the exclusion of general supervision.

2. Curriculum programs for elementary grades are developed with no regard to programs for secondary grades, and vice versa. Programs for certain subjects are developed with no relationship to programs for other subjects. The program is fragmentary and highly compartmentalized. Some subjects or grade levels are emphasized at the expense of others.

3. The supervisor in counties where there is only one general supervisor hesitates to work at a grade level where he or she has had no experience. Also, there is hesitation to work with teachers of subjects in which the supervisor has had no experience.

4. The program of supervision makes no provision for working toward improving the quality of living in the community. The school is assumed to be independent and apart from the daily life of the people. Lay citizens are not encouraged to share in school planning.

ordinating and integrating special supervisory services so that all phases of the program are directed toward commonly accepted goals.

2. Curriculum programs reflect a high degree of articulation and coordination between subject areas and grade levels. In building a unified program, all areas of human experience have been analyzed for their potential contributions to the growth of young people in desirable directions.

3. The supervisor does not claim to be a specialist in every subject and grade level, but *is* a specialist in working with teachers on such things as the requirements of successful teaching and the purposes of education, which are substantially the same at all levels.

4. The program of supervision reflects the understanding that the community educates as well as miseducates the young, and that one of the important clues to improvement of the quality of living and learning in the school lies in the improvement of living and learning in the community.

1	2	3	4	5
Inferior Program	Moving Toward	Average Program	Moving Toward	Superior Program

Materials and resources. The supervisory program should make use of appropriate materials and resources available for operating its program.

Inferior Program

1. Concern for materials of instruction is limited to providing a textbook for each child in each subject.

2. Concern for materials of instruction is limited to printed materials only.

Superior Program

1. Provision is made for securing a wide variety of both textbook and supplementary materials.

2. Provision is made for an adequate supply of maps, charts, globes, films and filmstrips, recordings, and the like.

3. Available consultants from the state department of education and from the state universities and other state agencies are not utilized.

3. Available consultants and resource people from state agencies and institutions are frequently used. Plans are made in advance for securing the maximum contribution from these people.

4. Available resource people from local agencies and the community at large are neither known nor utilized.

4. An inventory of human resources in the community has been made. Teachers know who is available and use him frequently.

5. There are no professional materials for teachers available on a county-wide basis.

5. There is a county materials bureau with an adequate supply of appropriate materials for the use of teachers. These materials are readily available and widely used.

6. There is no medium for sharing ideas and experiences on a county-wide basis.

6. Provision is made for sharing ideas and experiences on a county-wide basis through newsletters, teachers' meetings, personal conferences, and the like.

7. Necessary but expensive materials and equipment are not available to smaller or rural schools.

7. Some types of materials and equipment which cannot be purchased for all schools are placed in the county materials bureau and made available on a rotating basis to all schools.

8. Teachers are not kept informed about free and inexpensive materials.

8. Teachers are kept informed about available free and inexpensive materials.

9. Little use is made of first-hand observation in the community.

9. Facilities and information relative to field trips are readily available.

1	2	3	4	5
Inferior Program	Moving Toward	Average Program	Moving Toward	Superior Program

Long-range plans. The supervisory program should provide for cooperative development of both immediate and long-range plans which are continuously adapted to the needs and conditions in the county.

Inferior Program

Superior Program

1. Activity proceeds according to the exigencies of the moment, or in response to immediate pressures.

1. There are carefully developed, comprehensive long-range plans. Plans for immediate action are always

There are no cooperatively developed, comprehensive, long-range plans which serve to give direction to the program. The program is on its way, but no one knows where it is going.

made in terms of long-range goals. Specific next steps are set up for short periods of time, and achievement is evaluated in terms of accomplishment of these.

2. Whatever plans exist are static and routine in nature. Plans are not subject to revision although conditions may have changed to such an extent that they are no longer valid.

2. Plans are flexible and subject to adjustment in light of changing needs and conditions.

3. All county plans are made by the administrative and/or supervisory staff and handed down to teachers. Teachers do not understand these plans or see the relationship of present activities to an over-all long-range program of improvement.

3. Teachers and parents know what the supervisory plans for the county are and understand and support them because they have had a part in making them.

4. Activity proceeds for its own sake. Much "busy-work" goes on which is fleeting and fragmentary and in which there is no continuity. Passing fads and fancies are taken up with no appraisal of their real significance to the county program.

4. There is a balance between activity and reflection upon activity. The criteria for determining the relevance of specific activities are found in long-range plans for improvement of instruction in the county.

5. Whatever plans exist are so vague and indefinite or so out of tune with the experience and ability of the teachers, the social outlook of the community, and the financial status of the county school system that there could be little likelihood of their realization.

5. Plans are concrete and specific. They are consistent with the capacities and thinking of the teaching personnel and the lay citizens. Plans for immediate action are those which are judged to have the best chance of succeeding.

1	2	3	4	5
Inferior Program	Moving Toward	Average Program	Moving Toward	Superior Program

Research and experimentation. The supervisory program should base planning as far as possible upon realities of the situation which are discovered through the use of simple research techniques and careful experimentation.

Inferior Program	Superior Program
1. The necessity for securing factual information as a basis for planning is ignored. Planning is done largely on the basis of unsubstantiated opinion and subjective judgment, even in instances where accurate, objective information could be secured.	1. Factual information needed in planning is secured whenever possible. Readily available data as to such things as holding power of the schools, age-grade distribution of pupils, and census data about the county are always kept up to date and widely disseminated to teachers and lay citizens.
2. New programs are hurriedly devised or borrowed from somewhere else *in toto* and imposed on a wide scale without preliminary experimentation to determine suitability for local schools. There is no attempt made to develop means of appraising the success of new programs at frequent intervals.	2. New programs are always developed on a tentative basis and given a trial run on a small scale before being widely adopted. Teachers are encouraged and assisted in devising experimental programs and in sharing their findings. Whenever a new program is tried out, some method of determining the degree of success has been worked out to go along with it.
3. The findings of research on many of the common problems of teaching are largely unknown to the supervisory staff. There is no means of disseminating and interpreting to teachers what is already known.	3. The supervisory staff is informed as to the findings of educational research which are pertinent to problems being worked on in the county. These findings are made available to teachers in easily understood and usable form.
4. The supervisory staff is not acquainted with elementary theory and techniques of educational testing and with standard research and statistical procedures.	4. At least one member of the supervisory staff or someone in the county school system knows enough about testing and evaluation techniques and about standard research and statistical procedures to help teachers devise simple methods of appraising the outcomes of learning.

1	2	3	4	5
Inferior Program	Moving Toward	Average Program	Moving Toward	Superior Program

Purposes of education. The supervisory program should contribute to the development of understandings relative to the purposes of education in light of the nature and needs of our society.

Inferior Program

1. The functions of education as one of the basic institutions of society for its own perpetuation and improvement are not clearly perceived. Information and skills are taught as ends in themselves without reference to what they have to contribute toward the growth of the individual and the improvement of society. The supervisor is chiefly concerned with how well the teachers cover certain bodies of subject matter.

2. There is no provision for systematic study of the needs and resources of the local community. Information as to the social and economic conditions of the county which have a direct bearing on what the school should do is largely unknown.

3. The supervisory staff is not equipped or disposed to assist teachers, pupils, and parents in reaching common agreement as to what the school should do and how to tell to what extent it has been done.

4. Parents are not consulted as to what they think the school should do for pupils. Where parents have limited conceptions as to the purposes of education, no attempt is made to broaden their thinking.

Superior Program

1. There is county-wide study going on at all times relative to the purposes of education. Such study is on a voluntary basis and findings of competent authorities as to the purposes of education are widely disseminated among teachers and parents. Teachers are encouraged to select knowledge to be taught in terms of the needs and capacities of children and the needs of society.

2. Study guides, state bulletins, and supervisory assistance are available for making studies of the community and developing an educational program which better serves its needs.

3. The program makes provision for continuous work toward widening the area of agreement among teachers, pupils, and parents as to the purposes of education. The aim is always a broadened vision of what education might be.

4. Parents are consulted to find out what they think the school should do. Through study and discussion groups, parents are helped to understand our society better and needs which must be met if its problems are to be solved.

1	2	3	4	5
Inferior Program	Moving Toward	Average Program	Moving Toward	Superior Program

Human growth and learning. The supervisory program should contribute to the development of understandings relative to the essential factors of human growth and development, particularly with reference to the nature of the learning process and its implications for teaching.

Inferior Program	Superior Program

1. The supervisory staff does not recognize that parents and teachers are frequently opposed to newer teaching techniques because they do not understand how children grow and how they learn.

2. The supervisory staff does not recognize that supervision is a form of teaching and that activities which are designed to bring about changes in people are learning situations. Supervisory activities frequently violate the principles of good teaching, thus revealing an inadequate conception of the nature of learning by supervisors.

3. Curriculum programs and materials developed in the county ignore the growth characteristics of children at various age levels.

4. Professional materials relating to learning and growth are not available to teachers for study. There are no study groups working in this area at the county or individual school level. State bulletins which have sections devoted to growth and learning are not used.

5. No member of the county supervisory staff or the individual school staffs is prepared or seeking to become qualified to initiate and lead groups in child study. Available consultants in this field are not utilized.

---

1. The supervisory staff recognizes that one of the obstacles to wider acceptance and use of modern teaching practices is largely due to the lack of understanding on the part of parents and teachers of how growth and learning take place.

2. The supervisory staff recognizes that activities designed to improve instruction are frequently learning situations and, as such, must be consistent with the principles of good teaching. Educational experiences are planned which demonstrate the characteristics of a good learning experience.

3. Curriculum programs and materials developed for use in the county are constructed in terms of their consistency with the known facts of child growth and development and the nature of the learning process.

4. Professional materials in the areas of child growth and development and learning are readily available. Teachers are encouraged to join voluntary study groups investigating child growth and implications for teaching. State bulletins and other professional materials for study are available and extensively used.

5. At least one person in the county is prepared to organize and conduct child study groups. Out-of-county consultants in this field who are available are utilized.

1	2	3	4	5
Inferior Program	Moving Toward	Average Program	Moving Toward	Superior Program

Coordination of effort. The supervisory program should contribute to the coordination and integration of efforts of all agencies and institutions in the community which are interested in the improvement of education.

Inferior Program

1. There is no conscious effort made to coordinate and integrate the efforts and services of the various community agencies interested in the welfare and education of young people. There is frequent conflict in youth activities of these groups, and young people often find several organizations competing for their time and energy.

2. There are no clearly defined procedures and policies whereby the wishes and demands of various groups interested in certain learnings being provided in schools may receive consideration. The schools frequently find themselves at the mercy of pressure groups which do not represent the consensus of the community. There are no policies regarding the consideration of requests for the cooperation of the schools in enterprises sponsored by certain groups.

3. Community agencies are permitted to come into the schools and carry on educational activities which bear no relationship to, or duplicate, services already provided in the schools.

Superior Program

1. Through community planning, the efforts and services of such institutions and agencies as P.T.A., service clubs, Boy and Girl Scouts, churches, welfare agencies, health department, and the like, are coordinated and integrated so as to utilize effectively the contributions of all.

2. There are carefully worked out policies and procedures for considering the wishes and demands of groups interested in getting certain things taught in the schools, or in getting the schools to take part in enterprises sponsored by certain groups. The policies and procedures used by the schools make specific provision for discrimination between pressure groups and community consensus.

3. Learning activities carried on in the school by other agencies are not permitted unless they are carefully integrated into the school curriculum.

1	2	3	4	5
Inferior Program	Moving Toward	Average Program	Moving Toward	Superior Program

Cooperaton with other agencies. The supervisory program should cooperate with local, state, national, and international agencies in the improvement of education.

Inferior Program	Superior Program

1. There is a low degree of cooperation with other agencies which are interested in the improvement of education. The supervisors seldom attend meetings of these groups and do not participate in the development of programs formulated by these groups. While willing to enjoy the benefits secured by these groups, no help is offered.

1. There is a high degree of cooperation with all agencies interested in improving education. Supervisors belong to and encourage teachers to join groups such as F.E.A., N.E.A., A.C.E., etc. Provision is made for supervisors and representatives of the teaching staff to attend meetings of these groups. Those who attend take an active part in furthering the work of these groups.

2. There is a low degree of cooperation with the state department of education. Supervisors attend statewide and regional meetings only when required to do so. Invitations to participate in the development of state-wide plans and programs are ignored.

2. There is a high degree of cooperation with the state department of education. Provision is made for the supervisory staff and teacher representatives to attend statewide and regional meetings called by the state superintendent. There is active participation in developing state-wide plans and programs of improving the state system of education.

3. Requests for information needed by research workers in the state department of education and in institutions of higher learning in the planning of improved programs are ignored.

3. Provision is made to secure prompt return of information requested by representatives of reputable agencies and institutions seeking data to be used in improving education.

4. The supervisory staff makes no attempt to keep informed as to the aims and programs of other agencies interested in improving education. No attempt is made to explain and interpret the work of these groups to teachers and lay citizens.

4. The supervisory staff is informed as to the work of other agencies interested in education. Information is shared with teachers and lay citizens.

1	2	3	4	5
Inferior Program	Moving Toward	Average Program	Moving Toward	Superior Program

Appraisal of Administrative and Supervisory Performance, Cincinnati, Ohio

Personnel evaluated: All administrators below the rank of assistant superintendent.

Frequency: In the first and third year of three-year probationary period; every four years thereafter (board policy). Also evaluated in second year of probation if performance is marginal or unsatisfactory.

Procedure: Directors are evaluated by assistant or associate superintendents; principals by directors; assistant principals by principals; all others are evaluated by their immediate superiors, usually the director in charge of a division or department. On the evaluation form, the evaluatee indicates the major areas of his responsibility. In those areas in which he wishes to improve his performance, he identifies specific job targets (performance objectives). He submits these to his evaluator for reactions on or before November 30. If both agree on the targets, efforts are made to achieve the targets during the year, and the results of these efforts become the basis for the evaluation at the end of the year. By March 31, the evaluatee completes his self-appraisal which he sends to the evaluator. The evaluator completes his assessment of the individual's extent of achievement in the major areas of responsibility and in his job targets; he also assesses the individual's over-all performance on a five-point scale according to nine performance factors. The evaluator then confers with his immediate superior who serves as reviewer on the tentative evaluations he has made. When they agree on final evaluations, the evaluator schedules an appraisal conference with the evaluatee at which time the self-appraisal and final evaluation are discussed.

Appraisal: In addition to the evaluator-evaluatee appraisal conference described above, the evaluatee signs the evaluation form to indicate completion of the process, not necessarily consensus. He also receives a copy of the evaluation.

Appeal: The evaluatee may dissent in whole or in part with the evaluator's appraisal judgment and may request a conference with both the evaluator and the reviewer.

SUGGESTIONS FOR FILLING OUT APPRAISAL FORM

The following suggestions may be useful in the filling out of the appraisal form. Assume that the appraisee is an elementary school principal.

Page 1
1. Fill in data at top of page
2. Read instructions
3. Fill out bottom of page at completion of appraisal process

Page 2
1. Suggested areas of major emphasis might be:
   a. Instructional leadership
   b. Administration and organization of educational program
   c. Staff personnel relationships
   d. Pupil personnel activities
   e. Business administration of school
   f. Community and parent relations
   g. Public and professional relations, etc.
2. Space for "General Comments" is provided for amplifying remarks related to major areas.
3. Evaluation scale is self-explanatory.

Page 3
1. "Job targets" are specific tasks or activities related to major areas of responsibility. For example:
   a. Working with intermediate grade arithmetic teachers to improve instructional program
   b. Reorganizing staff meetings
   c. Revising pupil handbook
   d. Setting up study committees to review current materials in language arts and social studies
   e. Systematizing parent conferences, etc.
2. Space for comments by appraisee is provided for pertinent amplifying remarks.
3. Space for comments by evaluator is for same purpose as that of appraisee.
4. Appraisal scale is self-explanatory.

Page 4
1. Page four is for the use of the evaluator in making a general evaluation of the appraisee. The appraisal scale is self-explanatory.

CINCINNATI PUBLIC SCHOOLS

Appraisal of Administrative and Supervisory Performance

Name _____   Position _____

School or Office _____

Period Covered by Appraisal: 196__ - 196__   Appraisal Status_____

Instructions: Appraisal form should be completed in duplicate. Original for Evaluator; carbon copy for Appraisee. Original copy, when completed, sent to Division of Staff Personnel.

To Appraisee:
1. Prepare list of major areas of responsibility (Page 2)
2. Identify specific "job targets" (Page 3)
3. Clear above with Evaluator
4. Work to achieve "job targets." Seek help when needed
5. Complete self-appraisals (Pages 2 and 3)
6. Submit completed self-appraisals to Evaluator (both copies)

To Evaluator:
1. When requested, react to Appraisee's identification of (a) major areas of responsibility; (b) "job targets"
2. Provide Appraisee help and assistance
3. Analyze Appraisee's self-appraisals
4. Make tentative evaluation of Appraisee (Pages 2, 3 and 4)
5. Review tentative evaluation with Reviewer
6. Complete final evaluation of Appraisee (both copies)
7. Schedule and conduct appraisal conference with Appraisee (Original copy to Division of Staff Personnel; carbon to Appraisee)

To Reviewer:
1. Become as knowledgeable as possible with performance of Appraisee
2. React to evaluations of Evaluator
3. Question Evaluator as to validity of evaluations

Signatures:
Signatures indicate completion of appraisal process. If Appraisee is dissatisfied with appraisal conference, he may request a review of the appraisal with both Evaluator and Reviewer.

Appraisee: _____   Date_____

Evaluator: _____   Date_____

Reviewer: _____   Date_____

Scope of Job — Major Areas of Responsibility

Instructions: To Appraisee 1. List major areas of responsibilities (scope of job)
2. Indicate extent of achievement in each (self-appraisal)
To Evaluator 1. Indicate an estimate of accomplishment in each
(Evaluator's evaluation)

Evaluation Code: Use the number that best describes extent of achievement

```
Low                                              High
  L_____|_____|_____|_____|
  1        2        3        4        5
```

MAJOR AREAS (List in topical form; elaboration not required)	Column 1 For Appraisee					Column 2 For Evaluator				
	1	2	3	4	5	1	2	3	4	5

Explanatory Comments (as desired)

Appraisee	Evaluator

Job Targets

Instructions: To Appraisee   1.   List specific targets upon which you plan to work
                                           2.   Assess results attained at end of appraisal period
                                                (self-appraisal)
                    To Evaluator   1.   Evaluate appraisee's achievement of job targets
                                                (Evaluator's evaluation)

Evaluation Code: Use same code as for major areas

JOB TARGETS (List in topical form; elaboration not required)	Column 1 For Appraisee					Column 2 For Evaluator				
	1	2	3	4	5	1	2	3	4	5

Explanatory Comments (as desired)

Appraisee	Evaluator

General Evaluation

Instructions: To Evaluator   In terms of your general knowledge gained in your contacts with the appraisee, assess his over-all general leadership qualities and performance

Evaluation Code: Use same evaluation code as for previous sections

Performance Factors		Encircle				
1. Knowledge	Extent of information and knowledge needed to function as an educational leader	1	2	3	4	5
2. Planning	Degree to which careful planning is done before an action is taken	1	2	3	4	5
3. Follow-Through	Evidence that planning and actions are carried out to a successful conclusion	1	2	3	4	5
4. Organization	Extent to which own work is well-organized as well as that of those supervised	1	2	3	4	5
5. Initiative	Evidence of ability to originate and develop constructive ideas and actions	1	2	3	4	5
6. Decision Making	Degree to which decisions are sound, timely, and effectively carried out	1	2	3	4	5
7. Communication	Extent to which both superiors, subordinates, and staff are kept well-informed	1	2	3	4	5
8. Ability to Motivate	Evidence of ability to inspire and challenge those whose performance is directed or supervised	1	2	3	4	5
9. Ability to Develop	Extent of ability to promote development and growth of those directed or supervised	1	2	3	4	5

General Comments of Evaluator

appendix *6*

Simulated Activities

During the past several decades, attempts have been made to give students in educational administration courses more realistic experiences during their preparatory programs. The ideal situation would be for all students to serve an internship. Unfortunately, this has not been possible except to a very limited degree. As a substitute, case studies, role playing, simulation, and game theory have been introduced.

In order to provide as much realism as possible, the authors are including in this handbook some simulated activities and recommendations for role playing in some of the situations.

The organization of this section of the Appendix will include background material for a large city system and a suburban school district.

A series of simulated activities will next be presented. In order to make them more realistic they are directed to individuals in a particular school. At the discretion of the instructor, however, students may relate each episode to either one or both of the districts described, depending upon the appropriateness of the situation. Students also should be encouraged to write original simulated activities and respond to them in terms of the background information.

All the episodes presented are related to the supervisory function as presented in this text. Although it is the role that should be emphasized, various supervisory personnel may be involved in the episodes.

The exercises will prove more beneficial to the students if, during the discussion and the execution of the actions required by the episode, constant referral is made to Chapter II which deals with theory and research in supervision. It is in this chapter that the basis for action may be found.

GRANTLAND CITY SCHOOL DISTRICT, GRANTLAND, NORTH DAYLAND

Grantland, a large seaboard city, lies at the northeastern tip of the state of North Dayland. It has its share of decay, racial strife, inadequate financial support, crime, and corruption.

The citizens of Grantland are representative of many different nationality groups. The present population is approximately 1,500,000. Of this number 30 percent are members of the black race. A number of Cuban refugees live in one section of the city and a number of Puerto Rican families also live in Grantland.

There is a large Roman Catholic population and sizable Jewish segment.

Nearly every type of occupation may be found in this great metropolis. Approximately 750,000 earn their living in business offices, retail and wholesale trades, public administration, communications and transportation, construction, and service industries. Grantland's chief industry is manufacturing. Machinery, metal products, electronics equipment, and textiles and clothing are among the chief products.

Because of its location on a large river with direct access to the sea, Grantland is a shipping center.

The city government is of the mayor-council type. One political party has controlled the political scene for thirty years. Three of the twelve council members are black. By religious preference two are Roman Catholic, two are Jewish, and the remaining ones claim either Protestant church affiliation or none at all.

There is an eleven member board of education. Appointments are made to the board by the mayor from a list of names submitted by a fifteen-member citizens panel. The membership of the present board includes four Negroes and seven Caucasians. The president of the board is a Negro, three members have children attending Roman Catholic schools, and two board members are women.

Financial support for the schools is derived from state and council appropriations and additional state and federal subsidies. Relationships between the school board and city government fluctuate considerably. The school district has been turned down on numerous occasions by city council when requests for additional funds were made. Several bond issues for construction purposes have been defeated due to lack of support from the party in power.

Educational policy is set by the board of education based on recommendations made by the superintendent of schools. The new superintendent, Dr. James Turner, is a Negro, forty-five years of age, who previously served for five years as superintendent in a city of 120,000 population. He came highly recommended as an individual who had been successful in satisfying and unifying groups with divergent interests.

Prior to Dr. Turner's arrival, all chief school administrators for the city had risen through the ranks and strong central administration had been the rule. However, several second-echelon administrators had been imported from other sections of the country.

Superintendent Turner and his central office staff are responsible for the education of 289,000 children and youth. Of this number approximately 62 percent are non-white.

Although some mention had been made of decentralization, in the true sense of the word this has not taken place. However, for the convenience of administration only, the city school system has been sectioned into six sub-districts of less than 50,000 pupils each.

Subdistrict A

District A which is located in the western section of the city has been a rapidly changing area in terms of population. On the fringe of the district may be found light industries. The school community with which we will be concerned is residential with no industrial plants. There are however a number of independently-owned stores near both the Nixon Elementary School and the Hawkins Senior High School.

Dr. Ted Sarner is Assistant Superintendent in charge of District A. He is fifty-five years of age and holds an earned doctorate. He has previously served as a secondary-school teacher, elementary principal, and secondary-school principal. All of his professional experience has been in the Grantland School District. He is of the Jewish faith.

Dr. Sarner is directly responsible to the city superintendent, Dr. Turner, and his deputy superintendents for the administration of the public schools in his district.

There is a considerable value range in the residences in the school community. Some families live in row homes with a market value of $9,500 and very small lots. Many of them are in a dilapidated condition. The more affluent individuals live in homes that range in market value from $15,000 to $40,000.

The population of the attendance area of the Nixon and Hawkins schools is approximately 9,800 which is about one-fifth of the total population of District A.

Ten years ago, the school community was a stable one with very little turnover of population or teaching staff in the schools in the area. At that time this area was all white. In many of the families one or both parents held college degrees. In addition, there were families who because of financial setbacks were having difficulty keeping up with their neighbors.

During the past ten years the neighborhood has changed considerably. Many white Protestant and Jewish families have filtered out to the suburbs and their former homes are now occupied by Negro families. Those who moved into the section of the community near the southern boundary of the district are sharing multiple-family dwellings. A number of these families are culturally disadvantaged and economically distressed. Many of the children in this area are being cared for in foster homes. It has been estimated that the present population of the area includes 68 percent non-white. The white population includes approximately 30 percent Jewish, 20 percent Roman Catholic, and the remainder Protestant or of no religious affiliation. The black population likewise embraces the same three faiths. St. Christopher Catholic Elementary School is in the area.

There is a very active neighborhood association in the area with membership from both races. There is a good climate for improvement.

Nixon Elementary School. One thousand pupils attend Nixon School in grades K–6. Approximately 54 percent of the student body is non-white.

Thirty-three teachers comprise the staff of the school. Ten staff members are non-white. A majority of the teachers completed their undergraduate education in Grantland State College. Eleven hold Master's degrees from Dayland University. Two teachers do not hold degrees and three are liberal arts graduates teaching on limited certificates. Eight staff members are male including one who teaches in first grade. The years of teaching experience of the staff members cover a wide range. Three teachers are beginning their first year of experience including one of the liberal arts graduates. The range of experience for the remaining members of the faculty are as follows: (a) 1-5 years—four, (b) 6-10 years—three, (c) 11-15 years—four, (d) 16-20 years—three, (e) 21-25 years—six, (f) 26-30 years—six, (g) 31-35 years—three, and (h) over 40 years—one.

In addition to the 33 regular classroom teachers, the staff includes a full-time secretary; and a nurse, music teacher, art teacher, and physical education specialist who work in the school three days a week. There also is a full-time guidance specialist and a full-time professional employee in the library-instructional materials center. A school psychologist is on-call, but he is badly overworked and, consequently, is not readily available. The AFT is the bargaining agency for the teachers.

The Nixon School is organized on a self-contained classroom plan. Some mention has been made of the team teaching and non-graded plans but no action has been taken.

The school is situated on a one acre site. The original section of twenty classrooms was constructed in 1950. Last year a wing was added which included a library-instructional materials center, auditorium, gymnasium, cafeteria, and thirteen additional classrooms. The original section has been kept in good repair. At present, the building is taxed to capacity. There is some talk of erecting several temporary classrooms on the site.

Dale Thomas, thirty-five years of age, is the new principal at Nixon School and a product of the local school district and institutions of higher education. Dale, who has completed all the requirements for his doctorate except the dissertation, was formerly assistant principal in a larger elementary school in District B in Grantland.

When the announcement was made concerning the appointment of Dale Thomas, some of the members of the black community expressed dissatisfaction because the new appointee was not a Negro. Likewise, the Jewish segment of the population would have preferred a member of their group. However, after hearing Dale speak at the first PTA meeting of the year, most of the parents in attendance thought a good choice had been made.

Dale has no assistant principal but does have the assistance of a full-time intern in educational administration from Dayland University. The intern also is at the dissertation stage.

Hawkins Senior High School. Three thousand students attend Hawkins Senior High in grades 10–12. Approximately 70 percent of the student body is non-white.

One hundred and twenty teachers comprise the staff of the school. Approximately 24 percent of the teachers are non-white. A majority of the teachers completed their undergraduate education in one of the three institutions of higher learning located within the city limits although a number of the black teachers were recruited from a large city in the South. The staff is well balanced in respect to the sex of the teachers with approximately 50 percent of each sex. In terms of experience, the average number of years is twenty. Twelve teachers are beginning their first year of teaching. Nine staff members are in either their first, second, or third years of the intern teaching program in Dayland University. This is a program for liberal arts graduates which enables them to secure certification and a Master's degree in Education while they intern in the city schools. During their internship they receive supervisory assistance from representatives of the University in addition to the help received from local supervisors.

Because of the change in composition of the population, 75 percent of the staff have come to Hawkins during the past ten years. About 30 percent have been there from 1-5 years and 15 percent are new at Hawkins this year.

The teaching staff includes the usual subject-matter and other specialists found in a large city high school. The AFT represents the teachers as the bargaining agent.

Hawkins is a comprehensive high school. An attempt has been made to group students homogeneously by subjects. Some team teaching is being employed and a transition from department heads to some plan of differentiated staffing is being discussed.

The student body and community are very proud of Hawkins' athletic teams. The football team has won the city championship for the past two years. The basketball team also has won the championship once in the last five years.

The school plant leaves much to be desired. The original building was erected in 1925 on a site of four acres. Since then the following additions have been made to the building—ten rooms in 1935, twenty rooms in 1955, and ten more classrooms, two large group instruction rooms, an instructional materials center, new boys gymnasium, and swimming pool this past year. The old boys gymnasium was converted into the instructional materials center. A program of renovation of the older sections of the building is in progress, but it will take several years to complete.

Gayle Edwards, forty years of age, who has been principal of Hawkins for the past two years is black and holds an earned doctorate from Yalevard University. Before his appointment to Hawkins, Gayle served as principal of an all Negro junior high in a ghetto section of Grantland. At the time of Gayle's appointment there was some opposition from the white parents in the service area. The black community was jubilant because it represented a victory for them after their hard fought battle for a Negro principal.

Gayle has two assistant principals, one male and one female. Although they are given specific responsibilities and the authority to act, Gayle believes that the assistant principalship should be the training ground for the principalship; therefore, the assistant principals are encouraged to share the total job of the principalship. This, of course, includes supervisory activities.

FAIRVILLE AREA SCHOOL DISTRICT, FAIRVILLE, NORTH DAYLAND

Fairville is located in the northeastern part of New Dayland. It is situated approximately 10 miles west of Grantland City. Therefore, it has naturally become the "bedroom" for numerous commuters. Fairville encompasses nearly six square miles and houses approximately 28,000 people. Socio-economically the residents largely are classified in the middle to upper-middle income bracket. Because so many junior executives, executives, and Ph.D.'s from a large experimental laboratory selected Fairville as their home, the community has become known as "Smartville." The people very proudly have accepted the nickname and take great pride in the intellectual resources of their town. Since Fairville is considered a desirable community in which to live and because it is located near the metropolitan area of Grantland, the district is growing very rapidly. Just five years ago the population was only 20,000.

Because Fairville is largely residential, heavy industry has not been permitted to develop. There is, however, some light industry on the fringes. Fairville supports two large shopping centers, three supermarkets, five banks, numerous small clothing specialty shops, two Catholic churches, a large synagogue, and eight Protestant churches.

The community government is the commission type. The two major political parties are fairly evenly matched. At present, there are three Democrats and four Republicans on the seven man Board of Commissioners. The president is a Republican.

There is a seven member board of education. Its present composition consists of five men and two women. Dr. John Hudson, Superintendent of Fairville School District is sixty-two years of age. He has served the District faithfully for the past sixteen years and plans to retire in two years. Dr. Thomas Kane is Assistant Superintendent in Charge of Instruction and Mr. Joseph Moyer is Assistant Superintendent for Business. Dr. Kane who is forty-two years of age has taught on both the elementary- and secondary-school levels; he has also served as principal of an intermediate school. Mr. Moyer was a business education teacher before assuming his present position. He holds a Master's degree in Educational Administration with an emphasis on Business Management. He is thirty-eight years of age.

The recent incorporation of the borough of Lawton into the school district as a result of the County Redistricting Plan has created a few problems for the school authorities in terms of space. Up until the time Lawton was taken into the school district, the building program was keeping ahead of the population increase. Now the board of education suddenly finds that additional classrooms are needed in the secondary schools. No immediate problems exist on the elementary level because Lawton has its own elementary school. Lawton secondary-school pupils had previously attended other districts on a tuition basis.

The addition of Lawton Borough has added to the school population children and youth with socio-economic backgrounds that are different from those of children residing in Fairville. For the first time non-white children are attending Fairville Schools in discernible numbers. Less than five percent of the parents in Lawton have schooling beyond high school. It is basically a blue-collar community.

A majority of the residents of Fairville welcome the addition of Lawton children to the school. There are some who opposed the move from its inception.

As one would expect in a town where nearly 60 percent of the residents continue their education beyond secondary school, the citizens have a sincere interest in the educational system of their community. They want quality education for their children and youth and they are quite willing to pay for it.

The Fairville Area School System is comprised of four elementary schools housing grades K–5; two intermediate schools accommodating grades 6–8; and one large high school which provides for grades 9–12. The present enrollment in the public schools in the enlarged district is approximately 4,500. There are two Roman Catholic elementary schools in the district and a large high school just outside the district.

Palmer Elementary School. There are 650 pupils enrolled in grades K–5 in the Palmer School. Less than 2 percent are black and the fathers of these children are either in the professions or executive positions.

Twenty-one teachers comprise the staff of the school. All teachers hold Bachelor degrees in education from a variety of institutions. Four of them hold Master's degrees. Four staff members are male. Two teachers are beginners. The range of experience for the remainder of staff is as follows: (a) 1-5 years—one, (b) 6-10 years—one, (c) 11-15 years—one, (d) 16-20 years—five, (e) 21-25—four, (f) 26-30—five, (g) 31-35—one, and (h) 36-40—one.

In addition to the 21 regular teachers, the staff includes a full-time secretary, a nurse, music teacher, art teacher, and physical education specialist who work in the school two days a week. There is a full-time head of the library-instructional materials complex. A school psychologist is on-call. The Fairville Teachers Association is the bargaining agency for the teachers.

The Palmer School is non-graded. Some large group instruction is being used but, at present, great stress is being placed on individualized instruction. The school is a pilot school in the district for individually prescribed instruction (IPI). It has been working with the Far Out Educational Laboratory in this project. Instruction is computer assisted (CAI).

The Palmer School is situated on a twenty acre site. It was completed in the spring one year ago and this is the second full year of occupancy. In selecting the staff to occupy the new building teachers were asked to volunteer. In fact, a representative group of the elementary teachers had assisted in the development of the educational specifications for the new school plant.

The school which is modern in every respect is built around the library-instructional materials center. There are no "egg crate" type classrooms in Palmer School. Here is a school that really is functional, flexible, and adaptable. It includes large group instruction rooms, seminar rooms and standard size classrooms. Study carrels are to be found everywhere and most of them have dial access to both audio and visual materials. There are several rooms especially equipped for CAI and IPI. Closed circuit and regular TV may be viewed almost anywhere in the building.

In addition to the facilities previously mentioned, there is a gymnasium and swimming pool, auditorium, cafeteria, science laboratory, music room, and art room.

Clair Carter, thirty years of age, is principal of Palmer Elementary School. Clair has a Master's degree with a major in elementary school administration and taught in the intermediate grades in another suburban community before coming to Fairville four years ago as principal of the smaller Maplewood Elementary School. The young principal demonstrated such great talent in developing good staff morale in Maplewood School that Superintendent Hudson thought Clair would be the right person to weld together a new faculty and to head the pilot project in IPI.

Locust Grove Intermediate School. Approximately 900 students attend Locust Grove Intermediate School in grades 6–8. Less than five percent of the student body is non-white.

Sixty-three teachers comprise the staff of the school and only one teacher is black. The degrees held by the teachers were earned in at least twenty-five different institutions of higher learning in various parts of the country. About half the staff hold Master's degrees. There are 31 male teachers and 32 female. In terms of experience, the average number of years is eighteen. Five teachers are beginning their first year of teaching. There also are six teachers who have taught in Fairville School District for thirty years or more.

The teaching staff includes the usual subject-matter and other specialists found in a superior suburban intermediate school. The Fairville Teachers Association represents the teachers as the bargaining agent.

Locust Grove utilizes a form of differentiated staffing. Team teaching is employed extensively and some individualized instruction is encouraged. There is no lack of instructional supplies and equipment.

The school plant is five years old. It was built as an intermediate school and planned for team teaching. The instructional materials center is particularly well designed and equipped and was considered a show place when the school opened. In addition to the usual facilities, the building includes a swimming pool and outdoor theater. The auditorium is in constant use by community groups.

Lynn Lafferty, fifty years of age, has been principal of Locust Grove School since it opened five years ago. Prior to that Lynn was principal of Fairville Junior High for fifteen years. Lynn who began teaching social studies in Fairville High School right out of college has a Master's degree in secondary-school administration. Principal Lafferty has not taken graduate work since that date. Lynn's appointment to Locust Grove was based on seniority rights rather than on ability. When the new school was in the planning stage several board members put strong pressure on Superintendent Hudson to appoint Lynn as the principal of the new school. Dr. Hudson reluctantly agreed, thinking that a new challenge was just what Lynn needed to get rolling again. Now five years later, Dr. Hudson knows and the community is aware that the appointment was a mistake.

NIXON ELEMENTARY SCHOOL
Memorandum

10/2/75
2:30 p.m.

Dear Dale:

I thought I should inform you that I have asked Mrs. Johnson to meet with me after school today. I am at my wits end because of her son Jim's laziness. He refuses to do any of his written work here or at home. Would you like to be a third party in the conference?

RP/s

Rosella Parks

---

1. How would you respond?
2. Will you attend the conference?
3. What are your assumptions concerning this situation?
4. How could you as principal best help Rosella in this situation?
5. Write out your probable dialogue with Miss Parks.

4684 Trite Lane
Grantland, N. D. 17604
December 15, 1975

Dale C. Thomas, Principal
Nixon Elementary School
Grantland City Schools
Grantland, N. D. 17604

Dear Principal Thomas:

My son Aaron has informed me that his teacher Rose Allen read the Christmas Story to the class yesterday. She also is letting the children sing Christmas Carols. You and she both know that this is against the law since the Supreme Court decision on Bible reading and prayer.

If it is not stopped immediately, I will go to higher authorities.

Very truly yours,

(Mrs.) Althea Goldstein

1. What are some of the issues on this case?
2. How will you respond to Mrs. Goldstein's letter? Write your letter.
3. What other action will you take if any?
4. If you plan to hold a conference with Mrs. Allen, write out the probable conversation. Role play the conference.

NIXON ELEMENTARY SCHOOL
Memorandum

1/24/76

To: Dale Thomas
From: Ruth Adams, Secretary

Mrs. Finch dropped in the office while you were out. She was blazing mad. She said that Miss Slow, the art teacher, didn't show up again today. This is the second time this month. She was particularly upset because she wanted to go to the bank during the art lesson.

1. What issues are at stake?
2. What action will you take?
3. Write out any dialogue you plan to have with the parties concerned. Role play a conference with Miss Slow.
4. What implications are there for handling the special subjects?

NIXON   ELEMENTARY   SCHOOL
Phone Message

Date: 3/10/76
To: Dale Thomas
Taken by: Ruth Adams, Secretary

Terry Hill, Chairman of the Education Committee for the American Legion phoned to say that a social studies text his son brought home is subversive. He wants an appointment as soon as possible to discuss the matter with you. He threatened to go straight to Dr. Hudson if you didn't take all copies of the text out of circulation, but I persuaded him to wait until he saw you.

---

1. What issues are at stake in this situation?
2. How will you react to Terry Hill's phone call?
3. Write out what you plan to do or say.
4. What other members of the administrative staff will you involve?
5. What implications are there for the selection of instructional materials?

Episode: Altercation between Teacher and Student
Setting: Hawkins Senior High School
Primary Participants: Gayle Edwards (Principal), Tom Crandall (Math Teacher), and Rod Jensen (Student).

A student from a tenth-grade math class comes running into your office shouting that Rod Jensen is having a fist fight with the teacher Tom Crandall. You know that Rod has been in trouble a good many times and that Tom Crandall is one of the least likely of your teachers to engage in a slugging match with a student.

---

1. What immediate action would you take?
2. What longer term action would you plan to take?
3. What would you say to Mr. Crandall? Write out the probable conversation.

HAWKINS SENIOR HIGH SCHOOL
Phone Message

Date: 12/4/75

To: Gayle Edwards

Taken by: Edna Jacobs, Secretary

Mrs. Stephen Evans called about an appointment with you to discuss the possiblity of expanding the unit on Africa in the World Cultures course to a full blown African Studies course.

---

1. What issues does this situation present in regard to decisions concerning the curriculum?
2. What immediate action would you take? Write out your probable phone conversation. If you agree to an appointment, what preparation would you make for the conference?
3. Write out the probable dialogue you will have with Mrs. Evans.
4. What long term action will you take?

HOLY PENTECOSTAL CHURCH
1621 FERN ST.
GRANTLAND, N. D.

Reverend Thomas J. Jones   *March 10, 1976*
        Pastor

Gayle T. Edwards, Principal
Hawkins Senior High School
2091 Fern Street
Grantland, N. D. 17604

Dear Gayle:
I dislike very much bringing this to your attention, but since it affects a number of the families in my congregation, I have to do it.

In a tenth grade health class recently, Mr. Boner said he did not think that smoking marijuana was harmful. He even mentioned that he has smoked it. It is hard enough to keep our youth on the straight and narrow path without teachers corrupting their morals.

Can you do something about this incident so it won't occur again?

Sincerely yours,

TJJ/e   Thomas J. Jones, Pastor
                              Holy Pentecostal Church

---

1. What issues are at stake?
2. How will you respond to Reverend Jones? Write the letter or write out the phone call.

3. What other action will you take?
4. Write out any dialogue you plan to have with Mr. Boner and/or other individuals with whom you will discuss the case.
5. Role play appropriate conferences.

HAWKINS   SENIOR   HIGH   SCHOOL
Memorandum

4/4/76
1:30 p.m.

Dear Gayle:

I called a meeting of the members of the eleventh-grade social studies team for this morning during our scheduled period for preparation and team meetings, and only one of the other three members showed up. This is not the first time this has happened. I guess I am not a very good team leader. May I discuss the matter with you at 3:30 today?

TH/sms   Ted Hunter
                                                Team Leader

---

1. What are some of the basic issues involved?
2. Write out your probable dialogue with Ted Hunter.
3. To what extent should the principal participate in team meetings?
4. Would you talk to the delinquent team members? If you would, write out what you would say.

GRANTLAND STATE COLLEGE
GRANTLAND, N. D.

October 10, 1975

Dr. Thomas A. Kane
Assistant Superintendent in Charge of Instruction
Fairville Area School District
Fairville, North Dayland 19026

Dear Dr. Kane:

After meeting for two Wednesday afternoon sessions with the staff of Palmer Elementary School for their in-service program, I have decided to withdraw as consultant. Only a few of the teachers seem interested in learning about child study. Others come late, sit and knit or whisper during my lectures, and leave early. There are other schools that appreciate my services. I prefer to give them the limited time I have available.

Sincerely yours,

TAC/mr

Thomas A. Childsee
Professor of
Educational Psychology

FAIRVILLE AREA SCHOOL DISTRICT
Memorandum

10/11/75

To: Clair Carter, Principal
From: Thomas A. Kane, Assistant Superintendent

I received the original of the enclosed letter in the mail yesterday. Since we dismiss early each Wednesday, something must be done to fill the spot. Would you like to discuss the matter with me?

TAK/mot

---

1. What assumptions have you concerning the possible causes for the teachers' behavior?
2. Should the in-service meetings be discontinued?
3. Write out the probable dialogue with Dr. Kane. Role play it.
4. How will you inform your staff concerning the change in plans? Write out what you will say or write to the staff members, if you decide to send a bulletin.

November 1, 1975

Clair C. Carter, Principal
Palmer Elementary School
Fairville Area School District
Fairville, North Dayland 19026

Dear Clair:

As you recall, I visited the social studies class of my daughter Cynthia yesterday. Miss Campbell was introducing a unit on map reading. Her use of oral English was atrocious and she apparently is not a good speller either. There were at least three words spelled incorrectly on the blackboard. One of the pupils called her attention to a misspelled word, but she did not change it.

I realize that Miss Campbell is an inexperienced teacher, but I don't want Cynthia getting misinformation. I would like her transferred to another group so she won't be taught by Miss Campbell.

Sincerely yours,

Agatha C. Horn

1. How will you respond to Mrs. Horn's letter? If you decide to respond in writing—write the letter. If you plan to hold a conference, write out the probable dialogue. Role play the conference.
2. What will you do about Miss Campbell? If you decide to hold a conference with her, write out the probable dialogue.
3. Will you need to involve other administrative personnel in the solution of this problem?

Episode: The Case of the Older Teacher
Setting: Palmer Elementary School
Primary Participants: Clair Carter (Principal) and Henry Hasben (English Teacher)

As principal you have recognized for several years that Henry Hasben has been failing in his work. With only two years until retirement, he takes little interest in his work. He just has not been able to keep up with the newer trends in the teaching of English.

You have just observed Henry teach a group of pupils who are achieving on what in a graded school would be seventh-grade level. The lesson was uninspiring of the "drill on grammar type." You feel certain that if you had not been in the room the situation would have been chaotic.

You are now preparing for a follow-up conference.
1. What do you plan to say to Mr. Hasben?
2. Write out your probable dialogue.
3. What action might you take in this situation?
4. What can be done for the older teacher?
5. Role play your conference with Mr. Hasben.

433 Denton Drive
Fairville, N. D. 19025
February 10, 1976

Clair C. Carter, Principal
Palmer Elementary School
Fairville Area School District
Fairville, N. D. 19026

Dear Principal Carter:
As you probably know, we are new residents in your district as of January 1st, and my children, Sue and Tom, are attending Palmer School. Their father and I are quite disturbed that they are participating in a research project. We don't want our children to be guinea pigs. Could they be transferred to the Lawton Elementary School?

Sincerely,

Hettie L. Fox (Mrs.)

1. What issues are at stake?
2. What action will you take?

3. Put in writing what you plan to write or say to Mrs. Fox. If you plan a conference, write out the dialogue.
4. What implications are there for the orientation of parents to the instructional program?
5. Role play a conference with one or both parents.

Episode: In-Service Education Days
Setting: Fairville Area School District
Primary Participants: Dr. Tom Kane (Asst. Supt.), Lynn Lafferty (Principal), Clair Carter (Principal), and other building principals.

It has been the custom for a number of years in Fairville to have two in-service education days a year for the entire district. In addition, each building may have its own in-service program. In order to plan for next year's meetings, Dr. Kane sent out a questionnaire to teachers requesting topics and names of possible consultants for the in-service days. There was also a box teachers might check indicating that they preferred two personal work-study days instead of the in-service days. Teachers were not required to sign the questionnaire. The questionnaires have all been returned and tabulated. Dr. Kane has called a meeting with all principals to discuss the results of the poll. After initial greetings the meeting opened as follows:

Dr. Kane: "Well I am afraid there won't be any in-service education days next year."

Clair Carter: "What happened, did the teachers vote it down?"

Dr. Kane: "Yes, by an overwhelming vote of 2 to 1."

Lynn Lafferty: "I believe the in-service days are of little value. They are just like the old county institutes, they have outlived their usefulness."

Dr. Kane: "Certainly we can find something that will prove helpful. If we expect to use IPI in the other schools, it will require a lot of in-service work."

Clair Carter: "You know how some of my teachers reacted to our weekly workshop. They were unable to see the relationship of Child Study to IPI.

Assume the role of Dr. Kane and respond to the following:
1. What district-wide issues are involved?
2. Complete the above dialogue until some decision is made concerning the next step.
3. Take the next step in writing.

LOCUST GROVE INTERMEDIATE SCHOOL
Phone Message

Date: 9/20/75
To: Lynn Lafferty
Taken by: Ruth Pate, Secretary

James Smith of the Veterans of Foreign Wars called to see whether Locust Grove will participate in the poster contest for Veterans' Day. He wants you to return his call. (747-8921)

---

1. What are some of the basic issues involved?
2. What course of action would you take?
3. Write out your probable phone conversation.
4. Is a poster contest a legitimate form of motivation for art?
5. If you agree to allow your school to participate, what effect might it have on the instructional program in the future?

Episode: Observation and Conference
Setting: Locust Grove Intermediate School
Primary Participants: Lynn Lafferty, Principal and Mary Lehman, Science Teacher.

You have recently observed Mary Lehman present a science lesson on our solar system to 120 seventh-grade pupils in the large group instruction room. Although she had all kinds of audio-visual learning aids available, she chose to lecture without using any aids except the blackboard. You remained for the entire fifty minute period.

You know that this is Mary's second year of teaching and that if her contract is renewed, she will receive tenure.

---

1. What issues are involved in this situation?
2. How will you prepare for your supervisory conference with Miss Lehman?
3. Write out the probable dialogue you will have with Mary.
4. Will you recommend her for tenure?
5. How much responsibility should the other team members assume for Mary's apparent lack of preparation for the lesson you observed?

243 Stock Avenue
Fairville, N. D.
February 3, 1976

Lynn T. Lafferty, Principal
Locust Grove Intermediate School
Fairville Area School District
Fairville, N. D. 19026

Dear Principal Lafferty:

My husband and I were shocked to learn about the content material in the unit on sex education that our daughter Elizabeth is being exposed to in sixth-grade health class. We knew that Locust Grove was beginning sex education, but we did not understand that the bare facts would be so brazenly presented.

As you know, our church is not favorably disposed toward sex education in the schools. We believe that this is a very private matter to be learned about in the home.

In addition to the content, we don't believe that Miss Youthful is qualified to teach about sex. If it has to be taught at all, girls should learn about it from a mature, happily married teacher with children of her own.

Cordially yours,

Mary E. Fitzpatrick (Mrs.)

1. What issues are at stake?
2. What action will you take?
3. What additional information, if any, do you need?
4. If you reply by letter, write the letter.
5. Role play any conferences you plan to hold.
6. What implications are there for the participation and orientation of parents?

Index

Bruner, Jerome S., 37n
Budget, of instructional program, 91, 96
Bulletins, supervisory, 184–87
Burr, James B., 102n, 111n
Burton, William H., 2n, 16n, 171n, 186n, 217n
Business manager, 91
  as assistant superintendent, 94–95

Campbell, Ona L., 44n
Campbell, Roald, 24n, 88n, 110n
Certification requirements, for superintendents, 88–89
Change. *See also* Innovations
  adult impatience and, 153
  automation and, 292–94
  child development and, 298–99
  desire for approval through, 153–54
  discontent and, 154–55
  effect of fear on, 149
  factors influencing, 147–55, 289–301
  individual differences and, 148
  insecurity and, 148–49
  lack of skill for, 150–51
  lack of understanding and, 150
  leisure time and, 297–98
  nature of, 145–46
  past influence on, 149
  philosophy of education and, 152–53
  population increase and, 290–92
  principal's role and, 105
  process of, 145–46
  resistance to, 149–50
  scientific discovery and, 294–96
  sense of accomplishment through, 154
  superintendent's role in, 84–85
  technological revolution and, 292–94
  time required for, 151–52
  translating thinking into doing, 146–47
  urban renewal and, 290–92
  work load and, 151
Characteristics
  of intermediate size school district, 58–68, 79–80
  of large district, 71–73, 80–81
  of small district, 50–52, 78–79
Chief school official, *defined*, 19
Child development, 298–99
Claremont teaching team, 129
Clark County school district (Las Vegas, Nevada), 256–57
Classification of pupils, 90, 96
Classroom experimentation, 7–8, 103, 169–70
Classroom visitation, 7, 8, 53
  as individual technique, 161–63
  procedures, 164–69

Claye, Clifton M., 44
Climate, educational, 86, 103–4, 105, 142, 155
Coffield, William H., 102n, 111n
Collective negotiations, 17–18
College courses, to improve instruction, 170
"Colorless" teachers, 192–93
Committee
  Steering, 231–32
  Work, 242–45
Committee for Economic Development, 49
Communication, concepts of, 28
Community
  orientation to, 202
  power structure, concepts of, 28
Computer-assisted instruction, 270–71, 293
Conferences
  to improve instruction, 170–72, 178
  supervisory, 8
Consultant
  assistant superintendent as, 91
  coordinator as, 96
  outside, 87
  as specialist, 135–36
  utilization of, 87
Contacts, informal, 187–88
Cooperative Development of Public School Administration in New York State, 15
Coordination
  of curriculum, 232
  district-wide, 7, 20
    desirability of, 13
    topics for, 13–14
  of special services, 8
  by superintendent, 85
  of total school program, 4
Coordinator
  job analysis of, 95–96, 98
  K-12 subject area, 124–26, 136, 274–75
  in large district, 72
  qualifications of, 96, 98
  relationships of, 97, 118
  role of, 95–97, 98
  use of term, 19
Corey, Stephen M., 204n
Council, of principals, 15
Counseling, 26–27
Course outline, 304
Creativity, in pupils, 191
Creativity, in teaching, 189–91
Crosby, Muriel, 162n
Crucial subject areas, 238
Cruickshank, Donald R., 223n

Principal *(cont.)*
  in small school district
    cooperation between, 56–58
    improvement of instruction by, 54–56
    responsibilities of, 54–55, 78–79
    supervision by, 54–56
    teaching by, 11, 51, 56
    various tasks of, 53, 55
    when needed for, 51
  as staff or line official, 14–16
  unique aspects of job, 109–10
Problem census, 237
Problem teachers, 191–95
Professional activities, 178
Professional background
  of assistant superintendent, 92–93, 98
  of principal, 107–8
  of superintendent, 88–89, 97
Professional growth
  of assistant superintendent, 91
  of coordinator, 96
Professional library, 91, 96, 178, 207–8
Professional reading, 178–79
Professional staff, 184
Professional writing, 9, 179
Programmed learning, 269–70
Project, group study, 161
Projects, curriculum
  determination of, 85
  encouragement of, 86
Promotion, of teachers, 91, 96
"Proprium," 33
PTA committees, 91, 216
Public
  interpretation of program to, 10, 216, 225
  reports to, 91, 96
Publication
  of curriculum aids, 91, 96
  professional, 9, 178–79
  responsibility for, 91, 96
Pupils
  creativity in, 191
  evaluation of needs of, 280
  evaluation of progress of, 279–80
  and innovation, 142–44
  readiness, 148
  relationship with principal, 115–16

Qualifications
  of coordinator, 96, 98
  of department head, 126–27
  personal
    of assistant superintendent, 92, 94–95, 98
    of principal, 106
    of superintendent, 88, 97

professional
  of assistant superintendent, 92–93, 94–95, 98
  of principal, 107–8
  of superintendent, 88–89, 97
Quality education, 296–97

Redfern, George B., 300n
Reeder, Edwin H., 146n
Release time needed, 228
Reller, Theodore L., 113n, 120n
Reports
  to board of education, 91, 96
  to lay groups, 91, 96
  to superintendent, 91, 96
Requirements, for certification, 89, 93
Research
  action, 7, 203–7, 224
  belief in, 87
  in classroom, 7–8
  defined, 42
  on linc-and-staff administration, 14–16
  nature of, 41–42
  place for creativity, 42
  and professional growth, 43
  and supervision, 41–44
Resistance to change, 149–50
Resource materials. *See also* Learning Resources Services
  computer-assisted instruction, 270–71
  electronic push-button instruction, 270
  films, 268
  overhead projection transparency, 268
  programmed learning, 269–70
  providing of, 9
  television, 268–69
  textbook, 267
Resource personnel, supervision of, 76–78, 90–91, 118–20
Resources
  in small district, 54
  utilization of, 90–91, 116
Responsibilities
  of federal government, 230
  of local government, 230
  of principal, 53, 78–79
  of state government, 230
Revision, curriculum, 301
Rose, James P., 209n
Rosenzweig, J. E., 39n
Ryan, Kevin, 175n
Ryans, David G., 36

Salisbury, C. Jackson, 102n, 126n
San Diego (California) unified school district, 74–78, 221–22
Santa Monica (California), 132
Satlow, David, 127n